Michael Bodey is film editor and media journalist at *The Australian*.

He was previously arts editor, showbiz editor and media editor at the *Daily Telegraph* and a film critic for *The Age*, and has interviewed Australia and Hollywood's biggest stars. In 2010, he wrote *Broadcast Wars*, about the stars and spats of modern Australian television, and in 2005 he co-authored *Aussiewood: Australia's Leading Actors and Directors Tell How They Conquered Hollywood* with his wife, Michaela Boland.

He lives in Sydney with his wife, son and daughter.

EDDIE
THE RISE AND RISE OF EDDIE McGUIRE
show business, politics & footy

MICHAEL BODEY

hachette
AUSTRALIA

Published in Australia and New Zealand in 2015
by Hachette Australia
(an imprint of Hachette Australia Pty Limited)
Level 17, 207 Kent Street, Sydney NSW 2000
www.hachette.com.au

Copyright © Michael Bodey 2015

This book is copyright. Apart from any fair dealing for the purposes of private study, research, criticism or review permitted under the *Copyright Act 1968*, no part may be stored or reproduced by any process without prior written permission. Enquiries should be made to the publisher.

National Library of Australia
Cataloguing-in-Publication data:

Bodey, Michael, author.
Eddie McGuire / Michael Bodey.

978 0 7336 3254 9 (pbk)

McGuire, Eddie, 1964–.
Collingwood Football Club President – Biography.
Television personalities – Australia – Biography.
Businessmen – Australia – Biography.

791.45092

Cover design by Christabella Designs
Cover images courtesy of Getty Images
Typeset in Goudy by Kirby Jones

for Michaela

CONTENTS

Author's Note ... ix

Chapter 1	A Broady Boy	1
Chapter 2	Eddie McGuire, Boy Reporter	19
Chapter 3	Counting on Ten	28
Chapter 4	Eddie Everywhere	45
Chapter 5	More than a Nice Haircut and a Good Smile	56
Chapter 6	Nine Comes After Ten	64
Chapter 7	*The Footy Show*	69
Chapter 8	Outrageous Fortunes	89
Chapter 9	Man on the Rise	97
Chapter 10	'Austraya'	111
Chapter 11	Collingwood Forever	121
Chapter 12	Rumblings	136
Chapter 13	Eyes on the Prize	157
Chapter 14	Bullets, Booze and Lies	182
Chapter 15	The Handover	197
Chapter 16	Changes Brewing	220
Chapter 17	Jumping on a Grenade	236
Chapter 18	Back to Basics	284
Chapter 19	A Finger in Many Pies	299
Chapter 20	Regrets and Recriminations	303
Chapter 21	Building on Success	322
Epilogue	The Son Keeps Rising	330

Acknowledgements ... 333
Endnotes ... 335
Bibliography ... 345
Index ... 347

AUTHOR'S NOTE

Everyone has an opinion about Eddie McGuire.

As a journalist, mine has changed in an unexpected way. My admiration has grown the more I learned or heard about the man. Which is unnerving; that's not how it's meant to be. Journalists are taught to start at cynical and dig down.

The more you dig into Eddie McGuire's life, the more his achievements overwhelm his foibles. His achievements for the Collingwood Football Club and the city of Melbourne are public. His achievements as a broadcaster are lauded, debated and pilloried daily. And his achievements for charities and the country's underprivileged are largely private.

Which is not to say this book is a hagiography. Far from it. Just that some of the known foibles – the temper, the vicious tongue, the occasional abuse of workers of lesser status – don't illustrate his broader story. One of Eddie McGuire's favourite sayings is 'If I'm upset, everyone's upset'. Even Kerry Packer chided McGuire for being too hard on others.

The shortcomings are also outweighed by his empathy. Many speak of favours done or doors opened by McGuire with nothing asked in return.

In some respects, Eddie McGuire's story is little different to those of so many other high achievers in that it is built on an intense work ethic. Sam Newman says he is 'the most driven person I have ever met'.

Where his story differs from others is in its ordinary beginnings. He is not driven by childhood absences or abuse, vengeance (although he can be a good hater), or any other negative spark. It is a simple rags to riches tale driven by the love and lessons provided by two strong parents. His father admired effort, not success.

Effort would bring its own rewards; McGuire is a living example of that. He enjoys the trappings of success but he's quick to note that money does not define him. Activity, progress and achievement define him.

He seems to have an honest desire for improvement, not success. He wants to make things better, for his family, for Collingwood, for Melbourne, for Australia, for the less-fortunate, for Indigenous Australians. He is a progressive, because that improvement requires change. And he doesn't believe any problem is as monumental as everyone thinks.

Consequently, the perennial questioning of his conflicts of interest becomes moot. He argues that a man with many masters will always have conflicts of interest. Besides, the many interests denote activity. Action. Progress. How can you question that?

If you're part of that progress, he'll do anything for you; if you're not, he just wants you to get out of his way. McGuire doesn't tolerate obstruction or criticism. Such is his self-belief, criticism can't be assessed coolly. It becomes personal.

Only recently has he learned to pick his fights. A decade ago, it was not unusual for McGuire to spend 20 minutes on the phone discussing or berating a journalist from some far-flung newspaper who'd slighted him. He learned in Broadmeadows that if you allow people to stand over you, they'll kick you to death.

His father told him to run away from attackers at a hundred

miles an hour but that the day would come when you had to fight – so make the first one count. If you hit, make sure they stay hit. And Eddie says he did at school once, belting a classmate who 'wanted to have a crack', just to let him know Eddie McGuire doesn't back down. He once asked radio host Steve Price during an argument whether he wanted a left from Toorak or a right from Broadmeadows.

What you see is what you get. Despite his reach, there is a simplicity to him. He's not a superman, he just commits entirely to the three priorities in his life: family, Collingwood and work. Not always in that order. And he just goes.

Friends speak of a stable, consistent man who they don't have to second guess. 'If you scratch the surface of Eddie McGuire, you know what's underneath? More Eddie McGuire,' said Harold Mitchell.[1] They know that Eddie can be easy to read, even if many try to read in too much. His language, like his priorities, is simple. He deals in stock phrases – 'Don't you worry about that!', 'Only the best for Collingwood' – and sporting analogies because they cut through. He is not only an effective communicator, he is efficient. And if you truly know him, you know the briefer the sentence, the clearer he aims to be. When he uses a three- or four-word sentence, he means business.

The confidence that came from a stable, loving childhood propelled him. For a 13-year-old boy to sit in press boxes with hardened journos and believe he could join them – and, very soon, beat them – is testament to his drive.

Indeed, McGuire is a quintessential optimist, someone who believes they are never involved in something that doesn't work while anything they do is guaranteed to succeed. And if it doesn't work, a quintessential optimist has the ability to disassociate themselves from the failure and plough on. As Sam Newman explains, 'I expect the worst and hope for the best. He expects the best and then expects it to get better.'

That optimism is also a curse. Some friends warn that his constant need to attempt something, no matter how difficult, can also lead to his undoing. He tries to play out of position, and can be smashed for it.

Yet McGuire's inner belief allows him to prevail. The optimism keeps him moving forward and not looking back. Not regretting. The messes are for others to clean up. The fights aren't worth continuing.

'You never look down the ladder of life and try and kick people off the rung behind you, you just keep going as high as you can and enjoy it,' he said in 2004.[2]

His drive encounters doubts, though. He admits to opening his diary at the beginning of a day and fearing he won't make it. More than once he's stopped his car while reversing out the driveway, looked at his diary again and steeled himself, saying 'You've just got to keep going.'[3]

Eddie McGuire has lived the most private of public lives. Since marrying his wife, Carla, his family life has been largely out of view. Beyond their weekly appearances at Collingwood matches, Carla and sons Joseph and Alexander remain out of his spotlight. McGuire has not sold his family's story or been seen in magazine features, and his primary fear when hearing about this book was the invasion of his wife and children's privacy. Carla was once misquoted by *The Age* and vowed not to be interviewed again. Behind all the bluster, McGuire cherishes his family. When he travels overseas for work, more often than not the family comes too. What hurt him most among the criticism of his stint in Sydney as Nine CEO was the accusation that he was an absent father.

And the two boys are their father's young men. As Eddie did, they respect their elders; look you in the eye and shake your hand. Unlike those of almost all modern celebrities, his family is not a commodity, so this book respects that privacy. *Eddie* is about Eddie, not his young family.

Author's Note

Eddie McGuire is a solid citizen. He has an unnatural memory for names, trivia and events and has had since primary school. He remembers people and is disarming, with a rare skill of being able to make anyone feel special. That has ameliorated many of his professional sins. He knows a simple drinks party for staff is the most effective of employee satisfaction tricks. He lives in a macro world, yet doesn't ignore his micro relationships.

So far, McGuire has balanced the strange dichotomy of being everyone's mate but still a boss and a leader. That's why his term as Nine CEO hurt him. At his television peak, he was the most egalitarian star since Bert Newton. They share many traits: strong belief in family, loyalty, and a sensitivity to criticism balanced by a resignation that blows will come.

Two of the major blows in his life hurt hard. The accusation he used the term 'boned' and his mistaken insult of Indigenous footballer Adam Goodes are the mud that stuck.

His actions across a long period show McGuire is neither derogatory to women nor racist. But in the broad sweep of his extraordinary life, Eddie McGuire has got away with other things he should have been slapped for. Life evens up. And it does so more quickly if you keep going, relentlessly, like Eddie McGuire.

McGuire holds dear US president Theodore Roosevelt's paean to the doers:

'The credit belongs to the man who is actually in the arena ... who, at the worst, if he fails, at least he fails while daring greatly, so that his place shall never be with those cold and timid souls who knew neither victory nor defeat.'

Eddie McGuire is still in the arena, tasting many victories and few defeats. He is an extraordinary, unfolding, very Australian story.

Michael Bodey
July, 2015

CHAPTER 1

A BROADY BOY

The outer Melbourne suburb of Broadmeadows remains an indelible marker in Eddie McGuire's life, just as Glasgow marked the journey of his father, Eddie Snr.

But the suburb didn't define Eddie – his parents did. If someone is a living embodiment of nurture over nature, it may just be him. There are good people in all suburbs, but the nature of the suburb in which the McGuire children were raised suggested the four siblings could easily have become just more anonymous grist for the manufacturing mills.

Bridget and Edward McGuire were an odd couple, the product of a marriage that defied the 1801 'Act of Union' defining the United Kingdom's disparate countries. They ignored any Scottish/Irish prejudice and simply formed their own union.

Eddie's mother, Bridget Brennan – known as Bridie – was the eldest daughter of an Irish farmer in County Roscommon, the stereotypical mid-western heart of the republic of Ireland, an area of rolling green paddocks and low stone fences. Like many other young women at that time, Bridie was taken out of school at the age of fourteen to help on the farm and look after her younger siblings.

It is not surprising that she later left home determined she would not replicate the fate of the other poor women in her county, escaping with a cheap ticket on a 'cattle boat' that was taking stock to market to England.

The man who would become Bridie's husband, Edward McGuire Snr, was born in 1918, and grew up in Hamilton, in the Scottish lowlands just outside Glasgow. He began work as a thirteen-year-old during the Great Depression, leading a 'pit pony' in the coal mines below Glasgow. Like Bridie, Edward was determined to forge a better path.

Glasgow manufactures hard people: it is Scotland's Struggletown against the white collars, castles and culture of Edinburgh, but Edward's optimism belied the gravity of his upbringing and softened those hard Glaswegian edges. However, that hardness has another side – loyalty to a cause – and that was something Edward took to heart. McGuire was Catholic, so one of his most passionate causes was the Glasgow Celtic Football Club, whose enmity with the Protestant Glasgow Rangers constituted one of sport's most brutal rivalries. The hostility between the two clubs began as a PR exercise to excite interest in their early matches; it later resulted in fights, murders and ultimately the inexplicable bankruptcy and winding-up of the Rangers in 2011.

Edward did not want a miner's life, and he worked hard to graduate from the mines to become a tool maker. He was still in his teens when he realised he had to leave Glasgow to find a better life, as the religious gulf also divided opportunities. He recalled applying for jobs with Protestant employers and being shown the door if he let slip that he supported Celtic, thereby showing his Catholicism more loudly than if he had held a rosary as he spoke.

Such witless discrimination angered him; the banality of any kind of discrimination would be impressed upon his children. Conversely – and in a sweet moral contradiction – so too would the joys and benefits of passionate and blinding loyalty to people or a cause.

Edward served as a Scottish soldier in World War II, and in his later years his eldest son, Frank, would talk of him firing his .303 rifle into the air at the massed enemy overhead in the Battle of Britain. But, like so many men who experienced the horror of war, he didn't discuss his service with his family.

When Edward met the young Bridie Brennan at a Butlins Holiday Camp, neither of them was holidaying. She was working as a waitress, he as a toolmaker doing maintenance. They started married life together in Glasgow and later dreamt of opportunities – not so much for them, but for their two young children, the eldest, Evelyn, born in England, and first son, Frank, born in 1957 in Scotland.

At the time, brochures and advertisements were floating around pointing out the benefits of a life in Australia. The wide blue skies Down Under appealed to Edward and Bridie, and so did the promise of a better future, so they saved the ten pounds needed for the family to sail to a new life. They left from Southampton on the *Castel Felice* in 1958, and landed in Port Melbourne with two children, two suitcases and five pounds, 40-year-old Edward's innate optimism again to the fore.

Theirs was a meeting of personalities and intelligence. The couple appreciated the possibilities of a new start, away from the sectarianism, bigotry and drudgery of northern Britain under the conservative Macmillan government. Decades later, Bridie was very clear about why they migrated: to give the kids a chance.[1]

The McGuires took a year to the day from arriving to move into their allocated three-bedroom pale-pink concrete Housing Commission home at 74 Gerbert Street, Broadmeadows on 6 March 1959. It was one of Edward Snr's proudest days, walking into his own version of paradise (even though he thought the suburb was 'tombstone territory'),[2] and vindication for leaving everyone behind (although two of Bridie's brothers had also moved to Melbourne, one of whom they camped with while awaiting their new home).

Almost as soon as they moved in, they planted a plum tree in the yard to help colour the barren landscape of the new industrial suburb on the windswept northern outskirts of Melbourne. They were next door to the grasslands acquired by the Menzies government to build a new 'jetport' at Tullamarine (which would open in 1970), in a suburb in which the first house was built in 1953. The plum tree was the extent of any external adornments because Edward wanted the yards clear for family cricket and football in his own 'castle'.

Back then, Broadmeadows wasn't literally the end of the line – it was in fact on the country line to Wodonga built in the late 1800s – but it was the end of Melbourne: a fringe suburb lacking basic infrastructure beyond a train station. It may have taken the title Struggletown in the 1970s from Richmond and Collingwood, but to Edward and Bridie it was a dream come true.

Edward landed a job at the Board of Works as a 'powder monkey', and he started working explosives a week after alighting from the ship in Port Melbourne. He stayed with the same employer until he retired as a storeman at 65, but held other part-time jobs along the way to help the family get ahead; he was a hard worker and a loyal man – traits all his children would inherit. Edward Snr respected hard work above all else. He didn't admire success per se, rather the 'goers' who strove for it.

Teachers and friends recalled the sunburn around Edward Snr's neck and up to the shirtsleeves of an otherwise pale Scot who was not bred to dwell under the Australian sun. Edward would later tell his kids that with 'a job, a house and the sun on your back', nothing could be finer. He laughed when he said he could never be homesick for Scotland because Broadmeadows had 'so many scotch thistles'.

Edward and Bridie were of the generation that had endured the war and survived the Great Depression, and both had learned to be grateful for all they had. Their good fortune would be ploughed not into their own indulgences, but into their children's future.

And they had reason to be grateful. Such industrial Housing Commission suburbs were booming in the 1960s on the back of full employment and the realisation that the world – or at least the distant island of Australia – might not need to repeat the deprivations of the first half of the twentieth century. Work was steady in Broadmeadows, but many basic services were lacking. Communities made do, and did so happily in many of those outer suburbs that consecutive governments appeared to set and forget. Driven by determined women like Bridie, those in the community fended for themselves. The men didn't wait for others to deliver; they joined forces and did whatever needed to be done. Edward helped to build the local Catholic school, St Dominic's, to which he would send his children.

Something as basic as a footpath was a luxury. Bridie, like other workers from the suburb, left her muddy shoes on the Broadmeadows station platform and changed shoes to travel to the city. That was their lot: make do. The family settled in and quickly Broadmeadows became home.

The suburb was invented in 1952 by the Housing Commission to supply workers for the big manufacturers in the area – Yakka, Nabisco and Ford, to name a few. Occasionally Bridie worked shifts on an assembly line to supplement Edward's income. Evelyn and Frank would walk to school each morning with the smell of Nabisco's baking biscuits propelling them on.

The third of the McGuire children, Edward Joseph McGuire, was born at the Royal Women's Hospital on 29 October 1964 (his younger sister, Brigitte, was born four years later). Though his birth certificate might have registered his name as Edward, he was always going to be Eddie.

The new child slotted into a happy family. Bridie was always there for the kids but, when she worked afternoon shifts, Edward Snr would load all the kids into the car and drive to the Nabisco factory so they could have dinner together in the car during her break.

Once they were all at school, the boys would run home from St Dominic's at lunchtime to eat with their mother before she left for work. Bridie was the kids' great educator, and it was no surprise that one of them – Evelyn – would later become a teacher. Bridie taught all her children to read aloud before they went to school, and took great pride in both her sons' first television reports. Eddie recalls his mum telling him to 'read with expression'; she was proud of all her children, and showed this often. She photographed Eddie's first TV news report on Ten off the television screen in the lounge room.

Television provided Eddie one of his earliest memories. He has a scratchy memory (it must have been because he was a toddler) of urgent news reports of a missing Prime Minister, Harold Holt, in December 1967, when the telly was camped in his sister's bedroom as his dad relaid the linoleum in the kitchen.[3] Like many kids of the 1970s, the novelty of global events coming alive in his home via the wonders of satellite – Muhammad Ali's fights, the 1972 massacre of Israeli Olympic athletes – made a lasting impression as news, sport and television coalesced in his young mind.

The McGuires were a close family because they didn't have other relatives within coo-ee and a young Eddie could sense his parents' loneliness. He had his brother. Frank was eight years older than Eddie, and already a local sporting hero when Eddie carried his footy gear to training for him. They shared the same tiny bedroom until Frank left home, and as they grew up they would joke about how they'd had to take turns getting up in the morning because they didn't have enough space to stand in the room together.

Edward Snr told Frank that his duty was to take care of his younger brother, but that was an easy task when your younger brother idolised you. One of Eddie's earliest memories was of an eleven-year-old Frank carving up a football match the first time St Dominic's won the local premiership. Frank kicked seven goals and was feted from the Jacana Reserve, with his young brother beaming.

It was also an easy task for Frank, knowing his younger brother could fend for himself. After trailing Frank and his mates to the Broadmeadows Swimming Centre one summer's day, a young Eddie was thrown into the deep end and bombed by each of the boys. Frank looked on from the side of the pool knowing his kid brother wouldn't cry and wouldn't drown.[4]

Frank allowed Eddie to tag along as early as five, despite the age difference, as they wandered through paddocks and stormwater drains and hung out at the prehistoric local BMX track. Eddie appreciated he grew up a little faster under his big brother's tutelage, seeing a little more of life when Frank was a teen than most little brothers.

As they got older, Frank's aura only bloomed in Eddie's eyes, but so did the magic of footy. The young Eddie idolised boxer Lionel Rose but years later, when Nine's *This Is Your Life* asked McGuire for his three heroes, he named Muhammad Ali, Frank and Collingwood full-forward Peter McKenna. Footy trumped boxing as far as local heroes went, but it was inevitable that Frank would still be in the mix. It is telling that Eddie nominated Peter McKenna as one of his favourites, as McKenna's showbiz demeanour would unwittingly influence Collingwood decades later.

While Frank and Eddie shared a bedroom in Broadmeadows, incredibly they didn't share a favoured football team. Frank was a passionate Essendon supporter, and the Essendon home ground, Windy Hill, was the closest Victorian Football League (VFL) stadium to the McGuires' Broadmeadows home. Eddie may have wanted to follow in Frank's footsteps in most aspects of life, but not in this case. As far as footy goes, Eddie McGuire has always known his own mind.

Collingwood's Peter McKenna was the VFL's rock star. Essendon's full-forward, the bespectacled Geoff Blethyn, had nothing on Collingwood's rangy full-forward with the long hair, who played with a grace that seemed out of kilter with the hard edge of the Collingwood Magpies. Off-field, McKenna was a different cat too, embracing television, co-hosting GTV-9's *Hey! Hey! It's Saturday* with Daryl Somers before an ostrich replaced him, and even releasing his own singles, 'Things to Remember' and 'Smile'. Despite being photographed in an Essendon jumper as a three-year-old, Eddie was fascinated with McKenna, and Collingwood would become his team.

The passion the two McGuire brothers shared for footy was divided by their separate club loyalties, and it was inevitable that there would be tears. Eddie recounts hearing the final siren of the 1970 Grand Final, after playing along with his brother in the backyard to the call on the radio. He reacted to Collingwood's unlikely loss to Carlton with the naiveté and confusion of a young prep student, believing – as his neighbour had misinformed him – the loser had another chance: 'Never mind, there's always next week.'

McGuire ran inside to be coolly told by his elder brother there was no second chance: Collingwood was done (as a Bombers' supporter, there would have been considerable joy derived from pointing this out). It was the first time that McGuire recalled feeling a pain other than being physically hurt. Losing still hurts.

Frank thought the young Eddie would get over his Collingwood affliction. He was wrong. When Evelyn came home from school one day with a typewriter, Eddie asked his brother to type 'I love Collingwood' on the new machine. Without looking, Eddie proudly took the sheet to show his father, who read out what Frank had typed: 'I hate Collingwood'. Eddie was incensed. A psychologist might be able to decipher whether Frank's slights prompted a lifetime of underdog rhetoric from Eddie, but after the day his dad returned home with a Collingwood jumper there was no turning back.

His mum dutifully sewed the plastic number 6 of Peter McKenna on the back and Eddie stood proudly at the front gate wearing his new black-and-white guernsey as he awaited his brother's return from school. The passion and loyalty displayed by this young Broadmeadows kid would never leave Eddie McGuire.

If the jumper set young Eddie on his path, his first live VFL game sealed the deal. In round two of 1971, Collingwood played Richmond at the MCG in front of 82 000 people and McKenna kicked nine goals. Eddie was there. He could almost touch McKenna as he lined up from the boundary line just around from the infamous Bay 13 in the dark, cold Southern Stand. McGuire still lights up at the memory of the curve of McKenna's back and the dead-straight drop punt spinning backwards and glistening in the low winter sun peeking through the Members' Pavilion.

Any hope Frank had of Eddie's Magpie obsession waning was gone. Eddie laid his Collingwood jumper out at the foot of his bed the night before a big match. He'd found his tribe. The MCG and Victoria Park would become Eddie's mythical, magical places. Young Eddie had been to Arden Street, Windy Hill and Princes Park, which were all near the Broadmeadows line, but Collingwood's home ground, Victoria Park, was something else: two train rides away.

Victoria Park held a particular pull for Eddie because he deduced that almost every time Collingwood's name was first in the Friday night tips on the TV news, the team would win. Later Frank would disabuse him, pointing out Collingwood's sizeable home advantage.

Subconsciously perhaps, McGuire also wanted to belong, just as his dad belonged to Glasgow Celtic. He had grown up absorbing his dad's passion, and the loyalty, strength and identity his father gained from that club was what would appeal to Eddie. He would come to appreciate the same kinship his father felt at Celtic Park.

When one Friday night Edward ventured that Eddie might like to go to the footy the next day, the youngster was suspicious that his dad would renege when he realised Collingwood was playing at the distant Victoria Park. He hesitantly told his dad the next morning that Collingwood was playing at Victoria Park, not the MCG. His dad knew. Eddie couldn't believe it. His father had taken Frank to many games but this was something else. This was Collingwood's home ground.

After wrapping their supermarket lemonade cans in newspaper to keep them cold next to the fruit and nut chocolate, PK chewing gum and a bit of cake packed by Eddie's mum – Dad's little rituals after the Saturday fry-up lunch – Eddie practically floated with joy as they walked to the Broadmeadows station.

Broadmeadows was the first station on the line and, as they went further, more people would alight on their way to Windy Hill or Arden Street. Then Collingwood fans started jumping on board, including someone with a Collingwood cheer squad duffel coat that excited the young Eddie no end.

They alighted at Flinders Street to change for the Hurstbridge line, although Eddie panicked as they arrived at Collingwood station, urging his dad to get off. Eddie Snr told his son to sit down. Young Eddie feared his wonderful day was about to be destroyed because they'd missed their stop until he realised no one else had moved.

The next stop was Victoria Park station. McGuire couldn't believe the club and ground even had their own railway station! Edward Snr took Eddie's hand and guided him across the footbridge, the youngster too small to see anything above adult belts but enthralled by the cacophony and activity.

Just like the yellow brick road turning to reveal Oz, the footbridge dropped away and Eddie was confronted by Victoria Park's black-and-white-striped stands for the first time. He was agog.

Eddie and his dad made their way down to the right forward pocket, ending up next to the police horses, and the youngster took in every smell, sound and sight – which were always a little different from the norm at Victoria Park. Where the MCG was an amphitheatre, Vic Park was a cage fight.

Old-timers looked out for the kid, finding him a place where he could see something of the game, away from the farting horses. As his heroes ran onto the ground, the roar enveloped the young boy. He felt it and he was hooked. It was the first time Eddie ever felt part of a community – one he'd never let go.

For all its familiarity, Broadmeadows was not the entirety of the McGuires' community. It was home, and they felt connected, but Bridie and Edward had different aspirations from most in their suburb and it rubbed off on their kids. They believed their children – if not themselves – could move beyond the confines of their home suburb to aspire to something greater. It was why they'd made that long sea journey in 1958. They wanted more for their children and they expected their kids to work hard to get it. They instructed them not to behave like the others down Gerbert Street; they did not want them following the crowd and getting into strife.

And Broadmeadows could be a tough place. Eddie recalls seeing one fourteen-year-old kid in tears in his backyard one day after being given a belting by his drunken father, who'd pulled him out of school. 'No kid of mine is going to be smarter than me,' he was told.

Edward and Bridie knew the way they did things was not the way everyone around them did them but they didn't care. They would do it the right way for their children. Edward wasn't a father who skived off to the pub after work drinking; he returned home to be with his kids and kick the footy with his boys.

Everything about the Collingwood kinship drew Eddie in: the crowd banter, the humour, the achievements of a team that, crucially, attained a level of success that made them easier to support as McGuire progressed through high school in the late

1970s. The wooden spoon year of 1976 was merely a blip before Grand Finals in 1977, 1979 and 1980, and heavy-duty matches most weekends provided an impressionable youngster with enough to talk about and idolise during the week.

'Fabulous' Phil Carman was signed to spice up the Pies and fill the void for fans heartbroken by Peter McKenna's defection to, of all clubs, Carlton. In disgust, Eddie asked his mum to cut McKenna's number 6 off his jumper and turn it upside down so it represented Carman's number 9. Disappointingly for Eddie and his fellow Magpie supporters, Carman didn't deliver as much as promised; crucially, he was suspended for two weeks for striking and missed both Grand Finals in 1977.[5] It was a further blow, as Peter McKenna hadn't displayed such flaws.

McGuire remembers standing at the back of the Southern Stand directly opposite the time clock as the siren sounded on the drawn Grand Final between North Melbourne and Collingwood. Years later, he would experience the same feeling as president of the Pies during the 2010 Grand Final. His study of the 1977 matches would set up Collingwood to perform far better in 2010 than they did in 1977.

If the players didn't always provide the young McGuire with something to love, the supporters would. The twelve-year-old was standing at the station after Collingwood's 1978 first semi-final victory over Carlton at the MCG when Ray Shaw dominated with five goals and 25 touches. As Eddie stood near the train door in the scarf knitted by his mum, Collingwood jumper and beanie, an aggrieved Blue reached in, ripped McGuire's beanie from his head and threw it under the train before the door closed. As the train pulled away, the Collingwood tribal unity kicked in. Another supporter offered the kid a new beanie and, through the window, McGuire's gaze was fixed upon the offending Blue having the bejeezus beaten out of him by Collingwood supporters still crowded on the platform.

McGuire would go to more matches at Windy Hill – which was closer – with his dad taking a piece of wood that he'd balance between two beer cans so Eddie could stand higher and see better (ironically, a tale another Nine star, Daryl Somers, tells of his time watching Geelong at Kardinia Park). Footy fans had to be innovative at their primitive tribal grounds.

Football taught Eddie lessons away from league grounds too. He has a vivid childhood memory of a talk given by colourful St Kilda coach Alan Killigrew at a 'pie night' at Broadmeadows. 'Killer' was not a devout man himself, but he was Catholic and told the impressionable kids to go to Mass and be good Catholics, and that whatever they did in life, to just be the best at it. Nine-year-old Eddie took the legend's words to heart.

These were idyllic days for a young boy. His dad was employed, his brother was the sporting star of the suburb and he ran home each afternoon to watch *Cartoon Corner*, unknowingly beginning a lifelong fascination with TV.

He threw himself into everything he could: judo on Saturday mornings, school footy, and his role as an altar boy at St Dominic's. Like his brother, Eddie was a better-than-average under-age footballer.

He also hoovered up information. During primary school, he read Frank Hardy's *Power Without Glory*, the story of John West, a boy from the desperately poor fictional suburb of Carringbush (a thinly disguised Collingwood) who rose through cunning and bribery to a position of power and wealth. Eddie didn't identify with the criminality, but he was impressed with 'the way (West) was able to do things. I thought: Oh, OK, he saw an opportunity and took it.'[6]

Eddie recognised opportunity when it came along, and his entrepreneurial flair was evident early in his life. He sold his parents' old lounge to neighbours, adding a fee for use of his billy cart as he rolled it three doors up the street. He bought and sold a little more. He ran a 'lucky numbers' competition in the corner of St Dominic's primary school playground and rigged the numbers so that he wouldn't lose.[4] An old schoolfriend once told a newspaper reporter that the young McGuire was also an accomplished amateur light-fingers, a claim McGuire hurried to deny. A Grade 3 report gave him an N ('needs to improve'), although the youngster liked its statement that 'Eddie always wants to win'.

Like many of their neighbours, the McGuires didn't have a telephone until 1976, but Bridie and Edward Snr worked hard for their children and Eddie didn't go without. He had Adidas footy boots, not the clunky plastic boots of so many of his mates.

The siblings were taught to compete and learnt that hard work paid off. The McGuire kids knew to aspire to something and work hard to make it; Eddie aimed higher than most. In Grade 4, he wrote a policy speech outlining what he would do when he became prime minister. His teacher, Sister Therese, liked it because he argued teachers should be paid more.[7]

Life wasn't always easy, though. When Eddie was in Grade 5, Bridie fell ill and couldn't work, meaning money became tighter. It wasn't footy boots or new footy jumpers that were at stake. Eddie was told if he couldn't win a scholarship, he wouldn't be following his siblings. Evelyn, the oldest, was among the first in Broadmeadows to win a Commonwealth scholarship to secondary school, setting the bar for the rest, which Frank jumped over, gaining entry to the Christian Brothers College (CBC) in St Kilda. His brother was expected to follow.

Eddie could sense his parents' apprehension, but he also had a strong competitive instinct that would not allow him to be out of step with his brother. A series of events heightened the stakes, as Frank was doing his Higher School Certificate, Edward Snr's job at the Board of Works was under threat and Eddie himself was having a tough year at an overstretched school.

He wasn't the best student at St Dominic's but, as any parent knows, individual teachers can influence an education immensely. In their opinion, Eddie didn't have a good one that year.

When Frank was admitted to CBC, Brother McCarthy, appreciating the McGuires' financial circumstances and Frank's talent, implored Mrs McGuire not to let Eddie go to the local Therry College when he was of age. Now, given the family dramas, it looked like Eddie might not even make it there but would have to attend Broadmeadows High instead.

In March of Eddie's Grade 6 year, he had his CBC entrance exam. Months earlier, he had confided in a stern nun, Sister Matthews, that he had to win the scholarship for his family's sake. He picked the right woman as his confidante.

She pulled him aside and said 'Right, you sit here' and proceeded to test him. She then told her young charge that every day he would sit in a seat near the side of the blackboard where there would be a separate board and books set aside for him. He was in an accelerated learning class two decades ahead of it becoming the fashion. By the time of his exam, Eddie was practising on Form 4 scholarship exams, while at home Frank gave him English essays, his dad taught him long division and his mum worked on his reading and expression. His own innate intelligence combined with all this study meant Eddie nailed the CBC exam; however, he still had to wait nervously for the results. At the time, Eddie used to run home during the school lunch break to check on his sick mum, have lunch with her and do shopping errands. He timed himself as he ran to and from school because he was so competitive. He kept striving to beat his best time while, in his twelve-year-old mind, he was training to become a VFL player.

One day, he ran around the corner of Widford Street into Gerbert Street and saw his mum waiting at the letterbox with the letter from Christian Brothers in her hand. They looked at each other, knowing what this one letter could mean.

Bridie opened it while he watched on, and for Eddie the contents were more valuable than Willy Wonka's Golden Ticket. He was in! He felt as if he was floating on air. Even then he knew:

from now on he wouldn't be defined by Broadmeadows or luck. Now he had the opportunity, his future was in his own hands.

Eddie McGuire Jnr wasn't one to waste opportunity – but a school friend recalls his first encounter with him at CBC the following year. McGuire turned round from his desk and put out his hand: 'Hi, I'm Eddie McGuire. I'm from Broadmeadows.'

Eddie was never going to deny his roots – no matter what. He prided himself on saying he was from Broadmeadows, which was some distinction at a school largely drawn from wealthy suburbs heading in the opposite direction along the leafy Sandringham line. Similarly, he proudly wore his Collingwood jumper in the St Kilda stronghold.

His path at the inner Melbourne private school was eased by the reputation of his elder brother, who had dominated in both sport and scholastically, eventually becoming the school captain.

Schoolfriends and teachers recall Eddie as the same bloke we know today: personable, charming, cheeky and very talented. He wasn't the smartest student in the class, but he had a capacity for the humanities. His wit was always in full tilt and he had a keen eye for detail. He had a passion for facts, absorbing them quickly, and appreciated history and its context. Particularly school history. Even at school reunions today, McGuire remains the old boy recalling the minutiae of who did what when. McGuire did a lot, all the time.

He played the euphonium in the school band, dabbled in the theatre group (playing the president of the football club in the Alan Hopgood play *The Big Men Fly*), was a house prefect and competed across most sports, including athletics, cricket and football. The skinny student at one point held the Associated Catholic Colleges 4 x 100-metre record and he was vice-captain and best and fairest of the football team, although it still rankles that he didn't follow in his brother's footsteps to become school captain.

Frank was the one everyone anticipated would go on to do incredible things, although CBC expected that of all its students.

The expanding list of high-achieving old boys includes News Corp CEO Robert Thompson, TV host Daryl Somers, author Morris West and documentary filmmaker Damien Parer (whose *Kokoda Front Line!* was Australia's first Oscar win). Four old boys would be AFL club presidents during the 2000s: McGuire, Melbourne's Paul Gardner, St Kilda's Greg Westaway and Greater Western Sydney's Tony Shepherd.

He may have participated in many activities, but footy was everything for the young McGuire and he threw himself into the Wednesday afternoon matches, arriving home as his mum waited with a big bowl of soup to soothe his red-raw gums, cut up by his rudimentary mouthguard.

Eddie's teachers loved his spirit. One of them challenged him to a game of squash and McGuire cheekily said he'd thrash him. The opposite was true, with the teacher saying if he won 9–0 it would be written on every blackboard in the school. Reminded of the consequences when down 8–0, McGuire willed himself to win the next four points.

The young McGuire was studious, optimistic and fitted in easily. His charisma was on show early. Teachers could see where he got it from: his mum was quite a formidable woman, not dominated by her partner.

He fitted in, yet felt slightly out of step with those around him, at school and at home. Walking to the Broadmeadows train station at 6.30 a.m. in his CBC cap and tie, and returning at 7 p.m. made him an outsider in his own suburb.

The train ride was instructive though: a literal journey from his present to what could be his future. Eddie would wake up and walk down the muddy paths to the train station. He'd see friends from Sunday mass or the local footy team heading to the factories, some in overalls. On the train, he would see the different strata of society. At Broadmeadows and Glenroy, the working class jumped on, before suits and suitcases started appearing at Moonee Ponds and

Essendon. The student holding his euphonium would theorise about what kind of jobs they held: were they lawyers, clerks, somebodies?

Rattling past the Newmarket slaughter yards, everyone smelled the blood and guts of primary industry before the workers alighted for the factories and port around North Melbourne. Eddie would change lines at Flinders Street. A different kind of passenger altogether alighted from the Sandringham line as Eddie jumped on the train that went past South Yarra and the brothels that backed onto the train line, through to Prahran, before getting off at Windsor, at the shabby end of Chapel Street. It was a daily lesson in Melbourne's many social and economic strata. His parents might have thought they'd left class distinctions behind in Glasgow, but they were alive and well every morning for young Eddie to observe.

Eddie spent forty minutes more than any other student travelling to school, and that journey was a transformation. In winter, he'd leave home in the dark and arrive home in the dark at a railway station not known for its hospitality. If Frank was home, Eddie would call from the public phone at the train station, letting it ring three times then hanging up to save money while still alerting his brother to pick him up in the car.

That daily journey from Broadmeadows to CBC was as distinct as a ride from Liverpool to Eton. And Eddie had his own 'Mr Chips' in the form of a dapper teacher, Bill Humphreys, who inspired the young Eddie McGuire with English and the writings of Shakespeare.

One view of destiny stayed with the student: 'There is a tide in the affairs of men, which, taken at the flood, leads on to fortune. Omitted, all the voyage of their life is bound in shallows and in miseries.'[8]

In his mind young Eddie knew he was going to go somewhere – Broadmeadows might have been his home, but it wasn't his destiny.

CHAPTER 2

EDDIE McGUIRE, BOY REPORTER

That bright future Edward and Bridie McGuire wanted for their kids looked like it was going to happen – not that Edward Snr ever doubted it would. With Evelyn set to teach and Frank working for the *Herald*, two of the four McGuire kids were on their way. And Eddie wasn't far behind, even though he was still at school. Eddie had been taught to take advantage of opportunity and, as a teen, he pushed that maxim to its breaking point, making Jimmy Olsen look like a sop.

Frank's employment working for Melbourne's venerable afternoon broadsheet paper, which even published a late edition on Saturday afternoons to include the VFL results, gave Eddie his first break.

Frank was writing those VFL match reports, and he hired his thirteen-year-old brother to compile 'stats' for him – such as they were back then – and act as a runner, bolting down to the change rooms after the game to compile the injury lists and news of umpires' reports. Frank filed his stories to copy takers in the Flinders Street office, and the paper soon knew to hold the match being covered by the McGuires until last 'off the stone' because it would include additional late-breaking news supplied by Eddie straight from the angst and elation of the change rooms. Typesetters gave Frank's games a little extra space because they knew Eddie would have information they wouldn't get from other grounds.

Sometimes after an MCG game, Eddie would even sprint back along Wellington Parade and up the hill to the *Herald*'s offices overlooking Jolimont, to be there as journos filed their stories.[1]

Already, Eddie was setting himself the task of bettering his peers and elders. It was an easy game for a keen teen. Match reports were an addendum for many old writers – a simple way to earn some extra weekend coin. Indeed, Frank – who was making waves on the state political round – worked the extra shift filing VFL football on Saturdays for the money. An enthusiastic youngster could run rings around the old-timers by reporting from the change rooms, and the *Herald* loved it. The paper prided itself on being the first for footy and home to the doyen of VFL print writers, Alf Brown, so anything that set it apart from the rest was good news.

The McGuire brothers had a strategy to scorch the opposition with a dual-pronged attack. Frank taught Eddie a few tricks as his younger brother filed match reports for reserves games and stats for the seniors: look for different post-game behaviour among the players; hit up these people for a quote or a chat; watch the journos who don't stand with the pack – they're usually onto something; follow Trevor Grant – he's a pro; tell me who has ice packs on and where they have them; make sure a big-name player wasn't reported by the umpires.

The lead-up to Eddie's first front-page by-line was typical of his frenetic life. He played a game himself on the Saturday morning and then went to cover the second half of a reserves match at South Melbourne's Lakeside Oval, with mud still caked on his knees under the suit he'd borrowed from Frank. The Lakeside's press box was among the more rudimentary in the league, perched above an alcove where the police horses stood during quarters.

On the job, Eddie was exposed to some 'rustic' behaviour, including the day a sports writer with a gammy leg and a taste for a drink, Jack Dunne, asked everyone to lift their feet. A minute later, a policewoman knocked on the door to ask what was dripping down through the floor onto the horses.

That day at the Lakeside, Richmond player Ray Ball (Collingwood player Luke Ball's father) was told to get off the ground by an umpire, and was reported when he flashed his bum at the umpie in an act of complete disrespect. Eddie had the story: 'Ball bares all'. He filed from the ground then went on to the MCG to cover the seniors match, surely thinking this was one grand adventure: playing in the morning, reporting and sitting in the press box in the afternoon with news legends like Mike Sheahan, for whom Eddie would get the occasional coffee.

That summer, Australian Associated Press (AAP) needed a district cricket reporter for match reports that would go into the Saturday *Herald*, as well as the AAP wire copy for the *Sunday Observer* and the *Sunday Press*. They asked Frank whether his brother would be interested; management only knew Eddie through his by-line, not by age.

Would he ever. This was a step up from working with Frank; these were his own singular match reports. Frank guided him through his first day, but left him alone after that. Eddie's first cricket report was published on the Melbourne Cup weekend in 1978. He was yet to complete Form 2.

His parents were happy. His dad encouraged Eddie to forgo traditional teenage part-time jobs in the suburb, telling his son he'd much prefer him to write for the newspaper than deliver it.

The teen tyro unwittingly took advantage of a longstanding newspaper convention: editors didn't really care where the story came from if it was a good yarn. And young Eddie was filing good yarns.

Two seasons later, Eddie was invited to cricket's Ryder Medal because he was an 'established' writer. He went along and was asked whether he was there with his dad, the cricket writer Eddie McGuire. As he was in VFL circles, the teenager was quickly adopted by the sports media and his age proved no barrier.

Aged fifteen, Eddie was assigned his first international match, a Victoria versus England game, in which he sat in the press box next to some of the greats of the sports writing game, including Peter McFarlane and Henry 'Blowers' Blofeld, who took him to lunch in the MCG Members' Long Room afterwards. With beer.

Eddie was on the path to newspaper journalism, and he couldn't be held back. He was raring to go, and often burned the candle at both ends to maintain all his commitments. He would sometimes even cycle the 9 kilometres from Broadmeadows to Windy Hill to cover games. His dance card was overflowing; for one cricket match at Arden Street, he had to persuade another reporter to take notes for him while his dad drove him to Aberfeldie to run in the 800-metre race at the inter-school sports carnival before he returned to fudge the story.

He couldn't always keep up appearances, though, and one teacher remembers the days the teenage McGuire would fall asleep in class, recovering from a weekend of playing sport and working for the papers.[2] The school wasn't always amenable to Eddie's lapses. He somehow escaped detention after avoiding a cadet camp because he needed to work for the *Herald*, but he couldn't understand the grief he received from some brothers at CBC. Many pointed out that his elder brother glided through school, and they expected him to do the same. Sleeping in class wasn't the way to do that.

It wasn't just through getting him jobs that Frank showed he was still looking out for his younger brother. Frank was assigned to report on the Under-19 Grand Final in 1979, before Collingwood was due to play Carlton in the main event. Eddie couldn't get a ticket to the game, and it looked like he was going to miss out on seeing his beloved Magpies go for the premiership until his brother assigned him to carry the battery of phones the *Herald* would require to file copy throughout the day to the press box.

A gatekeeper insisted Eddie produce a ticket he didn't have before Frank told him he'd need to answer to the great Alf Brown if the *Herald* missed a moment of the Grand Final due to this impasse. That got Eddie in the gate, and once the phones were delivered he took off his jacket to reveal his Collingwood jumper. It proved another lesson in feeling pain that wasn't physical for Eddie when Carlton won 11.16.82 to 11.11.77, handing Collingwood its second Grand Final defeat in three years. Magpie supporters were sure they'd been robbed.

Though he was gaining immense experience as an aspiring journo, Eddie was still at school, and his weekends during his final year's schooling were frenetic. He still found time to carpet bomb the city in preparation for the end of his CBC days, applying everywhere for a job. Decades later, he can't comprehend what he was thinking, although it was the first inkling of a tenet that would subconsciously drive his life: the Glaswegian working-class fear that a job was never to be taken for granted and was always tenuous so you had to have options. His mass job applications worked, though: at one point he had six jobs to choose from. But not the one he wanted or expected.

Eddie was due to conclude his part-time stint at the *Herald* at the end of the home-and-away VFL season in September 1982, and he thought he'd easily walk into a job at the newspaper for which he'd written for five years. It wasn't to be. The man who had hired Frank wouldn't hire Eddie, who was flummoxed, believing this was another battle he'd have to overcome after his older brother had seemingly sailed in.

After that, Eddie wrote to every newspaper he knew – and every newspaper he didn't know. He enjoyed being interviewed at *The Age* by some of its legends, including editor in chief Creighton Burns, Robert Haupt and Michelle Grattan.

The interview obviously went well because *The Age* wasn't as reticent as the *Herald*, offering a cadetship when Eddie finished school, though it wasn't available until the next financial year (starting in July 1983). That was okay by Eddie, as he decided he'd have a red-hot crack at making the North Melbourne VFL squad while he was waiting.

The Kangaroo Under-19s were becoming a force to be reckoned with under the direction of future premiership-winning coach Denis Pagan. In the days of zoning, the Roos had access to a northern corridor through Melbourne, stretching from Arden Street through Broadmeadows and on to Craigieburn. It could have been worse. If Eddie had grown up across the road, he would have been zoned to Carlton.

The zoning rules brought some rough and ready players from tough clubs like Therry, which occasionally terrorised more genteel amateur clubs from south of the Yarra. Yet Pagan remembers Eddie presenting as a well-mannered, hard-working aspirant, memorable with his cheeky grin and his long-sleeved CBC jumper.

The jumper didn't hide much. He was a thin kid in an era of hefty thighs and beer-fuelled biceps. Sure, as a centreman he was a quick athlete with a straight kick, but his size – yes, he was a 'Collingwood six-footer', just nudging six foot (182 centimetres) – and lack of bulk counted against him. He was one of the 100 kids who didn't make the final squad. It was a telling blow for a young man who had invested so much into the game, and thought his hard work and dedication could be enough.

With the *Herald* out, *The Age* on hold and his footy career over before it had begun, another news organisation responded to Eddie's blitzkrieg of job applications.

Channel Ten news director John O'Lone asked him to come in for a chat. Edward Snr took a day off work, and Eddie a day off school, to drive across town to Ten's Nunawading studio.

Father and son arrived, and Edward waited in the car while Eddie went in. The teenager was wide-eyed at the sight of *The Roy Hampson Show* and practically speechless when he saw Logie winner Annette Allison. The bedazzle of television had him in its thrall already. O'Lone's secretary informed Eddie that something had come up and he couldn't see him today; Eddie started strategising in his head how he would break the news to his dad before she added that the deputy director of news, David Johnston, would see him instead.

Johnston, a veteran newshound from Seven who had only recently returned to television and started with Ten, grilled the youngster, asking him what questions he would ask Prime Minister Malcolm Fraser if he were to interview him there and then. McGuire's bluffing worked, and Johnston was mightily impressed — although Eddie had no inkling of this at the time. At the end of the interview, he walked out of the studios and he and his dad headed home, wondering.

A month later, the phone rang at their Gerbert Street home. The voice at the end of the line asked for Frank McGuire. Eddie said he'd be home in an hour before Johnston announced himself and asked if that was Eddie. 'Yes,' the boy replied.

Johnston said he was actually wanting to speak to him, but only had Frank's number.

'So, Frank still lives at home, does he?' Johnston inquired of the *Herald*'s rising star, as Eddie thought to himself, 'Live at home? He still lives in my bloody bedroom and won't leave!'

Johnston asked Eddie whether he'd like to work casually on weekends in the Ten Sports department to 'see if you like us and if we like you'.

It was perfect. The next day he finished at the *Herald* and the following Saturday started working as a copy boy at Ten on weekends, while completing the final two months of his school life.

Edward Snr's car turned into the driveway only minutes after Eddie hung up the phone. Dad thought the house must have been on fire given the speed with which his son tore through the front door and ran towards the front gate to meet him. 'Dad! Dad! You won't believe what's happened!'

His father and the car would be crucial for the months to come. Edward drove almost an hour each way to get his son to Nunawading at weekends. Some days he'd even let Eddie drive, with the L plates on.

Eddie – being Eddie – still had a few jobs to juggle on top of his upcoming Higher School Certificate (HSC). In the last few weeks of school, he told Ten's news director Tony Banks he might need some weeks off to catch up with his study. Banks told him to bring his books into work. So he did. Of course, Eddie didn't open his books there, being too busy chopping telexes and writing stories. He was always determined to be ready for the next opportunity, so wore a suit to work too – just in case the newsreader fell sick and he was called upon to step up.

Ten still hadn't committed to offering him anything permanent, but that didn't matter too much to Eddie. He had *The Age* job in his back pocket for July, after receiving standard pro forma knockbacks from Seven and Nine. The economic crises of the early 1980s were having an impact, and most TV chiefs weren't hiring – even Ten (which was faring better than most financially) warned Eddie that there may be nothing forthcoming. So, despite the thrill he was getting from TV, Eddie was coming to terms with a newspaper future.

With one option definite, you'd think Eddie would sit tight and be happy to wait. But that wasn't his way. Despite also being accepted into the RMIT Journalism course, he sent out another job application. Evelyn, then living in Sunbury, showed him an ad in her local paper for a job at the *Macedon Ranges Telegraph.*

He applied for the job and won it, warning the editor he'd need time off to attend RMIT and to play footy on Saturdays. He didn't tell the editor his plan was to work there for six months in order to soak up as much as he could to be match-fit for his cadetship at *The Age* in July. It was done and settled. Then Ten called, asking whether Eddie could work on Thursdays and Fridays.

He said no – he had a new full-time job and he needed it. As far as Eddie was concerned, he'd been living off his parents long enough. Ten rang back later that night and asked whether he could come and see news management on Friday. That was his full day at RMIT but he said yes anyway.

On that Friday, O'Lone and Johnston asked whether Eddie would work for Ten News if they gave him a cadetship. He couldn't say yes quickly enough, with the caveat he had to settle things with the *Macedon Ranges Telegraph.* The first story Eddie wrote for that paper was about his recruitment to the local paper; the second was about the Macedon journalist who'd been poached by Ten. Eddie wouldn't take his wage for that last week, apologising to his editor, who replied he hadn't thought the paper would keep him long anyway: 'I thought you might have been here more than two weeks, though!'

Eddie's future didn't lie in newspapers after all: the bedazzling world of television offered him his chance, and he was going to take it and run with it.

CHAPTER 3

COUNTING ON TEN

On his first day in the newsroom, deputy director of news David Johnston assigned the seventeen-year-old Eddie McGuire a test. Johnston asked Eddie to go out to the front of the building with a cameraman and record a piece to camera about any story from the front page of the newspaper. The vision emerged years later at a reunion and has since made its way to YouTube. It is instructive to watch the first on-screen hallmarks of determination and quick frustration for which Eddie McGuire would become known.

Trying to impress, Eddie chose a complicated story about economics. The pimply kid with a centre part wearing a navy suit is determined to get it right, and becomes mightily frustrated when he doesn't, pulling a scrunched face in anger. The emotions that cross his face suggest he really thought he'd have a one-day career at the TV network once the footage was assessed. He'd already learned that at consequential moments you only get one chance, and in that moment he thought he was blowing his.

However, his mixture of charisma, chutzpah and intense work ethic convinced Ten he was worth keeping. And he would eventually get it right. Years later, the first time Eddie read the sports news on television, he proudly called his mother after the bulletin and said: 'Thanks for teaching me to "read with expression", Mum!'

In the early 1980s, the Ten network was flush with cash and bonhomie as owner Rupert Murdoch spent his way to success, although Ten wasn't quite the sports presence it aspired to be. The eager Eddie looked a keen type right from the start, showing older news hounds a willingness to do anything he was asked, down to the most mundane task.

To Ten staff, Eddie's greatest attribute was his street smarts, the cunning that – especially back then – was even more crucial than having shorthand or perfect diction. It was about contacts, confidence and the tenacity to make a story work at a time when there was no Google search engine to help find sources or background information.

Eddie's first live TV appearance was the kind that disturbs sports journos even today: standing outside a footy tribunal for a live cross, reporting that there was, as yet, no news. Of course, an eighteen-year-old doing his first live piece to camera wouldn't be encouraged by his peers; newspaper journos stood behind the camera making faces – one even dropping his pants to try to elicit a response from the newbie.[1]

Eddie learned to maintain concentration despite such distractions. Indeed, his ability to look down the barrel of a camera and focus while all around are losing their heads remains one of his more unique and admired talents.

Even so, work had its frustrations for a young man with forthright opinions and a desire to get ahead. Eddie wasn't bashful about his ambitions. One colleague recalled having a drink with the new recruit and being told he wanted to be prime minister some day.[2] Before that, though, Eddie had grand plans for Ten.

Unfortunately, others weren't as open to these grand plans and new ideas. Eddie once recounted driving home from the station with his knuckles turning white as he strangled his steering wheel in anger and frustration. He thought his youthful exuberance was being stifled by his older, stodgier peers, who were telling him what he could and, more importantly, couldn't do. Already the progressive kid cadet felt he was being held back.[3]

He was young but he didn't think that should count against him; he wanted to make things happen. Eddie was smart enough to see the sports department as a way to build contacts, expertise and a quick name for himself in a distinct area rather than be lost in the morass and diversity of general news. He could see a future where he could make things happen in sport. General news didn't offer such options or specificity, so didn't excite him. Subsequently, he urged the news department not to treat sport as the light penultimate segment of the bulletin but as a platform for breaking news.

His time would come soon enough, as would *Eyewitness News*, which was assembling a sports department and a news team of rare quality.

But first Eddie had to extricate himself from his study. He continued the RMIT Journalism course until Ten told him to drop it; he was breaking too many stories – he didn't need theory to help him get that done. He told his then lecturer, the *Herald*'s Les Carlyon, that he was off, adding that he really wanted to complete his degree at some stage. Carlyon wasn't so sure, but told him if he wanted it he could catch up down the track. For a man who would go on to make a formidable career multi-tasking, Eddie's degree became one of the rare tasks he didn't complete. Not that it mattered; RMIT University awarded him an honorary doctorate in 2013 as a Doctor of Communications *honoris causa* (as a mark of esteem).

In his early days at Ten, Eddie still harboured an ambition to be a footballer; he really thought he could make it, and he was torn between the opportunities his employment was offering him and his one last chance to push towards a VFL career. Finally, as his career started to steady, he had to admit to himself the moment had passed him by, much as it hurt him.

Eddie made waves as a reporter with an obvious feel for sport and an uncommon ability to network and make contacts. His workmates knew he would be something – even as a hairy, skinny youth. And so did he – Eddie McGuire certainly didn't possess the doubt gene.

His beloved Collingwood provided him with an early lesson in reporting on the many layers of a football club. Eddie helped to cover the 1982/83 putsch to take over the club by a syndicate called 'The New Magpies', led by media proprietor Ranald Macdonald and his 'Magnificent Seven' candidates. While covering the brouhaha, Eddie befriended a number of influential Collingwood families, including the legendary Roses. Those connections would stand him in good stead in the years to come.

Eddie was rough, but he was ready; he wasn't the smoothest talent, yet he still earned the moniker 'super cadet' in the newsroom. He was often the last one working well after the bulletin began, and was so well regarded that he featured in a 1985 *Eyewitness News* 'Turn to Us' promo, pictured among the big guns, including Jo Pearson and David Johnston, as the whippet-thin jogger shown briefly in his singlet and shorts bounding along in front of the Yarra River boat sheds.

That promo was an indication Eddie's star was ascending, and he rose quickly within a Ten sports department not without its own already established stars. Bruce McAvaney, Mike Tancred, Peter Donegan and Rob Astbury were firing, as veterans such as Clem Dimsey made way for this new and very talented generation.

In late 1984, another young buck joined the team. Stephen Quartermain was twenty-two when he was head-hunted from the ABC. The sports team at Ten had noticed him doing crosses from the VFL tribunal, and he came in to join a now-formidable sports team led by the 'god' of the group, McAvaney.

Rupert Murdoch owned Ten at the time and, as would be his wont throughout his career, he invested heavily in news and promotion to lead the network to the top. It was still coming a long third when McGuire arrived but staff were happy to celebrate with parties for a solid third result in the ratings. It was the 80s after all.

The decade proved to be a boom time for Ten – at least on screen. It was the Olympic network, dating game show *Perfect Match* was a massive hit and its Melbourne *Eyewitness News* was flying in the ratings, with consistent high 30s. ATN-10 in Sydney had a similarly strong sports team, led by Ray Warren, Tim Webster, John Newcombe and Graeme Hughes. The Melbourne *Eyewitness News* team showed more than ratings leadership; the show had the audacity to hire the first meteorologist as a weather presenter: Rob Gell.

The turnaround at Ten was deliberate, and money was no object. Johnston, for instance, had been brought back at some cost after a career at Seven to read the news in Melbourne, and many of the journalists coming through the ATV-10 newsroom would become perennials of the business, including Mark Burrows, Neil Kearney and Jennifer Keyte.

It was a great testing ground for Eddie, learning the skills of television, stand-ups, writing scripts, editing and ensuring, unlike his earlier newspaper stories, the TV report had to source compelling visuals. Eddie adopted with vigour the early lesson not to come back from a job empty-handed – something that was important when you were looking to get ahead in a volatile, competitive newsroom in which strong personalities played hard. Eddie was forced to adopt a 'take no prisoners' attitude in those early newsroom days, and many would say he has never shrugged that off.

His greatest strength was apparent from the start – notwithstanding that first test report for Johnston. Off the cuff, Eddie had few rivals, even as a young journo, and his passion for and knowledge of footy were obvious. An older journalist from Sydney, Mike Tancred, latched onto him because he was a rugby boy; in exchange for footy information, Tancred would teach McGuire about television. It was an easy deal for the young Eddie to embrace.

Bruce McAvaney was particularly influential on the young cadet, and Eddie still refers to McAvaney as a mentor even though he would have learned more as a TV journalist from Rob Astbury when he was a copy kid, given that Astbury was all over the clubs in the years before the AFL Commission, working board members and club personnel in a way that was instructive to Eddie. From him, Eddie discovered sports reporting wasn't just about talking to sportspeople.

But within *Eyewitness News*, McAvaney was on another level, and was one of the few who could cut through Eddie's cocksure attitude and pull him into line, impressing upon him the importance of professionalism and preparation at all times.

Eddie soaked it all in, and pushed himself harder. On weekends, he also filed match reports for the Sunday papers. In the 1980s the Sunday paper wars were intense in Melbourne as the *Sunday Press* battled with the *Sunday Observer* for readers.

The *Observer* was rebuilding its sports section when Eddie McGuire got the call to cover a game every Saturday for about $150, with a $50 bonus if he managed to find a back-page lead story. Well, that was his sweet spot; he'd been doing that since he was thirteen years old. He grabbed about four back-page splashes in his first year (1987), again impressing newspaper types with his hunger and nose for a yarn.

His hunger for Collingwood wasn't so healthy, though. Saturday afternoon in sports newsrooms can be entertaining places when the footy and horse races are pumping. The young Eddie often enlivened Ten's newsroom with his enthusiastic special commentary and not-suitable-for-broadcast sledges of opposition teams, particularly Essendon. But if the Pies lost, McGuire was not good for much before the bulletin. More than once, his colleagues would take scripts from under his nose as he sat slumped over his Remington typewriter. 'Fuck it, I'll do it then,' they'd yell at the crestfallen junior who had been completely deflated by a Magpie defeat.

Despite these occasional moments of melancholy, Eddie's passion and ability to be across all aspects of VFL news soon led to his boss, Neil Miller, acceding to Eddie's request to have his own segment covering the Victorian Football League.

Miller called Eddie with the assignment and its name: *Doing the Rounds*. In the early days, Eddie was the expert at ringing players and officials on Monday morning for a casual chat about the weekend's game while prying subtly for the titbit that could lead to a story. These were the days when daily deadlines allowed a journalist the luxury of time to piece together and validate a story. With the sports segment being extended on Ten, Eddie had the scope to extend the gossip and news component of his pieces.

After earning the right to host *Doing the Rounds*, Eddie's modus operandi was simple: go to as many clubs as he could visit each day and cadge as much news as he could find.

It was what he was good at and he had a few advantages. First, he had a way with the players – later fuelled by his shrewd nightclubbing – that earned their trust. And, unlike another gun VFL reporter of the period, Eddie didn't burn the players by breaking confidences when he reported about them. Where journalists had players as contacts, Eddie had some as mates. To the players at least, Eddie appeared to be on their side, and he appreciated the rigours and confidences of the game. It was clear to players McGuire had played and studied the game. Indeed, colleagues who might have criticised a player would receive a disapproving eye from Eddie McGuire after a broadcast. And Eddie knew the best way to find the stories was to be with the players, whether at training or at after-match functions, or partying at nightclubs. He understood how to approach and cajole players differently, depending on a win or loss. He was able to court and seduce contacts in a fashion beyond many of his peers. Collingwood captain Tony Shaw saw the seduction and warned his team at one point that Eddie might be a Collingwood man who would protect the club, but he was also a journalist who should not be trusted. As dogged a journo as he was, history suggests Shaw's fear was unfounded; McGuire's fierce loyalty means he has always been a Collingwood man first.

Eddie's professional friendships with players extended in odd ways. In 1988, he offered to testify at a tribunal rehearing for suspended Magpie Craig Starcevich. McGuire reported on the game in which Starcevich was deemed to have hit the Hawks' Darrin Pritchard. The Tribunal refused to reconsider the charges, so Eddie didn't have the chance to state his evidence and Starcevich's suspension stood.

Time and again, Eddie showed he was interested in more than just the game and the results (except when it came to the Pies). Ten management noticed he was as intrigued by the motivations of club executives and the VFL management as he was by Saturday's game. That too distinguished him from other sports reporters. So did his mobile phone: he was the first person in the *Eyewitness News* newsroom to have one – a big brick of a thing – to cope with his countless hours stationed outside the VFL Tribunal.

His intrepid reporting almost had him speared when he ventured to Moorabbin in 1988 to talk to the injured Saints' full-forward and recent Brownlow medal winner Tony 'Plugger' Lockett. Lockett was unaware the club had set up the interview, and he had just arrived at the hospital to find out whether his season was over. He was on crutches and not prepared to talk to anyone other than a doctor or a nurse. Seeing McGuire head towards him with a cameraman close behind was enough to set him off. The sight of Plugger spearing a crutch through a doorway at Eddie as Lockett's father looked on remains one of Australian television's most infamous 'doorstops'. It helped propel the image of McGuire as a dogged newsman as well as a sports reporter of note, and ran at the start of that day's news bulletin.

McGuire was on the make at Ten, and he knew when an opportunity came along you grabbed it. He cancelled an overseas holiday in order to cover the Swan Premium Sun Tour bike race with daily reports for the channel – it was somewhat out of his area of expertise, but he wasn't going to let that stop him.[4] With his usual verve, he threw himself into the sport, even taking up cycling as a recreation.

Deep down, though, Eddie McGuire was desperate to call football matches. After a childhood calling them off the radio as he played simultaneously in the backyard on Saturday afternoons, now the possibility of really doing so was tantalisingly within reach.

Ten didn't have an appetite for the VFL broadcast rights, which were historically tied to Seven, but it snagged the rights to broadcast the 1987 post-season match in London between Carlton and North Melbourne. Officially, it was known as the Fosters International Cup Qualifying Final, and it was supposed to be a friendly exhibition game to introduce a wider international audience to the game; soon it would become known as the Battle of Britain, or 'the Bloodbath', after a brawl sparked by a bit of push and shove between Stephen Kernahan and Stephen McCann resulted in a brawl in which Alastair Clarkson king-hit Ian Aitken. Eddie won the gig to commentate, along with McAvaney. 'There's a shocker behind play,' McGuire called. 'Clarkson has come in and king-hit and Johnston's in there now and this is going to develop into a wild melee here.'

It might have become a huge spectacle, but Eddie almost didn't get the chance to call his first VFL match at the Oval. When Carlton chief executive Ian Collins arrived, he spoke to Ten staff about where the Fosters signs should be placed around the ground, pointing out where he thought they should go. He was also adamant radio veteran Harry Beitzel should call the game. Ten objected, saying Beitzel wasn't part of its network, and McGuire and McAvaney were their men. Ten had its way and the rest is football history.

Eddie was definitely Ten's go-to man, at least behind McAvaney, as he extended his range. He was part of Ten's Melbourne Cup coverage, reporting from the starting barrier, and he filled in for Stephen Quartermain as the nightly sports-reader while Quartermain was away covering the Seoul Olympics and the 1989 Ashes cricket series.

Eddie's rapid rise continued. He won the Electronic Media or Television category of the VFL Media Awards in 1989, 1990 and 1991, and it was becoming apparent he was a rare TV reporter: one who wasn't content to just report the news of the day. McGuire wanted his story to be THE news of the day.

In 1989 he was elevated to the chief weekday sports news-reading role after McAvaney left for Seven, a move that upset his buddy Quartermain, who was also angling for the role. The two were tight but competitive, although many thought the rivalry's heat came more from Quartermain. Eddie was always a step ahead because he had a mongrel instinct that Quartermain didn't possess. Eddie was the street-wise, funny scoundrel, whereas 'Quarters' was the polished performer. While no one anticipated McGuire's later achievements off screen, many knew Quartermain would one day settle in as a newsreader.

Despite the workplace rivalry, the pair had their fun on and off screen. They combined for one unlikely story in 1990 that actually won an award: a re-enactment of Collingwood player Craig 'Ned' Kelly being reunited with his presumed lost dog, Jazzy.

The duo kept pushing the Sydney-based network for a local footy show on Ten's Melbourne channel, but the idea didn't find any traction in the Sydney head office, which pointed out Ten didn't have the rights to the AFL. Eddie argued this fact didn't matter, given the access the station had to players and clubs through his *Doing the Rounds* segment.

Ten was bumbling its way down from its position of power under Murdoch – who had to sell the network when he became a US citizen – and was dealing with a chain of owners, including Frank Lowy's Westfield (Lowy would say owning Ten was 'like trying to hold a fish. The tighter we gripped the more it slipped out of our hands'.)[4] And a consortium led by former journalist Steve Cosser, who led the network for a year before the banks put it into receivership in 1990 and into the hands of the Canadian Izzy Asper's CanWest company.

At a time when Eddie McGuire was established enough to push the footy show idea again, Ten's management in Sydney was more interested in its own ideas and survival. Ten was a network in name only, and Eddie and the news division felt they worked for ATV-10 Melbourne, not Network Ten or Sydney's TEN-10. However, Eddie believed the footy show was a great idea, so it was one he wouldn't give up on as he continued to dominate his footy round.

Eddie always went the extra yard with everything, and his footy contacts were no different. As Footscray finally won its fight to stave off being merged with Fitzroy in 1989 and the VFL had to give the club its licence back after it raised money to pay its debts, Eddie asked Bulldogs saviour Peter Gordon to agree to be interviewed for the 5 p.m. *Eyewitness News*. Gordon said it was too far to travel to Nunawading, so Eddie sent the Ten helicopter to the Western Oval to pick him up. Waiting for Gordon in the Ten studio, via satellite from London, was the chastened VFL boss, Ross Oakley.

Through such initiative, by 1990 Eddie had established his reputation as one of the game's most prolific news breakers. Yet, in a tight newsroom, his frustration at people not meeting his expectations was a flaw – sometimes outrageously so. His ranting was legendary, yet he was always sharp enough to assuage hurt egos with a heartfelt apology.

Yes, Eddie was the man who got the story and nailed down the sources, but occasionally his work sailed close to the wind. His peers admired his work ethic, but he also pushed them to the limit. He was the classic late-filer, always working right to deadline. Editors would scatter as he came down the corridor of editing booths at Nunawading twenty minutes before the bulletin with arms full of tapes and a script he needed done precisely as written. He knew exactly how he wanted them edited.

Indeed, he taught himself how to edit stories because he became so frustrated with editors wanting to do things differently. That exacerbated problems in the newsroom, as they'd call for work to be stopped when they saw the journalist 'playing' on their equipment.

Eddie piled immense pressure on his editing team. Despite his proficiency live to air, he had an odd habit of not being able to deliver a voiceover in one take. Yet the tension was always alleviated somewhat when, like clockwork, he would come back to the editing booth after the bulletin concluded at 6 p.m. to apologise sweetly and sincerely. He could burn people yet was always savvy enough to extinguish the fire quickly.

This anger at workmates when they disappoint him is a trait Eddie McGuire hasn't shaken. Even today, only the occasional on-air equal or boss has been bold enough to confront Eddie about it. But he displays an anger born out of frustration rather than an evil intent. He just wants the job done to his standards: perfectly. And tomorrow is always another day. Eddie doesn't hold a grudge – partly because he knows his reaction is often tempestuous and unreasonable, and partly because it isn't in his nature … at least not at work. Footy is another matter.

None of this affected Eddie back then. On screen he was gold. He worked it hard, offering to call VFA matches with Phil Gibbs for nothing. The kid who had once called matches next to the radio and then off the TV was not going to let any opportunity to call football pass. This was his dream come true. He later called the 1990 VFL Grand Final for 3AK radio alongside Don Hyde, Michael Roach and Jim Main, and there was a chance he would continue there before 3AK pulled the plug on the 1991 season.

Eddie McGuire's audience appeal even led to Ten allowing him to jump networks – which was just not done back then – to appear on Seven's popular late-night talk show, *Tonight Live with Steve Vizard*. But Eddie wasn't focused only on himself; his success also allowed him to work for the greater good. It might have been token, relative to the often quiet charitable work he would do in later decades, but becoming the number one ticketholder in the inaugural year for the newly aligned, and short-lived, VFA club the Brunswick–Broadmeadows Football Club was a proud moment for this Broady boy. It meant something to that community because they hadn't had their own senior team, and juniors who grew up in the area had to disperse to play for other clubs once they graduated into older teams. This connection to footy was a major perk of Eddie McGuire's job – it gave him the ultimate access, and it hit its nirvana in 1990 when his beloved Collingwood won the VFL Premiership.

Ten minutes after Collingwood won the Grand Final, player Mick McGuane and director Wayne Richardson gave Eddie the Premiership Cup, which he hid in streamers and snuck out of the bowels of the Members' Stand into the MCG car park for a live cross to *Eyewitness News*.

Eddie opened his segment holding the cup aloft, breaking all rules of journalistic objectivity but providing a great live TV moment, as one ecstatic journalist relayed the joy of overcoming 32 years of Collingwood heartbreak. Eddie also smuggled the cup to show his dad; a photograph of the two Edwards with the cup is still among the family's most valued possessions.[5]

He couldn't have done it if the players and club didn't trust him.[6] Later that night, McGuire mused with colleagues about how the premiership was a reward for years of patience, theorising at just how monstrous the Collingwood Football Club could be. As the players' bus was stopped by a heaving mass of supporters on its way to Victoria Park later that night, Eddie was not alone in dreaming of an unstoppable future if anyone could harness this beast called Collingwood.

At the team dinner, president Allan McAlister declared Leigh Matthews coach for life and Lou Richards said it might be the first of ten premierships in a row for the Magpies. Eddie McGuire listened and dreamt of what could be.

But this particular dream did not come true; none of the victorious 1990 team played in another winning final. Eddie wasn't to know it then, but the possibilities for his club were right in front of him.

Meanwhile, he had work to do. On the following Monday, he implored some of the partying players to come to the Ten studios to present the sports bulletin. That was a Whitehorse Road too far away for the weary Pies, who'd been celebrating in the city for two days, so Eddie again commissioned the Ten helicopter, this time to pick up the sozzled Michael Christian, Craig Kelly, Peter Daicos, Denis Banks and Darren Millane from the Tunnel nightclub and deliver them to Nunawading.

Only Christian thought that this, in all its absurdity, could be an audition, while the others were still half-cut and baffled by the whole experience. After the broadcast, they ambled to the helicopter to fly back to their buddies. 'Sorry boys, it's a taxi home,' they were told. Eddie was nowhere to be seen.

It was apparent Eddie was becoming too big for the Ten sports desk. He knew it too. Perhaps in an attempt to keep him happy, Ten manufactured a VFL league teams show that Eddie hosted with Simon Madden and Ted Whitten, although it was short-lived.

After the 1988 Seoul Games, Ten lost the rights to the Olympics, and that alone meant the network would find it harder to retain its stable of sports stars. It couldn't keep McAvaney, and Ten didn't have the sports programming that would satisfy Eddie's itches either, as rumours abounded of him being poached by Seven.

Ten wasn't going to give up without a fight, and launched a new sports show, *Sportsweek*, hosted by Eddie and Stephen Quartermain, that would wrap up the weekend's sport with a focus on footy. However, the 10.30 p.m. Sunday-night slot wasn't optimal.

The following year – 1992 – Ten planned the launch of an hour-long mid-week sports preview show from Sydney featuring the odd trio of McGuire, David Fordham and Wayne Pearce. It hoped to leverage its NBL basketball rights into what would become *The Sports Show*, subsequently hosted by McGuire and Sydney-based Mike Gibson after some horse-trading.

McGuire showed his intent, noting that, 'Too many other sports shows in the past have become too matey and don't ask the hard questions.'[7] Ten didn't have its heart in it, though, and it showed. It didn't want to ask the hard questions either.

Eddie kept moving from show to show, hosting Ten's coverage of the Uncle Toby's Iron Man Super Series or whatever else he could get his hands on. He was clearly a restless soul, yet remained oddly loyal to Ten.

Before the launch of *Sports Tonight* in 1993, what would become a relatively long-term late-night beacon for Ten was merely expected to be a cheap and cheerful filler format imported from the land of ice hockey and suggested by the Canadian owners of Ten. Local news management argued that *Sports Tonight* was created in the Sydney newsroom, but the reality was ESPN's *Sportscenter* was the model for all sports news shows at the time and Ten was not breaking any new ground.

Initially, Eddie was to be part of a group of sports stars including Kieren Perkins, David Campese and Nick Farr-Jones rolling through the show hosted by Tim Webster from Sydney,[8] with Russell Fairfax, Mary-Anne Dibbs and Amanda DePledge, Peter Donegan, Quartermain and Anthony Hudson reporting. McGuire and Quartermain were among those suggesting the show should be broadcast from Melbourne. Logically, it should have been – that's where Network Ten's sports news-breakers were. But Webster was Sydney's man, and he would host the new program, which debuted in August 1993 and did as much to exacerbate the Sydney–Melbourne divide as Graham Kennedy's *In Melbourne Tonight* decades earlier.

Sydney management thought the Melbourne sports bureau was leaking information disparaging Webster, but some of Webster's Sydney-centric bumbling and mispronunciation of VFL names put Melbourne viewers and critics off-side immediately – the peak would be announcing on air that Collingwood star Nathan Buckley had resigned, not re-signed.

Of course, a Sydney sports program would never cut it in Melbourne – McGuire or no McGuire. The *Herald Sun*'s Jon Anderson wrote:

> What a pity Channel 10's new sporting program *Sports Tonight* isn't hosted and produced in Melbourne, which by then was becoming a beachhead against the mounted police coming from Sydney in the form of the network's new Canadian owners.
>
> Reporters Eddie McGuire, Steve Quartermain and Peter Donegan, plus producer Steve Pritchard, have proven themselves far and away the best news-breaking television team in this town, yet we must suffer Tim Webster presenting the show from Sydney each night. Another golden opportunity missed.[9]

Ten would soon miss another opportunity as Seven and Nine circled the Melbourne reporter. In his years at Ten, Eddie McGuire became TV's hottest young sport-reporting property. A couple of years later, as his star rose on *The Footy Show*, *The Age*'s Peter McFarlane wrote, 'At the risk of causing his head to expand even further, it must be said that Eddie McGuire was the last television reporter to devote all his energies to news gathering.'

From a leader of his craft – an intimidating creature who Eddie looked up to and first met as a fifteen-year-old – it was some accolade. And Ten's competitors agreed.

CHAPTER 4

EDDIE EVERYWHERE

As an ambitious teen, there were few moments when Eddie McGuire was the shrinking violet in the corner of the room.

One of those moments was at the Football Writers' Association Awards held in Jack Hamilton's office at the old VFL House near the corner of Brunton Avenue and Jolimont Terrace, four decent torpedoes from the MCG Members' Pavilion.

The young Eddie had just earned his driver's licence, but it was when he was still a part-timer at Ten, before he grabbed his cadetship. In this room, though, he was a fan. The first man he brushed past was Footscray legend Ted Whitten! McGuire was mesmerised and shrank back into a corner until the ABC's Drew Morphett, the dashing host of the weekly footy show *The Winners*, saw the lonely young figure and started the introductions: 'I'd like to introduce you to Jack Dyer ... meet Neil Roberts ... this is Ian Major and Harry Beitzel', and so on. Eddie was in his element. Meeting radio icons 'The Captain ('Captain Blood' Jack Dyer) and The Major'. That was grand, but Eddie also met Collingwood icons and *World of Sport* panellists Lou Richards and Bruce Andrew. 'That's Collingwood premiership captain Richards and dual premiership player Bruce Andrew!' McGuire thought.

The Football Writers' Association numbered no more than 25 journos in those days, but what names they were. McGuire was incredulous. And he was not only meeting them, but being treated respectfully by them. They knew who he was; he'd made a name for himself already, and the hardened sports journos could recognise his by-line from his coverage of district cricket matches and helping with Frank's VFL match reports.

Richards later wrote of McGuire: 'From the moment you lay eyes on Eddie McGuire you had a feeling that he wasn't going to stop until he hit the heights.' Most thought the same when they met him as a teenager.

After the 'awards', a few younger revellers decided they needed some food, so Morphett and former Geelong champion Sam Newman led a posse in Sam's Corvette to Topo Gigio's on Toorak Road. Eddie was worried; he had only seven dollars in his pocket and that almost stopped him joining in. He drove his Dad's old Toyota and jagged a park right outside the restaurant, a habit he would maintain during his next decade frequenting Toorak Road's bars and eateries.

Sam recommended the pepper steak to Eddie. It was an exotic choice for the tastebuds of a Broadmeadows boy who'd grown up on Irish stew and fried meat. He burnt his mouth. And it was $10. He was quietly terrified until Newman noticed and showily said, 'We're picking up the bill tonight, young man.' Morphett stumped up the cash for McGuire's dinner.

Dinner finished, Newman asked, 'Now, Ed, would you like to join us across the road?'

'What's across the road?' McGuire asked hesitantly.

'Well, we're going to Silvers discotheque,' he replied. And here's where a decade of carousing and working the nightclubs and bars of inner Melbourne began. Newman led the group past the queue and straight through the door before the group was handed drink cards, the holy grail of 1980s nightclubbing. Eddie was introduced to the manager, who said he would welcome him any time; McGuire didn't forget. He later joked that he was back there at 7.30 the following night, taking up the offer.

Eddie stood back and watched the dashing Newman in full flight as women flirted with him and men stepped out of his way. Sam asked a hostess whether he could hear that new song by Johnnie Cougar. The next song played was 'Jack & Diane'. In one night, Eddie McGuire was introduced to the joys of drink cards, nightclubs, the pulling power of Toorak Road and the charisma of Sam Newman.

The relationship between journalist and protagonist has changed markedly in recent decades, across most fields. Canberra's Parliament House physically separates journos from politicians; Hollywood stars ask for questions to be vetted ahead of their three-minute television interviews; and AFL footballers lead largely monastic lives, and only liaise with media when a media manager decrees that it will happen.

Eddie rose as a journalist in arguably better days, a time when news subjects trusted journalists and going to a nightclub was a legitimate news-gathering exercise. And he worked it hard. The roots of so much of what came good for him in later years with *The Footy Show*, the Collingwood presidency and his domination of Melbourne networks came during these early carousing years.

McGuire worked and played hard. Legend has it that when the young Ten sports reporter realised the station didn't have a publicity department, he set out to attend functions and openings to improve his profile.[1] He became his own publicity department. He made sure he was everywhere he needed to be, and his networks were already beginning to help. The *Herald Sun's* social pages photographer Fiona Hamilton gave Eddie a prominent run, partly because her father, the VFL's general manager Jack Hamilton, loved Eddie.

McGuire had some willing accomplices at Ten, including the older journalist Mike Tancred and shy eastern suburbs boy Stephen

Quartermain. Eddie McGuire taught him a thing or two – most importantly the whys and wherefores of drink cards. The pair proudly boasted at one point they didn't pay for a drink for five years as they caroused Toorak Road, King and Chapel Streets. In their early days, the Ten journos frequented the Star and The Roxy in South Melbourne; Redheads at Albert Park was also popular among footballers. They lived in each other's pockets for a decade.

This was a golden age for Melbourne nightclubs, when the clubs were infamous for late 80s excess, liberalised licensing hours, cocaine and boom-and-bust club nights. If it had gone badly they wouldn't have been the first journalists to be ruined by drink, but Eddie was disciplined. He was particularly upright, carrying on with the best of them but not once being seen wasted or reported out of control on alcohol (although he did break his nose in a 1992 nightclub stoush and fall down the stairs, and years later a couple of photos of a glazed-eye TV star circulated in Melbourne). He could be exuberant; The Metro was a favoured haunt, just up the hill from Triple M, and one night, McGuire grabbed a beer hose and sprayed patrons exultantly from atop the bar. Yet he maintained his decorum and friends sense that, even then, Eddie did not want to accumulate skeletons for his closet. He may have already anticipated his possible trajectory.

Eddie and his nightclub posse were happy rapscallions. McGuire surrounded himself with mates who were young, good-looking and notable for their good manners. He learned well from Newman. Even when he was a pimply nobody, he would pull the 'Don't you know who I am?' gambit at nightclub doors, more as a bluff than an expectation. Even when nobody did know, his braggadocio always seemed to work.

'I'm Eddie McGuire from *Eyewitness News*,' he would say, and the red velvet rope would part. 'My face is my medallion,' he'd tell friends – and it was. He became a king of the Melbourne nightclub scene.

Eddie's nightclub years were just as much a professional venture as a young man's folly, because he befriended VFL footballers – particularly his beloved Collingwood players – through the pubs and clubs. He loved the experience of talking to players and getting to know them away from the sometimes constricting club environments. And the players liked Eddie. He was respectful of their privacy, respectful of the game, appeared to know the game better than most, didn't ask stupid questions or push particularly hard after losses, and was their age. Eddie was drawn to them and the culture, noting that, 'I haven't met too many [AFL footballers] I wouldn't stand at the bar and have a drink with. I really like that culture.'[2]

While Ten news chiefs appreciated a journo who wouldn't say no, his seeming inability to refuse an invitation also saw him earn the moniker 'Eddie Everywhere'. Some may have thought this nickname came much later, from his screen omnipresence, but it was a tag he carried long before that time as he spread himself thin after dark.

Such were Eddie's hours that he became known for living out of his car. He would keep changes of clothes in his battered vehicle just in case he didn't make it home, and he'd often spend the night on a friend's couch or in their front room.

Later, his friendship with Adidas rep (and former Footscray captain) Ted Whitten meant the back of that car was usually brimming with oodles of free Adidas sports gear and tennis racquets, while his shirts, ironed ready for work, were hanging in the window. His Datsun was only good for one passenger, as the back seat was full of clothes and sports gear.

The only thing that seemed to slow him down was having to be at his breakfast shift at Triple M. Eddie presented the sports news on *The Richard Stubbs Breakfast Show* in the late 1980s. He was disciplined enough to not look out of control on screen, but he could look shabby rushing in to do this show. It was not unknown for Eddie to roll out of a city nightclub and walk straight down the hill into the Bourke Street studio of Triple M.

He'd work hard at Ten and be seen again that night at The Underground, the Carousel, the Saloon Bar or Silvers. He kept himself sharp, having his hair trimmed at celebrity hairdresser Edward Beale's Toorak salon even from his early days at Ten.

Like the teachers at CBC, Ten management rolled their eyes as Eddie came close to being disciplined after turning up after all-night sessions and going to sleep at his desk. Yet his capacity for breaking stories always saved him. And, as friends recount, he had 'a good engine'. However, his routine was noticed, and the *Herald*'s chief football writer, Mike Sheahan, suggested he slow down a little. Months later, during his 30th birthday speech, McGuire laughingly dismissed the gratuitous advice from an elder that he was 'getting ahead of himself'.

Eddie McGuire looks back at this time as a 'Boy's Own Annual' period. In the late 1980s, a group of media types, including *The Flying Doctors* star Peter O'Brien, the *Coodabeen Champions*' Ian Cover and Greg Champion, and Stephen Quartermain christened themselves the 'Mouse Pack', an Antipodean piss-take of Las Vegas's famed Rat Pack. Tennis, cricket and golf were just as likely to be had as a night on the tiles and it wasn't always with 'celebrity' mates in the spotlight. McGuire became close with nightclub regular Colin DeLutis and for a period Eddie had a quiet Friday golf foursome with three of Melbourne's greatest carousers – St Kilda star Trevor Barker, Skyhooks' lead singer Graeme 'Shirley' Strachan and Hawk bombardier Dermott Brereton – at the Elsternwick Golf Club. Among them all, Eddie was seen as the sensible one – always in relative control. Another striking aspect of the young troupe is they all progressed individually to very successful careers.

Footballers were happy to join the fun, knowing McGuire, Brereton and DeLutis would be holding court at the Saloon Bar or elsewhere on a Sunday because DeLutis's new Mercedes would be parked at the front door with two wheels up on the gutter.

Eddie was burning the candle at both ends, working seven days a week and accumulating a reputation as one of the town's original playboys. And why not? He was young, had a good disposable income and was employed in a high-profile job.

It wasn't just his elders who were noticing the young journo's antics either. Eddie was a perennial contestant in the *Cleo* Bachelor of the Year competition, once voted runner-up (perhaps after his response to the question, 'Give us the opening line to a love letter', which was, 'My dearest Lisa, the time we have been apart may only be short, but still my heart longs like the summer equinox.')[3] His 1992 bachelor profile listed his biggest vice as 'Going out too much'. Eddie embraced it all, and he was even prepared to take his shirt off for the occasional Triple M promo shot. He was a good bachelor, more likely to switch a girlfriend than cook a meal at home. He arrived on the doorstep of mate Trevor Marmalade's home one morning, in a suit with his shirt unbuttoned to the navel, with bare feet, saying: 'I've broken up with my girlfriend, I've got two weeks off, and I'm moving into the area.'[4]

He hosted Triple M's Desperate and Dateless Ball for 5000 people on Valentine's Day, came third-last in the 1991 Grand Prix celebrity race (ahead of Robert DiPierdomenico and Elle Macpherson) and continued to be in high demand hosting sportsmen's nights and other functions.[5] As far as Eddie was concerned, it was all part of his career development, not partying.

He began mixing heartily with the Collingwood players and, after the 1990 premiership, they were partying hard. That team was a group of rogues who managed to turn it on in September and heist a flag; they had good reason to party.

The social side of life mixed his passions for sport and his profession. He was part of the short-lived Collingwood coterie group The Magpie Monochromes, and in 1991 a member of the select, all-male fund-raising group The Crux Club, which brought together key sporting, media and business personalities to raise money for young sportspeople and charities (although some of the lads, including Simon Beasley, Michael Roberts, Michael Nettlefold and McGuire, happened to hold occasional functions at Silvers Nightclub).[6]

McGuire was becoming a very confident presence in Melbourne. As Chris Handy joked at a Melbourne sports debate in 1994, 'Eddie fell in love with himself 20 years ago, and he's remained faithful ever since.'[7]

As Eddie's career later moved to another level at Nine, his profile exploded and even more doors opened. He swapped his battered Datsun for a BMW, moved to South Yarra and lived the bachelor's life – socially chaotic and unable to cook for himself.

The cliché says footballers own pubs, so it follows the host of *The Footy Show* should own a nightclub. After all, a couple of his mates were in the game. In 1994, McGuire and Newman became part-owners of the Chevron Club, the famed St Kilda road venue newly renamed Club Chevron. They had plans for a revamped sports bar, nightclub and diner featuring a section devoted to a Sporting Hall of Fame that was no more than a storage space for their accumulating sports memorabilia. 'It's great because it's a combination of the two things I love the most – sport and socialising,' Eddie said.[8] Alas, life got in the way and the investment was short-lived.

Yet, just as his partying brought him connections and access to some great times, the downside of Eddie McGuire's very social life was being linked with some unsavoury moments – moments he would later wish hadn't happened.

Eddie was out late in 1991 with Collingwood champ Darren 'Pants' Millane and Denis Banks, who had been 'celebrity barmen' at The Tunnel that night – after being dropped there by coach Leigh Matthews – before bidding adieu early in the night. The Pies drank on until late in the morning and, in a fit of exuberance, 'hijacked' a bus – or at least drove it a couple of metres; they didn't realise six paying commuters were seated in the back. The incident, however minor, was manna from heaven for the newspapers, but McGuire believes the subsequent faux hysteria hurt Millane who, after having being charged with assault in 1990, was just wresting back control of his life. The coverage of the hijack set him back on his heels, and 'Pants' believed his chances of earning the Collingwood captaincy were gone. Some believe this incident was the catalyst for him again taking up the booze.

During another night out, Millane called Banks from The Tunnel, leaving a message on his answering machine on which he sang 'Goodbye Yellow Brick Road' and urged his mate to join him on the town. Early on the morning of 7 October 1991, Millane gave up on Banks and decided to drive his car home. It was a fatal decision; he killed himself driving into the back of a truck. McGuire would later co-write Millane's biography, *Pants: The Darren Millane Story*, in 1994, as a tribute to a great mate.

The worst outcome of McGuire's work after dark was being dragged innocently into a rape trial as a friend of the defendant, Stephen Millichamp. Millichamp was acquitted of raping a woman at his house after an all-night party in 1997, but it was a public and humiliating moment for McGuire and Stephen Quartermain as the duo gave evidence, saying they had seen the woman at a party at Millichamp's South Yarra home after they had been to a Channel Ten reunion and moved on to the Imperial Hotel. They were both sober during the busiest time of their year – football finals – and not implicated in any wrongdoing, but it was a sobering event, played out in the press and by their competitors with a little too much schadenfreude.

By then, McGuire was long past his jolly days. He could still pull a long night, but it was now for work rather than the sake of a fun time. His direction changed dramatically when he met Carla

Galloway at a fortieth birthday party for his mate Mike Tancred in his Mont Albert backyard in 1995. McGuire attended with another woman, but fell for Carla as soon as he laid eyes on her.

The couple hit it off immediately, and McGuire was tamed quickly – although deep down he was ready to settle. Their first public outing was soon enough, at that year's Cox Plate, and they were engaged in December of that year and married in 1997.

Galloway started her own fashion label, Endless Spirit, when she was 21, and was successful in her own right and attracted to Eddie's work ethic. It contrasted with the entitlement of those men she'd met who were born into money and status. As it happened, she matched his 1992 Bachelor of the Year profile of an ideal woman: 'Somebody who has a life of her own, a sense of humour and a fair bit of ambition. I'm not a real big fan of these girls that don't get past what they look like.'

They travelled in the 1995 off-season overseas, including trips on the Concorde and the Orient Express, and international holidaying has remained a constant in their lives – if only to extricate them from the bubbles of fame and work in Australia.

They honeymooned in Prague, expecting to be relatively anonymous – until someone yelled 'Eddie!' as the couple passed the only McDonalds in town. Two backpackers from Adelaide wanted a photo with him.

During their wedding speeches, McGuire reiterated what his parents had taught him: Australia is a place where you can achieve anything. Galloway spoke of the two words summing up her new husband – loyalty and commitment – but also her fear that everyone wanted a piece of him.[9]

After almost twenty years of marriage, those two words have defined their relationship. With Carla by his side his success has been sustained. 'Carla is so resolute', Eddie said in 2013. 'She stands beside me on everything. She's very worldly in the way of people. She picks people very well. I'm probably a person who starts with the glass completely full and works my way back; she starts with it half empty and makes you work to your position. I probably barrack for things; she sees things more realistically. She can see the foibles in football where I tend to see the romance of it. She's been a fantastic partner for me in facilitating everything that I can do. I couldn't do anything without Carla's full support.'

Carla would be the final piece in McGuire's personal puzzle, a leveller, confidant, cautious and the stability his life required if he was to truly take advantage of his talents. She would help take him to a whole new level.

CHAPTER 5

MORE THAN A NICE HAIRCUT AND A GOOD SMILE

It wasn't just his social life bestowing upon Eddie the name Eddie Everywhere. He was simultaneously conquering a number of media platforms.

The wireless had been Eddie McGuire's window into football. Like many youngsters across Victoria, he played with his own footy in his backyard while listening to Saturday afternoon VFL broadcasts on the transistor radio.

Radio has held an allure for Eddie McGuire ever since, and he would transform that fascination into an integral part of his professional progress. He would become a thoroughbred broadcaster who not only created a unique 'sports entertainment' format for FM radio, but also used his position on the airwaves as a crucial part of his being and personal growth. He built heady influence and clout in Melbourne – and it wasn't by accident. He fought a long campaign on radio to become the influence he is today.

As early as 1987, McGuire began reporting for Triple M as the breakfast sports guy attached to Triple M's newsroom while juggling his work for Ten and the *Sunday Observer*. He shifted to presenting morning news sports reports for Triple M in 1988; it was a move that tested his nightclubbing stamina, as the young buck often arrived at work moments before he was due on air.

Triple M program director Lee Simon and Rob Sitch, a key writer and performer with the tight-knit D-Generation comedy troupe, recruited him to do the sports reports on the D-Gen's FM radio show, but soon realised Eddie had much more to give, and his role expanded.

Triple M didn't want to let Eddie's talent go when the D-Gen moved on; he became an essential element of what would evolve into FM's leading breakfast show in Melbourne, led by comedian Richard Stubbs. It even toppled the dominant 3AW duo of Ross Stevenson and Dean Banks in one survey in 1994.

The light, bright show from Bourke Street featured his workmate, friend and for a short time flatmate from Ten, Brigitte Duclos, and an ever-rotating cast of fourth bananas, including Triple R graduate Leaping Larry L, Tim Smith and Brad 'The Young Idiot', together with a lot of good-natured, whip-smart ribbing. The show wasn't breaking any ground with its format but the talent was strong. They were young and flying.

The show succeeded despite the Triple M radio network's ownership problems: the network was sold by FM Australia to Village Roadshow in 1993 after going into receivership. Its success helped McGuire to build his presence in town, although he stayed in breakfast radio longer than he needed. Stubbs was the star – and allegedly an increasingly difficult one as time wore on – and he wasn't always at ease with McGuire's growing profile and knack for publicity. Stubbs' pointed on-air jibe that Eddie was often 'lunging over 100 metres' to pose for social photographers caused more stress between the two, resulting in a heated exchange at a

Triple M party. The friction between Stubbs and McGuire would rear its head again in 1995 when Stubbs co-produced Seven's rival to *The Footy Show*, *Four Quarters*.

Part of the problem was McGuire knew he was a big enough drawcard himself. He harboured a desire to package his own radio show, and if he could pinpoint a moment when that idea crystallised, it was during a long summer's lunch at the Red Eagle Hotel in Albert Park with Trevor Marmalade – with whom McGuire had struck up a friendship after following him in Melbourne's burgeoning comedy clubs – and TV producer Steve Marshall. It was a boys' lunch full of gossip, arguments about the footy and politics, and occasional forays to the pub's TAB. They all joked the session would make great radio and keep the lawyers busy.

Six years later, McGuire finally convinced Triple M to let him loose on Saturday mornings. The station was keen for a sports show in that slot, and McGuire assembled a crack team. He was fired up while tossing around ideas for a future football show on TV that combined entertainment with sport; he realised there was a big-enough market in Melbourne for footy alone, but knew there was also an audience that wanted footy as part of their bigger world. Saturday morning conversations in a share house weren't always about football.

The format and timeslot would unwittingly become a precursor to *The Footy Show*, with its combination of sport being done in an entertaining manner some way from the old-school *World of Sport*'s pie night vibe. The format and timeslot would also become a training ground for comedians trying out for FM stations, including the Today and Nova networks, for years to come. Most comedians making it to prime-time breakfast or drive on FM, including Hamish and Andy, were given space to develop on Saturday mornings.

McGuire recruited producer Steve Pritchard from Channel Ten sport, although there was little producing to do. Pritchard had a list of guests on his rundown sheet and little else. McGuire convinced Marmalade to jump from Fox FM – a move that made more sense knowing *The Footy Show* might launch in a couple of months – and also convinced his former D-Gen partner Jane Kennedy to return to Triple M while Marshall became the scurrilous gossip Sergio Paradise. Marmalade borrowed the show's name, *The Grill Team*, from the spoof spy series *Get Smart*, in which the 'Grill Team' is a bunch of CONTROL agents who employ extreme measures to extract information from spies, including Maxwell Smart.

The loose mix of Saturday morning talk attracted a diverse crew of regular and irregular contributors over time, including Roland Rocchiccioli, Lisa Hensley, comedians Glenn Robbins, Anthony Morgan, Darren Casey and Matt Quartermaine, Eddie's brother Frank McGuire, 'Racetrack Ralphy' Horowitz, Nicky Buckley, Nicole Stevenson and even Eric Bana.

And it worked. The show was scheduled against the seminal footy comedy troupe *The Coodabeen Champions* (at that point on 3AW), and improbably *The Grill Team* knocked off *The Coodabeens* in the first radio ratings survey of the 1994 footy season.[1]

The appeal of radio increased dramatically for McGuire when the station announced its desire to call football from 1997 after the Austereo board finally relented to management intentions. The move was bold; it would be the first time a city commercial FM radio station had broadcast AFL games (although Geelong's K-Rock did Cats matches after taking 3GL's licence). But the philosophy of rock, sport and comedy was a no-brainer for a station targeting under-40 males, and the station didn't want any listeners tuning to AM on weekends.[2]

Triple M wanted McGuire to lead the charge with former footballer Brian Taylor. This decision was more consequential than anyone thought at the time. It helped push Triple M towards a more commercial sports entertainment format and away from its classic rock format across the next two decades. And its irreverent, sometimes indecipherable, calls of matches would also attract a key younger demographic to AFL broadcasts – an outcome the AFL wasn't exactly anticipating in 1997. At the time, McGuire just saw it as a means to continue his true love: calling footy.

Triple M made the right noises from the start, proclaiming it would take on 3AW, 3LO and Magic to win, filling the space between 3AW's entertainment, led by Rex Hunt, and ABC 3LO's more sober analysis.

McGuire led the team, and speculation mounted he would poach *The Footy Show*'s Sam Newman from 3AW. That station sensed the pressure, with program director Steve Price telling a Melbourne Press Club luncheon there was more to football calling than 'a nice haircut and a good smile'.

As big as the boy from Broady might be on the small screen, Price said, he wouldn't cut it as a footy caller on radio. But 3AW had reason to be scared, with Triple M adding Stephen Quartermain and Taylor as callers, with special comments from Dermott Brereton, David Rhys-Jones, Doug Hawkins, Craig Kelly and Ricky Nixon and, in what became an industry-leading move, the president of the Australian Sports Medicine Association, Peter Larkins, as the boundary medico assessing injuries.

McGuire was bemused by Price's comments. 'Maybe he's going to find out there's a lot more to Eddie McGuire than a nice haircut and a good smile,' he said, in a rare instance of third-person rhetoric.[3]

McGuire and 3AW had ongoing stoushes in Melbourne's radio battles. In 1995, McGuire asked for an on-air apology from 3AW breakfast announcer Dean Banks,[4] and at the opening of the Crown Casino, McGuire stood over Price and told him, 'If you want, I'll whack you twice: once from Toorak and once from Broadmeadows. You pick the difference.'[5]

McGuire was furious that 3AW's *Rumour File* had alleged just after McGuire's wedding to Carla Galloway she was pregnant at the time of the nuptials. Added to that were drive host Price's jibes about 'Eddie McCrown' and jokes about his upward class mobility from Broadmeadows to Toorak.[6] As he would prove time and again, McGuire always snapped back at any personal slight, but when the attacks involved his family, he was ferocious.

Establishing a substantial presence in the AFL radio ratings battle wasn't enough for him, though; McGuire had the temerity to believe he could transfer *The Grill Team* to the weekday drive slot to take on the all-conquering kings of drive-time radio, FOX FM's Tony Martin and Mick Molloy.

The *Martin/Molloy* program had been the reigning drive champ for eighteen months, and was unassailable as the Austereo network – now including FoxFM and Triple M in the same offices in Melbourne – wheeled the duo out across its national network.

The comedy duo, who made names for themselves on ABC TV's *The Late Show* with the D-Generation team, combined unnatural talent with an incredible work ethic that would eventually burn them out. But in 1996, they were unstoppable.

Molloy said in passing at Austereo the only thing that could stop the duo – at least in Melbourne – was a show talking about footy. Austereo's program director, Jeff Allis, thought that concept dovetailed perfectly with McGuire's ambition to host in radio's prime time.

McGuire believed he could stop *Martin/Molloy*. Triple M wasn't so sure – and, to be frank, didn't need to beat the show, given they were in the same company. But the network hoped the sizeable Saturday morning following for *The Grill Team* would transfer to the drive-time slot between 4 p.m. and 7 p.m., and give the broadcaster a Melbourne drive duopoly.

The only doubt McGuire had was about the demands on him of a seven-day work week across Nine and Triple M – a qualm he dismissed in a second.

Triple M combined a relaunch of its broader sport, rock music and personality-based channel format with *The Grill Team*'s new line-up of McGuire, Trevor Marmalade, Dermott Brereton and Brigitte Duclos. Internally, some people – including the talent – doubted Duclos and Brereton would work well together, but McGuire had a knack for casting and backed them.

The formula worked. The show did the impossible and won the drive slot in Melbourne in a mid-year radio ratings survey in its first year. *The Grill Team* put out a press release crowing, 'There is only one place to be in radio: numero uno'.

And that they were – for just one survey. Alas, *Martin/Molloy* returned to an imperious and long-running lead in the following survey. On air, Tony Martin and Mick Molloy joked how galling it must be if you're 'numero duo'.

Even so, *The Grill Team*'s immediate success was so stratospheric that when Stubbs confirmed he would leave his breakfast show at the end of the year, *The Grill Team* drive show combination emerged as a possible replacement.

It was not a serious thought, though, and *The Grill Team* continued into 1998 and out of its honeymoon period. The show's ratings slowed, although that was arguably a function of both a weaker station and a focus on marketing dollars going to FOX rather than Triple M.

Management also suspected its trio of hosts – particularly McGuire – were too committed elsewhere. Network program director Allis called them in for a dressing down as they recorded their worst ratings result late in 1998, dropping to fourth. He told the *Herald Sun*, 'We will invest in people who put Triple M no. 1 in their list of priorities, not fourth. *The Grill Team* could learn a lot from Tony and Mick's day-in day-out commitment to make a great show every day.'[7]

That interview still ranks among the grander public dressing downs by a program director in Australian radio history. In commercial radio – at least publicly – PDs are usually subservient to the talent. McGuire conceded his workload juggle was 'a challenge', but denied his commitment was a problem despite a year in which he also hosted the Commonwealth Games for Nine and was elected to the Constitutional Convention.

On the flip side, his AFL calling for Triple M was boiling. It beat the invincible team of Rex Hunt and Sam Newman at 3AW in a surprise ratings result that year.

Another surprise late in 1998 was McGuire's election as president of the Collingwood Football Club. Something had to give and, oddly enough, it was unlikely it would be his football calling.

In November 1998, McGuire pulled the pin on Triple M's *The Grill Team*, ending a ten-year run working weekdays on the station. 'I've taken on a lot of other work and I want to devote enough time to the presidency of Collingwood,' he said.[8]

Later he wrote in his weekly column for the *Herald Sun* about his sadness at leaving the first radio show he had hosted and produced.

'*The Grill Team* was an idea and a philosophy that became a trademark and a brand,' he wrote not so humbly, although Triple M has retained the branding and the name continues to this day on the network in Sydney.

The decision to leave showed some maturity, and also reflected the influence of Carla McGuire. Eddie realised that, apart from dropping sports news reading on Nine, it was the first time he'd actually *stopped* doing a job. But he wasn't slowing down.

CHAPTER 6

NINE COMES AFTER TEN

Network Ten was simply not big enough for Eddie McGuire. Even some of his managers appreciated he was arguably the best sports reporter in the country, yet they couldn't contain him.

His *Doing the Rounds* segment was consistently breaking stories, and the frequency of its broadcast helped McGuire keep on top of contacts across the league. Talented, affable and well liked, he had Melbourne covered.

Some at Ten still shake their heads at what might have been had the network tried harder to keep him – particularly with the fresh memory of Bruce McAvaney moving to Seven. But McGuire's mind was made up, although his loyalty to Ten nagged at him incessantly and clouded what should have been an easy decision. He knew Ten was no place for him to expand his career as Tim Webster was the anointed network star, hosting *Sports Tonight* and ensconced in the Sydney *Eyewitness News* team.

Nor did McGuire want to be a gigging news reporter when he was 35 – although that was still some years away. And the Canadian owners of Ten, CanWest, weren't making many friends, with their aloof and all-knowing approach to Australian television

– including clueless cost-cutting. McGuire wasn't alone in believing the network would not provide him with increased programming opportunities or career growth, particularly in sport. Ten had lost the broadcast rights to the Olympic Games and showed no intention of going after the AFL. It was also coming last in the ratings among the three commercial networks.

So when Nine's Melbourne chief Ian Johnson came knocking late in 1993, McGuire was already halfway out the door. Seven also made a play, but couldn't squeeze McGuire's proposed $100 000 salary into its already hefty sports team costs, then featuring McAvaney, Peter Landy and Sandy Roberts.

McGuire's networking skills struck Johnson as crucial to his talents, as were the fire in his belly and his ability to connect with the audience. Nine News Director John Sorrell couldn't have given a toss about another sports reporter, but that was Sorrell. McGuire's work ethic and the way he worked had become known across the news sector, and now his popularity had grown. One newspaper critique of the Ten news team years earlier had described the dynamics of that 'family' in Melbourne lounge rooms: McGuire was 'everyone's favourite brother'.[1]

Johnson made a number of entreaties across the years, and McGuire would unfailingly joke them away. In a characteristic he would display throughout his career, McGuire was overly loyal to Ten, giving the network every chance to renew his contract and not talking seriously with Johnson at Nine until it became clear Ten, whether by default or design, was going to let the agreement expire. The Ten negotiations even regressed to ultimatums before McGuire relented and rang Johnson, asking 'How serious are you about me coming across?'

'Extremely serious,' Johnson replied.

Opinions within Ten digress on the degree to which it attempted to hold McGuire. Many suggest the contract renewal was left to Ten's Sydney-based head of news, who – either due to the chaos of a pressured news division or incompetence – failed to offer McGuire another contract.

He was off and Nine was waiting. Johnson and McGuire played the negotiations like pros, being seen at lunch together as a rumour emerged that McGuire might even host a Friday night footy show in 1994 – on Nine.[2]

McGuire borrowed a 'flash' green convertible Toyota to drive to a meeting to ensure Nine would raise the compensation, saying the car was part of his Ten package.[3] Johnson, who was in the café watching McGuire drive up and down the street so he could find an ostentatious park outside, saw right through that. By July 1994, though, the lucrative Nine deal had allowed Eddie to trade in his daggy car for a new BMW 325i convertible.[4]

McGuire told Johnson he wanted to take the next step in his career, and Johnson could deliver it. Nine's modus operandi was to spread its stars and not box them in. McGuire could see that he wouldn't be stuck in the sports department, and he was impressed that Johnson wasn't disloyal enough to his own staff to offer him the lead sports reading job held by Tony Jones. A future footy show was discussed, but Johnson told McGuire he would have to do some time in the newsroom first. Nevertheless, Nine's AFL coverage was in desperate need of rejuvenation if it was to ever seriously contemplate contesting the AFL broadcast rights. McGuire could be a start.

Eddie prides himself on his handshake deals. Yet the most consequential deal of his life – his signing to Nine – didn't even extend to that formality: it was delivered on a beer coaster. McGuire signed an informal contract with Nine – or at least a guarantee that Nine would employ him if Ten allowed his contract to expire. Johnson signed on the back of that beer coaster what would become McGuire's first contract at Nine. It said simply, 'Eddie, you're in'.

McGuire rang Johnson on 1 January and told him Ten hadn't spoken to him or even offered a new contract, so he was Nine's. He'd rung friends on New Year's Eve to tell them 'It's over'. He was emotional about leaving Ten, but the Canadian owners of the network, based in Sydney, had little interest in Melbourne – let alone a sports journalist.

'I'm going to go to Channel Nine and I'm going to do a footy show,' he told friends.

His colleagues at Ten felt his frustration; they knew McGuire's leaving wasn't just the loss of a talent, it epitomised the degradation of the network under the new owners.

In February 1994, after eleven years at Ten, McGuire moved across to head the football team for a network that didn't have any football. It was a large leap of faith, but the precocious talent was leaping most days. When Nine finally presented him with a contract, Johnson pushed it over to him and told him to sign it. McGuire asked for time to read it. Johnson asked whether he trusted him. McGuire did, and signed the back page before looking at what Nine was paying and blanching. 'You're kidding, aren't you?' he asked. 'Well, if the footy show or other things happen, you'll be fine,' Johnson replied. And he was.

His arrival in February coincided with and assisted a conscious move by Nine into AFL. The network felt Seven was being complacent, and it could see any positive moves to promote the code – however minor – could only help establish its bona fides for the next time Nine tried to win the AFL broadcast rights.

McGuire's first day at Nine began oddly – stuck in a lift for fifteen minutes with his new boss, Johnson – but McGuire quickly picked up his rhythm, continuing to break news, including one story that stuck in his throat: arranging the return of the stolen 1970 Premiership Cup to Carlton.

The Blues beat Collingwood in a match Pies supporters still lament after being up by 44 points at half-time. A Collingwood supporter stole the premiership cup from a Carlton social club disco in 1977, hid it up a tree and returned to collect it. Embarrassed Carlton officials didn't reveal the theft, but the replica cup was also stolen years later, sparking a very late-onset attack of the guilts. The thief, who stole the original cup because he believed Collingwood was robbed in 1970, contacted McGuire to tell him he had returned the cup in a plastic bag he left in a Princes Park toilet block. McGuire arranged the handover with Carlton.

Despite the commitment Nine made to McGuire not to white-ant Tony Jones, McGuire did present sport in Jones' absence early in 1994, and it was one of the most nerve-wracking moments of his life. He'd presented bulletins countless times before, but this was different: McGuire was sitting next to the living legend of Melbourne news reading, Brian Naylor. The debonair newsreader had guided Nine to its unassailable ratings ascendancy in Melbourne. He was the channel's real star, despite the noise made by various tonight show hosts. McGuire was rattled by the aura until Naylor's smooth demeanour and welcome to the 'new boy' settled him down.

McGuire remained busy away from Nine, co-authoring with Jim Main their biography of the late Collingwood premiership player Darren 'Pants' Millane. The hagiography cleared up a few misconceptions about the rumoured darker side of the player. For McGuire, the book was a cleansing experience too.

Early in the year, Nine confirmed it would extend its popular formula for the Sunday version of *The Footy Show*, featuring Max Walker, Lou Richards and Ted Whitten, into a 'league teams' program on Thursday nights with Sam Newman, a host of current players as panellists and Eddie McGuire hosting.

Nine offered new possibilities and McGuire was alive to them. He even joked self-deprecatingly in 1994 that one day he might host the TV Week Logie Awards. 'Yeah, Ray's in trouble,' he laughed. 'No, to use the coaching vernacular, I'll take it one show at a time.'[5]

Actually, how self-deprecating was he? Eddie anticipated a brighter professional life. But he had no inkling that 'one show' would not only set his life on its extraordinary path, it would also help transform Australian Rules football.

CHAPTER 7

THE FOOTY SHOW

Even today, it is not quite clear whether *The Footy Show* emerged by default or by design. The design theory says a large component of Ian 'Johnno' Johnson's compelling case to woo McGuire was his concept for a football-themed show, one that combined the heritage of Seven's old VFL shows with the heritage of Nine's shiny floor variety shows.

It was a melding of two grand formats: the casual, sportsman's night mayhem of Seven's *League Teams* with Lou Richards, Jack Dyer and Bobby Davis and the variety appeal of the stars and programs of which Melbourne's GTV-9 was so proud – *In Melbourne Tonight* with Graham Kennedy and Bert Newton and *The Don Lane Show*.

The default part of the theory comes from Nine's earlier necessity to fill a window in its Sunday morning edition of *Wide World of Sports*. Nine was the NRL broadcaster and devoted twenty minutes of its show to rugby league post-mortems. That wouldn't wash down south, so Nine created a simultaneous twenty-minute AFL segment featuring Sam Newman, Dermott Brereton and Simon O'Donnell.

In 1993, when Nine Sydney decided to broadcast a full-blown one-hour rugby league wrap on Sunday mornings, GTV-9 fell into line with an AFL wrap for the southern states.

Former *The Age* journalist Harvey Silver was co-opted from Nine's newsroom to create what would become the *Sunday Footy Show*, featuring some of the legends from Seven's old *World of Sport*, Lou Richards and Newman, Ted Whitten and others, including Brereton, Sam Kekovich, Mal Brown and Mark Jackson. The show, hosted by cricket legend Max Walker, rejuvenated some of their careers as it popped – as much as a Sunday morning program could – and dominated its timeslot as AFL rights-holder Seven dithered.

Johnson suggested Nine do a Friday night spin-off of the Sunday show before the 1993 Grand Final. It was a major rating's success, and incorporated some of the elements that would blend into what became *The Footy Show*, including the wise-ass at the bar, Trevor Marmalade, bringing a touch of *Hey! Hey! It's Saturday*–type mischief (his role increased after he heckled from the wings during rehearsals in the new year), a band and current players, and crosses to the competing coaches, Kevin Sheedy and David Parkin.

The show gave Johnson the confidence to further push into Seven's territory. The groundwork, though largely accidental, had been done.

Within the week, Johnson sat Silver down and mused about whether the format could transition to prime time the following year. Silver thought so, but not with the old-timers. It had to be different. Johnson asked him to come back with a concept.

Silver suggested current players could be the new show's currency. They would be the point of difference from TV football shows from times gone by. Silver then argued Max Walker wasn't the right host either.

Johnson replied, 'Don't worry about the host. We've got the host.'

When McGuire arrived at Nine, all systems were go as he, Johnson and Silver assembled their ideas for the new program. Nevertheless, it was a punt. Convention said sports programs didn't work in prime time. But Johnson knew the sportsman's night circuit still thrived in Victoria, and that football – at least on screen – had lost its *joie de vivre*. This wouldn't be a sport show, it would be a tonight show.

McGuire wasn't intimidated by the prospect of hosting – indeed, when has he ever been intimidated? He'd been preparing for just this kind of break for eight years, hosting sportsmen's nights gratis in order to learn how to work a live crowd.[1] Golfer Gary Player's maxim that the more he practised, the luckier he became held for McGuire.

McGuire suggested Newman as a potential co-host and had Johnson call him. McGuire had been in Newman's thrall as a person since that first nightclub outing, but his mate Mike Tancred had alerted him to the genius of Sam Newman as a TV performer back on Seven's *World of Sport*. 'Look at this guy with his hair sticking up as though he's just arrived from someone else's bed!' On *World of Sport* and later Nine's *Sunday* panels, Newman appeared to be working at a different pace and intellectual level to other former footballers. Johnson told Newman the show needed someone mature to balance the youth of the footballers and McGuire.

Sam was the last man in – and he was happy to be there. He was still trying to rebuild his life after a bad business investment sent him stone broke. Newman had just turned 50 and had nothing to show for it but memories of a grand football career with Geelong and an itinerant job writing for the *Herald Sun*.

McGuire has wondered about the sliding doors moment of his first encounter with Newman on Toorak Road as an eighteen-year-old. If Newman had been a prick to McGuire, would his life had been any different?

McGuire had clear ideas about the format of the new show. He, like Silver, wanted current players rather than the conventional former players.[2] He knew they would provide freshness and, hopefully, modern insight. For the most part, too, they were good-looking young men – just right for TV.

He also knew them socially, and had an insight into who would be suitable on-camera talent – even if some, like Footscray immortal Doug Hawkins, were incredulous that anyone would want them as 'talent'.

Indeed, the players didn't have high expectations for the show at all. The pre-season pilot on a Friday afternoon was just another gig for Tim Watson, Hawkins and Jason Dunstall. They didn't believe the show would even get to air. But at a post-mortem at Pellegrini's after the taping, McGuire's enthusiasm could not be contained. He was supremely confident he had something, even if few shared his enthusiasm. Nine's sales department certainly didn't. The major sponsor of the first episode was the Melbourne strip club Top of the Town.

A few more at Nine jumped off the bus in the fortnight preceding the premiere, when AFL broadcaster Seven confirmed the show would not be allowed to show match footage. Screening other networks' sports broadcasts remains a constant flashpoint, but Seven's decision in this instance was defensive, churlish and almost successful.

Despite their outward bravado at the time, McGuire and Silver were fully expecting to screen highlights whenever they wanted. Senior production personnel suggested Nine pull the show when the footage was denied. But the team ploughed on as word filtered down from Sydney management that a clearly defined noose was being placed around *The Footy Show*'s neck: it had six weeks to rate a 20-share; otherwise it was gone.

A pall might have descended if McGuire's determination and confidence hadn't helped drag the production towards its first show. Newman was less confident, but McGuire believed the time was right for the show they were producing.

Johnson told his team it would be little more than a variety show hosted by football players. Don't complicate it. And the production team followed with the basic advice to keep it light, keep it fun and keep your eyes on the player, not the ball.

Looking back, McGuire's suitability for the role was clear even in the hours before the first show in March 1994. Instead of fretting about scripts or wasting emotional energy, McGuire moved through his day as usual, hosting a lunch for the Melbourne Football Club with an easy confidence.

And as he stood backstage with Newman before walking on set to host *The Footy Show* for the first time, McGuire felt the pressure but had the calm that confidence and security bring. At the top of his mind was stepping into Nine's glorious TV lineage – Thursday, 9.30 p.m., Studio Nine at Bendigo Street, Richmond – with the spirits and echoes of Graham Kennedy, Bert Newton and Don Lane reverberating.

McGuire's positive stoicism kicked in. He thought to himself, 'Well, I might only walk in their footsteps once, but at least I've done it.'

Newman looked to McGuire as plaintively as Newman could and asked, 'What are we going to do?'

McGuire responded, 'Just pretend we're at a sportsman's night.' And they did.[3]

There were a few too many people at this opening sportsman's night though: six players accompanied what would become the core trio. And the 'cage' of boisterous fans next to Trevor's bar would be dropped soon enough.

But the show worked, winning its timeslot, out-pointing *The X-Files*, with a 19-share. That was good; a 20-share was attainable from there.

It was clear within two weeks *The Footy Show* was a going concern. By May, that 20-share appeared humble. TV columnists dubbed *The Footy Show* 'an essential part of the fixture for footy fans'[4] and 'the television success story of the year'.[5]

The reasons for its immediate connection with the Melbourne audience were obvious, although one wouldn't have banked on them. First, it celebrated its localism, doing much to confirm Nine as Melbourne's station – AFL or not.

Newman was a rare television presence, if in the slightly off-kilter manner that hints at, and delivers, dangerous television. Marmalade was a natural fit, revered in comedy circles as the 'Joke Doctor', a wit with a line for any occasion and a laconic delivery that couldn't offend. He was a rare stand-up in not craving attention desperately (which appealed to McGuire who, as a general rule, tends not to like stand-ups). Like McGuire as host, Marmalade was always aware of the dynamics for the greater good.

Crucially, the three lead men provided comic contrasts, bouncing off each other. The perky clashed with the laconic, the earnest with the world-weary, the young with the old, the disciplined with the undisciplined.

The tone was right: it wasn't entirely serious yet remained respectful of both guests and the game. And the show was live. It recalled the what-will-happen-next appeal of Graham Kennedy's live ads and the irreverence and wrinkles of Lou, Jack and Bobby on *League Teams*. It was risky and real.

McGuire was up to it, able to wrestle the competing egos and aptitude of his guests with an unnatural aplomb. He acted as the doughty centre-man who didn't win the best and fairest but was prepared to farm out the handballs and set-ups to the flashier receivers and forwards wearing the white boots. That style would stand him in good stead throughout his hosting career; while some expect a host to be as explosive as Graham Kennedy, in reality the majority of television's long-standing successful hosts have been linkmen (and yes, men – but that's another story).

Newman became problematic for McGuire, but that was his charm. The host would quietly tear strips off Newman during ad breaks for being unprepared, and not having read 'Sam's Mailbag' or the rundown before going to air. But as soon as the red light above the camera lit up, McGuire would be all charm and bonhomie to his partner. And that was real; he truly admired the man who frustrated him.

Newman said at the time, 'If you put Ed's ability and ambition in an Olympic event over 100 metres, there would only be a millimetre in it.'[6] His ability was key. He could stare down the barrel of the camera and deliver news off the cuff: no autocues, no writers.

The beefcake appeal of the program was left largely unsaid, yet the casting of current players met the zeitgeist. It elevated the players, even if some weren't ready for the spotlight. As the corporatisation of the AFL continued to shake off the 'amateurism' of the VFL, *The Footy Show*'s contribution to the marketability and professionalisation of players was elemental. The show arrived as the player management sector was starting to flourish.

Player agent Ricky Nixon had recently established his Club 10 stable of stars, hoping to wrestle some marketing rights and money from the AFL and the clubs (McGuire would host the launch of Club 10, including signings Gary Ablett Snr, Wayne Carey, Glen Jakovich and Gavin Brown in early 1995). Craig Kelly countered with his AFL-backed Pro Squad stable of players, establishing his business with a kick along from Collingwood and McGuire at Nine. The players' time had come; the AFL had abused its power exploiting the player's marketing rights.

They emerged as *The Footy Show* developed a new genre of 'footy-tainment' that coalesced with the AFL's moves to broaden its audience. McGuire and *The Footy Show* would ride the crest of that commercial wave while also blowing the winds that created the wave.

Silver wanted to show the players had personalities. McGuire agreed coaches had dehumanised the players over the last decade, turning them into automatons. He chose players he believed would bring something to the table – Watson's ease, Hawkins' *joie de vivre*,

Dunstall's intelligence, Brereton's mischief. Their success was quite an accomplishment, given they weren't trained or mentored. More care went into selecting the loud ties for each panellist than on honing their presenting skills.

Initially, Eddie, Sam and Trevor were the glue allowing the players to prosper. Yet the stars didn't get the early notices; the players did. Very quickly, Hawkins became the most popular panellist, Watson the most accomplished, with an easy rapport with Ed and Sam, and Dunstall the most surprising.

Initially, the players thought the show was merely an extension of the panel shows and interviews that were part of the game. As the season progressed, though, some became a little uncomfortable realising they were being taken out of their sporting comfort zone, where a 'one week at a time' quote would suffice. Others were struggling to discuss issues they considered serious in the lighthearted manner the program required. A number of players felt like actors.

Some of the players were uncomfortable when their comments and behaviour on *The Footy Show* were quoted back to them or newspapers wrote about them. Suddenly the players understood this was something far bigger than talking to a journo after a match. Now they were being thrust into the world of showbiz, which brought a different level of expectation and performance. For the first time, they felt like performers having to bring something to the table.

Not all the AFL clubs appreciated at first how the show benefited the players and the clubs. Carlton denied Stephen Silvagni his chance to become a panellist and coaches were reluctant to let players appear.

The anachronistic notion that poor form could be attributed to a player walking 'Media Street' still surfaced. A number of players were torn about their appearances after coaches and management noted when their form wasn't great that perhaps they should focus on something other than a TV appearance. McGuire spent a bit of time on the phone appeasing players before their appearances. It took some time for clubs to appreciate they could turn the show to their advantage with marketable players.

Even on the field, the players' higher profiles could work against them. One player sledged Melbourne firebrand forward Allen Jakovich during one match by telling him he was a 'dud' on *The Footy Show*. It worked, putting him off his game.

The players also negated Nine's fears *The Footy Show* would be a male-dominated bastion. Viewers could barrack for players rather than teams now. The show played up its 'peek' into the change rooms and female viewers lapped it up, even as the program made some spectacularly sexist faux pas through the years. The program was often forgiven because it was also so self-deprecating, and it slipped easily into a style of entertainment with which the audience was familiar – the manufactured chaos of *Hey! Hey! It's Saturday*. It respected the heritage of variety television and respected the game without being beholden to it. Because Nine wasn't the AFL broadcaster, strong opinions could be expressed and uncomfortable news broken.

The Melbourne audience lapped it up. *The Footy Show* accelerated to a 30 per cent share, as Seven and Ten began to program *Fawlty Towers*, *The X-Files*, *Heartland*, *NYPD Blue* and other strong performers against it.

Nine loved it. It promoted its success as a 'win against the odds' after Seven's 'refusal' to allow Nine to use game footage. That was disingenuous because, first, Nine limited other networks' access to its cricket or NRL vision in converse circumstances, and second, McGuire didn't believe they would require much vision – if any – in a one-hour program anyway. Ultimately, *The Footy Show* didn't use AFL vision, although the show would mischievously use vision from training and elsewhere.[7] The talent would be the key.

By June, one in six Melburnians was watching the program and the waiting list to join the studio audience grew dramatically. A table for eight – with party pies and soft drink – was auctioned for $3500 at the Irish Ball for the Open Family Foundation.[8] (The money raised by *The Footy Show* for charities and local sporting clubs was an ongoing, and usually quiet, achievement.)

By the end of its first season, *The Footy Show* attracted 896 000 viewers in Melbourne for its Grand Final edition – only 125 000 fewer than the Brownlow Medal telecast and 560 000 fewer than the West Coast Eagles' Grand Final win.[9] The show was also working well in the other two AFL states, Western Australia and South Australia (it buoyed the two Nine affiliate stations that were not part of the Nine Network while only boosting one of Nine's own east coast stations; an NRL Footy Show was consequently a must for Nine's Sydney and Brisbane stations). Nine's programmers and sales team loved it, but the show wasn't entirely popular within Nine because some sports executives were not enamoured of its irreverence; they were missing the emergence of 'sports entertainment'.

Such was *The Footy Show*'s popularity in its first year that Nine toyed with continuing the series beyond the football season in a revised form. The show returned in 1995 with new regulars, including Essendon's James Hird, the Eagles' Guy McKenna, Tony Hall from the Crows and the Swans' Paul Roos.

It maintained its ratings in the high 20s and became a major embarrassment for Seven, which entered the fray with a Friday night fireside chat show, *Four Quarters*, featuring recruit Tim Watson, Sandy Roberts and McGuire's mate Brigitte Duclos (and co-produced by McGuire's former radio boss, Richard Stubbs).

Nine tried to keep Watson with the promise of work on a travel show to supplement *The Footy Show*, but he thought that wasn't for him. He was one of the players who appreciated it was best to stick to sport. The subsequent Seven show had AFL vision, but couldn't generate any heat.

Meanwhile, at Nine, success meant the team quickly recalibrated. This wasn't a sports show; it was a broad entertainment program in which the hosts felt their laughs generated per minute ranked with any comedy on Australian television.[10] (This displayed a little hubris, considering 1996 was the height of *The Simpsons*, *Cheers*, *Frasier* and *Friends*.)

The viewing numbers were astonishing. In 1995, *The Footy Show* recorded a 36 rating, or 755 000 Melburnians, after 9.30 p.m. on a Thursday night, which is traditionally one of the lesser viewing nights of the TV week. Today, a network would be exultant with 750 000 viewers at 9.30 p.m. on a Thursday night across all five capital cities. A peak of 720 000 viewers for one episode in 1995 was larger than Seven's audience for any home-and-away match that week. *The Footy Show* was proving itself bigger than the game.

The show truly boomed in 1996. The Nine publicity department did a sterling job ensuring that whatever news or controversy played in Thursday night's episode swamped the newspapers and radio the following day. McGuire helped by not resting on his laurels. He wanted the show to be talked about for its news, not for its pranks or Newman's misdemeanours. Although they helped.

The 1996 Grand Final episode rated a 47 and the *Herald Sun*'s Jon Anderson said it was 'as good a piece of live television as you'd wish to see'.[11] The broadcast filled the then-Flinders Park stadium with 15 000 rabid fans and claims it was the biggest live broadcast in Australian TV history. McGuire describes it as 'the most electrifying night of my career.'[12] 'We were just living the dream at that stage and pinching ourselves knowing we were presenting a footy show on television and that it had got to this.'

Nine's introduction of an NRL version of *The Footy Show* – although an obvious move – caused friction as Fatty Vautin and his panellists turned their incarnation into a less-serious panto show with homophobic innuendo, dress-ups and silly pratfalls.

Whereas the southern version drew on Nine's variety tradition, the northern version appeared to draw on Sydney's drag queen tradition. 'I don't say "No" to anything, but you won't see me dressing up as a woman,' McGuire said pointedly.[13]

The fact that the NRL version won more *TV Week* Logie Awards than the AFL one as the most popular sports show, due to the broader market in New South Wales and Queensland, rankled with the higher-rating Melbourne team through the years.

The southern *Footy Show* became untouchable. It began to run well over time, something Nine management encouraged with a nod and a wink because it added another half-hour of timeslot-winning ratings late in the night.

And the feeling internally that the show's success made it seem above the law somehow worked for it. Nine backed the show, encouraging its talent to go for it and be as controversial as it wanted to be. It left *The Footy Show*'s team to clean up any messes, though. In all the later controversies, Nine's Sydney management was always silent, not willing to infringe upon Melbourne's peculiar dynamics and the show's ability to deliberately inflame headlines.

Creative talents in any medium need confidence and freedom to thrive. *The Footy Show* had those qualities: the team lacked fear. That confidence was emboldened by its lack of affiliation with the AFL. They could say whatever they wanted without retribution. And McGuire did say what he wanted because, deep down, he remains a fan of the game – albeit one who passionately defends his club first. He's Joffa (the leader of the Collingwood Football Club cheer squad) in a sharper suit.

McGuire knew where his program stood in the Nine hierarchy: at the top. Not only was it delivering ratings; it became a commercial powerhouse, bringing dollars through sponsored segments, prizes and corporate affiliations. Companies were desperate to host a table at the live program; it became more valuable than a private box at the MCG.

He also understood *The Footy Show* would not suffer the consequences experienced by other shows. That caused some internal friction – particularly with Nine's PR department, which was told *The Footy Show* was its own boss. However, McGuire had to be tethered from turning the show into a Collingwood variety hour for talent and the club's sponsors. That was a tough fight, though, given Collingwood supporters were a major segment of the show's audience.

An indicator of the show's standing at Nine came at the conclusion of the 1996 season, when a Sydney team, led by chief James Packer, Nine Network general manager David Leckie and director of sport Gary Burns, flew to join GTV-9 general manager Ian Johnson for a celebratory lunch with *The Footy Show* team in Nine's boardroom. Packer told them the show's budget would be raised, in a pre-emptive strike to keep McGuire and Newman on board. McGuire's contract was due for renewal within months, and was causing consternation because Nine management knew Seven would swoop. Packer's willingness to take the afternoon off to go drinking with McGuire, his cast and the footballers seemed to work.

'Everybody likes a pat on the head; everyone wants to feel wanted,' said McGuire. 'At Channel 10, you are on the expenses list; at Nine you're on the assets list.'[14]

There was nothing Seven could do to stop *The Footy Show*, so it tried to cut it off at the neck. Sure enough, news leaked in September 1996 that McGuire was considering a big offer from Seven. And he was, although such stories always emerge during media contract negotiations. The following day, Nine confirmed McGuire had agreed to new terms for a three-year deal. McGuire signed the deal with Johnson with a handshake after hastily brokering a deal on a Thursday night in December and wrapping it up on the Friday.

Unconfirmed rumours abounded that Packer's Crown Limited came on board to sweeten the deal. Certainly the new Crown

Casino, which opened in 1996 (and to which *The Footy Show* would eagerly cross during broadcasts, with Dermott Brereton famously taking out a rowdy punter during one segment), backed *The Footy Show* to the hilt as a sponsor.

Rather promptly, Sam Newman also signed a four-year contract worth about $2.5 million with Nine, which tied him to the network until 2001. By then, Nine valued McGuire and Newman so highly that when they needed to fly on light planes, the network insisted they fly in separate aircraft.[15]

McGuire and Newman appreciated they were essential to each other. Newman knew McGuire had pulled his flailing media career out of the gutter; McGuire acknowledged the show revolved around Sam and his willingness to do whatever it took. They weren't close buddies, but they had a professional and inter-dependent working relationship.

In 1996, they made a pact, via handshake, that neither would sign with another channel unless the other went too. McGuire's advice to Newman was sagacious: just make sure our contracts always expire at the same time; that way we don't have to go cap in hand to the network. Conversely, if we have a product to sell to other people, we can do so unencumbered.

In the late 1990s, Seven wasn't the smart network it would become a decade later. Back then, it couldn't even specify what it had planned for McGuire or Newman if they were to switch networks. So a shift was not a realistic option for the duo. As Leigh Matthews would later write, Seven was the football station at the time,

> but Channel Nine seemed to be where all the big stars worked, the network was great at self-promotion and it had a much bigger profile and following. It was the glamorous alternative and at the time I couldn't help but think that if I had a choice about where I would work, I would have chosen the pace-setters at Nine.[16]

McGuire was, and remained for many years, the chief pacesetter and a prickly thorn for Seven. Seven had to catch up, and it couldn't get McGuire or Newman, so it tried another strategy: attack the body.

Producer Silver had proposed a second show at Nine featuring its stable of 'lesser light' or veteran AFL stars, thinking it would be a way to keep more players tied to Nine. The station rejected it.

Silver was keen to spread his own wings, though. At the time, the holy grail for every TV star or producer was to own a show's intellectual property. It provided power and autonomy from being a network employee. Seven offered Silver the opportunity to own his own show as a producer. Nine wanted to renew his contract, but Seven's offer was too good to refuse. After all, McGuire, Johnson and Silver might have developed *The Footy Show* but Nine retained ownership.

Silver arranged to meet with Johnson on a Friday to inform him he knew the show could carry on without him and he was consequently negotiating with Seven as his Nine contract expired. However, they didn't meet. Melbourne being Melbourne, word filtered to McGuire on Thursday that Silver might be leaving. Even worse, McGuire realised Silver was pitching a show that would rely on poaching senior members of *The Footy Show* panel.

Rumours that James Hird, Jason Dunstall and Doug Hawkins — all part of the Ricky Nixon management stable — had signed filtered through to McGuire. Seven being Seven, though, almost shot itself when it was discovered another executive had made a separate offer to Jason Dunstall to host a nightly half-hour sports show. That was scrapped so Silver had the running on a new footy show.

Dunstall left Nine for the same reason McGuire left Ten. There were too many people in front of him — McGuire, Brereton and Simon O'Donnell for starters.[17] Dunstall could also do without a future in which he was merely Newman's antagonist; similarly,

Hawkins wanted to be more than a Nine clown, although his departure was a particular surprise to McGuire.

Silver took some big stars to Seven, including rising impressionist Andrew Startin, who had been a big hit on *The Footy Show* the previous year with his Newman impersonations. Oddly, his move annoyed McGuire intensely; he could understand professionals such as the players looking to advance, but Startin owed some loyalty to the show that had made him.

On that Thursday night, as McGuire and Nine heard the full extent of the coup, Silver was locked out of the Bendigo Street studios and his mobile was disconnected. He said farewell to some staff the following morning at a Richmond restaurant, Spargo's. Johnson let staff attend despite saying Silver's leap was 'a blatant act of disloyalty'.[18]

McGuire was ropeable. It didn't help when Silver said on 3AW, 'I am the creator of their most successful show in God knows how long.'[19]

The talent exodus would cause major instability on *The Footy Show* just as McGuire was preparing his tilt as Victoria's leading republican at the following week's Constitutional Convention in Canberra (see Chapter 10).

But he could understand. Seven was proffering big dollars and the opportunity to participate in its AFL coverage. Publicly, he was gracious, writing in his column, 'Harvey was there from day one and the show wouldn't have been the same without them. I wish them well at Seven and hope they have a small amount of success. It's going to be a big year in football.'[20]

The revolution, as it happened, was just the refresh *The Footy Show* needed after a year blighted by Newman's troubles fending off the jilted boyfriends of women he was dating and major injuries when a former girlfriend ran him over.

McGuire rallied his troops with a coach-like tirade in which he established the 'us against them' scenario, wherein the 'them' –

Seven – was trying to destroy Nine's show. He made a commitment to do everything he could, on and off the screen, to make sure the new show, *Live and Kicking*, had the hardest time possible.

McGuire added new regular faces – Wayne Campbell, Stephen Silvagni, Paul Salmon, Nathan Buckley and Matthew Lloyd – and used every network and contact to deprive Seven's new show of any oxygen. Admittedly, *Live and Kicking* did the same, but Silver underestimated just how hard McGuire would attack on all fronts.

The Footy Show needed to be self-reflective, though. McGuire was very public in his desire not to change something that wasn't broken, but audiences tire – as does the talent.

By 1998, the knives were out. Dunstall, Hawkins and Hird were bigger losses than had been anticipated. McGuire appreciated the show had lost its rhythm, and he missed the reliability of the trio as the player personnel were being rotated. Media criticism mounted that it was tired, not compulsory viewing and not so funny anymore. The new players were inexperienced, and finding the right mix was difficult.

Johnson defended the program hard, noting that 'Channel Seven doesn't get a 27 rating for anything bar *Blue Heelers* for the entire fucking week, including the $40 million investment in AFL football, yet *The Footy Show*, at 9.30 at night, does a 27 rating and we get all the media ringing saying it's shithouse.'[21]

But McGuire was burning himself out with his weekly column in the *Herald Sun*, hosting Triple M's *The Grill Team* six days a week and calling footy at least twice at the weekend on the same station.

Meanwhile, Seven's *Live and Kicking*, filmed live in a refurbished Art Deco cinema in Windsor on Wednesday nights, came at it hard, opening with Kylie Minogue as its lead guest. It debuted with a massive 38 per cent rating, double the audience of any show against it, including Nine's counter-programming of the Barbra Streisand special *My Life* (which peaked at 15). *The Footy Show* peaked with a 28-share the following night.

As the credits rolled for *Live and Kicking*, Newman's phone rang off the hook as McGuire, Marmalade and *The Footy Show*'s assistant producer, Ralph Horowitz, all called to trash the show, with one suggesting everyone on *The Footy Show* should apply for a pay rise.

Seven's show did have its problems: for her interview segment, a boom microphone was held over Minogue's head because producers were unable to clip her with a mic due to the skimpiness of her dress. Doug Hawkins' list of questions was written on his hand, but he was unable to deliver the final one – 'Do you have to leave Australia to become a big star?' – because he had begun to sweat and the question smudged.

The backgrounding to media began: the two blonde dancers on *Live and Kicking* had been pushed as an idea by Silver for *The Footy Show* – and rejected. Nine claimed it had even built a set for a Seven's 'Headkickers' segment, but ultimately rejected it. *The Footy Show* had also looked at *Live and Kicking*'s idea of funding a football club's end-of-season trip as part of a prize, but rejected it on the basis that a charity would be more deserving than highly paid footballers.

McGuire shouldn't have worried. *Live and Kicking* didn't last long. Late in 1999, Seven had another crack, recruiting Brereton to present a straighter footy show, *The Game*, programmed in the 8.30 p.m. timeslot on Thursday nights, one hour before Brereton's old employer at Nine, the six-season-veteran *The Footy Show*.[22]

And *The Footy Show* turned itself around, scoring its best ratings in years in 2000 and then finding a spring in its step as Nine won the rights to co-broadcast the AFL with Ten from 2002. Normal programming was resumed.

The background stresses on the show were beginning to mount though. It was an angsty set as McGuire became frustrated at Newman's off-road antics and the mounting controversies were beginning to take their toll, if only as their collective weight emboldened the show's critics. Within the show, there was a feeling many mountains were being made out of minor missteps. One producer recalled receiving a letter that began, 'Dear Sir, I don't watch *The Footy Show* but I must complain …' That was typical: the show became an easy target.

McGuire's tempestuous rants at staff weren't being indulged so easily. He was infamous for letting anyone and everyone know about it every time something went wrong, although the tantrums were often excused due to his drive and expectation that everyone should be as prepared and switched on as he was.

The show's autonomy was an issue too, as McGuire and Newman became tired of fighting every battle and not getting a 'chop out' from the network.

There were only two issues that concerned Nine. First, Johnson instructed his executive producers not to let McGuire employ any people from his own company, McGuire Media, on the program. Johnson was paranoid that McGuire wanted to take production control; the network had learnt from Daryl Somers' and Ernie Carroll's ownership of the out-of-control *Hey! Hey! It's Saturday* that Nine had to retain ownership of *The Footy Show*.

Second, Johnson implored his producers not to let the show return to London for a special edition. He said it was a waste of time and effort, bringing no more viewers at an exorbitant cost.

Then Johnson left Nine to go to Seven and was replaced by an inexperienced TV man, Graeme Yarwood. McGuire could wrench some power back under Yarwood, particularly after news of a talk given to students by Silver's replacement, Steve Perkin, was leaked to the newspapers. Perkin innocuously answered a question about *The Footy Show*'s stars in general terms by saying there was a danger egos could get out of control after success, but Nine was brilliant at coping with such issues.

The *Herald Sun* blew it up as a story about McGuire and Newman being overexposed and their egos too hard to handle.

Perkin rang Johnson immediately to offer his resignation, but a co-panellist at the talk, Robert Walls, had beaten him to the punch, telling Johnson the report was 'bullshit' and had been taken out of context.

Nevertheless, McGuire was rightly indignant; Perkin took two weeks' holiday.

Perkin would be punted in February 2001. McGuire didn't axe Perkin, but he could have helped him stay. He was replaced by one of the show's original producers, McGuire Media's Cos Cardone. Despite Johnson's warnings that overseas broadcasts were a waste of time and effort, the program returned for a special London edition in 2001. And again in 2004. It seemed nothing was going to stop the show – but others thought differently.

CHAPTER 8

OUTRAGEOUS FORTUNES

As much as *The Footy Show* flew on the back of the cast's dynamics, the news-breaking ability of McGuire and the thrall in which Melbourne is held to the AFL, its controversies propelled its notoriety and kept jaded viewers returning.

Most of the controversies were manufactured rather than random, although McGuire could feign ignorance of some of the doozies.

God was the first to complain. The Catholic Church called for a boycott of the show after it used the Last Supper as the promotional image to spruik the last show of 1994 – with Eddie as Jesus and twelve robed members of the panel on a long table mimicking the positions of da Vinci's painting *The Last Supper*.

Melbourne Archdiocese Vicar-General Monsignor Gerald Cudmore said the advertisement upset and offended him, particularly after Nine had produced such a quality show during the year: 'It is very sad. I liked *The Footy Show* and I think they have done an injustice,' he said.[1]

Cudmore urged a boycott; as would become its pattern, *The Footy Show* countered the criticism with the opinion of viewers; its final episode began a pattern of blockbuster ratings for its Grand Final editions.

The program flew by the seat of its pants – that was much of its appeal. And it laughed off such criticism, although in its flurry to celebrate the game, it took some missteps.

An early mistake was the return of former umpire, celebrated radio caller and convicted fraudster Harry Beitzel. The panel didn't quite know how to react to the segment, belittling Beitzel with some queasy jokes, as if to acknowledge he was one of them yet also a crim just out of prison.

Similarly, the proposed inclusion of independent MP Pauline Hanson with Sam Newman on a *Footy Show* off-shoot special caused Victorian Premier Jeff Kennett to blow a gasket, leading to the cutting of Hanson's segment from the show. Kennett saw Hanson on screen during the pre-record of a special *The Footy Show Awards* after recording his opening. He threatened to take it up with Kerry Packer before wiser heads prevailed. The offending 'Please Explain Award' segment judging players who had urinated in public that year, introduced by the anti-immigration MP, was cut because, as McGuire later said, it was 'universally decided that it didn't work and did not fit in with the rest of the show. As is always the case with *The Footy Show* we were running over and something had to go. Faced with this, it was an easy decision.'[2] The episode was made by Nine and McGuire Media, with Eddie's brother Frank co-producing it.[3]

Advertisers and sponsors piled onto the show as it grew, loving the 'halo effect' of having advertising near McGuire. He looked after sponsors' wishes, met them, remembered them and was a more effective revenue machine for *The Footy Show* than any advertising sales rep. His professionalism with clients would make him a far more valuable commodity for Nine than being a mere TV host.

His enthusiasm for sponsors would later cause Nine a few headaches as it became wary of McGuire dropping non-sequitur recommendations or plugs for advertisers aligned with Collingwood or *The Footy Show* on other Nine programs. There was no doubt Collingwood knew his ability to attract sponsors, including Emirates, Lexus and Westpac, to the club was heightened because they knew they would receive bonus exposure through *The Footy Show* and McGuire's radio segments.

Unwittingly, Newman counter-balanced McGuire's advertising aptitude with his random sledges and sarcasm about sponsors. Hyundai dropped its sponsorship after Newman joked on *The Footy Show* that its cars were made out of Coke cans. The Korean manufacturer was not amused.

Ford also dumped its sponsorship of Newman after he parodied Nicky Winmar in black face. Ford said the deal to sponsor Newman's car-racing endeavour was coming to an end regardless.

Nike wasn't a sponsor when Newman joked that it had introduced a new tennis shoe called Dykes, but they had been recalled because their tongues weren't long enough. Nevertheless, it sparked complaints – as would many episodes. But it spoke of Newman's willingness to deliver any line, no matter who it might offend, for the purpose of entertainment.

He would offend many women forevermore with lines like 'Arch yer back, Val, and get Norm's agates off the cold tiles', while still appealing to many women. He always played dumb, defending his miscued comments by saying he was an 'equal-opportunity offender'; he had no beef against any race, religion or minority.

That clashed with McGuire's superior moral line. He wanted to be known as a credible man who didn't step over the line ethically, morally, racially or sexually. Yet Newman thought anyone was fair game. If you were an idiot, he'd call you one.

Not everyone was convinced the show was so upright, however. Beverly Knight, the first woman to sit on the board of an AFL club, lashed out at the show's 'vilification' of a female football supporter, Jiin-Wen Ewe, in 2004 by mocking her name. McGuire defended Newman, saying, 'He does things in the Sam Newman way, and often over the years Sam's way has been inappropriate. We are doing a footy show, not trying to save the world.'[4]

However, Newman's decision in 2008 to pillory a constant critic of the show, *The Age*'s Caroline Wilson, was a step too far. Newman attached with a staple gun an image of Wilson – who also appeared weekly on Nine's *Footy Classified* – to the head of a lingerie-clad mannequin before proceeding to lift the mannequin by the crotch. McGuire was long gone then; new hosts Garry Lyon and James Brayshaw watched on.

Nine ignored calls by some of the AFL's most influential women – including Knight, Western Bulldogs director Susan Alberti, Sydney Swans director Lynn Ralph, Melbourne director Sue Natrass, Hawthorn director Janine Allis – for the cast of *The Footy Show* to be counselled on their attitude to women by an expert from the office of the federal Anti-Discrimination Commissioner and a code of conduct implemented.

Nine did apologise to Wilson, as did *Footy Show* co-host Garry Lyon, who made a public apology on *Footy Classified*, on which he appeared with Wilson.

McGuire was still host when St Kilda president Rod Butterss reacted angrily to Newman attending a news conference by coach Grant Thomas, saying Nine and *The Footy Show* were now 'persona non grata'. Newman attended the news conference to question the coach's ability after St Kilda refused a request for him to appear on McGuire's show. Butterss responded with colour and venom, likening Kerry Packer's support of *The Footy Show* to events in Frank Hardy's novel *Power Without Glory*. The novel (one Eddie had connected to when he was younger) is about a character based on John Wren, who ran gambling dens in Melbourne during the Depression and was a patron and backer of Collingwood.

'Some things just haven't changed in terms of a certain gambling (den). Well, it's not a den, it's more a mausoleum that's owned by a certain individual that also owns a television station,' Butterss said.[5]

It wasn't always clear whether McGuire and Newman colluded on minor 'controversies'. However, they certainly didn't on the biggest blue of the show's run.

The Footy Show invited the former St Kilda champ Nicky Winmar to appear to discuss his new club, the Western Bulldogs, and his achievement in becoming the first Indigenous player to play more than 200 games. The show negotiated with Winmar's manager Peter Jess, including an appearance fee, but on the day of the show, Winmar disappeared. Producers at *The Footy Show* realised at 4 p.m., when they rang to confirm he'd be there, and later at 7.30 p.m., when Jess confirmed that no one could find Winmar. McGuire knew that was a big story in itself, and the show reported and discussed the fact at the top of, and throughout, the episode.

McGuire kept promoting the fact Winmar was meant to appear but hadn't shown, until a break late in the show, when Newman walked off set, as was his habit. They returned from the ad break and Newman was not on set, prompting McGuire to ask the producers where he was. No one knew until, when back on air, there was a bit of a commotion behind McGuire and gasps and laughter from the audience. McGuire turned to look behind him and uttered a horrified 'Oh, Jesus!' under his breath as Newman waltzed in with blackface on. McGuire knew immediately that this act could cripple the show; Newman just thought blackening his face with make-up was the best means of mimicking Winmar. McGuire was sharp enough to calculate the consequences immediately; Newman wasn't.

McGuire later said it was too late to do anything: 'It threw me completely. Things happened in split seconds, but that's live TV. I didn't endorse what Sam did.'[6]

The incident became a lightning rod for racism in football. Certainly Winmar had been the protagonist of one of the most meaningful images in Indigenous sporting history when he pointed to his black skin in front of a rabid Victoria Park crowd in 1993 (see Chapter 20). But six years later, Winmar was hurt. Winmar said his children were taunted after Newman's antics on the show and he derided the episode as disgraceful: 'We have worked hard to stop this rubbish but what happened the other night has sent it backwards.'[7]

Winmar won an unreserved apology on the next week's episode, after a ninety-minute mediation session at the South Melbourne office of Western Bulldogs president David Smorgon between Winmar, Jess, his minder Oberon Pirak and *The Footy Show*'s Newman, McGuire and executive producer Steve Perkin.

The Winmar incident, and more extreme vilification in the same month by Blues president John Elliott, led to the AFL reviewing its vilification code, which only governs players' conduct on the field and not that of club officials. Despite the Bulldogs making a formal complaint to the AFL, it could not have punished the Collingwood president, McGuire, if it had wanted to do so.

Newman remained unrepentant, believing he was mocking the person rather than his race, with no intention of degrading the player. He described the process as a 'charade'. And some at *The Footy Show* remain adamant Winmar wasn't perturbed by the incident and the outrage was manufactured elsewhere.

Weeks later, tensions on set grew as Newman sought to paint the face of Aboriginal umpire Glenn James white live on air. Supervising producer Perkin and McGuire stopped him from doing so during a heated ad break. 'That's what happens in television, you have discussions in ad breaks,' McGuire said.[8] That led to Newman learning not to push some of his ideas past McGuire, sensing they might be shut down. Not telling him meant McGuire would be genuinely surprised.

Such Newman mayhem was impromptu, but other controversial incidents were not. For instance, the production knew Newman would come out naked apart from a football in one episode, but no one knew – not even Shane Crawford – the Hawthorn Brownlow medallist would 'dak' him on another, leading to a brief flash of Newman's manhood.

In 1997, Jason Dunstall's cuffing of Newman to a chair and shaving his head looked like a spontaneous act but was actually planned in advance. However, Newman's drunken 'Street Talk' segment at the Brownlow Medal ceremony was unplanned.[9]

The dynamic between Newman and McGuire was simultaneously rock solid and brittle. They knew they were both good for each other, and Newman felt he had a mentor who was 25 years younger than him, yet Newman's impetuousness frustrated McGuire. Nine's management, rather than McGuire, would heavy Newman to pull back or hold his tongue. McGuire had the difficult job of trying to corral Newman during 100 minutes of live television.

Another infamous stunt was planned, but the outcome was completely unexpected.

One tenet McGuire held dear through the life of *The Footy Show* was respect for the footballers. They were never demeaned or pilloried unless they did it themselves. The evening panellist David Schwarz copped a cream pie in the face, Newman and *The Footy Show* crossed the line. The Melbourne player knew the pie was coming, even if McGuire claimed he and producer Cos Cardone did not, but the verve of Newman's serve nearly pushed him off his seat and hurt him. Schwarz retaliated angrily, putting Newman on his behind.

The furore came hard and fast – and, peculiarly, was almost more indignant than that for incidents pillorying women or Winmar – with AFL Players' Association Chief Executive Dr Robert Kerr describing the incident as 'exceptionally demeaning'.

McGuire knew that was true. He conceded that for the first time in the show's nine-year history, the program had left a bitter taste. The show – particularly Newman – could often get away from McGuire, whose appreciation of pace in live TV meant he would never stop to question a moment as it unfolded. He would raise an eyebrow and occasionally express his displeasure, but as a host – a servant of live television – he would allow the contentious moment to keep running or move on promptly to the next segment or question. Was he complicit or just a knowing TV host?

The questions, arguments and retribution would come when the red light on top of the camera was off. And then be forgotten within a day as Eddie kept moving forward.

CHAPTER 9

MAN ON THE RISE

McGuire's ego and lean upbringing don't allow him to refuse a job easily. He appreciates any opportunity that can lead to the next role, the next contact, the next deal.

To be fair, it is not a purely commercial instinct: although his desire not to relive the financial insecurity of his forebears is paramount, his propensity for charity work is as keen as his passion for paying gigs.

Nevertheless, McGuire wasn't one to be content with only hosting *The Footy Show* and a Triple M radio program. As *The Footy Show*'s star rose at Nine, McGuire's rose along with it, and he worked it hard. He wanted to dominate not just AFL but sport. Then, seemingly, infinity and beyond.

In 1995, as *The Footy Show* took off, McGuire's commitments elsewhere didn't abate. He was appearing, for the moment, on a new sports show for Nine, *Sunday Scoreboard*,[1] which he co-hosted with Sydney's Ian Maurice, as well as on *Nine News*, the *Triple M Breakfast Team* and Saturday's *The Grill Team*, and even occasionally guest hosting *The Today Show*. And this was all while maintaining his fervour for breaking news as a journalist. Something had to give.

The first commitment to go was his regular gig on Richard Stubbs' *Breakfast Show*, although he continued to contribute a footy report at 8.30 a.m. each day.[2] But Stubbs' and McGuire's egos were clashing increasingly frequently as the program moved towards a more comedic take on sport than McGuire wanted.

Publicly, Eddie conceded his on-camera load was heavy. 'I'll be OK,' he said. 'As long as you pace yourself and learn how to switch off away from the camera you're OK.'[3]

Radio could go into hibernation. His raised status at Nine resulted in many discussions about new roles. If there was a new program in development, McGuire's name invariably would be attached to it. He wasn't limiting himself merely to propping up the Sports Department.

His name was floated as the replacement host of *Midday* in 1995 – as were those of Ken Sutcliffe, Richard Wilkins and Larry Emdur – before Tracy Grimshaw and ex-*Getaway* reporter David Reyne were named hosts.[4]

In 1997, McGuire even emerged as an outsider to replace Brian Naylor as Melbourne's *National Nine News* newsreader, although that was more misguided rumour as Naylor's deputy, Peter Hitchener, moved into the role without skipping a beat.[5] It spoke more of McGuire's ambition than of a reality.

In June 1995, McGuire co-hosted a rare piece of TV coverage as Nine and Seven jointly presented former Footscray great Ted Whitten's funeral service and procession from St Patrick's Cathedral. McGuire hosted with his former Ten mentor, Seven's Bruce McAvaney.

The changes kept happening at Nine, and McGuire was often front of mind. In 1996, he delivered sports reports for a re-energised *Nightline* with Jim Waley and Paul Lyneham, at the far end of the day from his breakfast radio commitments.

He wasn't becoming any more complacent as the commitments piled up. In preparation for Nine's telecast of the

Ted Whitten Legends game, McGuire and Brian Taylor took Nine production crews to North Ballarat and Traralgon to hone their kick-by-kick calls. Nine's and McGuire's commitment to score points with the AFL, and sow the seeds for the next AFL broadcast deal, was serious, as was McGuire's ambition to make it as an AFL caller.[6]

Nine locked McGuire into a new contract in 1996, tying him to the network until 1999 at more than $1 million a year, bumped up from an already healthy $650 000-ish. *The Footy Show*'s commercial success escalated his worth and, thankfully, Seven upped his price by coming knocking again with the sweetener that he could call AFL football and be involved in the 2000 Sydney Olympics.

McGuire had set himself a long-term ambition when he was a Ten reporter in the late 1980s: to work on the 2000 Olympic Games with whichever network had it and wherever it was held. It was a millennial milestone and a Sydney Olympics was very tempting.

But he was now a Nine boy and *The Footy Show* was a juggernaut. The Olympics would have to wait.[7] A few rocky headlines later, McGuire recommitted.

'Eddie had a few things to think about. He had been very happy here, he had enjoyed enormous notoriety through *The Footy Show*,' Ian Johnson said. 'The boy's done good.'[8]

The new contract affirmed that Eddie was the successor to Ray Martin, who was becoming an unhappy host in the chair at *A Current Affair* and certainly not the dominant force he was during his run of four consecutive Gold Logies up to 1996.

That ascension was clear when McGuire featured as part of Nine's federal election night coverage, reporting from the tally room as Martin anchored with Peter Costello, Graham Richardson, Laurie Oakes and Paul Lyneham. And early in 1998, he flew to San Diego to host Nine's coverage of Superbowl XXXII. Nine was pushing him – indulging him but also worried about him.

Late in 1997, Nine boss James Packer took McGuire to dinner to raise concerns about his star performer's workload outside the network. And that was before he became Collingwood president.

Packer reminded him he was first and foremost a Nine employee, and not to be distracted by other interests, including his nascent production company McGuire Media, which produced *The Grill Team* and AFL commentary for Triple M and the occasional footy special for Nine, or political ambitions via the Constitutional Convention.

His varying workloads and incomes would remain an ongoing issue for his employers. The only broadcaster to have left him to run his own race over the years is Southern Cross Austereo's Triple M after Jeff Allis sprayed McGuire and his *Grill Team*.

Back then, Nine was ambivalent about the issue. McGuire wound back his Triple M commitments, but that time would soon be filled by his increasing commitment to Collingwood. Nine's management believed he was young and energetic enough to juggle his responsibilities, and smart enough to realise Nine was his primary employer. In the short term, though, they worried he was not devoting enough time to his creative, news-breaking and performance duties on *The Footy Show*.

While the 2000 Olympics was now out of the question, McGuire co-hosted Nine's 1998 Commonwealth Games coverage from Kuala Lumpur. As co-host Ken Sutcliffe later wrote, 'That was Eddie's personal debut party, as the campaign began to turn him into a national figure.'[9]

McGuire walked into Nine's Malaysian studio directly after his bloodless coup in the Collingwood Football Club boardroom, tired but up for the job. The reviews for Nine's up-and-comer were very positive.

Ray Martin wasn't so positive when the Games coverage subsequently won the Logie Award for best sports broadcast. McGuire accepted the award, which mildly annoyed Martin because he had hosted Nine's telecast. He could read the tea leaves: McGuire was the man on the rise at Nine; Martin was not.

Indeed, McGuire was rising so sharply his notoriety made him a public target. The *Herald Sun* listed his combined earnings in 1997 as $1.2 million,[10] although his entry into *Business Review Weekly*'s annual survey of the Top 50 Australian Show Business Earners pushed that to $1.9 million, making him the 18th-highest-paid entertainer in the country. McGuire wasn't happy at the attention, and said the figure was inaccurate: 'When I was young, my dad told me it was the height of rudeness to ask people what they are paid, so maybe they should talk to their parents about what they're doing here,' he said.

'Actually, I hope I'm there (on the Rich List) next year and every year after that for the next 30 years.'[11] He's now been there for seventeen years and counting.

The money and fame arrived, but they weren't enough: McGuire clearly wanted to stretch his wings further professionally. He showed his keen study of variety programming when writing a column after the 1998 *TV Week* Logie Awards. McGuire defended the ceremony – as one would at Nine – before proceeding to assess, with some insight, Daryl Somers' hosting job:

> Somers is no Frank Sinatra, but neither is Billy Crystal, the undisputed world heavyweight champion of award show hosting. Somers showed first-class timing and ability to pull the complicated piece together … The art of being a successful host is to keep things moving and bring out the best in your guests. With Kathy Najimy, the star of *Veronica's Closet*, Somers was able to hit lobs to her forehand and Najimy had the talent to put away the smash. At no time did Daryl's ego get in the way of trying to trump her lines.[12]

That was McGuire's modus operandi, which has since been appreciated by producers and directors within television but not so much by critics, who long for TV hosts to be triple threats (dancers/singers/actors) who can also deliver a comic line. They're once-in-a-generation people, and even Graham Kennedy, Daryl Somers and Bert Newton weren't known for their song-and-dance skills.

McGuire realised early that he wasn't necessarily the key talent: that was Sam Newman or the footballer or the comedian. McGuire set them up for their smashes, but was capable of rushing to the net to put away his own volleys as required.

McGuire's screen empire grew. In 1999 he replaced Ken Sutcliffe as the host of Nine's coverage of the Australian Grand Prix, a move that ruffled the unflappable Sutcliffe. Then came another turn of 'luck' that would secure his status at Nine and deliver another reliable income and public visibility for decades: a game show.

McGuire couldn't believe his good fortune when Ian Johnson called him into his office to ask whether he knew about a show called *Who Wants to Be a Millionaire?* Of course he knew about the new British hit, although he had yet to see an episode. Johnson gave him a tape of the UK version and told him to decide whether he wanted to host it. He watched five episodes that night and was at Nine early the next morning to badger Johnson. McGuire could see this as a real opportunity to walk into a national, non-contentious prime-time show without having to be too serious. It was perfect.

He wasn't a walk-up start for the role. Other Nine personalities were being considered, including former *Sale of the Century* host Glenn Ridge, but Kerry and James Packer were beginning to warm to McGuire. The job was his for the taking.

Eddie took the gig and performed well in the show's first two-week run, in which any contestant, if they answered fifteen consecutive questions correctly, could win $1 million.

McGuire hosted effortlessly, making contestants comfortable and maintaining the show's pace and suspense. And the format was a classic, with its promise of a major payday in any episode rather than the smaller, incremental progress seen on other game shows. It also had a game show's essential element: broad at-home playability.

Its much-vaunted arrival was nearly usurped by Seven's ambush with its own $1 million quiz show, *Million Dollar Chance of a Lifetime*, hosted by Brisbane newsreader Frank Warrick. Nine was livid, but there was little it could do. Quiz shows are difficult to copyright; most are variations on a theme: answer general knowledge questions and win a prize. Seven's director of program development, Tim Worner, said his network deserved a pat on the back for 'a well-kept secret' that launched four days before *Who Wants to Be a Millionaire?*[13]

In the rush, *Millionaire* also had an issue with its gaming permits but it turned out to be a minor concern. Like *The Footy Show*, *Millionaire* began brilliantly, exceeding even the high expectations of it held internally at Nine. It won every night of its first six nights on air and, more surprisingly, had most viewers some nights in Sydney, where McGuire was still a nascent star. Even better, it took the gloss off Seven's game show, which came off second-best when programmed against another Nine hit, *Friends*, on Monday nights.[14]

McGuire's status at the network was confirmed as he sat next to James Packer at the 1999 TV Week Logie Awards. That was the evening host Andrew Denton made his way through the audience to sit on Packer's knee and pretended to be the ventriloquist's dummy in what McGuire described as a 'brilliant and polished performance in the most daunting hosting task in television'.[15]

McGuire's status outside the network was confirmed when it emerged that two journalists from *The Age* had notoriously registered the names of Packer and McGuire. There were better ways to be acknowledged, McGuire thought.

As his contract came up for renewal again in 1999, word leaked that Seven, just as it had in 1996, was again attempting to poach McGuire to head Seven's AFL coverage and host its Sydney 2000 Olympic Games telecast in September. Everyone in TV was jockeying to be part of Seven's Sydney Games, though, with Nine's out-of-contract star Ray Martin also putting his hand up. Of course, the leak conveniently happened as McGuire was renegotiating with Nine, resulting in a deal that made him Australia's highest-paid TV star (speculated at $3 million across four years) and tied him to the network until the end of 2004.

McGuire noted Nine had given him huge opportunities and been '100 per cent behind me in my position with Collingwood',[16] which was not in fact completely true. Johnson was worried Seven might get him, and McGuire was stressed by the negotiations with the opportunity to call the Sydney Olympics and AFL football again on the table. But loyalty counted for something significant in Eddie McGuire's mind. He had to stay at Nine. There was no way he could walk away from *The Footy Show*; McGuire would just have to work hard to help Nine bring the footy across to Nine.

The new deal unofficially anointed him as heir to the throne previously held by Nine's human logo, Ray Martin.

'He's of the Ray Martin ilk but he's the new breed coming through,' Johnson said. 'Ray is still very important to us but you've always got to have a couple of people and Eddie's got the ability, he's right up there with Ray. Whether or not he's had the same level of popularity at this point in his career, we think he will have.'

So did Kerry Packer, who began to take a serious interest in Eddie as his son James grew closer to him socially.

McGuire's friendship with James Packer led him to one of the more intimidating hosting gigs of his career, in front of an elite gathering of celebrities, business people and politicians (including Prime Minister John Howard) at the wedding of James and Jodhi (or Jodie as she was then) Meares at the Packers' Bellevue Hill compound in Sydney in October 1999.[17] McGuire did it as a friend, but that didn't stop Kerry at one point abusing McGuire in front of guests: 'I thought I fuckin' told you to get this fuckin' show on the road! What the fuck are you doing? Are you fuckin' incapable of taking orders?' In a perverse way, those around the bollocking could see McGuire had Kerry Packer's confidence.

McGuire became Nine's go-to man, co-hosting Nine's *Millennium Live* 25-hour broadcast at the turn of the century, in which Nine's New Year's Eve broadcast trumped that of the ABC, with a peak national viewing audience of 1.6 million people. Nine was relieved despite losing its bid to screen the Sydney fireworks at midnight exclusively after it had paid Sydney City Council $450 000.[18]

As *The Footy Show* barrelled along, recovering from a poor 1998 season and growing through to 2000 (averaging three times the Melbourne audience of Seven's *The Game*), *Who Wants to Be a Millionaire?* returned and swamped its rivals.[19] Together, McGuire's two programs were the dominant performers on a dominant network.

And he was hosting at a level that stunned international producers. A producer from the American ABC network's US version of *Who Wants to Be a Millionaire?* interviewed Sam Newman before the Sydney Olympics and asked about the Australian host of the game show. Newman noted McGuire was pretty good, knocking over the taping of four or five episodes in an afternoon. The American producer was incredulous, saying the US host, Regis Philbin, only recorded one episode a week, after extensive rehearsals. She thought Newman was making it up.

Then came the prospect of McGuire's holy grail: broadcasting the AFL. Nine swooped in 2000 to secure the rights to broadcast the AFL from 2002 in a stunning partnership with Ten and Foxtel. The bid ended Seven's forty-year run of televising Australia's own football code, and McGuire initially believed he could play a bigger role in the coming broadcasts than mere lead caller.

Early on in discussions, he believed his McGuire Media could be the single production house producing the AFL for the consortium. It was typical of McGuire's optimism, although some believed in this instance it was a sign of a ridiculous, over-reaching ambition.

McGuire Media had been formed years earlier as a vehicle to value-add to Eddie's deals. It packaged and produced the AFL broadcast team for Triple M rather than just allowing McGuire to be a salaried broadcaster. McGuire saw the possibilities of producing his own content way back in 1990, when he co-produced a commemorative video after Collingwood's premiership with the Video Entertainment Group.

Like the actors who only want to direct, the McGuire brothers could anticipate a time when Eddie wasn't so popular, or television would turn, and they might have to grind it out as producers or proprietors. The downturn at Ten in the late 1980s left an imprint on McGuire. He remembered a voice on the station intercom one day asking a list of people to go to the pay office. They received severance pay and were escorted from the premises there and then.[20] From that moment, he didn't want to be beholden to one employer.

McGuire Media's early days were scrappy, though. Nine didn't want the company to become a dominant player, yet it appeased its star by allowing it to produce the occasional *The Footy Show* spin-off special such as *More Than a Game*.

The company had office space at Nine, but wasn't really producing anything. It made the short-lived *Screema!* national footy show for youngsters with Foxtel and produced *The Grill Team* for Triple M. The company was many years away from being a viable broadcaster of a sporting competition, though. That would take more than a decade.

Professionally, McGuire was running at full tilt. One thing slowed him momentarily and it would sharpen his focus. Carla gave birth to the couple's first son, Joseph, in 2000. The boy with his mother's eyes would soften Eddie, slightly, and demand the attention and contrast his manic professional life required. And Eddie had the beginnings of something that defined his early years and remained central to his being: a family.

Football was now a second priority, although the wait to broadcast the footy was interminable. McGuire's dual responsibility as Collingwood president and as Nine's proposed lead AFL caller caused some consternation, both publicly and behind the scenes among other clubs. Kerry Packer came to Melbourne to meet Eddie at Crown so that, for the first time, he could really size up Nine's contentious multi-million dollar man and judge whether he deserved to juggle both roles.

McGuire's overexposure was foremost in the mind of his friend, manager and mentor Jeff Browne. In 2001, Browne implored McGuire to slow down or do less so he could endure for longer. 'Sooner or later everyone's empire runs down, doesn't it?' Browne mused.[21]

By this time, McGuire admitted to working pretty much every day from February through October. It was time to reassess and he knew that, with a young child, he was no longer the young, single man who felt he should be working for as many hours as he could. Slowing down for McGuire was a matter of inches though, compared with others.

In December 2002, Carla gave birth to their second son, Alexander, yet McGuire barely slowed his pace. Not until a few years later, when the brothers could kick the footy after school with dad or accompany him on work trips overseas, did McGuire adapt his working life visibly for them. And as his own boss, effectively, he had a schedule that afforded him more time with his sons than most.

The work at Nine, and his successes, kept rolling on. His hosting of the finale of the beached *Australian Survivor* in 2002 was forgotten promptly after he co-hosted the major TV event, the *National IQ Test*, with Catriona Rowntree later that year. The three-hour program had an average capital city audience of 2.8 million viewers, making it the most-watched show on television that year, more than the World Cup soccer final between Brazil and Germany (2.7 million) on Nine and the *Big Brother* final eviction (2.3 million) on Ten. *Who Wants to Be a Millionaire?* even cracked two million viewers in 2002.

McGuire hosted 143 television shows that year.[22] More came in 2003, including the poisoned chalice of Australian television, the *TV Week* Logie Awards. As one veteran producer noted, the program involves three months of politicking and ego massage, a month of planning, a week of high tension, twenty-four hours of unmitigated stress, 'and by 2 p.m. Monday no one gives a shit.'[23]

McGuire was a relatively safe choice after Wendy Harmer had bombed the previous year. As would become routine, reviewers in Sydney whined, with *The Australian*'s Amanda Meade carping that 'McGuire was dull, wooden and blokey'.[24] *The Age*, on the other hand, lauded McGuire's 'cool, capable hands', with the key being 'McGuire's great gift: his humble recognition that other people are funnier'.[25] Viewers appeared to agree, with ratings rising from the previous year to a peak of 2 479 661 viewers nationwide.

Whether the organisers knew it or not, the Logies ceremony changed the moment Andrew Denton pulled the curtain, literally, on the opening song and dance number of the 1999 awards ceremony. McGuire was not a song and dance man, nor was he a comedian. Comedians – including Denton, Harmer and Shaun Micallef – are high-risk, and not always high-reward, options as hosts. Consequently, the producers of the show made a conscious decision to change the direction of the event, so it was about the show and less about the host.

McGuire was the perfect man for that transition, appreciating the right pace was integral and knowing his job was to steer the show from one talent to another, not *be* the talent. The show was king and his job was to keep it brisk, as comedians such as Kath and Kim, Micallef and Dave Hughes provided the laughs.

Which is not to say McGuire couldn't add something. An amusing sketch featuring Steve Irwin with a snake on his arm went 'awry' as Irwin lurched off the stage and the snake 'bit' Tim Webster in the crotch. McGuire sharply noted of his former Ten Sydney nemesis, 'I'm not going to suck that wound.'

He backed up the following year and attracted the same divided reviews, but an even larger audience.[26]

By now, Sydney's media had latched on to McGuire's old moniker from his Melbourne nightclubbing days, Eddie Everywhere. It certainly seemed the Melburnian was omnipresent in 2004, although it said as much about the fragmentation and impatience of the modern TV viewer as anything else. Recall television in 1982 when Bert Newton appeared on *The Don Lane Show* on Monday and Thursday, *New Faces* on Friday and *Ford Superquiz* on Wednesday, while hosting a program on Melbourne radio station 3UZ five days a week. And this when television was the only real recreational option on dark nights!

On 26 December 2004, images started arriving from South-East Asia of a major disaster: the destruction of large portions of the Indonesian coastline by a tsunami. Seven's *Sunrise* proposed a fundraising concert on the steps of the Sydney Opera House until Nine suggested its own fundraiser during its cricket coverage. Seven boss David Leckie and *Sunrise* producer Adam Boland thought a joint event could be worthwhile, with network ratings suspended for the event. *Australia Unites: Reach Out to Asia* became an unwieldy telecast featuring hosts from all three commercial networks – including Ten's Rove McManus, who joked, 'Finally, Eddie McGuire on all three networks.'[27]

But it went so well – raising $20 million for tsunami victims – that the three key hosts, McGuire, McManus and Andrew O'Keefe, were chosen to host the 2005 Logie awards together. Eddie *was* everywhere.

Traditionally, the parking space closest to the dressing-room doors at GTV-9 in Bendigo Street, Richmond was allotted to the channel's prime talent. Previously, the spot had been assigned to Graham Kennedy, Bert Newton, Don Lane and Daryl Somers. Now it belonged to Eddie McGuire.

CHAPTER 10

'AUSTRAYA'

Eddie McGuire was brought up with a strong sense that the best means of progression was through your own toil. It was a lesson enhanced as he read Frank Hardy's *Power Without Glory* as a child and devoured sports biographies, which showed him that in Australia you could achieve your goals if you were determined enough.

The only caveat in McGuire's inquiring mind was you could not be the head of state. That job – at least in his lifetime – was reserved for the reigning British monarch, the Queen of England. It didn't sit well with someone who made plain his ambition to be prime minister as early as primary school, and reiterated it – much to his workmates' surprise – as a young journo at Ten.

Similarly, his brother Frank's political aspirations were motivated by an answer he received to a question put to the retiring head of the Premier's Department when he was working at the *Herald*. His biggest career mistake? 'Broadmeadows,' he replied. The journalist was staggered; Broadmeadows was his home. He asked the public servant to explain and the bureaucrat said the government's policies had been wrong – it could have done so much more for the suburb. The incident gave Frank McGuire a taste for politics and what it could achieve.

The brothers thought alike despite their age difference. So when they heard art critic and writer Robert Hughes and Malcolm Turnbull speak at a Melbourne republican rally in July 1997, they agreed this was an issue on which they could both work.

They also liked their nationalism. McGuire proudly talks of 'Austraya', a place where his working-class mum and dad could immigrate and establish a home for what would become a prosperous family. Eddie Jnr said:

> Dad always said Australia was God's own. I feel very lucky with the hand Australia has dealt me. You can do anything here, if you're prepared to step up to the wicket. We look back at some relos in Scotland who have all the go in the world but can't break the shackles. They used to export them here in shackles, now you leave them behind when you come out.[1]

In hindsight, the push for constitutional change and a republic happened rather too quickly, hastened by a looming new millennium and the Centenary of Federation in 2001.

After much gnashing of teeth within conservative ranks, the Howard government allowed the proposal to be developed and put to the people – although some, including Prime Minister John Howard, anticipated Australians would feel safer with the status quo and they would be confused by a new republican system.

The Australian Republican Movement (ARM), which would quickly assume the dominant position among republicans, assembled sharply from its Sydney base, although it realised it did not have 'a national spread of stars', as ARM president Malcolm Turnbull put it, to stand for delegate seats at the coming Constitutional Convention or to prosecute the Republican case. The ARM had earnest hard workers across the country, but none of the big names associated with the campaign in Sydney or a spread of ALP and Liberal delegates, as it had in New South

Wales. In Sydney, there was a surplus of diverse candidates including Turnbull, the National Party's Wendy Machin, former ALP premier Neville Wran, Democrat Karin Sowada, the ACTU's Jennie George, author Tom Keneally and former first lady of Australia, Hazel Hawke.

Turnbull met with ACTU powerbrokers Bill Kelty, Jennie George and ACTU assistant secretary Jenny Doran to nut out potential candidates.

'To win down here you need a real Victorian star, someone who everyone knows,' Kelty said.

Turnbull asked who that might be, fearing the name Jeff Kennett would emerge.

After a dramatic pause – or perhaps some improvised thought – Kelty exclaimed, 'Eddie McGuire!'

The group congratulated themselves on the magnificence of the suggestion. The host of *The Footy Show* was omnipresent and a wonderful communicator. Victorians liked him and he had the perfect working-class rags-to-riches story of great cross-party appeal. Turnbull couldn't bear it any longer. 'Who is Eddie McGuire?' he asked.

Another member of the ARM Victorian ticket, Steve Vizard, would also impress McGuire's suitability upon Turnbull. Turnbull soon appreciated McGuire's talents, later writing the man who would head the ARM's Victorian ticket was 'articulate, incredibly well known and well liked and very smart … he also came with a brother'.[2]

The McGuire boys were a key part of the strategy with Frank, a former media adviser for Victorian premier John Cain, in the backroom working on strategy and communications.

The showbiz candidature was criticised, but the ARM knew it had a natural communicator. And McGuire was in his element, embracing a cause that offered a little more in terms of existential consequences than a weekend football match. This was a forum in which he could test himself. And he passed the test gloriously; the ARM would later attribute its strong performances in Victoria to him.

Eddie had to overcome public mistrust that he was now a Toorak boy, despite his Broady beginnings, and he was on the ticket as a populist stunt. Rather, McGuire believed he could overcome the mistrust of politicians and become the one to whom voters could relate. After all, he was the host of the most popular show in town, *The Footy Show*. Additionally, he thought he could be part of a progressive outfit that would counter the cliché pushed by monarchists that republicans are 'over-educated, chardonnay-swilling Lefties'.

McGuire came out with the Victorian team at a press call in the, ironically enough, Royal Botanic Gardens in October 1997. Frank was the Victorian campaign director corralling thirty-nine prominent ambassadors – including Bryan Brown, Ron Barassi, Kate Ceberano, Max Gillies and Jane Kennedy – whose job was to move the debate away from politics and into mainstream conversation.

Executives at Nine and Triple M were not enthused, though. They feared his political bent could alienate particular segments of their audience. There would turn out to be very little to prove that was the case.

But even as late as January 1998, the month before the Constitutional Convention, James Packer, managing director of Publishing and Broadcasting Limited, which ran the Nine Network, took Eddie and Carla McGuire to dinner at Crown to remind him that Eddie worked at Nine. Ian Johnson, the general manager of Nine, agreed, saying 'I'd prefer that he didn't do it, but I'm certainly not going to stop him.'[3]

The ticket for the Convention formed, with former ALP national secretary Bob Hogg, a key ARM strategist, insisting McGuire should head the Victorian ticket, partly to counter the notion the movement was a Sydney push. Another TV host, Steve Vizard, joined the ticket, as long as he was given a winnable position, which bumped former Liberal premier Rupert Hamer down. Cosmetics entrepreneur Poppy King, ABC newsreader Mary Delahunty and transport tycoon Lindsay Fox also joined.

When Turnbull launched the national ticket at the Sydney Opera House, he said it was 'the ultimate unity ticket ever fielded in Australia',[4] although the ARM hierarchy was a little peeved at trucking magnate Lindsay Fox's financial contribution. Fox gave the campaign a relatively measly $10 000 compared with Vizard's $100 000 and McGuire's $30 000.

McGuire led the ticket well, pushing the cause across his many outlets and, to the ARM's eyes, not deviating from the script in a disciplined performance. The problem would be he was so identifiable, he became a key target. The leader of the Real Republican (RR) Party, the Reverend Tim Costello, attacked McGuire's ticket more than he attacked the enemy, the monarchists. 'It's a triumph of style over substance, of image over content. Get the most popular person, associate them with an idea, and that idea's right,' he said of McGuire's ascension.[5] Costello described the ARM ticket as a 'beauty contest': 'You can't imagine (Federation proponents) Alfred Deakin and George Reid saying "a bit boring – we'll have a front sports person running for us".'[6] He later admitted his relentless criticism of McGuire was a potent strategy. The RR couldn't get any media attention for its own cause, but it did every time Costello bagged McGuire.

McGuire did bring media professionalism to the campaign – for instance, answering phones that were not ringing when the cameras were on him in campaign headquarters while launching a new information hotline with Turnbull.[7] When he was prompting people to get out and vote, cameras were there covering McGuire and the news carried the Republican message.

Six hundred and nine candidates sought to be elected to the seventy-six delegate positions around Australia for the Constitutional Convention, to join seventy-six people appointed by the federal government.

Victorians took to the election for delegates with an enthusiasm unmatched by the rest of Australia.[8] The Australian Republican Movement ticket claimed victory for six of the sixteen Victorian Constitutional Convention seats, with McGuire top of the ticket elected with Delahunty, Vizard, King, Fox and unionist Jenny Doran. The Reverend Tim Costello's Real Republicans earned two seats.[9]

With the two largest tickets for the republic being the ARM and Costello's Real Republicans, those supporting the retention of the monarchy and the constitution salivated; they saw a split of the vote, attention and thoughts.

The ARM was criticised for placing McGuire and other celebs on the ticket, with a high rate of almost 400 000 primary votes – nearly double the number of its nearest rival – not translating into the necessary share of below-the-line or individual votes, which was down 9 per cent on the proportion of votes above the line (or for the 'party'). It didn't really matter. The ARM had the voice at February's Constitutional Convention, with forty-six of the seventy-six elected delegates supporting a republic, and twenty-seven of them from the ARM. Twenty-seven delegates supported the monarchy.[10]

McGuire upped the ante, writing in January 1998 of his hope of taking:

> the next step as a mature nation and [becoming] an egalitarian republic striding self-confidently into the 21st century with an Australian as our head of state. In making this change, the ARM wants to maintain the stability and strength that have served us well in the current system of Government.

The roles of an Australian president would be to act as a figurehead above and beyond party politics, conduct the civil and diplomatic duties previously carried out by the Governor-General and encourage debate on diplomatic duties and on community values in the public interest. Our preferred model supports the election of a president by at least a two-thirds majority of both Houses of Parliament, indirectly giving the public a say.

The ARM remains open to a popular election as long as the powers of the head of state are clearly defined and limited to the roles described above.

The road to the Convention was far from smooth. McGuire inflamed tensions when he said the voluntary national ballot had delivered the convention a mandate 'to come up with a blueprint for a republic'. The former independent member for Wills, Phil Cleary, who won a delegate's position, sniped, 'I would suggest that he get a copy of the Constitution and while he's down at Portsea read it in between playing tennis and golf with the superstars.'[11]

It was typical of the cheap shots lobbed at McGuire, although *The Age*'s Virginia Trioli was smitten with McGuire, noting,

> the appeal of the beaming McGuire visage – a '90s version of old Moonface – seems to be the only point of benign agreement.
>
> Comfortably Everyman, McGuire has a similar style to Bob Hawke – confident that his blokey intimacy crosses classes and genders without him having to adjust his approach even one degree. It does, too … McGuire was as genuine and disarming as Paul Hogan.[12]

But McGuire's 1998 entry to Canberra – his first time in the nation's capital for fifteen years – began badly. Ansett confirmed it had lost his luggage, along with Vizard's and King's.

The Convention itself wasn't particularly scintillating, with the first week bogged down in vanity, personal vitriol and semantics about the kind of republican model that would be put to the public. Essentially, too many egos dominated the debate and the Republican movement was irrevocably split over the idea of a popularly elected president.

'Realistic is the word now, rather than idealistic,' McGuire noted mid-way through the Convention.[13]

Some of the niggling was puerile, with Phil Cleary and Paddy O'Brien vocal against celebrity candidates like Vizard and McGuire, to the detriment of actual political debate. McGuire quickly tired of Cleary, telling others he was a grandstander who helped cost Coburg the 1986 VFA Grand Final after giving away a crucial free kick and being sent off. With Melburnians, it always comes down to footy.

One drunken night at the end of the Convention, O'Brien went so far as to grab McGuire by the throat after Eddie implored him to vote with the ARM or be seen as a 'charlatan'. McGuire didn't flinch and gave him a count of three to let go.

Turnbull agreed to step back somewhat to allow McGuire and the other seasoned media performers, Vizard and Delahunty, to step up during the convention. The ARM needed to assuage voter scepticism about Turnbull, and ease the politicking without his confrontational approach. As Turnbull himself later noted with some good humour, a journalist told him the only resolution 'that would get unanimous support at the convention was one disapproving of me'.[14]

Former Brisbane Lord Mayor Clem Jones, a republican, said Turnbull's position was troubling. 'He could have retained the title of father of the republic. Unfortunately, I believe he will become known as the mother of destruction.'[15]

Ultimately, the Convention voted for a referendum on a republic to be held in 1999, with a view to having any change in place before the deadline of 1 January 2001. A clear majority voted to make Australia a republic, but a collective majority of the elected delegates voted against the republican model adopted, with the split in the Republican ranks over the issue of who should elect the President not healing. Ultimately, it was a loss for the Republicans, as they were split over the notion of a directly elected President.

McGuire remained adamant the head of state must be appointed by a political process with bipartisan support.

Turnbull lambasted Prime Minister John Howard for missing 'the opportunity to lead Australia to its destiny'.[16] As it happened, he also heavily criticised Howard minister Tony Abbott, describing him as a 'Jekyll and Hyde character – deliberately, of course. When he is in the company of educated people he eschews extreme talk, but when he is addressing the gullible he pulls out the stops.'[17]

McGuire was as effective an advocate as any in the ARM, leading the state in which the Republican movement attracted most votes and also the most attention. He largely bore the slings and arrows of the campaign, and personal slights, in a serene fashion – something for which he wasn't known in his media and football circles in Melbourne. Republicans regarded McGuire as an effective salesman and weapon.

The process was also important for McGuire. He mingled with people and politicians who wouldn't normally cross his path. It broadened his world and his ambition. He could see that he wasn't just some lower-class upstart: he could mix it at a higher level.

Most illuminating, though, was his ability to play the sides – or at least not become embroiled in some of the uglier politicking. Despite being a friend of Vizard's, he was not drawn into the ugly disagreements between Vizard and Turnbull about strategy, or the very damaging story in *The Bulletin* reporting that the 'Yes' committee would remove Turnbull as chairman.

In November 1999, Australians voted a resounding 'No' in the republic referendum, killing off the idea in the short term at least. McGuire's political foray was over – for now.

Looking back at the many disparate individuals who participated in the Constitutional Convention while claiming no broader political aspirations is intriguing. Julie Bishop, Malcolm Turnbull, Marise Ryan, Mary Delahunty and Nova Peris-Kneebone (now Senator Nova Peris) are among the delegates to subsequently enter parliament. Many believe McGuire too will fulfil that destiny – he's just on a slower burn.

CHAPTER 11

COLLINGWOOD FOREVER

It is said the sticky stains on the floor of the Victoria Park Social Club were blood, not beer. The Collingwood Football Club's politics didn't settle easily.

As a green reporter at Ten, Eddie McGuire had followed his older colleague Mike Tancred as he covered the turmoil of the 'New Magpies' revolution at Collingwood Football Club. The 1982/83 putsch led by broadcaster and heir Ranald Macdonald to take over the club, like all new dawns at Collingwood since the 1950s, was bloody, newsworthy and doomed.

But McGuire was taking notes. He followed Tancred with the wide eyes of a trainee journalist and the passion of a frustrated Pies supporter. It was a seminal moment for McGuire, who in that moment understood both the power and animosity burning off the field at football clubs, and how he could tap board members and club staff for information beyond the predictable confines of Saturday's game.

This supposed new dawn at Collingwood proved to be yet another false sunrise. For all their pride and bluster, the Pies remained noble failures through the 1980s, having won only two premierships (1953 and 1958) since the ten leading up to their consecutive premierships in 1935 and 1936 and the glory days of wonder coach Jock McHale.

Collingwood was the most successful club of the 1920s and 1930s, appearing in thirteen out of a possible twenty Grand Finals during the period and taking the premiership six times, including four consecutive wins between 1927 and 1930, a VFL/AFL record. The club was more than a dominant sporting team, though; it was a cultural force – a movement that bound the inner Melbourne working class.

In the 1930s, needy players ended up working at Carlton & United Breweries' Abbotsford premises, a few hundred metres from Victoria Park, where Jock McHale worked and the notorious fixer, John Wren,[1] had influence. Locals played for the club. Harry Collier, captain of the 1935–36 premiership sides, went to school opposite Victoria Park and was 'so honoured to play for the club he was shocked to learn he would be paid.'[2] Lou and Ron Richards were third-generation Collingwood players.

Yet the club lived for too long off those boom years. The Magpies believed they had the right to expect success forever more. But the club was always bickering: its history was its undoing.

And the friction was religious as much as familial. The Masons fought against the Catholics and good friends Wren and Archbishop Daniel Mannix rallied Melbourne's Catholics in Collingwood's name – Dr Mannix would walk from Raheen, his home in Kew, through Collingwood to St Patrick's, dispensing shillings to the poor inhabitants of the suburb. Meanwhile, the McHale, Galbally and Wren families bickered intermittently with the Sherrin, Coventry, Collier and Merrett clans.

The feuding was at its greatest in 1950 when, at the Collingwood Town Hall, John Wren Jnr and Frank Galbally led a 'rebel' victory of the board and overthrow of executive positions. The Pies won two premierships in that decade, and reached many Grand Finals until 1976, when the club won its first ever wooden spoon under coach Murray Weideman. The coach at one point refused to work at the club because he couldn't abide president Ern Clarke. Meanwhile, no one at the club looked up and realised the club had only won two flags in 40 years.

Collingwood broke with tradition the following year by appointing its first non-Collingwood coach, former Richmond premiership coach Tom Hafey, and he led the club to Grand Finals in 1977, 1979, 1980 and 1981. But Hafey was nobbled by his board, which initially denied him the opportunity to recruit players from Richmond because it was the enemy. Hafey was sacked in 1982, leading to the short-lived 'New Magpies' and another period of instability with club legend Bob Rose even stepping in as interim coach.

The club maintained a profound attitude of arrogance despite its lack of success. AFL president Ross Oakley recounted Collingwood president Allan McAlister's offer to contribute the final $100 000 to the Save the Dogs campaign being run by Footscray to remain in the competition in 1989. 'All we ask in turn is you transfer [star player] Tony McGuinness to us,' he told a nonplussed Footscray saviour, Peter Gordon.[3]

Leigh Matthews led Collingwood to its drought-breaking premiership in 1990, but that only papered over the cracks off-field, while injecting an inordinate amount of money into the club. That was not the only required cure.

Collingwood under McAlister believed that without the club, the AFL would be nothing. As interstate clubs began entering the league, becoming behemoths, and Victorian clubs Hawthorn, Carlton and Geelong dominated the 1990s beside the West Coast Eagles and Adelaide, Collingwood was edging itself closer to nothing.

Television news directors appreciated that one of McGuire's key strengths as a sports reporter was his appreciation of the backroom games beyond the game. McGuire was fascinated with sports administration, the motivations and machinations of those on the other side of the white line. He took a keen interest in the goings on, on and off the field, at Collingwood. After all, Collingwood sold newspapers and attracted eyeballs to TV.

The first inkling of Eddie McGuire contemplating running for the Collingwood presidency emerged in 1996. He dismissed the prospect until '[President] Kevin Rose has won us a premiership and my days as a footy commentator are over.' Publicly, he also noted his journalism would be compromised, as 'none of the other clubs would have anything to do with me'.[4]

If the truth be told, McGuire was possibly contemplating the Collingwood presidency as early as 1990 – not seriously at that stage, but something had to fill the hole left when he couldn't fulfil his true desire: to play AFL football.

The tale of how he fell in love with Collingwood at his first game at Victoria Park, and the memory of holding his father's hand on the way over the footbridge towards the ground and into what at the time must have been a daunting, incredible mass, is McGuire lore.

As he grew, McGuire found more to appreciate in the Struggletown beginnings of the club, the tales of local labour building Victoria Park and then its dominance as not just a football club but as a bigger force. Collingwood's dithering 1980s and 1990s helped people forget the period from the 1920s to the 1950s, when Collingwood bestrode the competition and its supporters were meaningful Melbourne power brokers.

For McGuire, a Catholic son of working-class immigrants – including a Glasgow Celtic supporter – the parallels were too obvious. And, for a man of unfeasibly large ego and pride, who was now as dominant and connected a force in Melbourne as any other due to his success at Nine, the attraction to emulate them could not be denied.

McGuire also loved the notion of the Pies being the 'underdogs' – the battlers of the league – and still pulls it out as a rallying cry, although the idea that such a powerful club can still fancy itself as an underdog is now absurd. Certainly, in the years to come, McGuire would do much to confirm Collingwood was no longer an underdog but a powerhouse and leader of the Australian sports establishment.

But in the mid-1990s, McGuire's interest in playing a role in Collingwood started to solidify. His interest could be very public: he was not averse to revealing the manoeuvrings of the boards during the instability through the 1990s, despite Allan McAlister's constricting grip on the club's presidency. It was an era of amateurism and over-reaching.

Collingwood's property-buying spree around their old Abbotsford home at Victoria Park to create 'Maggieland', a Collingwood entertainment precinct, was a disaster. The debt carried from those purchases nearly broke the club, and it was forced to sell despite the fact that it would have generated a profit if it had been able to hang on to those investments for another five years or more. But in the mid-1990s, the property debts were consigning the club to parsimony. The failure to rebuild the playing list after the 1990 premiership also meant the club had to resign itself to on-field mediocrity.

At the same time, McGuire's success at the Constitutional Convention (see Chapter 10) broadened his horizons. After heading the Victorian republican ticket and performing well at the Canberra Convention, delivering a number of strong speeches, he began to believe he could offer far more to public life than just a smile to the camera. Eddie McGuire has always been fascinated by people who build their own empires or companies. As he mulled over the nation-building possibilities of a new republic, he found confidence that he might be a leader.

McGuire was already involved in Collingwood politics as an unofficial adviser to David Galbally in the criminal lawyer's bid to wrest the Collingwood presidency from the outspoken McAlister at the 1995 election that forced McAlister's resignation. But it was a member of another famous Collingwood family, Kevin Rose, who ended up with the presidency. McGuire was close to the Roses, and they were worth knowing too: the closest thing Collingwood had to the Kennedy American political dynasty.

There was talk the club's banker was looking to come in to investigate some irregularities and possibly even liquidate the club. This was a period when ghost invoices were being paid, club legends remained on under-the-table payments and Collingwood was bringing forward future sponsorship monies to prop up the books.

The club's administration was amateur off the field at a time when coach Tony Shaw was the first VFL coach to tell his players they must become full-time, professional athletes. The game was changing dramatically; suddenly the AFL and clubs had to find the money and the wherewithal to support a professional sport. Collingwood owed money; something had to give.

McGuire was right in among the 1997 board shenanigans in which a competitive ticket, including advertising boss Kevin Dutton and former players Barry Price and Jeff Clifton, campaigned against incumbent Jack Kennedy and Tim Loveless with the help of the president, Kevin Rose, who was not living up to McAlister's expectations. McGuire opined in his weekly newspaper column that his club's 'greatest tradition in recent times is for boardroom brawling, factionalism and disharmony'. Some board members weren't even on speaking terms. McGuire made his opinion clear in print:

> This board must overcome its rivalries and get to the business of football. As it stands the Magpie board is divided, the team has not won a finals match since 1990, it hasn't made the finals in three years, hasn't beaten Carlton in seven outings, the behaviour of its players off the field has been disgraceful and the rest of the football world wonder how long Collingwood can be

a 'sleeping giant' before greatness passes them by completely ... it's about time reality was faced. This board really does have the future of the club in its hands. Time has run out.[5]

He couldn't have made a clearer stump speech; the issue was how to enforce change without tormenting one of the club's great families, the Roses.[6]

McGuire later admitted his interest in taking an official position had grown gradually, although his hope was the club could right itself without him. History told him otherwise.

The 1997 election convinced McGuire his fears were justified and he needed to act. McGuire Media was shooting a documentary, *More Than a Game*, for Nine at the time, interviewing all the candidates, who he liked individually. But as a group, they were a rabble. The club was leaking stories reflecting badly on individuals, even as it managed to reduce its debt. Worse, McGuire felt the flame that burned so brightly in Collingwood supporters was flickering out. It was becoming harder to maintain the faith.

And Collingwood's bumbling was becoming terminal. Off the field, the club clumsily sounded out David Cloke to replace the struggling Tony Shaw as interim coach after the Maggies began 1998 poorly. Shaw, who still had twelve months on his contract, then won three games in a row, and the desire for change faded before the Pies slumped again. The leaking of the Cloke approach only emphasised the unstable culture – as did a report the players had lost faith in Shaw. Inflaming the situation, Shaw threatened to sack the player who told *The Age* he no longer had the support of some senior players.

The club doubled down after finishing the year with seven consecutive losses, telling Shaw it wouldn't look for a new coach without informing him, before news soon emerged the board had indeed interviewed Sydney assistant coach Damian Drum for the job and even Dermott Brereton was being contemplated. Shaw told Kevin Rose the relationship between coach and president was now untenable.

The personality clashes didn't trump management's disasters. The club's new major sponsor, Viatel, failed to deliver its promised cash before it emerged its boss John Massey had used an alias and was a discharged bankrupt.

The club was humiliated during the Shaw and Viatel shenanigans, and plans were already underway for McGuire's team to move in. He later said 'there was no straw that broke the camel's back', but it was 'unacceptable' for the former AFL heavyweight to finish fourteenth.

McGuire was broadcasting another Collingwood loss to Carlton at the MCG when he saw a thirty-something Magpie in the Members' Stand, wearing his black and white guernsey, stand up at the twenty-five-minute mark of the final quarter and say 'Get fucked, Collingwood', then turn and walk out.

The man's heart was broken, as was McGuire's. He loved the club; there is vision, used in a tribute video by Collingwood, of a grown McGuire in full Collingwood playing kit, including the number nine guernsey, kicking a banana goal from the social club pocket at Victoria Park. One kick wouldn't make a career, so if he couldn't play for the club, he could save it.

McGuire knew the club was shot: its list was poor; Collingwood didn't stand for anything; and it had alienated the people who would normally gravitate to the club. Collingwood had lost its power – its bragging rights. Even worse, the need for change was apparent but the personnel capable of implementing the change were not. Certainly McGuire felt, at least initially, he was too young and it was not the right move for his career.

Publicly, the story goes, president Kevin Rose approached McGuire to ask for help in 1998. He agreed to McGuire's idea he could take over. However, the reality was the transition wasn't quite so smooth.

McGuire and Nine chief James Packer's names emerged as Collingwood's possible saviours or irritants, depending on who you asked. The AFL was not happy, anticipating Nine's possible guerilla entry through Packer to a game then broadcast by Seven.

McGuire approached Packer in March during the Formula 1 Grand Prix and pestered him throughout the year with a plan to bring PBL in as major sponsor and align Nine – in a non-cash manner because its sponsorship couldn't clash with Seven's AFL deal – to help consolidate its AFL bona fides before the next broadcast rights to be negotiated in 1999–2000.

The most extreme plan was to help Packer secure broadcast rights to games featuring Collingwood at certain venues, as McGuire forecast a scenario from US sports whereby leagues, venues or cities were split between broadcasters. 'It would be fantastic to get a piece of that action,' he said.[7]

He also wanted Packer as a partner in building Collingwood into Australia's leading sports entertainment group, dominant in marketing, merchandising and, most importantly, the business of winning games of football.[8] Packer's potential involvement brought quick opposition from Seven chairman Kerry Stokes, who believed it to be a breach of its contract with the AFL and ambush marketing; he told the AFL this would replicate the Brisbane Broncos' move that led to the creation of News Limited's Super League – and years of ignominy for rugby league. Packer's involvement, and his interest, faded promptly. It was too much, too soon.

Speculation about McGuire's intentions mounted through 1998 and, when asked, McGuire simply said, 'At this stage, I'm not running.' And that much was true. Collingwood would come to him; he just had to be ready.

McGuire quietly sought counsel from his Nine Melbourne boss, Ian Johnson, and with AFL CEO Wayne Jackson and Commission chief Ron Evans. They gave him the nod – the AFL needed a strong Collingwood, as long as he did it through legitimate means. And he went to Nine owner Kerry Packer to tell him respectfully, rather than ask, he was going to follow his passion and become president. Packer told him if he was going to do it, he had better make a success of it.

Names linked to McGuire's push included his friend, and the AFL's legal adviser, Jeff Browne, who grew up as a Collingwood fanatic; Alex Waislitz, the chairman of Thorney Investments and son-in-law of multi-millionaire Richard Pratt; Greg Montague, director of Montague Industries; and Brad Cooper, CEO and chairman of FAI Home Security; plus past players Michael Christian, Craig Kelly, Craig Stewart and Brian Taylor. Yet McGuire denied he was orchestrating or even involved in a board takeover.[9]

As the drums beat louder, McGuire played his game well, noting if he was to join Collingwood, it would be with the imprimatur of president Kevin Rose and the current board. He knew he merely had to sit it out and keep quiet. More importantly, history told him another board insurrection would only perpetuate the club's malaise.

Rose didn't play it so gracefully, conceding he had approached McGuire but disparagingly adding that he was not ready to hand over to a 'young' and 'enthusiastic' man. He also didn't think his job was done. He was wrong.

By the end of June, Rose grudgingly conceded McGuire could be 'capable of leading the club.'[10] Rose faced re-election at the end of 1998, as did treasurer Peter White, while brother Bob was expected to retire.

In late July, McGuire told Rose of his intention to run for the board and that he still had his support. Well, not so much run for the board as calmly take his office. But the seven-member board had three factions. McGuire would need to clean things up if there was to be any progress. He had quietly assembled a 'gang of four' wherein he would become president, joined by three moneyed thirty-something corporate tycoons: Brad Cooper, Alex Waislitz and Ian McMullin.

Waislitz, McMullin (a former Collingwood player and then general manager of the Spotless Group, owned by AFL Commission chairman Ron Evans) and McGuire had discussed Collingwood's woes over the years at social functions, but only galvanised as a team late in the piece.[11]

McGuire pushed for a few incumbents to step aside without a whimper in an act portrayed as 'for the good of the club' – or, as he said quietly, 'natural attrition' – and the three existing directors who would remain for continuity would be Rose, Kennedy and Peter Hammond.

McGuire believed a bloodless coup would set a unified club on its way to the powerhouse status it deserved, and Magpie fanatic Cooper's Sydney business interests would help nationalise the team beyond its parochial Melbourne milieu.

McGuire had an ever-ready AFL media fraternity advocating his takeover, and powerful groups within and outside the club imploring him to fix the mess. And his media connections were influential, implying he could report any recalcitrance by board members on *The Footy Show*.

However, the board members didn't go quietly when McGuire met them on an unseasonably cold September Monday[12] at the club's Lulie Street headquarters.

McGuire outlined his plans for a smooth succession the day after Kevin Rose said he would not seek re-election as president and only hours after Bob said he would leave the board. McGuire would take the presidency and move in his three compatriots, despite five members of the seven-member board initially wanting to remain. And there would be no electoral contest. This needed to be presented as a fait accompli to the members if the club was to begin again as a united force.

The following night, after some angst, the revolution was accepted. The board met at 6.30 p.m. with McGuire joining them at 7.30 p.m. The board agreed to accept McGuire's four-man ticket with two current directors – former star player Barry Price and club historian Richard Stremski – standing down following vice-president Bob Rose's resignation and treasurer Peter White's decision not to seek re-election. Jack Kennedy and Peter Hammond continued on the board. Stremski was the hold-out during the twenty-four hours, needing the guarantee of a new position as the club's general manager, created following Graeme Allan's departure to Brisbane, in order to agree.

McGuire left the following day for Kuala Lumpur, where he would anchor the Nine Network's coverage of the Commonwealth Games, as preparations were made for an extraordinary annual general meeting to ratify the restructuring of the board. McGuire was rapt; it looked like the coup had been orchestrated without anyone leaving 'in a pine box'.

But his first public statement as president-in-waiting – again through his weekly column in the *Herald Sun* – was less as benevolent leader and more as dictator:

> People who try to destabilise the club will be dealt with. We won't be taking any nonsense from anybody who tries to leak information or undermine the club in the future. On the first rap, they'll get fixed up.
>
> We are in this to become a successful football club again.
>
> This is a changed club. The factionalism at Collingwood that was tearing the club apart will end. We want people to be proud of Collingwood again.
>
> It is no longer the team with the most premierships, the team with the most members, or the richest club …[13]

Tony Shaw's contract was endorsed for twelve months, but he was on notice; similarly, 'players who break hearts are also on notice'. McGuire was keen to stress that he was acting independently of PBL, James Packer and Nine.

He also noted, 'There are no dissenters or disenfranchised former board members who are going to be rabble rousing around the edges. For the first time for as long as I can remember, everybody at Collingwood is going to be moving in one direction.'

Collingwood being Collingwood, though, it couldn't all be smooth sailing. A few weeks later, financial planner Chris Kozaris confirmed he would stand as an independent for one of the four vacant board positions. McGuire felt he was hitting his head against a brick wall and knew he had to get in without an election. Kozaris reconsidered his position days before the election.

Unity was an easy platform to sell. Collingwood regarded itself as the country's most powerful sporting club, but the evidence showed it only used its power for Shakespearean bloodletting. A club in turmoil off-field rarely performs well on-field. Every minute of a sporting club's week needs to be devoted to the weekend's optimum performance; anything else is a distraction. Collingwood had been mightily distracted.

As if to raise the stakes, McGuire said before the election, 'Anything less than 75 per cent I'll take as a vote of no confidence. I want a clear indication from Collingwood people that they're fair dinkum about being a football club in the AFL. Otherwise, we're wasting our time.'[14]

McGuire didn't have to do too much preparatory work ahead of the election, merely reiterate an ominous warning that, 'Egos and high profiles are out. Collingwood Football Club is one, two and three. The first one who rats goes down the lift well. That's been part and parcel of the scene for too long and it stops now.'[15]

The unity was tested two weeks later when favourite son Gavin Brown was stripped of the captaincy (after taking over from

Tony Shaw in 1994), and replaced by Nathan Buckley. Brown still wanted the job.

McGuire's suitability as a club president then became an issue for debate. The *Herald Sun*'s Mike Sheahan raised the issue before McGuire was formally appointed president, noting:

> McGuire will be privy to a constant supply of confidential information as president of a football club. In addition to the club's board meetings, he will be invited to the league's quarterly information meetings, when presidents are updated on major issues, and he will receive copies of all sensitive documents, such as five-year plans and budgets. While Collingwood is a passion for him, Channel Nine is both a passion and his master.[16]

Eddie would swat away the conflict of interest his new role would raise for him as a journalist with what would become his rote response for decades: 'I'll manage it, thanks.'

The only real hurdle became convincing Collingwood members to waive the club's constitutional requirement that board members had a minimum twenty-four months' membership of the social club before joining. McMullin and Waislitz couldn't satisfy that condition.

McGuire then had to fend off occasional grenades. He told a social club gathering days before the election that: no, the Magpies would not play home games at the Docklands Stadium; no, the club would never change its name; and no, he was not a Packer stooge. He quoted Shakespeare and John F. Kennedy and spoke of passion and promised better days.

Finally, if things did not go McGuire's way at next Thursday's extraordinary meeting, was there a Plan B? 'Rum,' he said.[17]

But there would be no rum rebellion. On Friday, 29 October 1998 – the night of McGuire's thirty-fourth birthday – nearly 1000 members overwhelmingly approved the changes to the club's articles of association, allowing McMullin and Waislitz to join McGuire's ticket filling the four casual vacancies.

Only two of the 666 proxy votes received by the club did not support the changes. Rose, Hammond and Kennedy continued as directors while Rose stood aside for McGuire, who would face 're-election' in December.

This was a grand political coup. A team unaligned with any of the famous feuding families of Collingwood's long history took control without an election. And without an election, it could claim a mandate to do whatever was required to save the club.

At the EGM at the Camberwell Civic Centre, McGuire told the 1000 faithful the meeting was not political. But, of course, it was. He sold his case with strong rhetoric, noting the 106-year-old club had 'again been relegated to battler' and 'Tonight is the moment of truth in shaping Collingwood's future into the twenty-first century.'

McGuire screened a mini-documentary, which he narrated, about the success of the 1996 and 1997 premiers Adelaide and where Collingwood needed to improve to match them.

'What I can promise you from the bottom of my heart is that every decision made by the Collingwood Football Club will be made for the benefit of the club and nothing else,' he said.

'But I am not going to promise you a premiership next year or any year,' he said. 'There is no 100-day plan.'[18]

As McGuire and his new board linked arms and launched into a powerful rendition of the Magpie theme song, 'Good Old Collingwood Forever', the new president looked out and saw the expressions of joy and expectation on the faces of the members.

For once, he doubted himself, thinking, 'Maybe I am just a footy show host'. Now something powerful, substantial but wounded was relying on this Broadmeadows-boy-cum-TV host to restore it to past glories. It was the loneliest moment of his life.

CHAPTER 12

RUMBLINGS

The rumblings began before he became president of Collingwood. It was absurd to think a journalist – and not just any journo but one of the most dogged news-breakers in the game – could also be the custodian of one of the game's grand clubs. The rumblings have not ceased almost two decades later.

Mike Sheahan may have been the first to raise the issue before McGuire was formally elected. And this was coming from a supposed mate. He was not the last.

Kevin Rose squared up days after confirmation of the smooth coup, confirming he'd asked McGuire to guarantee that his many media commitments wouldn't undermine the boardroom at Australia's most famous football club.

Rose said he believed McGuire's numerous television, radio and newspaper duties involved a potential conflict of interest, 'But that is a problem Eddie has to sort out and I think he is capable of doing so.'[1]

AFL chief executive Wayne Jackson weighed in too, conceding the president-elect McGuire faced a conflict of interest. He added. 'That is not a position that is new to the AFL, having different conflicts of interests in issues, and they do have to be managed.'

Jackson also said he was 'wary' of McGuire's links to Packer and Nine, and possibly an infringement on Seven's broadcast deal.[2] Jackson's comments were particularly galling to McGuire, who had consulted with him about his move to run Collingwood.

Of course, the conflicts of interest were raised by the boss of the AFL, an organisation that was seemingly fuelled by them, from the AFL Commission down. AFL Commissioner Ron Evans ran Spotless Catering, which held the lucrative MCG contract, while another Commissioner, Graeme Samuel, was then a Trustee of the Melbourne Cricket Club and a key player behind the construction of the $450 million state-of-the-art football stadium in the Docklands, while also helping run the Olympic Park Trust. Samuel's son, Grant, later became an employee of McGuire Media, Ed's television production company. And McGuire's boss at Nine, Ian Johnson, was also vice president of the Melbourne Football Club.

McGuire was peeved: everywhere he looked he could see conflicts of interest within clubs and the AFL, yet he was being chastised.

He defended his own position by pointing at theirs, saying no one pilloried Evans. But they did: Evans' conflict was a blight on the former Essendon player's stunning corporate career. Nevertheless, it remains true that Melbourne is too tight a city not to be riddled with conflicts of interest at the highest levels. Corporate Melbourne works on the caveat that its mavens declare their interests when appropriate. Yet, even today, player managers and club employees 'commentate' on TV and radio without any acknowledgement of their interests. McGuire has been justifiably indignant that he is the poster boy for conflicts considering his labels – Collingwood president, journalist, broadcaster – are clearer than most.

Nevertheless, McGuire would work his networks to his, Collingwood's and his employers' advantage at every opportunity.

Initially upon his election as Magpie president, he said, 'It's only a problem because journos keep talking about it.' That's not what Nine and Triple M thought; they both commissioned market research on the subject, although there wasn't any significant public opposition to his move.³

McGuire didn't win many friends with his initial hubris about the role. During the 1999 pre-season launch at Crown, Seven's Jim Wilson asked McGuire whether he was talking to him as a peer, Channel Nine star or Collingwood president. Wilson reminded McGuire that as the Collingwood president he should provide equal access to all programs, including Seven's *Talking Footy*. McGuire asked why he would bring viewers to an opposition network, and did that mean Seven would free up access to its contracted stars Wayne Carey and James Hird?

McGuire told Wilson to piss off in a rowdy, end-of-evening argument. Fists were shown, but not thrown. McGuire resolved to give up drinking after that night, as much to improve his on-air performance and look as to set an example for the new players under his care. He quickly lost 7 kilos. But his prickly dealings with Jim Wilson, and Jim's sister, Sydney journalist Rebecca Wilson, haven't abated.

Seven remained unconvinced about the purity of McGuire's access to confidential information and inside running on any TV broadcast rights negotiations. McGuire confirmed he would walk away from such discussions, although the reality was club presidents entered such discussions at the end of the process; the dealing was the job of the AFL and its Commission.

McGuire tried hard to do the right thing. His first season was largely without a 'conflict of interest' incident, although the probability of such an event grew.

Within eighteen months of taking over the Collingwood presidency, McGuire had a burgeoning empire beyond his media contracts, as managing director of McGuire Media; a stakeholder in the internet company Sportsview; a director of tipping entity Footy Millions; and, through his Radio City Australia Pty Ltd, presenting football programs on Melbourne's Triple M.

He held his counsel on *The Footy Show* or Triple M when discussions turned to a sensitive or confidential matter to which he had been privy as president of Collingwood. And he didn't favour Nine, to the point of frustration for his Nine bosses, who were particularly annoyed when Collingwood coach Tony Shaw's departure was announced at a Thursday afternoon press conference rather than during that night's *The Footy Show*.

And the confidential information from AFL meetings? McGuire said he was surprised how transparent the game was and how little the journos didn't already know.[4] Journalists remained sceptical though, even if McGuire made a pledge – as a journalist – that he would do his utmost always to respond to his peers. And he didn't change his mobile number, which remained readily available.

But one week in April 1999 was instructive. After responding to two days of media questioning following Shaw's sacking, McGuire arrived as a journalist at the MCG to attend an AFL media information session. Two days earlier, he had sat down with the same AFL Commissioners and league executives as Collingwood president. Some senior journalists didn't want him at the media information session, particularly when Collingwood's poor crowds were questioned and McGuire defended his team – as president.

He was unrepentant. 'More power to the Collingwood members for voting in a president who can get them into places they can't normally go. I don't answer to the club presidents, I answer to the Collingwood members.'[5] He maintained his membership of the AFL Media Association.

The presidents were more forgiving than the journalists, with none registering complaints. Another nascent president who would see his team become much worse before it too improved,

Geelong's Frank Costa, even empathised: 'If Collingwood wasn't so damn bad and wasn't getting belted every week, the spotlight on him wouldn't be so demanding.'[6]

McGuire's role would always be complicated. When, early in 2001, Channel Seven's pay TV arm C7 was refused permission for McGuire to appear on a special pre-season football forum, Nine copped the blame even though the invitation was issued to E. McGuire, Collingwood president, and not E. McGuire, Channel Nine employee. A day later, McGuire took the fall, saying he was too busy to attend.

Two years later, *The Age* – which became a little obsessed with all things Eddie – conducted a poll on the matter. The Saulwick *Age* football poll found 35 per cent of respondents believed McGuire had a 'definite' conflict of interest between leading the Magpies and his role in the broadcast and written media. Another 21 per cent believed McGuire 'probably' had a conflict.

The issue rose to another level when Nine secured the rights to broadcast the AFL from 2002, with McGuire readying to be the lead caller. He told *The Age* he would 'take on board' the poll result, but the truth was nothing would stand between McGuire and his lifelong ambition to call the AFL.[7]

Nine's deal with Foxtel and Ten to broadcast the AFL was a coup, and Nine management wanted McGuire as the network's lead caller, but they were split on whether he should call Collingwood games. Ian Johnson was adamant he could call them; Nine's upper management, led by David Leckie, was not. The AFL expected that he would be advised by Nine to step down from the Collingwood presidency.

The proximity of McGuire to his friend and manager, Jeff Browne, who was also a lead lawyer negotiating the broadcast deal, also raised concerns. Browne worked closely with key league negotiator Graeme Samuel on the broadcast rights negotiations. He also helped McGuire to sign his multi-million-dollar four-year deal with Nine, which made McGuire the country's highest-paid TV star, as well as helped McGuire search for a new chief executive at Collingwood.

McGuire was the concern, though, and it was raised immediately. 'What does this mean for you, Eddie?' Richmond president Clinton Casey asked McGuire in the AFL's new Colonial Stadium boardroom the night the clubs were briefed on the new $500 million, five-year TV deal. Casey was one of a few club presidents who couldn't see how McGuire could be the face of Nine's AFL coverage as well as the face of Collingwood.

And Richmond was bitter because, a couple of years previously, McGuire led the 2000 Grand Final edition of *The Footy Show* with news that Richmond could be forced to trade a star player to escape salary cap pressure – hours after McGuire and Collingwood coach Mick Malthouse had spoken to Richmond's Nick Daffy about moving to the Pies. McGuire said the story came from another player.[8]

Publicly, McGuire said that, should he become the face of TV football, he would probably be forced to relinquish his commitments to Triple M and *Who Wants to Be a Millionaire?*

His ascension to the top of Nine's AFL coverage wasn't smooth. As late as the 2001 post-season, Nine had not confirmed whether McGuire would call football matches the following year. The situation wasn't helped by McGuire's occasional tirades, as president, against the AFL, including a claim in October that 'the AFL are blatantly cheating against the rest of the competition' with the draft concessions the league offered to Brisbane and Sydney. He later apologised to the league.[9]

The issue of McGuire's future AFL broadcasting role was conflated stupidly with new Nine caller Tim Lane's conscientious objection to calling a Collingwood game with McGuire. It was even a condition of his contract not to do so, as Lane's manager pointed out to Nine as they discussed McGuire's lead role. Lane was paid out for taking a stand of dubious merit, and departed amicably – as one can when facing a potential payout of a three-year, $200000 annual contract – copping an intense phone call from McGuire on the way out.[10] Lane timed it at 48 minutes and 55 seconds.

A well-known Carlton supporter, Lane then continued to call Carlton games for other broadcasters. McGuire reiterated that there was no one in football without some sort of conflict.

Nine would always side with McGuire in that battle, with varying degrees of enthusiasm, because top management realised the relationship with the network's number one star could be irrevocably damaged were it to jeopardise his lifelong ambition to call the footy.

But there was little doubt Eddie's needs as a football newsman clashed with his responsibilities as one of sixteen chairmen of the AFL. Melbourne chief executive John Anderson questioned McGuire's role after *The Footy Show* aired rumours of a possible leadership challenge at Melbourne, with Ron Walker challenging Joseph Gutnick for the presidency and vice-president, Nine's Ian Johnson, calling the meeting. The rumour was unfounded, and McGuire bit, calling some Melbourne staffers 'rats and wimps'.[11]

But McGuire was street smart; he was able to make something from nothing many times – he didn't need access to presidents' meetings.

His investment in another enterprise, TipStar, emerged after an English stockbroker, Ed Clark, spilt a glass of wine over McGuire's shirt at a Sydney barbeque in December 1999. Clark was on a sabbatical from dealing for the American firm Cantor Fitzgerald, and was discussing with a friend investing in the football pools lottery back in the United Kingdom. McGuire was immediately interested, and told Clark he had been thinking about doing something similar in Australia.

The new Labor government in Victoria had promised to introduce a football tipping competition, and McGuire wanted a piece of the action. Clark didn't know who McGuire was, except that he was the president of an AFL football team. The next night, he turned on the television to find McGuire hosting Nine's marathon coverage of the millennium celebrations.

The pair came up with an idea that would lead to a joint football tipping venture, called TipStar, with the Tattersalls organisation. At least to Clark, McGuire's involvement helped secure Tattersalls' backing, although he said he would have pursued the venture regardless.

In December 2000, McGuire's company, Footy Millions, in a joint venture with Tattersalls, won the licence to operate the competition for seven years. Footy Millions was a 75 per cent stakeholder in TipStar. The announcement came only hours before the AFL confirmed Nine had won its broadcasting rights, exacerbating concerns about McGuire's increasingly long and tangled tentacles.

The AFL's Wayne Jackson admitted there 'absolutely is a conflict' between McGuire's various roles, but insisted the involvement was transparent, and therefore manageable. Funnily enough, Footy Millions beat two other bidders partly because it had also secured an exclusive deal with the AFL, providing the 'opportunity to exploit the AFL brand and products'.

Victorian Gaming Minister John Pandazopoulos said an independent probity audit cleared McGuire of any concerns about a possible conflict. The opposition spokesman on gaming, Ted Baillieu, was one of many to criticise McGuire's conflict.

The real concern for McGuire was the viability of the project. It budgeted to generate up to $30 million annually, with 60 per cent of the tipping pool returned to punters and government takings expected to fund hospitals, women's sport and state initiatives.[12] It didn't generate that revenue, and McGuire soon sold down his interest, pulling right out by 2002, after Clark dropped out of the business by 2001. The reality was work and pub footy tipping competitions worked effectively enough and gave more back to the winners. By 2015, the AFL 'Footytips' website run by ESPN had one million registered users playing free.

Part of the concern about McGuire's conflicted interests was his early awareness of the possibilities emerging technologies might allow sports broadcast deals. From his international travels and interest in US sports, McGuire saw the standard sporting organisation broadcast contract with just one broadcaster was not the ideal future. Sporting codes had to utilise emerging platforms. So, as he broadcast, he also dabbled.

Sportsview.com.au counted McGuire and Steve Vizard among its shareholders (as well as the Granada Media and Stuart Simson business ArtSim and Vizard's and Chris Clarke's Virtual Communities).[13] It bought the internet rights to four AFL clubs, with a long view of being able to broadcast their matches over the internet. McGuire's Collingwood, for instance, should have been making money far more effectively from hundreds of thousands of hits to its website.[14]

Soon enough, the listed Web-development company MultiEmedia, itself featuring Microsoft co-founder Paul Allen as a minor investor, bought a 23 per cent stake in Sportsview.com.au, creating further interest. They aimed to create 'Australia's leading sportscasting Internet business.' They were a decade too early.

McGuire said the internet could allow the AFL's more popular clubs the financial edge they had been denied by the league's equalisation policy, predicting that an internet company rather than a television station could buy the AFL broadcasting rights when Channel Seven's contract expired in 2001.

The AFL was unimpressed with McGuire's Sportsview sortie. Four clubs – Collingwood, Carlton, the Bulldogs and Hawthorn – signed up while other clubs were more than mildly surprised to see McGuire suddenly appearing with a sales pitch at the start of presentations. The AFL believed McGuire's involvement was a disturbing conflict of interest, and chief executive Wayne Jackson, concerned the league had missed a valuable business opportunity, wrote to the clubs warning them to stay away from Sportsview.

Jackson feared the Sportsview clubs could be taking part in a webcasting pact with McGuire's company, which could challenge the AFL's multimedia ownership. He warned the four Sportsview clubs they stood to lose millions of dollars.

The AFL wanted those four clubs to come back home ahead of a digital deal with Telstra, just as McGuire was pitching his own company as the middleman to establish club internet sites in a joint venture with Telstra.

The dotcom MultiEmedia, partly owned by Vizard and McGuire, continued to try to acquire its way to growth and sustainability as it emerged from the dotcom crash (and a share price that dropped from a high of 96 cents in November 1999 to 7 cents in May 2001).[15]

But Sportsview was wound up in 2005 with assets of $45 150 after the internet rights to the Melbourne clubs had been rolled into a $30 million deal struck between Telstra and the AFL years earlier. Years later, McGuire would claim his actions prompted the bigger paydays for the AFL and clubs from Telstra. He was half right. But even by 2015, digital companies were still reticent to buy exclusive rights to sport.

At the same time, McGuire played nice with the AFL, denying that he was working with Carlton president John Elliott to undermine the AFL's bid to negotiate broadcasting rights.[16] That the speculation wasn't true – yet – reflected the wariness with which the AFL considered the ultra-connected McGuire.

The conflicts weren't all sparked by business. McGuire's flair for showmanship, or requirement to fill press conferences or airtime led to some uncomfortable contretemps. Invariably, it would be the AFL that was annoyed. After joking that Collingwood fans would 'pull the joint down' in an upcoming match at Docklands if

Pie supporters encountered the same chaotic queues that blighted a Footscray match the previous week, AFL chief executive Wayne Jackson bit back in an interview with 3AW: 'I think they're inappropriate comments for the president of a football club to make. Sometimes, I think our blokes try to out-do each other with the comments they like to make public.'[17]

Then Jackson had to rebuke McGuire and Elliott when they criticised the AFL for not sanctioning a live telecast of Sunday's sold-out Carlton versus Collingwood match. This time Jackson compared Elliott and McGuire to the characters in the Australian children's book, *Gumnut Babies*:

> One does get tired of the Bib and Bub show. Every time John says something, Eddie echoes it, and every time Eddie says something, John echoes it. I think sometimes Eddie is confused as to whether he's a TV host or a president of a footy club or, indeed, a supporter of the Carlton president. I'm quite confused.

Jackson also noted Elliott rang him to say he would cop a 'great big bollocking' from him on McGuire's *The Footy Show*.[18]

The truth was McGuire's consistent bollocking of the AFL had begun to cut through. But was it from a club official or a commentator?

He and coach Mick Malthouse were investigated after he said an umpire who had reported Chris Tarrant was 'up on the dartboard of every Collingwood supporter in the world'.[19]

He was cleared – although Malthouse was fined $5000 for similar criticism – but it was unseemly, especially Malthouse's defence to the AFL that the system, or lack of video evidence, had hurt the umpire in the eyes of fans. McGuire went on with it, telling a breakfast audience that Malthouse had been 'embarrassed and humiliated' by football operations manager Adrian Anderson's decision to fine him.

'If you're going to fine somebody of Mick Malthouse's stature, you'd want to be right, and if you want to take on Collingwood and fine them, you'd want to be very right, and we don't think that's the case,' a defiant McGuire said.[20]

So the 2002 AFL season came and McGuire commentated. He humbly assessed his call of a Friday night Collingwood match against Port Adelaide in round nine as unbiased. Talkback listeners disagreed, as did his peers – including Rex Hunt[21] and Nine's Dennis Cometti, who thought he was making an error of judgement. 'I've basically said this to Eddie. I think he's making a mistake to do Collingwood games, but that's just a piece of advice from my experience,' he told Perth radio before later claiming that his comments had been taken out of context.[22] Seven's Bruce McAvaney and Tim Watson also weighed in, with McAvaney saying, 'If I was Eddie, I'd like to take that [Port Adelaide–Collingwood] call back', a comment McAvaney later wished he could take back.

McGuire responded that he kept out-rating the likes of Tim Lane and McAvaney on radio and television. 'All I do is turn up and have a go ... I don't criticise or bag,' McGuire said.[23]

The complaints wouldn't dissipate, though. The AFL ordered the removal of a Channel Ten poll on its website questioning his performance, with 75 per cent of responding subscribers describing his call as biased towards Collingwood. McGuire raised it with the AFL. He fought hard to explain it all away, telling *The Australian*:

> I have conflicts of interest, yes. But it's how you approach them and how you deal with them. I try to be as honest as possible. Everything's up front and people can decide whether they like me – or not like me – or respect me – or hate-me-but-respect-me ...
>
> But you don't let critics decide what you do, you just get on and do what you think is right.[24]

Nine's management softened; its only concern now was that McGuire would exhaust himself. But the shellacking he received concerning his commentary duties hurt him. He lost his sparkle and sense of humour for months as something for which he had fought so hard – a rock-solid reputation and clean image – was being besmirched, particularly by some peers who, deep down, he respected.

His actual ability as a caller was not questioned but he couldn't rid himself of the muddy perception. It wasn't so much that he was a Collingwood supporter; the issue was that he was a club president. His every comment would be seen through that prism. In 2003, for instance, during a Collingwood match with Brisbane, he described a match official as 'the goal umpire from hell'. Ordinarily that would pass, but in this situation it became a club president lambasting an AFL official.[25]

Brisbane coach Leigh Matthews was unimpressed but the AFL did not act, arguing McGuire was working as a Channel Nine commentator at the time and not acting in his capacity as Collingwood president.

McGuire also continued to use *The Footy Show* as an influential mouthpiece; in one segment, he highlighted the 'zany, crazy' men of the AFL Tribunal while showing a number of inconsistent non-decisions – only days after Collingwood's Brodie Holland's penalty of four weeks for kicking.[26]

Then there was the non-disclosure on *The Footy Show* of details of Collingwood shenanigans in Queensland during a bye – several players were later referred to alcohol education programs and two senior officials reprimanded – heightened by the show's enthusiastic reporting of allegations about misconduct directed at St Kilda footballers at the Sorrento Hotel. This time, Australian Journalists Association president Alan Kennedy said McGuire had a clear conflict of interest.[27]

The appearance of his club presidency and advocacy for Nine overlapping was again apparent when he put the case for a night

Grand Final on the agenda of an annual meeting of the league presidents in 2005.[28] The benefits to broadcasters of a night Grand Final – an increased viewing audience and advertising revenue – are clear, even if players aren't convinced the conditions are optimal and AFL chief executive Andrew Demetriou said a night Grand Final would take place 'over my dead body'. To be fair, McGuire continued the case even when Seven held rights to the AFL.

When McGuire railed in 2005 – on *The Footy Show* – against Nine possibly losing the rights to broadcast AFL, he was using intimate knowledge of the finances of AFL clubs while pushing Nine's barrow. He said the future of three Victorian clubs could be endangered if there was no auction of the next round of AFL media rights. Again, McGuire was arguably speaking in the best interests of the competition as a club president, yet his argument was also in the interests of Nine in arguing that a Seven and Ten consortium would push down the price of the broadcast rights: 'For the sake of footy, Kerry Packer ... had better come up with something because I tell you what, we're headed straight for the bad old days if the money's not there if there's no auction.'[29]

McGuire was testing the wind of the 2007–11 deal, although, days later, Nine boss David Gyngell said Nine might not bid.[30] Ten chief John McAlpine called McGuire's lobbying 'pathetic'.[31] 'There are ways and means to get your message across and I thought he didn't do himself any favours,' he said. Ultimately, Seven and Foxtel won the rights to broadcast the AFL from 2007.

Simultaneously, McGuire Media, Eddie's company formed with brother Frank (who no longer has a direct stake), was attempting to develop its own products. Years later, this would place him in direct competition with the broadcasters who employed him. But in the early 2000s, Eddie had fingers in too many pies to develop the company that kept Frank occupied.

It wasn't so much a conflict as a breach of faith that saw McGuire and Collingwood dragged into a Royal Commission investigating the collapse of insurer HIH. The inference in the Commission was that money eked from the dying days of the failed insurance company was used to help HIH associate Brad Cooper win election to the Collingwood board in 2000.

Collingwood received a $2 million interest-free loan and a $250 000 sponsorship deal through two HIH Insurance offshoots, including FAI Insurance, in the company's dying days. The club furnished a statement to the Royal Commission saying 'Any inference that the timing of the payment was influential to the outcome of the club's election in 2000 is without foundation and completely incorrect. It should be noted that Collingwood president Eddie McGuire was not up for re-election in that year.'

While it deserved investigation, the Commission couldn't connect late payments to Cooper as the insurer played out its final days to money sent to Collingwood. The money provided by Cooper was to save the club money, and was paid back quickly by Collingwood.[32] 'It was just another sponsorship deal,' McGuire said, noting that the club received a personal interest-free loan from Cooper in March for $1.5 million to pay out player entitlements before changes to the fringe benefits tax. It was a shrewd move that saved the club tens of thousands of dollars but cost it a tad more in associated brand damage.

Cooper conceded that when McGuire announced the sponsorship, he might have said that it was a reason to support Mr Cooper's re-election. 'Someone may have said that, yes,' Cooper said.[33] FAI's $250 000 sponsorship of Collingwood was also complicated. It emerged that it essentially came out of the personal proceeds of a Cooper share deal with HIH.

'We fulfilled the contract, the matter is closed,' McGuire said. 'They had a contract with us, we provided service, they paid money – done.'[34]

It was an unseemly beginning of the end for a Collingwood director who did much good work straightening the club with

McGuire (and even paid $100 000 to bring Jimmy Barnes down from Sydney to perform at the MCG during a Collingwood game).

McGuire felt being dragged into the whole affair was manna from heaven for certain sections of the media, who were celebrating the muck. And Collingwood could have done without the commercial imbroglio because it was raking in sponsorships and building brands in the process.

The unlikely company that helped turn around Collingwood's fortunes in 1998 was the UAE national airline, Emirates, which backed the Pies when others were heading towards the door. Emirates' Australian boss, Eddie Lim, half-joked the red logo of Emirates put Collingwood back in the black. When it renewed its deal for a second time, McGuire crowed that Collingwood's guernsey sponsorships were now worth 70 per cent more than any other, making it 'the most valuable sporting real estate in Australia'.

McGuire and Collingwood essentially launched the brand in Australia, impressing upon the market its credentials as a serious new player in international travel. Certainly Emirates was ecstatic about the results, and only with Emirates' security did others follow, including Yakka (ball sponsor) Gillette, Bartercard and an increased commitment by Crazy John's. After Volvo, Toyota's luxury brand Lexus Australia signed an eight-year deal with the club, believed to be worth up to $16 million. It knew its sponsorship value was multiplied by McGuire's ability and willingness to use *The Footy Show* and his position at Channel Nine to push the company's cause. It became an issue for Nine, with the network in later years keen to send McGuire to Sydney to record shows, removing him from his Melbourne bubble, in which he invariably mentioned Emirates, Lexus or whomever on his numerous Nine programs, including *Who Wants to Be a Millionaire?* But Nine tended to give McGuire his head – as long as the network was also earning its cut from the same advertisers.

McGuire's tentacles were even reaching into areas that he had no idea about. Or so it was thought. In 2004, the Greek–Australian media was excited at rumours he would be involved in the new Premier League being established by the Frank Lowy-led Australian Soccer Association.

The speculation, on 3XY and in newspaper *Neos Kosmos*, caused enough buzz for South Melbourne Soccer Club chief executive Mark Patterson to ring McGuire to ask whether the rumours were true. McGuire had to say that, at least at that point in his life, he had never met Lowy and he had neither the 'time or the inclination' to get involved in soccer.[35]

Other sports were another matter. Steve Vizard helped bring Eddie McGuire to the board of the organisation responsible for bringing the Commonwealth Games and Formula 1 Grand Prix to Melbourne, the Victorian Major Events Company, in 2002. Vizard was chair and he ensconced McGuire among a suite of interconnecting and influential positions that could play off each other. That would be a cynic's view. The clearer view is McGuire was a tribal creature wanting to do the best for his city.

It followed a clumsy period of politicking to develop Collingwood's new home. The transformation of the Olympic Park area of Melbourne bounding the Yarra River between the city and Richmond was a slow-burning sore. After Premier John Cain announced the building of the National Tennis Centre on parkland beside the Jolimont rail yards in 1984, he vowed not one more inch of the parkland bounded by the Yarra, the rail yards and Punt Road would be turned over to development. Today, the entire northern side of Swan Street is developed (much of it now for car parking), while the southern side has a new stadium, and only a few acres of green space not devoted to training grounds for Collingwood or the Melbourne Storm.

The manner in which Collingwood became a key tenant of the prized area alarmed many, yet today members of the Melbourne and Olympic Park Trust are convinced the area would not be a going concern without Collingwood at its heart.

The deal to move Collingwood to the Yarra was classic McGuire. At a dinner, he sat next to Graeme Samuel, who was chairman of the Melbourne and Olympic Parks Trust. Samuel told him how, as a Melbourne supporter, he tried to get his club to take over the rundown Olympic Park pool and make it their new training home. It was all too hard for the Demons.

McGuire went to the dilapidated venue the following day and saw the opportunity. He didn't have any plan to pay for it all and the move was a massive risk for the club. But it was worth pursuing.

McGuire's roughshod approach was apparent when Collingwood later decided to name its Olympic Park training ground the Lexus Bob Rose Oval, despite objections from the Park's trust. McGuire said he told Rose on his deathbed he would do so, although Olympian Ron Clarke believed it was disrespectful to his sport.

The issue made great play in the *Herald Sun*, which went hard on the Collingwood move, although its commercial sense was strong: the Pies sold newspapers. But McGuire and Collingwood were delighted, realising the club and its sponsors were repeatedly on the front page of Melbourne's biggest newspaper. McGuire played the situation for all it was worth.

Yet it was difficult to defend some of the Pies' decisions: the club also planned to allow Lexus car owners use of the gym at the new Lexus Centre. Collingwood eventually reneged, allowing the oval to be named the Edwin Flack Oval, and Bob Rose's name was assigned to the training centre.

That one name change inflamed suspicions a few years later in 2005, when McGuire ascended to the board of Athletics Australia. It was seen as a stalking horse for Collingwood to gain greater control of the Olympic Park precinct (see Chapter 19).

Eddie McGuire's power connected but did not corrupt. Nevertheless, Patrick Smith wrote in 2005 that McGuire was now the most powerful person in the AFL.[36] It was hard to argue otherwise. The interconnections and conflicts were everywhere, yet they were never actionable. Business decisions stacked up and McGuire behaved properly. Indeed, McGuire conducts his personal commercial affairs as straight as possible, telling his advisers he desires his affairs to be as clean as a prime minister. Not that he necessarily covets that job; rather, he anticipates the kind of scrutiny a prime minister attracts.

The one business dealing that did go wrong, and sticks in the craw of many at Collingwood, was the most unlikely of all – a couple of pubs.

Once the cliché said footballers retired from playing to become publicans. But football clubs as publicans? Collingwood didn't make a good fist of it, to the point where McGuire and the club would be deemed unfit to hold a liquor licence and board members would have their ability to remain corporate directors threatened.

Collingwood had commercial interests in three hotels when it committed $14 million to buy the long-term leases on The Beach Hotel in Port Melbourne and the Diamond Creek Tavern in 2006. Within eighteen months, the club booked a $4.5 million loss, and was forced to sell in a fire sale.

The acquisitions were part of a grand plan to own satellite bases across Melbourne at which fans could congregate. Servicing the debt of $1 million a year (Collingwood had borrowed $12.5 million of the $14.5 million to buy the hotels) proved onerous, particularly with The Beach Hotel running at a loss.

The reasoning behind the purchases was dubious. The Diamond Creek Tavern had a little romance, being perched in prime Collingwood heartland, an area that produced the Coventry and Shaw families. The Beach was to be used for Collingwood entertainment and functions (*The Footy Show* even crossed live one night to a Collingwood function at The Beach). But the club was ill-equipped to deal with the complexities of gaming and licensing. And the particular messes a pub could throw up, including noise complaints from neighbours and liquor licence breaches, were not simpatico with the branding the football club was trying to establish.

The sale of the Beach Hotel was complicated by licence breaches for noise offences after previous allegations of fighting and violence. Victoria Police made an initial application to VCAT that considered the licensee (Collingwood) was 'not a suitable person to hold the licence'.[37] The club's right to own and operate pubs and pokies – and at the time, it had nearly 300 pokies across five gaming venues – was in jeopardy due to the licence breaches at the Beach Hotel.

A hearing was held to determine whether the Collingwood board, including CEO Gary Pert, Visy chief Alex Waislitz, Spotless boss Ian McMullin, insolvency expert Mark Korda, Starcom CEO Paul Leeds and Alisa Camplin, should be disqualified from holding a licence under Section 92 of the Liquor Licensing Act.[38]

The hearing was not good for Collingwood, with sales of both hotels stalling and the club being accused of trying to wriggle out of the lease for the Beach Hotel when, oddly, 38 of its poker machines were removed by Tattersalls.[39] Collingwood could then activate a clause in the lease meant to protect the lessee. Lawyers for the landlord, Bleake House director Peter Board, didn't allege fraud, just an 'incredibly fortuitous thing, coincidence.'[40]

As a result of their licence breaches, McGuire and his board of directors were ordered to alcohol compliance classes and had to pay $30 000 for the creation of a community alcohol education program after investigations by the Director of Liquor Licensing and Victoria Police. There was a feeling at the club the scrutiny was a particularly personal vendetta by individuals within the force. Yet the fact remains the club failed in its management of the hotels.

All up, the pubs cost the club $8 million across eighteen months, a figure that relates largely to operating losses on the 2007 and 2008 years, a huge devaluation on the leases, interest on the initial $14.5 million loan and capital expenditure on the venues and legal costs. It all but sent the club back to its dire financial situation in the late 1990s, and forced it to rebuild financially. The club retained the Diamond Creek Tavern, the Coach and Horses in Ringwood and The Club in Caroline Springs – all of which return profits.[41]

The directors who were on the board when it was decided to buy the leaseholds included McGuire, Jack Kennedy, Sally Capp, McMullin and Waislitz. Collingwood's chief executive officer and chief operating officer at the time of the hotel ventures, Greg Swann and Eugene Arocca, were also part of the decision to drive the pub deals though. Both left, to work at Carlton and North Melbourne respectively.

The debacle stung McGuire although he was able to deflect any responsibility onto Collingwood management, including COO Arocca. He defended himself by telling the *Herald Sun* he had let things slip while he was CEO of Nine in Sydney.

> When I got on to the plane to go to Sydney, I probably should have resigned for two years and then come back again. I was on top of everything before I went to Sydney, and then, for two years, perhaps I wasn't. But now I am all over it again, terrorising everyone.[42]

As far as Collingwood was concerned, Eddie McGuire wanted to always give his best, but by his own admission he'd taken his eye off the ball – and the club had lost out.

CHAPTER 13

EYES ON THE PRIZE

Addiction counsellors propose the first step towards recovery is admitting you have a problem. An addict has to admit they're at rock bottom before they can take control. Collingwood was a proud club addicted to the power of its history, a history steeped in premiership dynasties, generations of high-achieving families – the Colliers, the Coventrys, the Twomeys, the Pannams, the Richardsons, the Roses, the Shaws, the Sherrins, the Weidemans – and influence within the VFL/AFL.

This was a club that entered the VFL during one depression, in 1897, and dominated during the Great Depression, winning four premierships in a row under Jock McHale at the end of the 1920s. One of the poorest suburbs in Melbourne couldn't be humble after thriving during such deprivation. It gave the club an aura of invincibility for decades.

Admitting it was at a low point was always a difficult thing for Collingwood. Time and again, Collingwood turned to those familiar names and favourite sons from the field to resurrect the club from the coach's box and within the boardroom.

The slide from top to bottom through the 1990s was gradual, yet inexorable. The Pies were mid-table in 1993–95, a little worse in 1996. In hindsight, it seems bottoming out was a necessary evil. It is easy to kid yourself that you're okay while clinging by your fingernails to a rung in the middle of the ladder. The playing list essentially declined as the core of the 1990 premiership team aged. In 1996, then football director Graeme Allan warned Collingwood supporters that more suffering was in store – he estimated eighteen months of pain. It was more like five years. By 1998, the extent of Collingwood's degradation could no longer be denied.

It eased the entry of McGuire and his new board somewhat, partly because McGuire's vitality and novelty helped bind the club. Deep down, Collingwood stalwarts knew (even if it was a hard thing to admit) their favoured sons – Bob Rose, Neil Mann, Murray Weideman and now Shaw – had not delivered premierships.

It was more than three decades before the 'Colliwobbles' were despatched with a premiership in 1990, and it took an outsider, Hawthorn's Leigh Matthews – thankfully not someone from Carlton, Essendon, Richmond or Melbourne – to lead the Magpies to their first flag since 1958.

McGuire was also an outsider of sorts. Certainly he wasn't beholden to any of the Collingwood families, and in fact he ran roughshod over a couple of them on his way to the presidency. As the new president, McGuire had to face reality and find an outsider to replace Shaw. But first Collingwood had to concede it had hit rock bottom. And that would take some time. McGuire's ascension to the presidency buoyed the players, who anticipated change for the better from someone to whom they could relate. But McGuire was stressed.

Nathan Buckley was appointed captain, with Gavin Brown moving over despite still coveting the job. Brown saw it coming, as coach Tony Shaw wanted to breed a new wave and Buckley was the template for the kind of professionalism McGuire and Shaw wanted other players to emulate. And Collingwood had invested quite a bit in Buckley, making an under-the-table agreement with Brisbane to take the talented youngster after only one year up north. Former coach Leigh Matthews later admitted that the effort, and price paid, to get Buckley to the club was probably not worth it in terms of damaging club culture and dumping players. But McGuire would believe the opposite as Buckley became the club's talisman through very dark times.

There is no room for self-delusion when you're coming fourteenth, which is where Collingwood finished in 1998. If McGuire needed any confirmation of the size of his task, misfortune gave it to him early in the 1999 season. Captain Buckley broke his jaw and the team began the year with three consecutive losses, prompting prominent *Herald Sun* columnist Scot Palmer to write:

> This is the worst Collingwood side I've seen in 50 years of following the Magpies. It pains me to say it, but we have to face facts. And the fact is, this 10-match losing streak – stretching back to July last year – is the worst in the club's proud 107-year history.[1]

McGuire couldn't argue with Palmer's punch. 'This is the time for Collingwood to show what it's really made of, it's real back-to-the-wall stuff,' he said.[2]

The club was heading for rock bottom – which, if it needed a date, was Round 4 of 1999, when Richmond towelled up a woebegone Pies. The team had not won a game since Round 16 of the previous year, and headlines pointed to McGuire being 'under pressure' already.

The pressure was heavier on coach Shaw – although McGuire had guaranteed Shaw the job for the season, which left little room to move. McGuire said in April that Shaw would remain as coach 'until such time as the board of the club feels it is falling apart, and we're not at that stage'.[3]

McGuire was losing sleep and patience, increasingly irritable both at home and in public. In response to a regular doorstop question, 'Is Tony Shaw the coach of Collingwood?' McGuire snapped, 'A. Yes, B. Yes, C. Yes, D. Yes. Is that enough for you? Do you need a lifeline?'[4]

McGuire was still only 34, and felt he hadn't yet nailed his own career. Yet here he was overseeing the careers of many and the hopes of hundreds of thousands. And it wasn't simple. He was frustrated that he had walked into a structure that was established and couldn't be moved easily. This was unlike his nimble moves between TV, radio and print, where he said and did what he wanted. He dreamt of a time when he would have his own team running the club with him. One night, after another Collingwood drubbing, he returned home and drew on a sheet of butcher's paper how he would set up the club if he could start from scratch.

He'd often wake at 2 or 3 a.m., toss and turn with anxiety until he would have to rise and then write more notes for the club. He really believed he might have arrived at the club twelve months too late, and Collingwood needed a real businessman, not a TV host, in the driver's seat to turn it around. Carla would invariably be there with a cup of tea at 4 a.m., telling him to go back to bed.

It didn't help that McGuire didn't feel comfortable around the club during his first year as president. He felt awkward in the club rooms and still felt like an outsider. The appointment of a 'TV host' as club president was still being trivialised and patronised by some within, and outside, the club. But he'd been around football for 15 years, observing the successes and failures and how football people ticked. He was not a footy novice.

McGuire couldn't be seen to knife the most prominent incumbent, Shaw, as he'd promised a presidency of stability and transparency. When one board member was anonymously quoted questioning Shaw's future, McGuire even confronted the coach to check he wasn't the source of the leak. And Shaw wasn't going to go of his own volition.

As the injury list[5] and losses mounted, Collingwood played kids and rebuilt as McGuire implored supporters to hang in there as the club aimed to 'build a skyscraper and not a tent'.[6]

Yet in 1999, Shaw only had the players to build a tent. The playing list was poor, with hindsight showing that bright hopes including Tyson Lane, Glenn Freeborn, Mark Orchard, Jamie Tape, Brad Oborne, Craig Jacotine and James Wasley didn't deliver as anticipated. In April, McGuire prepared his club for the worst, noting the losing streak was 'the record we had to have'.[7] By June, Collingwood's home crowds had fallen to an average of 38 106 from the previous year's 57 702 and a particularly harsh winter was partly to blame; however, McGuire had to admit 'given the disappointment of the past four years, it's no surprise that figures are down'.[8]

Off field at least, McGuire was making minor inroads. His first two years in the role would transform Collingwood and professional AFL football in Australia. Bit by bit, deals were done, money flowed in and Collingwood shed much of its low-rent baggage.

McGuire applied what he'd done for his own career to the club. His transformation of Collingwood would be as much about rebranding as about kicking goals. He took all his knowledge about his own advancement and applied it to the footy club. As it happened, one of the first Magpie deals would involve suits, something which McGuire is never without. The old journalist dictum was that you should always wear a suit because you didn't know when you'd need to cover a state funeral, court case or meet a prince or president. McGuire always wore a suit.

European fashion house Versace came on board, creating an exclusive wardrobe for players and officials after initially discussing the design for a new club tie. As the Australia/New Zealand ambassador for the Versace Classic V2 range, Luciano Azzaro, said, 'It is time for footy fans to realise the days of the polyester tie are over.'[9] But McGuire thought it was time for Collingwood to sharpen up; club suits were window dressing, but he knew it would make a broader statement about his, and their, professional intent.

Collingwood couldn't make a positive statement on the field, though. It needed to win, but it didn't, registering the club's longest losing streak from Round 16 of 1998 to Round 8 of 1999. When it recorded its eleventh loss of the year in Round 12, McGuire had to act and Shaw knew it. It was tough for McGuire, who held Shaw high in his esteem as both a club legend and a man. But he also expected Shaw to be big enough to cope.

One former player advising both men warned McGuire that he too should have the ability to listen to people when, invariably, he was tapped on the shoulder. Ensure you exit gracefully too; though that day is yet to come.

On the second floor of the Collingwood social club, in the President's Room, McGuire announced, 'Tony has decided he won't be coaching the Collingwood Football Club in the year 2000,' as if Shaw had a choice. As the Roses had said when McGuire moved in, and as Shaw reiterated, 'the club comes first'.

McGuire spoke of the 'great bloke and great coach' who he'd chase with a chequebook in order to give him a job in the media.[10] 'We are delighted with the way Tony is coaching at the moment,' McGuire said.

The fifteenth coach in the history of the club departed on a wave of good tidings and mutual respect. For Collingwood, it was other-worldly. McGuire manufactured another coup. For once, a revered clubman hadn't been turfed from the coach's box in acrimony or disgrace (a vast improvement on the 1998 failed efforts to replace him with David Cloke or Damian Drum).

McGuire knew this was a significant moment for the club: treating a club great who had failed – Shaw has the worst record of any Collingwood coach – with dignity. He'd made a pact with Shaw pre-season not to entertain any discussion about his replacement before the club knew what Shaw was doing. And Shaw was honourable; he accepted the inevitable and didn't even discuss coaching beyond 1999 with McGuire.

Incredibly, Shaw even remained in the job, vowing with the match committee and McGuire to build for the remaining ten rounds by blooding young players and letting others play with the confidence of a secure position for a month. The core of the 2002–03 Grand Final teams would debut for the club (Paul Licuria, Heath Scotland and Tarkyn Lockyer), or benefit from extended stints developing their games in the seniors (Chris Tarrant, Mal Michael, Simon Prestigiacomo and Anthony Rocca), that year. He set the team up but Shaw would not be allowed the eleven years' grace his replacement would get to manufacture a premiership.

McGuire was beginning to assemble his team. Within twelve months of arriving, he would have a new captain, coach, board, chief executive and football director.[11] The hope was that the new chief executive and coach would help transform the club with McGuire. No one could anticipate they would all plummet even further before rising. McGuire would continue to hire as the club continued to fall, and angst built as the losses tallied.

The president couldn't help himself, though. After being trounced in the first half by the Eagles at the WACA in Round 18, McGuire stormed into the rooms. Shaw had just told his charges they should spend some time quietly contemplating how they could lift in the second half. McGuire noticed the calm and began an old-school gee-up, which left coach and players nonplussed. Buckley told the president afterwards to leave the team to those who were with them every day of the week and understood the training methods and what the coach was trying to achieve.

McGuire was stepping in and stepping up, believing he needed to lead the club because the coach was on his way out. He thought the players were being hypersensitive but the captain invited

McGuire for a coffee later that week to reiterate his point that the president's role was not to coach the players.

Their relationship was an odd one. Buckley, in his comprehensive fashion, had previously written a letter to McGuire asking Eddie to be his mentor. Their early days as president and captain were tempered, though. Buckley was focused on everything that would better help the team; he found some of McGuire's intrusions distracting. Conversely, McGuire felt Buckley was inclined to sweat the small stuff.

It was big stuff to move Collingwood away from Victoria Park. The club had been weaned off the inner-city ground since the early 1990s, when the AFL started restricting games at the dilapidated venue despite president Allan McAlister's protestations that supporters preferred Vic Park. Attendance figures showed they preferred the MCG, a deal that was negotiated with the say-so of some prominent Collingwood identities who would have done anything to deny mortal enemies Melbourne and Richmond sole rights to games at the home of football.

When a Collingwood and Carlton blockbuster was shifted from Victoria Park to the MCG, McAlister protested, saying his team would turn up at Vic Park. As AFL President Allan Oakley pointed out, that would be a forfeit; Oakley later agreed to 'give' the club five home games at Lulie Street the following year as compensation – just as he had always intended. But the club couldn't become a force as Victoria Park literally crumbled. Even worse, the crumbling was costing Collingwood money. During the 1999 season, a coterie group raised $35 000 to install a weights rack and gym on a clubroom wall. It fell down, costing the club $60 000 to have girders reinforce the wall on Abbot Street. New players entered the club in the 2000s astounded to find they'd left behind better facilities at their suburban clubs. Mouse droppings littered the rooms and players weren't allowed to sit in the stands because there were fears for their safety.

Meanwhile, the MCG was undergoing its own transformation with a new board and continuing renovations. It was hunting for new tenants to help it, and convinced McGuire of the financial case for moving there. It was harder to counter the nostalgia case. But nostalgia had brought Collingwood to a point of financial distress, and McGuire had little choice but to move the club. His Collingwood management team realised it could transform the club.

In August 1999, 'McHale Stadium' hosted its last game of VFL/AFL football against Brisbane. Collingwood lost, but celebrated with a ceremony in which a Collingwood flag was lowered and presented to captain Buckley, who passed it on to McGuire. The Magpie players linked arms in front of past Collingwood greats and joined in a rendition of the club theme song.[12] It was a defiant moment in a calamitous year – the worst in its on-field history.

Collingwood would win the wooden spoon, lose a favourite son as coach, play its last game at its fortress and spiritual home, Victoria Park, and realise its playing list was simply inadequate. Even worse, the Allan McAlister years were being spun as halcyon days. McGuire and the inner sanctum knew otherwise. And McGuire knew what was being negotiated behind the scenes.

McGuire was aggressive, preparing to spend whatever it took to attract the right coach and chief executive (with John May leaving): as much as $1.5 million a season.[13] He even briefly floated the notion of two coaches.

He called AFL Players' Association boss Andrew Demetriou for a coffee and offered him the CEO job. He nearly convinced him after unrolling, on the bonnet of his car in Bridge Road, the plans for the proposed Olympic Park training centre.

All kinds of names were being bandied about for the coaching role, from Kevin Sheedy, Malcolm Blight and Denis Pagan to – less seriously – Garry Lyon, Dermott Brereton, Peter Daicos, Mick McGuane and Neil Balme.

Incorrect rumours also surfaced that West Coast Eagles premiership-winning coach Mick Malthouse had bought a house in Eltham. But the fix was in. McGuire had been in contact with Malthouse earlier in the year, meeting him for a casual coffee at a café down from Subiaco Oval, although the friends' catch-up wasn't about coaching (and Malthouse's daughter Christi was even there for some career advice). Unfortunately *The Footy Show*'s cameras, following a wandering Sam Newman, caught them chatting.

Nevertheless, off camera at the end of their meeting, McGuire asked Malthouse, 'So how can I get you to Collingwood?'

Malthouse laughed. 'You can't.'

'One day I will,' McGuire declared.[14]

Malthouse was settled in Perth, and his Eagles were flying when Collingwood made a quiet mid-season approach after Shaw's departure. Malthouse didn't know whether the offer was genuine, and didn't think much about it. It was rejected immediately.

In late July, negotiations became more serious, with Malthouse's West Coast Eagles stalling (after opening 11–3, the Eagles won one more home-and-away match in the final eight rounds) and Collingwood anchored to the bottom of the ladder. McGuire only had Malthouse and Pagan in mind to replace Shaw.

Malthouse's circumstances changed when his wife's mother was placed in palliative care. As soon as he announced in August that he was leaving Perth to return home, Malthouse fielded offers from four clubs: Collingwood, Richmond, Adelaide and Hawthorn. Hawthorn was not a serious alternative, nor was Adelaide, and Malthouse felt Richmond lacked professionalism.

McGuire's persistence, his salesmanship of a future move away from the rundown Victoria Park to the Olympic Park precinct and a sly fondness for the club (Malthouse grew up in Melbourne and his local football club wore the same colours) turned Malthouse towards the black and white – as did the opportunity to lead the proud club out of its depths. There could only be one result in taking on Collingwood now: improvement. McGuire later said the club had spoken to only one potential coach.[15] Mick Malthouse became the best-paid coach in the league. It was worth it: he was regarded as the best and his appointment was the message to supporters that things would change.

His 'coming out' as Collingwood coach in the week after the Grand Final presaged the new, commercial Collingwood. Seasoned football journalists saw a car silhouetted under a glamorous, silky sheet, musing to each other that there was no way a man like Malthouse would submit to such razzle-dazzle. But as the cover was pulled off, Malthouse was introduced in the front seat of a Volvo beside Buckley, both of them dressed in Versace suits. They looked anything but the leaders of a club that was once nearly called The Purloiners because they were the suburb of thieves. And Malthouse looked anything but relaxed as McGuire boasted they were the best duo in the league.

Malthouse was uncomfortable, always preferring shorts to a suit. But the sizzle was compelling. The players had a sense that they could 'fake it 'til they make it' and were positive about the new image.

The show displayed Collingwood as the biggest and the best club – and Eddie would begin trumpeting his catchphrase, 'Only the best for Collingwood' – even if it was some way from being the truth. The supporters would follow.

The first time Malthouse arrived at Vic Park, he froze in his car for an hour, stuck solid by the memory of what he had said goodbye to in Perth: the might of the Eagles he was leaving behind as he moved to the sixteenth club in the league. He had to cut his umbilical cord to the Eagles, but it took him that hour to do so.

His first tour through the Victoria Park facilities with new CEO Greg Swann was even more depressing. The facilities were a shambles, with rotting floorboards, mould and an office fridge full of beer. McGuire warned him it would be bad; the coach just didn't expect it to be *this* bad. One comfort was knowing his former Richmond teammate Neil Balme was football operations manager.

The following weeks didn't offer much solace. Malthouse learned quickly the strength and fitness of the Collingwood players was deficient compared with the Eagles. He soon hired sports physiologist David Buttifant as the club's sports science director.

Conversely, Malthouse began to appreciate Collingwood's unique DNA from more than 100 years: 'hard work, mateship, survival and an ability to go on no matter how tough times were'.[16]

Nevertheless, in quizzing staff and players, no one could tell Malthouse why the club wasn't as professional as the Eagles. He thought the range of excuses offered for Collingwood's wan performance – blaming the AFL, umpires, drafting – was 'almost comical'.[17] He told McGuire that Collingwood was the worst side in the league because 'it was the worst side'.

As if to confirm it, after ending the year with the wooden spoon for the first time in the club's history, McGuire received a call from Buckley's manager, Geof Motley, in the post-season.

'Are you aware Bucks isn't contracted?' he told the president.

McGuire paused. In the CEO handover, previous CEO, John May, told the incoming Swann that Buckley was signed. He wasn't, and Motley had let it run surreptitiously to increase his market value. Buckley had no intention of leaving, but McGuire and Swann didn't know that.

The bungling was typical of Collingwood in the late 1990s. Motley had the upper hand and negotiated a contract wherein Buckley's salary was fixed at 12.63 per cent of the salary cap (which in 2000 was $4.75 million). It was the last time Buckley was uncontracted at Collingwood.

Malthouse wasn't the only person telling McGuire the club was in dire straits. Greg Swann was head-hunted from his partnership at Ernst and Young chartered accountants after being chief executive of CAMS, the country's motor sports authority. It took some wooing, but the former Williamstown player came, attracted by the opportunity to be CEO of the most famous club in the country – even though it was struggling. As an accountant, Swann was involved in winding up the Fitzroy Football Club in the 1990s; the despair of the Lions supporters had affected him and he could have done without repeating it. It also gave him experience of a footy club on the bones of its arse.

When he arrived at Collingwood with Malthouse in October, it quickly became apparent Collingwood could become the next Fitzroy, as shocking as that sounded. Swann found a club $1.7 million in debt, with no foreseeable way out, and limping along without dignity. It was so bad, he suggested to the board, that the club needed to have a shameless, tin-rattling appeal for funds. The board said no. Whatever pride was left wouldn't allow it.

Collingwood reported a trading loss for the year just shy of $1 million, largely due to gate receipts falling by $660 000 in a year in which they won just four games and home crowds fell by 20 per cent. The club was also being sued by catering company Spotless. There were spot fires everywhere. 'That year, 1999, was always going to be one when we drew a line in the sand,' McGuire said.

McGuire suspected, when he arrived with his new board, there were some deep, black financial holes to fill. He held his tongue – just. Swann's arrival brought some calm to McGuire. The first time Swann outlined the true extent of the financial disaster faced by Collingwood, McGuire slept easily. No longer would he be swinging at shadows.

McGuire and Swann invited AFL chief executive Wayne Jackson and football operations chief Ian Collins to Victoria Park for a meeting in which the club held out the begging bowl. The AFL dismissed the idea, a response McGuire later relished because it fuelled his us-against-them narrative.

Indeed, McGuire later railed at the AFL's imperiousness in suggesting Collingwood 'sell' a home game to Sydney to raise money – a mere $100000.[18] McGuire thought he was, in his euphemistic way, being forced to bend over and Jackson was revelling in chiding him. That non-deal alone precipitated at least two years of anti-AFL venom from McGuire.

Eddie also had his own internal worries. He found it difficult to fit in, a job made harder by his inquisitiveness and attempts to establish some financial rigour. McGuire is not known for his governance aptitude, but even he could see straight away the club was a series of unaccountable fiefdoms, with cash flowing but no budgets. Cash bars were rolling, backs were being scratched, and nods and winks were as good as cash. Volunteers expected their in-kind payments and old-timers clogged up some staffing areas. Match-day tickets were being used as currency.

For instance, the club had two full-time property stewards but only one sponsorship employee. The club was built on costs, not revenue. The cleaning up of the club became literal; players' jumpers previously sent to be dry-cleaned were now washed on-site in heavy-duty washing machines supplied by a sponsor. Some $750000 was cut from costs in the first year just by questioning things.

Swann said, 'The club was immersed in a culture of "That's the way we've always done it. And that's why we'll continue to do it." But the rest of the competition, and sport and business in general, had moved on.'[19]

And many staff did move on. By July 2000, forty of the fifty-two people who worked at the club when McGuire arrived were no longer there. In his first two years, virtually every major position from chief executive to property steward changed, with many resigning as McGuire brought some of the hard-headed ruthlessness of TV to the Pies.

Another key McGuire appointment was David Emerson as marketing manager. He came after Swann, and he too quickly realised the situation was far more dire than he'd been told.

Swann and McGuire put together a three-year plan in 2000 under three headings. The first year was 'Right the Sinking Ship'; the second year was 'Awake the Sleeping Giant'; and the third year was 'Become the AFL's Most Hated/Respected Team'. It was an optimistic timeframe, but they would achieve it.

Sponsorship was essential, and club management knew it could represent a sustainable competitive advantage because McGuire had so much exposure on TV and radio. They particularly benefited from the many rubes trying to get a leg-up during the dotcom bubble of 1999–2000 by sponsoring Collingwood. Every week it seemed a new start-up was throwing money at the club to host a product launch, or for access to a table at *The Footy Show* or match-day sponsorships.

McGuire worked hard for the money personally, taking Newman and Marmalade to regional footy clubs and venues with live, non-broadcast versions of *The Footy Show* to raise money for Collingwood. Nine turned a blind eye.

McGuire, Emerson and Swann remade every aspect of the Collingwood brand, from its membership structure through to the design and sponsorship of its jumper and the match-day experience for members and sponsors, which at one point included parachutists.

The plan was to welcome supporters to the biggest sporting club in the country at the best stadium in the world, the MCG. Collingwood games would be the big time. McGuire maintains a key catchphrase from the period, 'Welcome to Collingwood'. It showed McGuire at his PT Barnum best, selling a product that was not yet fully formed.

The new millennium began brightly for the club on-field, despite losing another hefty sum on its failed Millennium Eve match against Carlton that pushed it further into the red. The young team began its AFL season as well as could be hoped, thumping Hawthorn with a free-scoring style and four debutants.

The round one victory saw rare humility from the club, with McGuire noting:

> What you need around a club is realists – not people who will tell you what you want to hear or hope to hear, but people who will tell you what is actually going on, so that you can sit down and work things out …That's what we've done over the last six to twelve months: recruit people who tell it as it is. We're not hoping for the ghost of Jock McHale to come and save the day anymore.[20]

The team continued with five straight wins and shared the top of the table with Essendon before nine straight losses. It was a young team; inconsistency was anticipated. Then McGuire had to begin to defend the club again; his honeymoon was over.

'If we're not a great club, I'll go he,' he said in July. 'We're an unbelievable club.'

That was correct off the field. Despite the club's on-field slump, Collingwood recorded sell-out crowds for three successive weeks, its games were rating on TV, sponsors were happy and it had the top club website in the country. 'What more do we need to do, apart from winning games?' McGuire said.[21]. He'd hit the nail on the head.

By mid-year, the club regressed again, not helped by an outbreak of legionella bacteria from a contaminated spa in the players' room at the club. Four people were affected – none of them players – and Collingwood looked, both figuratively and literally, sick again.[22]

McGuire was looking everywhere for growth. And he was fortunate to have a flexible, well-remunerated media contract to allow himself the time and space to do it. He couldn't have devoted the energy to Collingwood's transformation were he a 'normal' businessman. Nevertheless, people at the club were amazed at his indefatigable energy through those bleak first years.

He submitted a club request to play three games in Sydney in 2001 to forge a presence up north if the Olympic Stadium was right to go. 'We want to have a presence in Sydney. I don't think you can get a presence with just the one game, so we would possibly look at playing one home game, one against Sydney and one against the Kangaroos,' he said.[23] 'If there was a club that Sydney would call its own out of Melbourne, it would be Collingwood, I reckon.'

Such initiatives were distractions: the situation was still bad. McGuire thought he'd reached a nadir in Round 18 when, in the 'battle of the suburban grounds', the dreaded Carlton thumped the Pies by 111 points at Princes Park in the final match the old foes would play at the ground. For some key figures at Collingwood, it remains the most harrowing day of football they've ever experienced.

As McGuire, Malthouse, Buckley, football manager Neil Balme and Swann walked across the ground to the after-match function, they were targeted by rapturous Carlton supporters. McGuire felt humiliated.

The furious five retired to a marquee to deliberate, and made a vow to make the changes necessary to never let it happen again. Sport likes its 'moments', when a game, a player, a season or a club changes; the truth is transformation is gradual, as it would be for Collingwood. But if one day marked the bottoming-out of the club under McGuire, this was it.

Four weeks later, Malthouse and Swann's first season closed with Collingwood finishing fifteenth, with seven wins. It was a year in which Malthouse figured out the worth of his playing list. That list would turn over sharply with some key retirements, notably the last two remaining members of the 1990 premiership side, Gavin Crosisca and Gavin Brown. They were significant retirements. Now Collingwood was McGuire and Malthouse's club, unshackled by its recent history (the following year, its 27-year-old captain would be the oldest player on the list) but not by its supporters' desire for something – anything – better.

It remained Collingwood, though, and a campaign to destabilise Buckley's captaincy peaked in November, of all times, as rumours of a player coup to replace him with Scott Burns as captain surfaced. McGuire defended Buckley in comments to *The Age*, while admitting he could be imperious and difficult for younger players, as he tried to 'coach' them during games. There was no coup, and Buckley argued vociferously with his president that there wouldn't have been a story if McGuire hadn't commented. Eddie thought otherwise.[24]

The club's finances began to look brighter though, with a $336 715 profit for the 2000 season after the previous year's $1.261 million loss, aided by gate receipts increasing by $150 000 and marketing revenue up by almost $1 million.[25] The spruiking was working.

But McGuire had to get through an election after his board members, Brad Cooper, Jack Kennedy and Alex Waislitz, were challenged for board positions by candidates Rick Sciessere, Nick Theodossi and Paul Murphy. Given the poor on-field performance, the election could have been dicey. In a letter to voting members, McGuire wrote, 'Too many times Collingwood has let emotion interfere with carefully laid out plans. This is not the time.'[26] McGuire's trio was re-elected handsomely.

Malthouse stamped his imprint on the club in 2000–01, delisting or trading three senior players – Paul Williams (to Sydney), Mal Michael (to Brisbane) and Saverio Rocca (who was cut and picked up by North Melbourne). A third of the list departed. Malthouse, Balme and new recruitment manager Noel Judkins could cull because they were new and had no emotional attachment to the decisions.

More importantly, the fruits of the club's dark days at the bottom of the ladder and picking up high-draft picks were ripening. By finishing low, Collingwood could start again with young talent. Across four years (1998–2001), Collingwood would draft the following players: in 1998, Nick Davis and Heath Scotland, trading in Paul Licuria; in 1999, number one draft choice Josh Fraser, Rhyce Shaw, Leon Davis, Ben Johnson and Shane O'Bree; in 2000, Alan Didak, Jason Cloke and Ryan Lonie; and in 2001, Dane Swan and some serious pre-draft trades, including James Clement, Brodie Holland, Jarrod Molloy and Carl Steinfort. They built a core list that would bring later success. Just as important as the playing talent were the leadership potential and expertise that would be assembled; Buckley, Burns, Rocca, Licuria, Clement and Holland would subsequently stand up as the leaders, dragging a young list to success.

McGuire had an amusing first encounter with one draftee, who would become a favourite. South Australian signing Alan Didak answered the phone on draft day at his Adelaide home to hear, 'It's Eddie McGuire here.' The seventeen-year-old thought it was a mate playing a prank and replied, 'Sure. Mate, I asked for the 50–50 lifeline, not phone-a-friend,' before hanging up. An hour later, his manager arrived with the papers to sign for Collingwood as Didak told him about his mate ringing pretending he was Eddie. His manager told him McGuire had asked for his number, so he'd hung up on the Collingwood president. If only that were the only inconvenience Didak would cause McGuire during his career.[27]

Inconsistent results in 2001 conspired to leave Collingwood one game out of the eight. It had a future, though, and McGuire was making further advances with his staff. At the end of the season, McGuire and club stalwart Kevin Rose were re-elected unopposed at the club's annual meeting. Just as importantly, McGuire told the AGM, after being quizzed by a member, that he had also received the blessing of the fifteen other club presidents to combine his role at Collingwood with commentating on football's new broadcaster, Channel Nine. The Pies declared an operating profit of $1 089 729 for the year, with Swann telling members 2002 was budgeted to be as good.[28]

Something stable was happening – at least until the opening rounds of the 2002 season. After Collingwood was beaten by an out-of-form and injured Carlton in Round 3 – the club's second loss after an unconvincing one-point win over the Eagles – McGuire left the Channel Nine commentary box and stormed to the change rooms, where he found the players doing their own post-mortem. After being invited in by Buckley, he weighed in, saying the party was over and if any player was not prepared to give his heart and soul for the Collingwood Football Club then he was free to leave, no questions asked. 'I'll be in my office at 9 a.m. on Monday and I will start the paperwork immediately,' he told them. He wasn't joking.

Collingwood promptly confirmed its father–son draftee Nick Davis had made it clear he wanted to move to Sydney with his family. McGuire played hardball, telling him he was contracted and 'If he wants to play for Collingwood we love him, we'll pay him, we'll look after him.'[29] McGuire used *The Footy Show* to announce that Davis was on the verge of splitting with his manager, Ricky Nixon, just to heighten tensions – although he raised the hackles of other player managers with his added comment that most players could do without managers, while saving football millions of dollars.[30]

Collingwood grunted its way to a 2-3 win/loss ratio when Greg Swann approached Malthouse to tell him there was a push at board level to get rid of him. It wasn't coming from McGuire.

Malthouse expressed his views to the board strongly, and didn't realise until later that the business-focused board members were focused on footy being results-driven rather than method-driven. Admittedly, fans don't understand that either, although Malthouse believed strongly that once the systems at the club were right, the results would come.

They did indeed. Collingwood then won five games in the next six during a year that would deliver unexpectedly good results while Malthouse was still rebuilding. The youngest list in the league was outperforming expectations.

Very little now bumped McGuire's train, including an astonishing false claim by former Crow Stephen Rowe on Adelaide radio station 5AA that Collingwood had bribed an umpire to get Nathan Buckley off at the tribunal. The station and Rowe apologised and Rowe was suspended.

McGuire busied himself with more consequential matters around the club. As the big-picture profit and loss began to strengthen, he could start massaging the egos and picking out the splinters that, however small, can debilitate sporting clubs if they're not heading in the same direction. So he acted as a peacekeeping force to align the four factions of the Collingwood cheer squad. They splintered again in 2002 before McGuire lobbed onto supporter message boards cajoling and pleading until he threatened to ban malcontents from matches. And he didn't dither; he left one serious corporate meeting at the club to deal with two rival factions in the cheer squad. A dispute dragging on for weeks was done in minutes.

Everything from the menu at the presidential lunches and dinners to righting the club's wretched relationships with the coterie groups and the past players' association – well-known sites of disharmony in the past – was put under Eddie's blowtorch. McGuire took a particular interest in building the Anzac Day blockbuster with Essendon, writing the banner messages himself and suggesting the teams enter the stadium in unison.

McGuire could see the club turning. 'Everyone felt bitter. What I've found is that everyone really just wants a cuddle,' he said.[31]

He knew he could fend off any negativity for a couple of years as the club tried to rebuild, and he believed he had a coach seasoned enough to accept Collingwood's thin list and endure the few years at the bottom of the ladder as the footy world revelled in or criticised Collingwood's failings.

Financially, things were good with money pouring in. Membership revenue had almost doubled in three years; merchandising revenue had grown 300 per cent in a year; the club's move to Olympic Park was budgeted to net an extra half million a year plus advertising revenue; and Collingwood had a $2 million bonus from the sale of VFL Park.

Even factors outside the club's control were working in Collingwood's favour. Indigenous player John Kelly Country, who nine years earlier had placed a curse on Collingwood after racist comments made by the Magpie president Allan McAlister,[32] chose to bestow a good-luck charm on the club in July. The Magpies had recruited Territorians like Nathan Buckley, their champion, and Robbie Ahmat, and made great progress on Indigenous recognition. 'This is all coming from the heart. I feel I've owed them something,' Kelly Country said.[33]

In July, Victorian Sport Minister Justin Madden unveiled plans for Olympic Park's $13 million upgrade to become the new base for Collingwood and the Victorian Institute of Sport, with an MCG-sized oval on the site of the old Olympic Park greyhound track (and scene of Michael Jackson's 1987 concert) and redevelopment of the Olympic Pool.

Of course, the state government would not contribute money to the project (that would come later), but it guaranteed loans that would be bankrolled by a multi-million-dollar sponsorship deal, including naming rights to be negotiated by Collingwood for up to $1 million a year.[34] McGuire hoped the Yarra Council would retain some element of Collingwood at Victoria Park, although that would take years of battles, schmoozing and ultimately money to eventuate.

The increasingly successful triumvirate of McGuire, Malthouse and Swann was hooked in more than emotional terms. Malthouse's new 2002 contract had a clause allowing him to walk if McGuire was dumped as president.[35] They were working well, with Balme adding calm to Malthouse and the sanguine Swann balancing the emotional McGuire.

'It's a good group of people whose egos don't get in the way,' McGuire said.[36]

And so McGuire's club marched to an unexpected 2002 Grand Final appearance. McGuire celebrated its unlikely season by inviting all players, partners and club officials to a team dinner on the Monday after the final round of the home-and-away season. He realised there hadn't been an actual moment when the team appreciated that it had made the finals or the top four, so this would be it. There was no gee-up, no stress, a different Collingwood. 'We believed in ourselves and we had a laugh and we went forward from there,' McGuire recounted.[37]

Collingwood had a stunning September after limping towards the finals. It was vindication – perhaps prematurely – for McGuire and Malthouse. They'd made some hard decisions and copped a caning for persisting with youth and building experience through second-hand players who didn't break the bank.

Grand Final week was a test for McGuire as both TV presenter and club president. His flexible media contracts allowed him the time and space to devote time to his presidency that normal CEOs couldn't afford but this week would make him earn his money, on both fronts.

McGuire and Nine mutually decided he shouldn't host the Grand Final Breakfast; Tony Jones earned that gig. Then came media interviews and preparing the machinations of player Jason Cloke's defence at the tribunal before hosting episodes of *Who Wants to Be a Millionaire?* and attending the Brownlow Medal dinner. And that was Monday.

Malthouse told McGuire he should be proud of what he'd achieved. He was. But McGuire's greatest achievement, perhaps, was choosing Malthouse. It would become clear Malthouse was able to coax something extraordinary from this playing list.

Ultimately, Collingwood was beaten by the better side. Gallant – and all those other clichés – in defeat, the Pies met a bigger, more accomplished team. Yet history would look as kindly on this Collingwood team as it did Brisbane.

It was a tough day for the McGuires on all fronts. Seven-month pregnant Carla was sick. She watched the game with heat bags on her stomach to help the nausea of gastro. Their youngest boy, Joseph, now 21 months old, had been sick with it on the Friday, and Carla picked up the bug.

McGuire, dressed in a black suit, white shirt, Collingwood tie and charcoal-black overcoat, was holding it together but hurting. Every supporter of a losing Grand Finalist team knows the feeling; it only seems slightly ridiculous later. In that week, on that day, in that moment, you believe you will, can, might win, no matter how unrealistic the prospect. If we knew the result, no one would watch. And McGuire was hoping – just hoping – his dad would be able to hold that Premiership Cup one more time – a time with aching significance.

Which made the reality of defeat all the more crushing, particularly with such an investment as McGuire's. This was the culmination of four years of emotion, of sleepless nights, shrewd politicking and cajoling, cursing and begging.

For a public personality known to bite back at every infraction or slight, or react to anything less than perfect, McGuire was polished and dignified in the aftermath of the grand final loss.

'I'm very proud,' he repeated and repeated.[38]

Eddie's dad, blind and frail, joined him in the rooms. Eddie was visibly moved.

> The eyes opened up, I can tell you. It's amazing. No matter how big and ugly you get, the moment you see your dad ... No, it was great, my brother and sister, they feel it because when they read

stuff in the paper, they know it's their little brother, whereas I read it, it's the third person half the time ...

McGuire was surrounded by friends at the post-match dinner at Crown – on table four at the Palladium, Rob Sitch and Jane Kennedy, Ian Johnson, his best friend Colin DeLutis, Jeff Browne, the production manager of GTV-9 and rampant Collingwood man Graham Trippett, and their partners consoled him.

However, McGuire was spent and needed a release. He reverted to 1980s Eddie, moving on to Heat Nightclub and partying with the players until 4 a.m. Just like old times – but not like the old times. Eddie McGuire was leading, not following.

But he wasn't slowing. The following Monday, he had a double recording of *Who Wants to Be a Millionaire?* followed by a players' and partners' night on Wednesday and the Copeland Trophy on Friday before heading to London and Ireland the following week to call the exhibition game and Irish series. There was no time to look back and mourn.

CHAPTER 14

BULLETS, BOOZE AND LIES

Success begets trouble, particularly at sporting clubs.

Professional sportspeople are protected and mollycoddled from a young age after they are identified as 'special'. It takes solid parenting or mentoring, or strength of character, to ensure that 'special' label doesn't lead to arrogance, hubris or irresponsibility. And winners need to be especially vigilant.

McGuire and his team successfully turned the culture of Collingwood around. It was only years later McGuire claimed that when he arrived in 1999, the club had the worst culture in the league, with ill-disciplined, unprofessional players and a lax management structure.

The club did well to keep its very young playing list on the straight and narrow through its two years of relative success leading to Grand Finals in 2002 and 2003. But the frustration of the 2003 loss to Brisbane hurt the playing group. It was particularly hard to keep emotions in check after the 50-point loss, so when a drunk punter taunted Chris Tarrant and Ben Johnson at the Lower Plenty Hotel, the result was predictable.

Tarrant bit back, holding two people in a headlock before scuffling with Johnson in the car park. It was all passed over as a minor scuffle as the club's 'Mad Monday' celebrations at Richmond's Rising Sun Hotel progressed without incident, although radio talkback lit up with unsubstantiated rumours of assorted nightclub stoushes involving players throughout the weekend.[1]

Drink-driving was an issue for Collingwood, as it was for many clubs. It was particularly problematic for Collingwood, though, because the club had a million dollar-plus sponsorship with the road safety organisation, the Transport Accident Commission (TAC). The ramifications of a breach heightened for all players and club officials. McGuire even carried his own personal breathalyser in his car, and all players were issued with smaller breathalysers to give them indicative alcohol readings, as well as fit-outs of hands-free mobile phone kits for their cars and wads of taxi dockets.[2] Unfortunately, it wasn't quite enough.

First to go in an era of player misbehaviour was Cameron Cloke, who the club fined $5000 after he was caught speeding – 144 kilometres per hour in a 100-kilometre zone[3] – just as the club was renegotiating its contract with the TAC. The TAC docked $10 000 from its sponsorship.

The TAC soon lost patience, downgrading its sponsorship with Collingwood in 2005 as Wizard Home Loans took over the Pies' jumper sponsorship. Collingwood was lucky; Richmond lost its sponsorship completely when one of its players was charged with speeding and drink-driving.[4]

However, in 2006 the TAC would dock another $200 000 from its sponsorship package, believed to total around $500 000 annually, after Chad Morrison blew 0.093 and lost his licence when being breath-tested while riding his motor scooter. McGuire was livid.

Collingwood wouldn't lose its TAC sponsorship until 2008 when nineteen-year-old rookie Sharrod Wellingham was booked in Lorne with a blood-alcohol reading of 0.13 while driving Hawks player Lance 'Buddy' Franklin and teammate Simon Taylor. Wellingham said he was moving the car to avoid a parking fine; the club fined him $5000 and McGuire was left with no choice but to walk away from the partnership with the TAC.[5] 'That we have transgressed means we've forfeited the right and the privilege of being associated with the Transport Accident Commission,' he said.[6]

The rot had set in well before that moment. The hangover from the 2002 and 2003 Grand Final losses began to tell off the field.

Early in 2004, reacting to an obvious trend, the club issued a warning to players about their safety in public places late at night, advising them not to be out after 1 a.m. A week later, Johnson broke his hand at a pub in the early hours of a Saturday morning, requiring surgery and missing several weeks of pre-season training.[7]

In May, Rhyce Shaw was punched in an Eltham bar while celebrating a teammate's birthday. The players were fined for drinking and ordered to dawn training.

In June, several unnamed players were referred to alcohol education programs and two senior officials were placed on 'final notice' after a late-night drinking binge in a Sunshine Coast hotel room went awry. As mentioned previously, McGuire also copped it for not revealing details of the incident on *The Footy Show* after revelling on the program in a similar story involving St Kilda players. The Collingwood players were on a mid-season break and their drinking binge resulted in one player vomiting onto an occupied balcony below his room and players having to pay compensation to another family. 'This is not new to life or football clubs,' a weary McGuire said.

He defended his decision not to disclose the incident as host of *The Footy Show*, saying he was regularly in possession of privileged information through his various work with Collingwood, the AFL and other boards, which he could not disclose in his capacity as a journalist.[8] In this case, it didn't quite wash.

Behavioural issues continued to dominate the president's time in office. McGuire's patience with one of his project players, Tarrant, stretched further after the forward was involved in a 4.00 a.m. pub fight with Essendon's Mark Johnson in August. And, post-season, young forward Tom Davidson pleaded guilty to assaulting a taxi driver in Geelong and was put on a two-year good behaviour bond with no conviction recorded.

Assaults were becoming a habit. In February, Dane Swan was ordered to serve a hundred hours of community service after pleading guilty to affray during a drunken brawl in 2003, with Malthouse telling him he was on his 'last legs'. McGuire would repeat the ultimatum to Swan almost a decade later in a testy meeting with the Brownlow medallist and his manager. McGuire couldn't stand seeing young men being led astray away from the club.

And in January, Brodie Holland lodged a guilty plea to charges of unlicensed driving and driving on tram tracks before contesting charges of assaulting a woman in a fight over a cab in the city at 3.30 a.m. the previous May.

Tarrant and Johnson were involved in another street fight the following year, leaving one man unconscious, needing hospital treatment for a head injury. The brawl outside a Port Melbourne nightclub resulted in $5000 club fines for both players and the opening of a cultural wound at the club that would take some time to heal.

The players were not the provocateurs; Tarrant was abused by a passing motorist as they left a nightspot at 4 a.m. on a Sunday after an eight-hour night out. Three men jumped out of the car to fight Tarrant, with Johnson jumping in to defend the outnumbered teammate. Again McGuire was distressed, not having been told of the incident until the *Herald Sun* broke the story. He told the duo they owed the club now.

Former coach Tony Shaw – who instigated a ban on King Street nightclubs for his players back in 1997 – condemned Tarrant and said he should be traded, saying he was a 'protected species' since he had walked out on the group (in 2002).[9] McGuire bit back, saying Tarrant was different:

> Shawy was the coach when Taz [Tarrant] got there and he walked into the worst culture in football. The club was in disarray. The kid was seventeen years of age ... the joint was rat-infested at that stage. The playing culture was appalling – off-field, on-field, every field. I was there in 1999. I know what it was like.[10]

They spoke on the phone and made up – for a moment. Shaw then accused McGuire of not telling him about the 'rat-infested culture' jibe. McGuire was adamant: 'I have no problem in saying that in 1999 that Collingwood Football Club's culture was the worst in football.'[11]

Shaw wore the comment about a losing culture, but not the one about ill-discipline, noting only that Tarrant and Mal Michael didn't follow team values. Michael was traded to Brisbane.

McGuire had to defend the club's overall behaviour, saying discipline was good. But he was hurt by the behaviour of particular players in whom he had invested so much. McGuire remains the last of another generation of club presidents who are fans first. His desire is to support his talented, sometimes wayward, charges. Even today, he might be seen unstrapping reserves players after a game at Victoria Park. He invests emotional energy, and sometimes his own resources, in his players, so when they fail him, he is wounded personally: 'They just got themselves into the wrong situation,' he said of Tarrant. 'There's no joy after 2 a.m. or 1.30 a.m. I know boys will be boys, but they should have known better.' By now, McGuire was in Sydney and unable to shepherd his favoured son to safety.

> He [Tarrant] has let me down and I'd be bitterly disappointed if either of them let me down again.

He was a young man lost in the early part of his life, which is why, as our song says, I'll be standing side by side with Taz and Johnno. If I'm the last bloke in Australia, I'll be standing next to them.

Maybe I've got blind optimism but if Chris Tarrant gets to the end of his career, hopefully at Collingwood, and has made a success of football and put some serious money away, then I will count that as one of my greatest achievements in my time at Collingwood. But if he lets me down again, I'll have to think a little differently.[12]

It would take a trade to Western Australia and a happy return before Tarrant would become one of McGuire's greatest achievements. Even so, the Collingwood rap sheet grew longer. Court documents showed Cameron Cloke instigated a nightclub brawl in Ringwood that left a young man with permanent brain damage.

Tensions were fraying everywhere. McGuire became involved in a push and shove with his own cheer squad after another season concluded with one more loss against the Bulldogs. McGuire went to the cheer squad after the final siren, asking to say goodbye to Jeff 'Joffa' Corfe. A brouhaha commenced as one member said there was more to the cheer squad than Joffa, and McGuire told them to 'get stuffed'. 'It was a long day for us all,' said the president.[13]

And so it went, until Alan Didak ventured on a mad night with some new friends. The incident took the crime at the Pies to another level. The scrutiny afforded McGuire's charges was immense. Didak, in the middle of a storming season (that would push him near All-Australian selection), made the papers after *Herald Sun* readers reported his blazing row with his girlfriend, Cassie Lane, outside the Boutique nightclub in Prahran – with a third man involved, as it happens. The club said nothing happened, everyone move right along. But this was two weeks after Tarrant and Johnson's run-in in Port Melbourne. Collingwood was volatile.

Later that year, Didak sent McGuire ballistic after being locked up in a prison cell for assaulting a taxi driver, twenty-four hours before he took out the club's best and fairest award. This time, an athlete's 'mixed emotions' on accepting an award was not a thin cliché.

'It's been a weird day – mixed emotions,' Didak said on accepting the Copeland Trophy. 'I was pretty upset when I rocked up to the club today and to win a Copeland now, what an absolute honour.'

McGuire didn't mix his message at the ceremony, frustrated at the continued off-field failings of the players. He told them:

> Those who do not give us every opportunity to achieve on-field success will no longer be tolerated. On-field and off-field discipline and commitment are essential to success in any business.
>
> Discipline and commitment and respect, respect for the club, respect for teammates, respect for the professionalism of those around … I put it on the players and the leadership group to take this club further.[14]

Yet it was a line in the sand that would be crossed again, infuriating McGuire, testing friendships and jeopardising careers.

After retaliating after being stung by a taxi driver at 1 a.m., Didak was charged on summons with being drunk and disorderly. McGuire's ultimatum haunted him eight months later as Didak was given one last chance, and then another one, when it emerged he was in the company of alleged city shooting killer Christopher Wayne Hudson while on a joy ride. Didak was with the Hells Angel just days before Hudson shot three people in the city – killing one. A drunken interlude then became a major outrage.

Didak told police he was in a black Mercedes with Hudson on 12 June after he left the King Street strip club, Spearmint Rhino, about 3 a.m. after the Queen's Birthday game. Random shots were fired from the car as they drove to a number of suburban locations, although Didak told the club he was essentially 'hostage' to Hudson.[15]

McGuire was informed of the incident by Arocca while returning from a Europe holiday. Initially, Didak's 'abduction' washed with Collingwood management, although McGuire and the executive, coach Mick Malthouse and the players' leadership group, compiled a list of rules and penalties for Didak.[16] McGuire said he would be 'rehabilitated' by his club following his 'profound stupidity'.[17] The club remained frustrated at how the story elevated – and was being leaked by the police – with the inference being the force was trying to distract attention from a procedural formality that allowed Hudson to elude arrest before the shooting.

Didak undertook not to drink alcohol, to seek alcohol counselling, to observe a 1 a.m. curfew and to avoid nightclubs. McGuire would have sacked him had he not done so.

'I think some of the decisions that I've made under the influence of alcohol haven't been the best,' Didak said with considerable understatement.[18]

The tale wasn't quite so innocent, though, with police believing Hudson befriended Didak with a drink before offering to take him to see a Hells Angels chapter. The night would not have caused the police much consternation had someone in Hudson's car not shot at a police car after the Hells Angel's vehicle ran a red light.

McGuire was incensed he had so publicly defended Didak and the club had backed the 'victim' when Didak's truth wasn't so edifying. Didak had further damaged a Collingwood brand its players were doing little to embellish. After the first Didak media conference, all sponsor logos were removed from subsequent briefings by the club.[19]

The incident split Collingwood, briefly hurting the relationship between McGuire and the newly installed chief executive he had muscled in against some board members' wishes, Gary Pert. Management bickered about the incident's handling, with some angry the president was the club's spokesperson, and subsequently fall guy, during such debacles. At other clubs, CEOs or football managers spoke on such issues. Conversely, the executive was particularly angry at how some players had again taken advantage of McGuire's faith and optimism.

Didak continued to make amends on the football field through 2006 and 2007, after McGuire asked him what he was going to do to restore the club's faith. Twelve months later, the club signed him to a new two-year contract, which dumped the subsequent alcohol and curfew restrictions forced upon him.[20] McGuire said: 'He has earned our trust.'[21]

Briefly, anyway. In the early hours of Monday, 4 August 2008, coach Mick Malthouse was woken with news Heath Shaw had crashed his car.

Shaw was drunk after drinking with brother Rhyce and another person at the Geebung Polo Club in Hawthorn. Shaw drove his ute home with the unnamed passenger, crashing into three cars and blowing 0.144 at about 11.30 p.m. McGuire and Malthouse were told of the incident early in the morning after Shaw rang Magpies football manager Geoff Walsh a short time after the crash.

The club came down hard in public that day, with McGuire noting at a press conference, 'We are embarrassed and absolutely furious ... There is no excuse and we're sick and tired of this behaviour.'

Captain Scott Burns went further, saying, 'Bugger him. We're going to make sure he cops it.'

Earlier in the morning, McGuire subjected the players to an expletive-riddled tirade expressing his dejection and rage. Emphasising their responsibilities to the players, he also highlighted the sacrifices so many others at the club made for the players, including himself as president. McGuire noted he had sacrificed winning four or five Gold Logies while devoting so much time to the club rather than to his own career.

He also laid into repeat offender Ben Johnson, telling him he was fat and that, after nine years at the club, McGuire himself could kick better with his wrong foot than Johnson. He reminded the by-now furious players of the value of their bounteous contracts while the rest of society was suffering an economic downturn.

McGuire was hurt, and he told them so. He couldn't understand why players didn't realise their behaviour hurt those at the club defending them and taking the hits – particularly the president.

That was all before the club realised Shaw had lied to them: Didak was in the car with him, despite Shaw's denials. The first inkling of this information was Nine's Tony Jones repeatedly asking about Didak during a press conference. He knew more than Collingwood.

That pained McGuire, who told the initial press conference that Didak hadn't been involved and joked he was surprised Didak had not been linked to the JFK assassination.

He said so with confidence. McGuire asked Shaw beforehand bluntly: 'Is that all? Is there anything else to the story that I need to know?'

'No, there's nothing else,' Shaw replied.

He warned Shaw, 'There comes a time in your life when you have to get rid of scaly mates.' McGuire would soon realise that mate was the player recently re-signed to an $800 000 Collingwood contract after a series of indiscretions: Alan Didak. It was the most debilitating of blows. After all the chances came this almighty lie.

'We've had enough of these blokes letting us down at the Collingwood Football Club,' McGuire said. 'They're not five-year-olds now; they're grown men. We are angry, we are furious, we've had enough, the public has had enough.'[22]

McGuire, Pert, Walsh and Malthouse, in consultation with leaders of the club, ended Shaw and Didak's season, saying they didn't deserve to play for Collingwood.

'When you have two of your key players looking the president, the coach and their own teammates in the eye and actually lying to them, it really destroys the essence of the club,' Pert said. Shaw's brother, Rhyce, was suspended for two weeks and all three copped fines for their two-day drinking bender and its ramifications.

The Shaw incident was embarrassing for McGuire: he'd gone hard in defending him. And accusations of a stinking culture hit Collingwood yet again. All the good work by McGuire, Malthouse – indeed, the whole club – was being unwound by a few footballers who weren't capable of holding their alcohol.

Former captain Nathan Buckley even criticised McGuire's handling of the week, while adding the players were at serious fault.

Buckley told Radio 3AW that Shaw and Didak's lies were 'unforgivable'. 'For those players to be out, from a football perspective, six days before a game, when they have had an eight-day break, is just unacceptable and then to top it off by being dishonest to the people in an environment where you rely on honesty and you rely on trust is unforgivable,' he said.

McGuire learnt from his previous stoush with Tony Shaw it wasn't good for the club to have rows with its former players. He texted Buckley his disappointment but kept his mouth shut.

Premier John Brumby, a Collingwood supporter, concurred Collingwood had a problem with alcohol: 'There is a problem, I think, with this culture,' he said. 'I would have thought all the players would be there just focused on trying to make the four.'[23]

McGuire spoke to the Premier to tell him he was wrong.

By 2008, Collingwood was employing security guards to protect its players, and most infractions were being self-reported to the club through Walsh, who had been brought to the club largely to oversee player discipline – and invariably to McGuire.

The blame was shifting, though, with players increasingly being picked off by the public. McGuire spoke to the AFL and AFLPA about the issue after a number of Collingwood players were assaulted.

Vice-captain Scott Pendlebury was king hit after leaving a Lakes Entrance hotel, left nursing concussion, broken teeth and cuts to his face only months after Travis Cloke suffered serious facial injuries after being punched while holidaying in Queensland.

'We're getting tired of our blokes getting targeted these days,' McGuire said. 'There's obviously been transgressions in the past by footballers, but we are finding more and more that it's the other way around now.'[24]

Dane Swan was also assaulted after a stranger insulted his partner, but he walked away from the incident and phoned the club straight away.

The club still had to counter the misdemeanours, however, and McGuire did it by paraphrasing one of his favourite sources: Theodore Roosevelt. He told a president's lunch:

> We would rather make a mistake protecting our players than enjoy the sanctity of indifference.
>
> This is a club that cares for the community. It is a club that will never turn its back on the disassociated or its own when they need us most. Far from being humiliated, as the headlines screamed this week, this club stands determined.
>
> We've copped our whack this week and we acknowledge our shortcomings. We acknowledge our failings but there is no effort without error or shortcoming.[25]

Didak organised to meet McGuire and Malthouse separately to plead his case to remain with the Magpies in 2009 before appearing on *The Footy Show* for a very public *mea culpa*. 'One thing I did regret was lying to Eddie when he asked me,' Didak told *The Footy Show*.[26]

McGuire always leaned towards keeping Didak; he was too good a player and clubman to let go. But, just as the club's culture was being questioned, McGuire went after disgraced West Coast Eagles captain Ben Cousins.

Cousins, who was deregistered by the AFL for bringing the game into disrepute with his confessions of drug taking, was looking to resurrect his career away from Perth with Collingwood as his major hope. Cousins met with Malthouse and Walsh, and admitted he would love to play under Malthouse again. But Cousins was unable to complete an initial fitness test due to a hamstring tweak. Even so, Cousins thought Collingwood was a chance until it emerged the club had a private investigator following him in Perth.[27] Cousins' manager Ricky Nixon was warmed by Collingwood's approach, as well as by how McGuire 'sniffed the deal and the benefits to Collingwood but also had a genuine compassion for helping Ben get back on the field, which he still has today'.[28]

But McGuire and Malthouse realised Cousins just wasn't ready and McGuire baulked after viewing a preview of the documentary on his drug addiction and recovery.

By the time Collingwood triumphed in the dual 2010 Grand Finals, post-premiership celebrations looked to be far more controlled than they were in 1990, when Collingwood jagged a flag and partied heartily.

After the 2010 celebratory club dinner at the Convention Centre, players and a select group of Collingwood VIPs moved to Tonic, a nightclub at Crown Casino, where a private room had been organised. Entry was by wristband only.

Some players left for Eve nightclub after that and some progressed to a private residence in South Melbourne, where the dastardly decade reached its obvious conclusion.[29] Premiership player Dayne Beams and emergency player John McCarthy would later be accused, and acquitted, of sexual assault.

The premiership celebrations ended quite abruptly for McGuire. 3AW's Neil Mitchell later revealed the names on his morning show,[30] provoking McGuire into a tirade on his own Triple M program:

> I'll confirm one thing – Neil Mitchell is a self-appointed, self-important windbag.
>
> Collingwood Football Club and the players involved have openly cooperated with Victoria Police in every situation that has been asked of us over the last few days.
>
> There is no hiding. There is no trying to cover up. There is nothing. It has been absolutely transparent. He talks about fairness there. This is the hypocrisy of Neil Mitchell.
>
> He gets on every day. He bangs on how he wants footballers to be treated like everyone else but then he bangs on that, 'No, they're special people' and names two young men who have not been charged or done anything wrong as far as the police are concerned yet. You're damned by your own words, Neil Mitchell.

The Magpie duo would later be cleared of any wrongdoing and another man was accused of rape. However, the damage was done.

Thankfully, disciplinary infractions turned to another area. The AFL has no tolerance for its 'employees' gambling, despite the hypocrisy of the game's revenues being turbo-charged by the gaming sector in the 2010s. The irony is delicious because screens at stadia and at home are full of ads and crosses to odds makers, yet the AFL restricts any players or club officials – even club mascots – from betting on games.

So when Heath Shaw placed a 'stupid' $20 bet at a TAB, he was suspended for fourteen matches, six of them suspended, and fined $20 000. Magpies captain Nick Maxwell was also fined $10 000, half of which was suspended, after his family members placed bets, causing a plunge on Maxwell kicking the first goal in a Round 9 match.

The misdemeanours mounted but they felt relatively minor after McGuire's messy 2000s mopping up after his players. Travis Cloke was booked for driving while on a disqualified licence in 2012, and Dane Swan received a two-week club suspension for arriving to training hung over, with McGuire stating, 'Anyone who thinks they're better than anyone else needs to be pulled into line.'[31]

The infractions kept mounting because the culture of 'boys will be boys' runs deep. But McGuire wasn't just any club president. He was selling the Collingwood brand and story – and often defending it – more virulently than any other club president. He was willing to jump on the grenades when necessary to protect others, but the bad behaviour by players was taking its toll – on the club's reputation, his image and, ultimately, his emotional well-being. Every incident chipped away at his love for the players; yet, inexplicably, even to some within the club, that love keeps regenerating.

CHAPTER 15

THE HANDOVER

Collingwood and McGuire had an odd year in 2003.

The club was coming off an admirable Grand Final loss and hoped to take the next step. Its ambition was writ large in its late-2002 push to recruit Wayne Carey, the seven-time All-Australian player shunned by North Melbourne and the footy world after having an affair with the wife of his vice-captain, Anthony Stevens.

Despite public ostracism, five clubs lined up to draft Carey after he bounced out of his alcohol-fuelled haze. Carey didn't entertain the financially struggling Hawthorn or the salary-cap-stretched Essendon, although Collingwood was a chance. McGuire insisted on going to Carey's Port Melbourne apartment in the anonymity of night, with Malthouse and a club delegation.

He flattered Carey, as Essendon had, telling him, 'The number of times you flogged us was ridiculous.' He also wanted Carey to mentor the young players, in the way Dermott Brereton did during his short stint at Collingwood – 'as long as you get more kicks than Dermie!'

Carey was impressed, and thought the Pies would be contenders that year. However, he also felt he had to leave Melbourne to make a clean break.[1] It was Sydney or Adelaide, and Adelaide won. Carey would come to the Pies as a short-lived assistant coach in 2006.

Another superstar, this one from Hollywood, was typical of the unique mix of on-field power and off-field stresses enveloping McGuire throughout the year. McGuire invited visiting American TV star Rob Lowe into the team circle to sing 'Good Old Collingwood Forever' after a rousing win against St Kilda at the MCG (the actor also heard Malthouse's pre-match speech and sat in the coach's box).[2]

Captain Nathan Buckley was livid. He told McGuire during the week in no uncertain terms, 'This is OUR circle.' McGuire countered by reminding his captain the image went around the world and would be valuable in securing major sponsorship. Buckley thought another image would have been fine. 'Everything in footy is for sale, but we want to own those moments for ourselves,' he said. Buckley wasn't about to compromise.

The following week, actors Tim Robbins and Susan Sarandon (sporting an Anthony Rocca badge) were also invited to the Collingwood rooms post-match. They weren't allowed into the victory circle.

The balance between club and corporate, between McGuire's big-picture imprecision for the club and Buckley's tunnel vision for his team, would remain a sticking point between Buckley and McGuire for some time, despite their closeness – which was genuine despite being played up for laughs on *The Footy Show*, primarily by Sam Newman.

'Why do football clubs exist?' Buckley asked his president before providing the answer: 'To win premierships, not make profit.' The captain and president had many testing discussions in their early years. They would always find a happy medium.

The Hollywood glad-handing wouldn't stop, though. Tom Cruise and Katie Holmes joined McGuire in James Packer's MCG superbox for a Collingwood vs Carlton match in 2009, and Lowe showed he was a genuine Collingwood fan after being introduced to the club by his brother Chad. Packer rang McGuire in 2010 while holidaying in Sardinia with news he'd just bumped into an inquisitive Pies fan who was asking about the team and Eddie: Rob Lowe.[3] Lowe messaged McGuire during Grand Final week later in the year to wish him luck.[4]

But 2003 had its ups and downs – trivial and less so. McGuire's peccadillo for maintaining the same mobile phone number, and being an ever-available president, resulted in a torrent of abusive and threatening phone calls in August, mainly from school children, after the number was widely circulated.

Collingwood became the first club to crack the 40 000-member barrier earlier in the year, and the first sod was turned on the old Olympic Park greyhound track, about to be transformed into Collingwood's new training ground.[5] The club also bought into its own travel agency, a Jetset franchise, which it planned to name Pie in the Sky Travel.[6] More than a decade later, it would still be a thriving concern, selling more Emirates flights than any other agency in the country.

McGuire's public presidency was continually putting out brush fires, such as defending Collingwood supporters who booed Brett Ratten after he was chaired off after his 250th game for Carlton. They were simply booing Carlton, as they had done for 100 years, McGuire said: 'Collingwood supporters will cheer Collingwood and boo the opposition. Be sure of that.'[7]

As the year progressed, McGuire's blood pressure rose, particularly when player Brodie Holland was suspended for two weeks for striking, and McGuire accused broadcaster Ten of hiding mitigating footage.

'They can't put it over me ... there is a code of ethics in journalism and one of them is you're obligated to report the facts fairly and accurately,' he opined. 'That includes omitting elements of a story.'[8]

Football remained the main game, however, and Collingwood played it well in 2003, progressing to a Grand Final rematch with the previous year's foe, Brisbane.

It was a particularly fine Grand Final week for McGuire, who hosted the Brownlow Medal telecast for Nine as his captain and friend Buckley won in a three-way tie with Mark Ricciuto and Adam Goodes, the year after winning the Norm Smith Medal.

But reality struck. Brisbane was one of the great teams of modern football – if not the greatest – and Collingwood would be exposed as not having the same pound for pound individual talent even if it was as good, if not better, in spirit.

McGuire didn't deal with this loss as graciously as he had in 2002. He sensed the moment, for this team, might have passed.

McGuire set upon Geelong president Frank Costa for barracking loudly for the Lions during the grand final; Costa countered that a Brisbane success was good for the national competition, and for all clubs.[9]

McGuire's malcontent surfaced again at the Magpies' annual general meeting after the loss. After confirming Malthouse had agreed to extend his contract for another three seasons, the president set upon his own members, who were furious at what they believed was a botched Grand Final ticket allocation.

'This club has always been the people's club and as long as I'm here – and I've got one more year to go and you can all stand next year if you want – that will be the way that I'll be running the place as president of this football club,' McGuire said.[10]

Yet the club announced a record profit of $2 million for 2003 – some distance from the $1.3 million loss it had recorded in McGuire's first year, 1999 (and a $26 million turnover, up from 1999's $14 million).

Now to get the team right. It was testament to Malthouse's talents that he cajoled this Collingwood playing list to consecutive Grand Finals, but he knew it wouldn't deliver him the premiership.

After that second grand final loss, Malthouse chose to start again, with the board behind him. This strength in unity would be something Malthouse sorely lacked at his next club, Carlton.

It was time to refresh the list and bring rookies in. And it would be tough. McGuire didn't publicly acknowledge until the club's 2005 annual meeting that Collingwood's recruiting was 'useless' in 2002–03.

McGuire's off-field strengths continued to make hay in 2004 as Toyota's premium brand, Lexus, began sponsoring Collingwood's new training ground at Olympic Park as Toyota sponsored *The Footy Show* and Sony signed a $500 000 a year personal endorsement deal for coach Michael Malthouse. Collingwood had to dump his Volvo deal, as well as another club deal with Renault, in order to bring Lexus on board. The Lexus deal to name the $20 million training and administrative facility the Lexus Centre was a massive coup, understood to be worth $16 million for eight years.[11]

McGuire also brought a woman onto the board, replacing former Carlton and United Breweries managing director Nuno D'Aquino. The 36-year-old Sally Capp was a corporate star, opening her own investment bank in the same year her second son was born before moving to the ANZ. McGuire described the former schoolgirl ruckman as the original 'Collingwood six-footer'.[12] McGuire's progressiveness at Collingwood was becoming starker. Such appointments would not have been made by previous presidents.

And his social liberalism might have gone unnoticed in some instances, yet its impact could be profound. How unlikely was it the open mind of Collingwood would give someone the confidence to come out as gay. Yet Molly Meldrum would reveal that McGuire's ease at a Collingwood Football Club president's lunch made him realise his sexuality was no longer something to hide.

McGuire invited Meldrum and his partner, Rui, to lunch at his table and introduced them to his 'VIP guests' as he would anyone else, Meldrum recalled: 'That astonished me because the Collingwood Football Club is ocker, ocker, and that would never happen down there.'[13] But that lunch gave him the confidence to later reveal his homosexuality. If they could cope at a Collingwood pre-game, anyone could cope.

What was happening off-field was the culmination of McGuire's dream to build a sporting behemoth. As Malthouse tried to refresh the list, poor performances dogged the club in 2004. But midway through the year, McGuire realised his grand plan as the club moved into the renovated Olympic Park facility with its ice baths, state of the art gym, altitude room, players' lounge and oval.

It was a key moment in McGuire's revolution – or, as he said 'one of the most significant announcements in the history of our great club, and it heralds a new and exciting beginning for Collingwood'.[14]

Collingwood was leaving its home of 122 years, the newly named McHale Stadium at Victoria Park. The move of home games from Victoria Park was acrimonious among members, which McGuire appeased back in 1999 with his simple question at a members' meeting: 'Put your hand up if you still live in the same house you grew up in.' No hands were raised, and that was his point. You aspire to progress and trading up; a football club should be no different. Victoria Park was its own argument, too. It was no place for a professional sporting organisation.

Collingwood shared the new facility in the old Olympic Pool with the Victorian Institute of Sport, but McGuire remained adamant about who was the key tenant. The state government wasn't particularly thrilled with the VIS anyway. Collingwood had fifty-two-week access to the training ground. It wasn't a bad deal considering the state government and the Melbourne and Olympic Park Trust had co-funded the facility on public land used for the 1956 Olympic Games, which now included a 25-metre, four-lane swimming pool, 80-metre indoor running track, theatrette, players' lounges, function centre and rather expensive café.

'Ed's Shed' was a triumph, even if the new name of the old Olympic park, the Lexus Bob Rose Oval, didn't exactly roll off the tongue[15] – or please some in the Olympic movement or across the road at the Rod Laver Arena.

Left off Swan Street and down Hoddle Street, Victoria Park rotted in what would become an embarrassing fashion. The club left the ground to the Yarra Council, before its disrepair and takeover by squatters and drug addicts. The lack of any future for the site resulted in recriminations between the council and club. The Yarra Council said damages to Victoria Park before the club handed it back to the council amounted to $10.7 million.[16] The spat brewed for years, with Collingwood's desire to build a community centre there shunned by a dysfunctional council. McGuire was the front-man meeting and turning around each councillor, one by one, until Collingwood was 'allowed' to spend $3 million renovating the social club, or Bob Rose Stand, into a major community centre.

McGuire couldn't impact the club's on-field performance, though. The 2004 season was a shocker, with a mere four wins coming into a Round 13 clash with Sydney before McGuire put the season on the line publicly, stating that if Collingwood lost to the Swans, its season could be 'down the toilet'.[17] The team lost by six points.

But McGuire and Malthouse continued to think laterally. They began speaking to Rodney Eade, the former Sydney coach, with a view to employing him in an innovative role as a match-day adviser or high-performance coach.[18]

The club ended the year thirteenth. It was the biggest drop a Malthouse team had suffered in a year, although it was a thoroughly reasonable result given two years of extraordinary zeal and performance. This playing list had run out of puff.

But at West Coast, Malthouse managed two premierships and did not miss the finals in ten years. Consistency would not be Collingwood's *métier*.

Financially, McGuire's club was consistent. He confirmed the club had recorded its fourth successive record profit, $2.07 million, after a $1.08 million surplus in 2001, $1.55 million in 2002 and a little over $2 million in 2003. He and the board were performing – particularly the marketing department.[19]

Ironically, given McGuire's disdain for interstate draft and salary cap concessions, Collingwood's financial clout was partly the result of the interstate giants. Collingwood was the Victorian club of choice for the big interstate teams, bringing audiences, travellers and enough animosity to stoke a potent marketing story.

The books were fine, and McGuire had bedded the club down in glamorous new digs, yet 2005 was looking difficult. The knives were out due to the high profile of the coach, the team and the president who presided.

And McGuire felt the heat, realising Malthouse and the club now couldn't afford the length of rebuilding afforded less experienced coaches and inferior clubs. He was indignant he had to defend his coach even before the season started.

McGuire was serious about the team's rejuvenation, making a serious pitch to Brisbane's triple premiership centre half forward Jonathan Brown, who tormented the Pies in consecutive Grand Finals. McGuire and chief executive Greg Swann flew to Sydney and met with his adviser, Glen Warry, at Otto, a showy restaurant on Sydney's Woolloomooloo wharf. It was pretty anonymous for three men talking AFL, despite the Hollywood numbers used to lure Brown back to Victoria: $6 million over five years bumped up by greater opportunities on *The Footy Show* and elsewhere. Brown remained loyal to Brisbane, but Collingwood's name was top of mind in trade speculation, with Brendan Fevola and Nick Dal Santo also mentioned as possible targets.

Time wouldn't be kind to the club's recruitment. McGuire was pinning his hopes on the players the club drafted as its next generation of names, including Travis Cloke, Ben Davies, Sean Rusling and Chris Egan. Only one of them would stand tall.[20]

Off field, the club was flying, with McGuire confirming a renewed five-year $8 million sponsorship with Emirates Airlines while in a first-class cabin flying 11 000 metres above the ground. It flew the assembled journalists business class to New Zealand to announce the deal. The club even negotiated to play a match in Dubai to kick off the 2006 season,[21] as well as signing a new jumper sponsor, Wizard Home Loans, worth nearly $8 million over five years.

The money wasn't everything, though. McGuire's ambition was broader: he saw the partnership with Wizard, part of GE Money, aligning Collingwood with the global giant General Electric, which would potentially allow Collingwood to broadcast its matches via GE's CNBC Asia sports channels through Asia. McGuire's corporate ambitions knew no limits.

But McGuire wouldn't take the year's capitulation well. The fall on the field came with obvious consequences. He started blaming the umpires, protesting that his forward, Chris Tarrant, was not protected enough – and that was after a win. He said Tarrant was almost unable to 'function as a footballer'. 'It's not a criticism of the umpires, but we just don't understand how he does not get free kicks,' he said.[22]

McGuire's ill temper hit a low in July, when he stormed down from the Nine commentary box after his team's meek capitulation to Essendon to tell his match committee and football staff the loss was 'totally unacceptable'.

'We can't keep serving up that crap. I want you blokes to go away and think about how we can fix it,' he said coldly.

McGuire made it clear to the group comprising senior coach Mick Malthouse, coaching staff Guy McKenna, Gavin Brown,

Brad Gotch and Adrian Fletcher, chief executive Greg Swann, football operations manager Neil Balme and football manager Mark Kleiman that two dismal performances within seven days were 'totally unacceptable to our club'. Malthouse, who was contracted for 2006, was under real pressure for the first time in his relationship with McGuire.[23]

The next day, McGuire called in an external consulting firm to review his football department.[24] The club was on notice because McGuire didn't believe there was enough accountability, with particular attention being paid to the performance of former recruiting manager Noel Judkins, despite McGuire saying there would be no scapegoating.[25]

Ten days later, in what was an intriguing aside, the lead news item out of Channel Ten's sports department – the workplace of another high-profile Malthouse, daughter Christi – claimed the Collingwood coach had offered to stand down from his post after the same match. The club denied it, and history would show Malthouse was not the type to resign. Indeed, the coach began to miss many team meetings as the year progressed, instead walking 'the Tan', the running track around the Royal Botanic Gardens opposite Collingwood's home, with his CEO, Swann, attempting to solidify his position.

Collingwood was in need of review. It was staring down its worst season since its 1999 wooden spoon, with five wins. McGuire wasn't sleeping; it felt like 1999 again and the pressure was intense. McGuire even sat in the coaches' box for one match to provide 'fresh eyes and ears' to review the operations of the box – not, McGuire said, to see whether Malthouse could coach.[26]

McGuire discovered his coaches were working under 'substandard' conditions at the ground with a poorly positioned TV and poor communications.[27] If the president required further ignominy for his club in a timid on-field season, it came from Network Ten, which decided to broadcast a late-season Adelaide–Port Adelaide showdown on Saturday night into Melbourne rather than the match between the two bottom teams, Collingwood and Carlton.[28] Ten's executive producer of football, David Barham, said Collingwood's previous two Friday-night games – against St Kilda and Essendon – were the lowest and fifth-lowest rating Friday night games of the year. 'We're very happy with our decision and we believe football fans in Victoria are interested in watching the best teams play,' Barham said. It was a crushing insult for a club McGuire had made a powerhouse off the field.

McGuire was livid, reminding the AFL just how important Melbourne-based clubs were to the league. 'We have to be very careful with this now, not to laugh at and push aside and underestimate just what football means in this town to the entire competition,' he said. But it had a whiff of 1985 Collingwood about it: you need us more than we need you. In 2005, that wasn't the case. McGuire was hurt and chastened.

And the season petered out. The club put players into surgery early and lost its last eight games. The slide down the ladder would allow the club to pick up Scott Pendlebury and Dale Thomas in the subsequent draft. Years later, in 2012 as Melbourne was placed under the knife for 'tanking', the latter stages of Collingwood's 2005 season would also be mentioned in passing. McGuire said the club had nothing to hide; it just had a dud run with injuries.

The review continued with greater fervour. McGuire said every position in the club's football operation was under the spotlight, excluding that of Malthouse, but the pressure intensified on the coach.

Ultimately, not one Magpies official lost their job in the post-season examination. Rather than looking for scalps, McGuire added to the football staff, bringing on Wayne Carey as a full-time assistant, and former player Alan Richardson as the new player development coach. Stephen Silvagni and Peter Daicos were interviewed for coaching positions but did not join, as the current assistants – Brad Gotch, Gavin Brown, Guy McKenna and Adrian Fletcher – all received new contracts. *The Australian* noted Collingwood now had the most expensive football department in AFL history.[29] Arguably, McGuire's strategy sent a mixed message that was ultimately positive: the club would invest for growth rather than cut for retribution.

One expensive program instituted at the end of 2005 was an innovation that would help player growth. It was a program four years in the making and would be copied across the league – at least by those who could afford it.

Malthouse and new fitness coach David Buttifant first began seriously discussing the benefits of altitude training back in 2001, after Buttifant mentioned how it had aided the 2000 Olympic team. Buttifant put together a presentation for McGuire and America's Cup captain John Bertrand (a Collingwood fan and confidant of the president's) about its benefits, but McGuire initially resisted the method and cost. Buttifant kept working on him until McGuire turned and the club could afford it.

Malthouse loved the idea, and the team left for Flagstaff, Arizona in 2005. McGuire joined the team and participated, not quite appreciating the labour a 15-kilometre walk at high altitude required – and the vast difference between his fitness and that of the footballers.

A walk up Humphreys Peak, the highest point in Arizona, was a timed test and Malthouse knew McGuire and some of his management team would struggle and deliberately pushed them hard. McGuire struggled more than most, and couldn't continue, sitting on a rock as the players pushed on. Malthouse loved it. Buttifant pulled aside his assistant, Mike Dugina, and whispered, 'Get Eddie to the top, I don't care how long it takes.'

The players reached the peak and McGuire was nowhere to be seen. Then Malthouse made it, but still there was no McGuire. Eventually the main group descended, passing a beetroot-faced

McGuire. Malthouse started sledging his president with joy, telling him he had no hope of making it. The competitive McGuire kicked in, responding in kind, telling the coach where to go. McGuire did make the peak, impressing the players. McGuire also realised Malthouse was there to lead the players, not him, and one forty-something soldier could always be sacrificed for the sake of the team.

Collingwood didn't miss the finals for the nine consecutive years during which it undertook altitude training. Its effect, physically or psychologically, couldn't be quantified across a season although the Pies weren't accused of being unfit; the essence of it was that the club thought it made a difference.

The Collingwood annual meetings were becoming a revelation under McGuire. His first was like an evangelical prayer meeting, and the positivity remained as the team played Grand Finals and the books brightened to make them feel more like corporate AGMs. But by 2005, they'd reverted to something like AA meetings replete with rigorous truths and mournful accusations. After this torpid season, McGuire had to defend vigorously, conceding previous recruiting had cruelled the team and Malthouse still had the faith of the players. But did the fans have faith in McGuire and Malthouse?

Others had faith in McGuire's management. Russell Crowe met with him in Sydney to cadge advice on how to transform a sporting team ahead of his and Peter Holmes à Court's imminent privatisation of the South Sydney Rabbitohs NRL club. They would adopt many lessons from McGuire's run for the presidency. And the new year came with new stresses as McGuire took on the onerous CEO role at the Nine Network in Sydney.

Collingwood lost its first match in 2006, and was losing at half-time to Hawthorn in its second match. Inexplicably, rumours later suggested McGuire called for Malthouse's head at half-time, before the Pies eventually won – ahead of four successive wins. It was back to 'Bad Old Collingwood Forever'.

During the vaunted Anzac Day contest against Essendon, Malthouse suffered serious chest pains, further ratcheting up tension at the club. After an emotional win, McGuire was a wreck. A memo he later sent to players and staff seemed to indicate he was ready to hand over the presidency while he was running a TV network in Sydney. At least that's what the players thought. 'You could say I'm agonising over this because it's an agonising thing,' he told *The Age*. 'Because I've loved every minute of it and if there is any possible way I could continue, I would and will. But my major focus now has to be as CEO of the Nine Network.' Board member Gary Pert and former player Craig Kelly's names emerged as possible presidents – and would continue to do so for another nine years.

The on-field year righted many wrongs from 2005, as new kids Pendlebury, Harry O'Brien, Heath Shaw and Thomas were blooded, and a middle generation including Nick Maxwell, Rhyce Shaw, Travis Cloke, Alan Didak and Dane Swan made inroads. The club stormed back to the finals in fifth position – as Malthouse had promised at the 2005 AGM – but finished seventh after losing its first elimination final.

Collingwood was bullish again, with its operating profit soaring past $2 million – its sixth consecutive profit – record attendances and revenue of $44.6 million, three times more than the $14 million turnover of Eddie McGuire's first year as president in 1999.[30] Suddenly, the club was aiming for a $100 million turnover, a figure from a five-year plan for the club by Eugene Arocca, who wanted the club to push into gaming and licensed venues.

It was an astoundingly stable year, considering McGuire's turmoil at Nine after taking the job as its CEO before a major shift in the business as James Packer prepared the network for sale. McGuire was no longer his own boss, able to devote as much energy to his football club, yet Collingwood was now stable enough for some to think the job was done and they could move on. And stable enough to breed a little complacency.

McGuire was flummoxed when chief executive Greg Swann, one of the three musketeers to turn the club around, flew to Sydney to tell him he was leaving the club prior to the 2006 season. The news that he was moving to Carlton was the greatest rub.

McGuire thought something important was bringing Swann to Sydney – perhaps a drugs issue at the club or Swann being recruited to the AFL. The news floored him. Already he sensed he was being hung out to dry at Nine, and Sydney was proving particularly unfriendly. Now his right-hand man at Collingwood was decamping.

Malthouse was particularly stunned. He and Swann were good friends, as were their wives. Swann saw Carlton as being where Collingwood was when he had joined in 1999: it was a challenge that could only improve. McGuire regarded Swann's departure on season's eve as particularly galling, despite outward claims the club didn't miss a beat, with executive Eugene Arocca stepping into the role. There was turmoil, down to the simplest things. For instance, young star Dale Thomas had to find a new home; he'd been lodging with Swann and his family.

'Swanny made a significant contribution to the club, but he is a Carlton person now,' McGuire said. 'I don't comment on Carlton people. I speak for Collingwood.'[31]

The person eventually poached to replace Swann (and the temporary Arocca) caused McGuire more friction. Board member Gary Pert, who had played 233 games for Fitzroy and Collingwood, had been reluctant to even join the board because the media executive thought football was unsophisticated compared to the business world. McGuire's board featuring millionaire business people convinced him otherwise, so he was ripe to be appointed CEO of Collingwood, leaving his role as CEO of the Nine Network's Melbourne operation. McGuire was his boss in both positions and the Australian Shareholders Association expressed its opinion there was an apparent conflict of interest.

'Shareholders in PBL want to see Mr McGuire totally focused on the businesses of PBL and Nine. They don't want to see private interests of Mr McGuire being used to either take away or adding to the company,' ASA spokesman John Curry said.

McGuire replied it wasn't an issue for Nine, and the reality was it was good to get the highly paid Pert out of what had become an almost ceremonial position. Pert also encountered precisely the chaos McGuire was going through at Nine – indeed, the day after Pert signed his contract, the new private equity owners of Nine were confirmed. The job both men had signed up for at Nine was not the job they walked into.

'I don't have a conflict of interest when it comes to Nine and Collingwood. They're both my major interest, if you can have two major interests,' McGuire said. 'I have a deep, abiding love for this football club, as I do for the Nine Network ... I would never do anything to harm either of those institutions.'[32]

It was an issue for the club, though, with the acting CEO, Arocca, expected to get the job. He resigned when he knew he had been overlooked, only to be convinced to stay at the club after all.[33]

Collingwood progressed brilliantly on the field in 2007, but off-field the club was only keeping up appearances. McGuire was back to his chipper best, having eventually unburdened himself of the Nine Network job after its sale and thrown himself back into the Pies in the final months of the season. It was all relative, though; McGuire was not as invested in the club on a day-to-day basis as he had been before he moved to Sydney. The northern capital beat him up, but his management baptism by fire at Nine had taught him something about the value of delegation. And he'd mellowed a little. Post-2007, McGuire was a little more flexible at the club and able to give those he'd hired greater autonomy.

In front of a microphone, it was back to usual Eddie, who decried the absence of any Collingwood players in the AFL's All-Australian squad as 'a disgrace'. The problem was the club itself had only nominated two players for the squad: Tarkyn Lockyer and Travis Cloke.[34]

The club finished sixth, won its first final and then had a stirring semi-final win against third-placed West Coast Eagles in Perth, only losing its preliminary final to the year's dominant team – and eventual premier – Geelong by five points.

As McGuire and his executives watched a replay of the famous victory in a Perth hotel late after the match – the players were already on a $50 000 low-altitude 737 flight chartered by McGuire, on their way back to Melbourne – the mood was exultant. The president knew the team was on its way up and the core of a premiership team was assembling. The retirements of Nathan Buckley, Paul Licuria and James Clement would destabilise the team in the short term, but he had faith in its youngsters.

The cream would be the recruitment of 24-year-old West Coast Eagles premiership captain Chris Judd, who was filling his dance card with prospective Melbourne clubs begging for his services.

The Magpies, led by McGuire, Pert and former Eagles coach Malthouse, went hard with a polished presentation, pushing the club's professionalism and leadership on sports science and conditioning. They were the frontrunners, although they didn't have the low-draft picks the Eagles expected from the trade.[35] In fact, the Pies had been working on Judd since 2005, when the unlikely rumour that the star may entertain returning home found credence. Swann did some subtle groundwork, inviting Judd to be a major guest of sponsor Emirates in its Derby Day horse racing marquee while all his Collingwood players were training in Arizona.[36]

He did it again on Derby Day in 2006, but in 2007 Swann was now with Carlton, which had the lower, tradeable draft picks – and Richard Pratt's company, Visy, to help line the pockets. Judd went to Carlton. As McGuire's Magpies prepared for the 2008 season with some confidence, another key executive flew the coop. Collingwood's second-in-charge, and the architect of the club's pubs strategy, Eugene Arocca, moved to North Melbourne as its chief executive officer. Arocca had been associated with Collingwood for 42 years, and quickly overcame his pariah status at the club, when he took on former president Allan McAlister over the club's finances at the end of 1995, by subsequently helping to recruit Nathan Buckley.

Like Swann with Carlton, Arocca saw a major challenge ahead at North. In a perverse way, it was testament to McGuire's turnaround of the club that two CEOs thought Collingwood was no longer a challenge. He went with McGuire's blessing, although the president told the staunch Pie in his office, 'When you walk out that door there's no coming back.'

Collingwood kept innovating. The club flew Emirates to Dubai for the AFL's Middle Eastern debut in the 2008 pre-season, playing in front of a crowd of 6000 as Adelaide thrashed its fatigued side in the first round of the NAB Cup. 'I wouldn't have imagined a day like this was possible five years ago,' AFL chief Andrew Demetriou said. 'It's been an unbelievable experience.'[37]

Many thought Collingwood's land grab of Olympic Park in 2008 was also unbelievable. The year before, Collingwood began secret negotiations with the state government to take over the entire Olympic Park, kicking out the Victorian Institute of Sport because the club had run out of space.

When the Victorian government wanted to fast-track a new rugby league and soccer stadium near Olympic Park, by bypassing council and public objections, Collingwood was caught in the crossfire.

The plan wanted Collingwood's then training ground, the Edwin Flack Oval, to make way for a new 25 000-seat rugby league and soccer stadium, with Collingwood being pushed further east to a new ground at Gosch's Paddock, turning further public parkland into training fields. That was a walk too far for McGuire. He wanted Athletics Australia moved from its spiritual home, allowing Olympic Park to be transformed into a shared training ground for Collingwood and the nomadic Melbourne Football Club, while Athletics Victoria would move to the windswept Albert Park.

Collingwood would then install its own MCG-sized training ground on the site of the old Olympic Park, next door to the club's Lexus Centre base. At the time, McGuire was sitting on the board of Athletics Australia, the governing body for Athletics Victoria. To be fair, behind the scenes McGuire was lobbying the state government to increase its financial commitment to athletics not for Collingwood's empire building. And Collingwood was happily training on the Gosch's Paddock ground with no intention to move until the new stadium was proposed.

Athletics Victoria CEO Nick Honey was livid. 'There is no doubt we live in a football town in Melbourne, but you've got to question how 50 professional footballers can have the power to move an Olympic venue that has been here for more than 50 years,' he said, flying the flag for his sport, ensuring it wasn't forgotten in the rush to appease Collingwood.

Most athletics officials knew the jig was up. The Olympic and MCG precinct now had a spectator strategy and its hold on the Olympic Park track was a participant strategy (with the stadium costing around $1 million a year to run, largely underwritten by the Melbourne Storm training there).

The Victorian Institute of Sport was another matter. It was stiffed by Brumby and Collingwood and knew it and couldn't do anything about it.

The construction of the new 'rectangle' soccer and rugby stadium next door meant Olympic Park tenants Melbourne Storm and Melbourne Victory would move, and the reason for Athletics Victoria being at the Olympic Park track would contract to just hosting school and occasional professional athletic events, which it had done for decades.

The Bob Jane Stadium being proposed as athletics' new home had been a dysfunctional venue for decades after being converted from the Lakeside Oval, former home to the South Melbourne Swans. And the March–April athletics season would clash with the annual Albert Park Grand Prix race. Meanwhile, Olympic Park – which was built for the 1956 Olympic Games – was witness to one of Australia's finest sporting moments in March 1956, when champion middle-distance runner John Landy stopped mid-race in a mile championship to help fallen rival Ron Clarke, but still won. Clarke, who set world records at the track, was devastated.[38]

Collingwood was quietly cock-a-hoop, knowing it had a trump card in its negotiations with government. It had already brought money and innovation to the Olympic Park site. Athletics only had nostalgia. McGuire also had a clause in a hefty lease that stated Collingwood's 'oval [was to] be easily accessible from the Lexus Centre and that it have the ability to access the oval whenever it requires'.

With the new stadium being built, and squeezing Collingwood's patch of grass further east, and the National Tennis Centre raring to take over the Old Scotch oval next to the tennis centre, there was nowhere else for the Collingwood-supporting Premier John Brumby to go. Brumby confirmed a $50 million plan to shift the VIS and Athletics Victoria to Albert Park and give Collingwood sole access to Olympic Park.[39] It was some retraction, given the $13 million in taxpayer funds that had already been spent redeveloping the old 1956 Olympic Games swimming pool into a facility for the state's best athletes and not just Collingwood footballers.

McGuire argued Collingwood had bent in allowing the new soccer and rugby stadium to be built. Meanwhile, athletics officials remained quiet, fearing retribution, despite the Albert Park plans falling well short of the 'world-class' standard required to compete for international track events.

The move came under scrutiny when a request for documents obtained by *The Age* under freedom of information laws revealed the state government and Collingwood had secret meetings to decide the fate of the venue without the input of Athletics Australia or the VIS. Collingwood privately negotiated with the government in mid-2007 to take control of the Olympic Park precinct, briefing then Sports Minister James Merlino of its desire to take 'over the entire [Lexus Centre] facility' because it had run out of office space.

The VIS and Athletics Victoria did not learn that they were to leave Olympic Park until April of the following year. The documents showed even the AFL was aware of the move before the VIS knew about it.

Today, athletics officials remain mixed about the move to purpose-built facilities at Albert Park. Collingwood continues to pay commercial rent at what is now called the Westpac Centre, but the investment of tens of millions of government money in the infrastructure of what is solely Collingwood's facility is either a masterstroke or merely smart politicking.

Four years later, McGuire and Collingwood would become embroiled in another minor political imbroglio as a Senate Estimates Committee hearing revealed the Melbourne and Olympic Parks Trust – which controls the publicly owned land and had just extended Collingwood's lease at the site by twenty-one years (to 2033) – knew nothing of the club's plans to develop the site further with a community centre. The centre fronting onto the new training oval received a $10 million funding grant from the federal ALP government's Minister for Employment, Bill Shorten, which was later compared to an infamous 'sports rorts' ad hoc decision by former Labor Sports Minister Ros Kelly.

The Trust didn't know of Collingwood's plans until a few days before the announcement, and when federal Sports Minister Kate Lundy was grilled about the decision at the Senate hearing, a government official stepped in to note that 'It was our understanding that Collingwood Football Club would have squared that away with the government in Victoria.'[40]

Somehow communications had broken down, but the result for the club was terrific. It would spend $35 million upgrading the Westpac Centre precinct, with $11 million funded by the Parks Trust under a deal struck with the former Brumby state government, and $10 million in federal funds for the community centre.

Ultimately Olympic Park was demolished in 2010 and a new training oval was in use in 2013. The new community centre adjoining it, including public change rooms, a netball court and training facilities for women, opened in 2015. Athletics lost the home to so many of its memories but benefited from a $50 million Lakeside Oval development.

As Collingwood's training grounds transformed again, the 2008 season didn't pan out as planned on the field. A youthful squad stumbled into eighth position, and had a stirring elimination final win in Adelaide before being bundled out in the semi-final. Consistency is youth's failing, although the standard of the youth was good – so much so that, at the club's annual general meeting after the finals, McGuire committed the club to winning a premiership inside three years. It was part deflection – Collingwood had reported an $8.3 million slash from its accounts in eighteen months due to its failed hotel investments (see Chapter 12) – part expectation and part hope.

Eddie McGuire didn't absolve himself of responsibility. In a sense, the expansion was part of Collingwood's DNA and Arocca's plan was to build self-sufficiency and club connections through a network of hotels and venues across Melbourne. It didn't sound too dissimilar to Allan McAlister's 'Maggieland' concept of a club-centric precinct around Collingwood's old Abbotsford home at Victoria Park in the early 1990s. The debt back then nearly broke the club and hastened McAlister's exit. The pub purchases might have done the same to McGuire if they'd occurred in 1998 and not closer to 2008.

Six months later, McGuire conceded the club would have been in serious financial trouble if a new $3 million sponsorship deal for two years with Aussie Home Loans had not come through. 'Let there be no mistaking whatsoever, that the juggernaut that is Collingwood would have started to grind to a halt unless John Symond and Aussie Home Loans decided to get on board,' he said.[41]

Collingwood could look outwards again. It reclaimed its holy ground, Victoria Park, in a 2009 deal that brought a tear to McGuire's eye after years of undignified personal schmoozing of City of Yarra councillors. The Magpies' VFL side returned to play there, and not at the uncomfortable home of Carlton, Visy Park. It continues to call the ground home.

Leaving Victoria Park remained one of the toughest things McGuire has ever done, breaking ties with the club's spiritual heart. After the bitter stoush with the Yarra City Council over the lease and repairs, a $7.2 million facelift, jointly funded by the federal government and Council (including a couple of million from Collingwood), transformed the ground into a 'community recreations space'. 'John Wren [the architect of Melbourne] would be happy,' McGuire said. 'To walk back in today … is just one of the most wonderful moments in the time that I've been Collingwood president.'[42]

The year brought its joys – a progression to the 2009 Grand Final and a financial bounce from its pub debacle – but also continued stresses, as members complained about the appointment of an unelected board member, aerial skier Alisa Camplin, who replaced Sally Capp.[43] Lexus cut its long-term sponsorship of the club's training home, while McGuire bickered with his board as a potential replacement sponsor was debated.[44]

The Collingwood natives, and the board members, were getting restless. McGuire had been president of Collingwood for a decade. He had righted the ship, but he was yet to deliver the premiership he'd promised.

CHAPTER 16

CHANGES BREWING

There was no way Eddie McGuire would allow Nathan Buckley to leave Collingwood. The club's most decorated player delivered more than the club could ever have hoped when it negotiated with the Brisbane Bears to take the highly prized junior after one year up north.

McGuire and Buckley discussed his transition during his final years as a player. Coaching was top of his wish-list, although McGuire noted that he 'has some areas he needs to learn to make the transition from Buckley the warrior to Buckley the coach'.[1]

As early as 2006, McGuire nodded to his star there would be a coaching apprenticeship available should he be willing. At the time, Mick Malthouse was contracted until the end of 2007 and he made it clear he wished Collingwood to be his last coaching job. Inherent in that statement was his unspoken expectation he would choose the moment he retired from the job – and it was some way off.

Malthouse's demeanour and performance weren't helping his cause at Collingwood. As his young team struggled for consistency through 2006 and 2007, his intemperate behaviour behind the scenes and at press conferences was annoying Collingwood management. McGuire expressed his frustration to Malthouse late in the 2006 season, imploring him to chill out.

At the start of the 2007 season, McGuire and the board extended Malthouse's contract through to the end of 2008. It offered security with a caveat; it wasn't the three- or five-year contract Malthouse believed someone of his stature deserved.

Malthouse knew in 2007 the club had to improve on its seventh placing in 2006 but Collingwood was still in transition. Even Buckley was a reticent captain in 2007, believing it was time for others to step up and shoulder some responsibility during what would be his final year.

The 2007 season didn't see much change in Malthouse's attitude – or, more importantly, in the team's performance. The coach's lament that he was tired of opposing teams lifting for blockbuster games on event days such as the Queen's Birthday surprised McGuire.

'You don't get an easy one at Collingwood; you don't creep up on a club,' McGuire said. 'What people call blockbusters, we call home-and-away games.'

The club pushed upwards through 2007 until a plucky preliminary final loss to eventual premiers, Geelong. While the Cats were the dominant team of the year, Collingwood's performance showed McGuire that Malthouse might have the list to obtain the longed-for premiership.

The stability required for such a push wasn't present in 2008. Malthouse's accomplished coaching staff – including Guy McKenna, Brad Scott and Alan Richardson – were being tipped to take up vacant positions elsewhere, and Buckley retired to the Seven commentary box. The playing list was also undergoing a major transition as Shane Wakelin, Brodie Holland and Ryan Lonie retired after Buckley, James Clement and Paul Licuria.

The culling continued after a wan 2008, a year in which the club finished sixth. The clock was ticking on both coach and president. In the 2009 pre-season, McGuire raised the stakes, telling a briefing of journalists, in front of Malthouse and CEO Gary Pert, the club aimed to win the premiership that year: 'We are not saying we will win it this year but we are aiming to win it this year.'

It was effectively the line in the sand for Malthouse. He was in the last year of his contract and in his tenth year at the club – without a premiership. Anything less than a premiership in 2009 could mean the end of the Malthouse era.

It wouldn't be done on a whim. The spotlight was just as much on McGuire. His autocratic presidency was being questioned by a board that wanted to introduce new processes to ensure greater transparency. Directors would not be kept in the dark after a corporate facilitator was brought in over summer to improve the workings of the board.[2] He too was without a premiership, despite his extended tenure as president. When *The Age*'s Caroline Wilson pointed this out, suggesting that Collingwood should look at succession plans, McGuire denied her newspaper's reporters access to its players after a pre-season victory.[3]

Yet the club was looking up, despite the rumblings. Malthouse began his twenty-sixth year as senior coach by reaching the Grand Final of the pre-season NAB Cup, thereby meeting early expectations that the club would be a premiership chance. Buckley began his second year in the commentary box unaligned with any club, but the Pies' most decorated player stated there was no way he would remain a commentator, and intended to coach in 2010.

The intrigue began with the prospect of Buckley replacing Malthouse countered by the strange notion the duo might work together as current and future coach. McGuire floated the idea publicly in March to see whether it sank or swam.[4] Buckley said he could countenance it and Malthouse held his tongue[5] before McGuire had to backtrack, saying, 'We believe we've got, if not the best, then someone who is as good as anybody in football in Michael Malthouse.'[6]

Collingwood's management privately decreed Malthouse's future would be known by the Queen's Birthday bye weekend, a decision made after a slow 1–3 start to the year. A top four position by Round 11 would keep Malthouse alive. McGuire was intrigued by Malthouse's intentions himself, as the coach began to sing from a different song sheet to the club. He was particularly puzzled when the coach suggested before the annual Anzac Day clash in April that the fixture should not be reserved only for the Magpies.

McGuire spent a bit of time trying to muddy the waters on transition options, noting in April, 'When I first came to Collingwood, I said our philosophy will be "Only the best for Collingwood". If that means my best friend in the world is the second-best bloke for the job, bad luck.'[7]

But McGuire was testy. He knew the club had a difficult choice to make to fulfil his romantic vision of him and his mate Buckley securing Collingwood's 15th premiership cup together.

In May, the wheels started turning. McGuire had breakfast with his coach to talk their way through Collingwood's parlous 3–5 win–loss record and his future. Personally, Malthouse was having an awful year, with one of his close friends, David Buttifant, losing a son and player Harry O'Brien's father taking his life. Malthouse's grandson also required serious surgery. And his team also had a disastrous injury list – at one point, its entire forward line was sidelined – although that was placed in perspective.

McGuire began contract talks via Malthouse's manager and friend, Peter Sidwell, with Sidwell's expectation to renew for two years. McGuire had other plans; he thought Mick was showing signs of blowing up and it was starting to affect his health and his family. Simultaneously, McGuire's board established a coaching sub-committee that would make its recommendation to the board. Future coaching decisions would be made by the entire board, not just by McGuire and his CEO, as had previously been standard practice. But McGuire was the mastermind of a 'handover' deal, believing Malthouse's time had come and this would be a most noble exit. He took the idea to the board, along with other potential outs for the coach as Buckley entered – including giving Malthouse a board position. The board thought such a handover hadn't been done before (it would later emerge a Brisbane Lions plan to do the same changeover between Leigh Matthews and Michael Voss broke down over timing), but believed it was worth investigating.

Instability at other clubs hastened the process. Buckley's name was touted as a potential coach of North Melbourne or Richmond, so McGuire and his board rushed to tell Malthouse's manager of their plans for succession. Malthouse was astounded; he'd been expecting a contract extension and believed the team to be on the verge of great things. Footy manager Geoff Walsh had said as much, noting in a recent meeting with Malthouse and McGuire that a premiership wasn't far away due to the age-profile of its talented list.

He couldn't have it both ways, though. Malthouse had put many offside with his imperious nature and dismissive attitude towards journalists. Collingwood couldn't have a coach who was an enemy of the media. He raised eyebrows when he declared earlier that year he would look to coach elsewhere should Collingwood not retain him. Those eyebrows hit hairlines when he subsequently wrote in his column for *The Australian* clubs such as Geelong and St Kilda should be applauded for sticking with their coaches through good times and bad.

But when the transition was first floated, the club was not travelling well. Earlier in the year, Malthouse knew he was on the nose at the club – although he had his players on side, as always – and he was unlikely to find another head coaching role if he was turfed by the Pies. In a handover, he could survive two more years guaranteed despite his then-precarious position – and that was two more years than he might get elsewhere – and if, as many hoped and expected, the club jagged a premiership or sustained success, chances were the deal might be voided. The unseemly alternative was he would be dumped at the end of 2009.

The contract negotiations, or suggestions of them, were played out, often cryptically, in public. Malthouse expressed his family's – not his – frustration at the ongoing negotiations. Conversely, McGuire was constantly asked about them and always bit, even saying assistant Mark Williams was a viable alternative coach.

In July, McGuire told members the coaching imbroglio would be sorted 'in due course', hinting slyly that a pending decision would 'set the club up for the future'.

Negotiations commenced only when Malthouse agreed to the possibility of the tapered retirement. He could have said no and rolled the dice, but he knew it was his best option. If he said no, Buckley would have entertained other offers and Collingwood would have faced the greatest moral challenge of McGuire's time.

As was McGuire's way, the details would be worked out over time, by others. This was another of McGuire's grand ideas that sounded good, so it would be good.

But Collingwood started winning – six games in a row – and Sidwell started pressuring the club, telling the CEO that Malthouse was now a valuable commodity and could walk. Suddenly a one-year handover was extended to two years.

By July, the deal was firming. McGuire called captain Nick Maxwell to his East Melbourne office, a terrace within a kick of the MCG. McGuire raised the possibility of Buckley serving an apprenticeship under Malthouse. The possibility of Buckley taking over coaching the VFL team was discussed, if primarily to keep the two bulls, Buckley and Malthouse, out of the one paddock. Maxwell was taken aback by the plan and doubted whether the club could keep both coaches.

Afterwards, he met Malthouse at the Lexus Centre and asked his coach how he felt about the plan. 'Well, I don't have much choice,' he replied with a smile of resignation. Collingwood had set the timer on Malthouse.

A week later, Malthouse and Buckley met as Buckley continued to contemplate an offer to coach North Melbourne. Could they work as coach and assistant coach for the 2010 and 2011 seasons? They still didn't know. The details were sparse, with the finer detail about Malthouse's role as director of coaching yet to be considered. Malthouse's immediate concern was clarification of Buckley's role as an assistant and who he would replace. He wasn't happy Buckley would displace one of his team, but as it happened assistant Brad Scott was appointed North Melbourne coach a few weeks later.

The duo met with Pert and Walsh at McGuire's offices on a Saturday morning, hours after Collingwood had clocked its eleventh win of the year. The breakfast meeting reached a breakthrough when Buckley and Malthouse made concessions to each other in a private room. Buckley asked the coach if he wanted him around for the two years; if not, he would go elsewhere in the interim. Conversely, Malthouse told Buckley he would not countenance white-anting.

They emerged together ready to commit, however reluctantly. Malthouse would coach for the 2010–11 seasons and step down, premiership or not, to the role of director of coaching in 2012–14. Buckley would be an assistant coach before assuming the main coaching role from 2012.

In vague terms, Malthouse believed his post-coaching role was outlined as all-encompassing, including recruitment, match-day involvement and as a mentor. He told others he could not possibly sit in the coach's box on match day under Buckley; nevertheless, he asked Buckley at that breakfast whether he wanted him in the box. There was an awkward silence, representing both the unpreparedness of McGuire to clarify the details and Buckley's reticence. He said no, which Malthouse would later use to justify his contention that the deal was effectively stillborn. McGuire would remain unfailingly loyal to Malthouse through the negotiations, yet most within the club felt Malthouse had turned against the club months earlier as soon as he realised his coaching career was done.

McGuire, Sidwell and Malthouse formalised the deal in a series of emails and phone calls during the following two days. It was both a relief and a burden for Malthouse. At the time, he was driving the one and half hours to Ballarat most days to see his mother, stricken with cancer. Malthouse signed the contract in an 'anything can happen in two years' moment. The next day, Buckley told North he was heading to Collingwood.

On 28 July, McGuire held a press conference with a smiling Buckley and reticent Malthouse announcing the board had voted unanimously to keep its coach until the end of 2011 and appoint him director of coaching after that. McGuire had got his men.

Not everyone at Collingwood was happy with the deal. Essentially, it would be throwing Malthouse a massive annuity for a few years while doing not much under Buckley. The deal would leave Malthouse second to Collingwood legend Jock McHale in AFL history as coaching the most matches, and he had two and a bit years to secure his third premiership.[8]

The players were scared of Buckley's potential as a coach. Most had played with him and were intimidated by his hard, direct manner and intensity on the track. For the remainder of 2009, they played for Mick, reaching a preliminary final in a year St Kilda and premiers Geelong were a step ahead of the rest of the competition.

That was the first year of McGuire's three-year window to win the club's first premiership since 1990.

The club was bolstered in 2010 by the addition of former Swan Darren Jolly and ex-Saint Luke Ball as Malthouse stacked the playing list for the here and now. There was no point in him planning for a future. Off field, McGuire managed to extend the club's sponsorship with Emirates for another five years as well as secure a five-year naming rights deal with Westpac for its training facility. Board member Alex Waislitz committed to a second donation to the club of $5 million across five years.

But McGuire's script was being upset by Malthouse. As soon as Malthouse had the expiry date placed on his senior coaching career by Collingwood, he agitated internally. At first he told *The Footy Show* he would contemplate coaching elsewhere after the 2011 season. McGuire responded hard and fast, threatening legal action if the coach broke his five-year contract.[9]

Sidwell back-tracked, saying in July, 'It is Michael's intention, absolutely, to honour his contractual responsibilities. He has absolutely no intentions of coaching anywhere else. He's got a five-year, unequivocal contract – and it has no variations should Michael, or when Michael more particularly, is successful this year or next year in winning a premiership.'

But Sidwell and Malthouse thought his stocks were rising as Collingwood rose; effectively, he would see out his two years as coach and then all bets were off. McGuire's loyalty, and the romanticism of keeping a club legend on side, was being abused.

When Malthouse was fined for calling St Kilda player Stephen Milne a 'fucking rapist' during a quarter-time break in a fiery match, McGuire and his Collingwood management knew they'd made the right decision in calling time on Malthouse. He'd denied speaking to Milne in his post-match press conference but later apologised. McGuire knew his coach was cooked and hurting the Collingwood brand, yet the president was all but alone at the club in defending him. Those below McGuire questioned his loyalty to Malthouse, given his bullying and the lack of respect the coach showed within the club. Malthouse was creating two clubs: the team versus the administration. And among the team, even his assistant coaches were defiant. Assistant Guy McKenna pointedly praised Malthouse as Collingwood entered the finals series top of the ladder, saying his style taught him that 'you can't have a team of Nathan Buckleys'.[10]

And Malthouse himself was beginning to belittle Buckley within the club. The issue remained front of mind and a challenge for the players. They had to work on focusing on the present and what they could control rather than the imminent loss of their coach and the fear of Buckley.

Ironically, the expiry date changed Malthouse's coaching strategy too. It lit a rocket under him and he made tough decisions in early 2010 that he would not have made with the luxury of a longer-term outlook. Quietly, he said the club could win the 2010 premiership but it would do so without loyal servants including Shane O'Bree, Tarkyn Lockyer, Leon Davis, Paul Medhurst and Josh Fraser in the side – a notion some in the playing group thought absurd. Malthouse also intensified the team's defensive pressure and methods to counter Geelong and St Kilda, including a revolutionary increase in the use of the interchange bench.

It worked. Collingwood destroyed Geelong in a preliminary final to book its first grand final appearance in seven years. McGuire was relatively humble and restrained in Grand Final week, privately telling friends that a Collingwood victory would mean 'I can finally get on with the rest of my life'.

That would be postponed for a week after a pulsating Grand Final that hinged, ultimately, on the bounce of a Lenny Hayes' kick, jerking to the right and through for a point to level the scores rather than into the hands of a St Kilda player, Milne.

In the moments after the game, there was disbelief at the drawn result. As the Norm Smith Medal was being presented – to Hayes – Malthouse, Geoff Walsh, captain Nick Maxwell, Eddie and David Buttifant gathered to talk through the hours and days ahead of the Grand Final replay. CEO Gary Pert was dealing with a sewage explosion that swamped their rooms, meaning the Pies had to stay on the ground before Pert could find another change room at the MCG.

Maxwell was gutted and said he didn't want his players to attend the post-match function at Crown. McGuire pointed out that after the last Grand Final draw in 1977, North Melbourne did attend the function and Collingwood didn't, which meant North worked through the disappointment of the draw and subsequently won the replay. Pert argued for the function to go ahead, primarily because he couldn't get phone coverage at a chaotic MCG to actually cancel the function if required.

When the players finally entered their new change room, they were drained and disorientated. They were in no state to make a rational decision about whether to attend the function and see their families and friends, or go straight home. Malthouse agreed they should attend but the decision was left to the players – none of whom spoke up strongly either way because they were still in shock. Malthouse said, 'If no one has a strong view, let's go.'

The club didn't know whether it was commiserating or celebrating as it assembled at Crown, until McGuire stepped onto the stage and said 'What great news, we're in the Grand Final next week!' The mood in the room lifted immediately. The drawn Grand Final was no longer an opportunity lost; the replay was an opportunity to be taken.

McGuire's speech and attitude eased the players' family and friends, who no longer felt they were tip-toeing around fragile players, and it steeled the players. The night became a positive for the team as everyone looked forward, not back. Even Malthouse complimented McGuire's motivational, graceful speech in which he noted this was only half-time in the Grand Final and the president and the club had every faith in the players.

The next morning, the players were still a little sore and jaded in their recovery. On Monday, Maxwell came to the club to inform McGuire and the Collingwood executive that, after chatting to his players, he just wanted to tell them: 'We will win this one. I've never been so certain of anything in my life.'

On Saturday, 2 October 2010, the players delivered the cherished premiership. McGuire watched the game with his family. Carla began crying as Chris Dawes kicked the first goal of the last quarter to give the Pies an unassailable 47-point lead. Eddie began crying two minutes later when Dale Thomas added another goal. He reached his arm around his sons to squeeze his wife. 'That was the acceptance that we could be happy now,' Carla McGuire said.[11]

McGuire's childhood hero Peter McKenna, the man who ensured Eddie McGuire would barrack for Collingwood and not Essendon, presented the Premiership Cup to Mick Malthouse and Nick Maxwell.

The aftermath of the premiership was joyous, and it sealed Malthouse's fate. His churlish behaviour alienated many Collingwood faithful and ensured the final year of his coaching career at Collingwood would be difficult.

In his post-match acceptance speech, he acknowledged the vanquished opponent, St Kilda, because it was, he said, convention to do so. Later, at the celebratory function, Malthouse further ingratiated himself by lauding his players and every one of his staff, quipping, 'I can say this now because there is only one year to go I think, Ed.' Among all his thank yous, that was Malthouse's only mention of McGuire – the man who brought him to Collingwood, allowed him to spend more on his football department than any other coach in the league and was his sole and final protector at the club when all others dropped off.

In his final year, critics lined up to express their doubts Malthouse would move aside to become Collingwood's director of coaching, or even want to have Buckley around in 2011. Former coaches Leigh Matthews, Malcolm Blight and Paul Roos, who handed over the Swans to his assistant John Longmire, questioned Malthouse's commitment to the deal as the prospect of breaking Jock McHale's coaching games record loomed.

McGuire continued to meet the coach to establish Malthouse's post-2011 duties, but the details were never quite clarified. Meanwhile, Buckley made it clear he would change the game plan.

Then Malthouse told *The Footy Show* there was a slight chance he might leave the club the following year. He wanted to clarify that Buckley would be coach in 2012, but he couldn't help himself opening the door to a stint elsewhere.

'I cannot turn the passion off like a tap. It will always be there,' he said. Buckley, McGuire and several members of the board were furious.

The fallout was horrendous and Malthouse, as would become ritual for the year, was criticised mercilessly. Furthermore, Malthouse said his manager, Sidwell, had fielded offers from rival clubs – although the reality was that only one, Carlton, was serious.

Simultaneously, Pert and Buckley were having quiet meetings about the future, and Malthouse wasn't happy when he saw new office equipment being delivered to the coaching offices. The coach worked on his power base – the players. They responded as he rejected all the enticements being suggested to keep him as director of coaching – overseas scouting trips, recruiting influence and, insultingly, the lesser match-day speeches to coterie groups.

As rumours began circling mid-season that Malthouse would coach elsewhere in 2012, Alan Didak knocked on Malthouse's door to tell him several senior players wanted to sign a petition to have him reinstated as senior coach in 2012. It wasn't the consensus among players, with a couple suggesting the coaching appointment was a matter for the board, not the players. Nevertheless, Didak had most players behind him and he told his coach the players wanted to approach the board with their proposal. Malthouse told him it was futile. It remains unclear whether he said so because he was readying to move to Carlton.

In August the *Herald Sun*'s Mike Sheahan wrote, 'Michael Malthouse won't be at the club next year – in any capacity.'[12]

McGuire played it straight, saying the deal would stand and inciting his members to bind as the football world tried to destabilise the club before the finals. 'It is us against the world,' he told members. The truth was, at that point, it was more Collingwood against Malthouse.

Malthouse chose a moment after Collingwood's twelfth straight victory in Round 21 to tell McGuire he would retire after the current season. Malthouse told him his new job was muddled and, while he accepted he was handing over 'his' team and team selection and game strategy, he felt that in order to be an effective director of coaching, mentoring coaches and teaching, he needed to be involved on match day. He was not happy with what appeared to be a glorified promotional role.

McGuire was sanguine; he'd expected it but didn't accept it. He asked the coach to sleep on it. He took at face value Malthouse's contention that he wouldn't coach elsewhere because he couldn't coach against 'my boys'.

Malthouse then asked a senior player how the players would react if he told them he was leaving. He was told it would motivate them, perhaps, but it was better to save it until after the finals.

The players rallied and finished the year top of the ladder, winning two tight finals to qualify for the Grand Final against Geelong. Malthouse confirmed his retirement decision to McGuire before the preliminary final against Hawthorn. He cried visibly after the tight victory, knowing it had secured him a chance at two premierships in his final two years at the club.

Before the Grand Final game, Malthouse was asked whether he thought the game would be his last game as a coach. 'Yes, I do,' he told Channel 7. Forever? 'Yep.' He didn't guarantee that he would be at the Westpac Centre in 2012.

McGuire continued the charm offensive, comparing Malthouse's influence on the club to Jock McHale's and saying his contribution would resonate for years:

> I think Jock McHale set the scene for Collingwood in the early part of last century, and I think there is no doubt Mick Malthouse has been a person who has rebuilt the football culture at Collingwood.
>
> There is no doubt Mick Malthouse's influence on this football club is absolutely profound.[13]

The lead-up to the Grand Final was unsettled when the coach discovered Rodney Eade had been hired to accompany Buckley into the coach's box in 2012, a role not offered to Malthouse. And the Grand Final was horrendous as a tight match was turned Geelong's way in the space of a quarter.

After the debilitating Grand Final loss, Malthouse spoke to the players, board, staff and volunteers:

> I didn't want to make this about me but I'm not coming back, boys. I'll leave it to some great people in this football club, they'll take you forward … I know deep down we'll be hurting like hell right now and tomorrow morning, but boys you've made this football club from sixteenth, broke and shithouse and you've converted it into a powerhouse. Thank you so very much.

The next day, he said goodbye to Collingwood fans at the wake at Gosch's Paddock. He was asked to clean out his office the same day.

When many at the club wanted Malthouse gone and Buckley secured in 2009, McGuire lobbied to allow the coach the two years to deliver on the report suggesting the Magpies would be firmly in premiership contention for that period. After the game, McGuire noted his admiration for the way Geelong handled its coaching transition after Mark Thompson departed and Chris Scott came on board, saying they got the succession plan 'we wanted without all the bullshit'.

The bloodletting and legacy building began immediately.

McGuire said Malthouse was leaving because 'He's hit the wall mentally, emotionally. He gave everything – there's no more.' Malthouse was incensed.

Then McGuire told his Triple M radio audience in the Grand Final aftermath that Malthouse had approached him in 2009 to tell him he was struggling and doubted he could continue. It had been a year of great personal stress and McGuire said Sidwell suggested he could only do two more years. Malthouse denied that claim, but conceded he and Buckley only had a 'very good working relationship'; they had not been friends. That was no secret to those who'd seen Malthouse belittle or embarrass Buckley in front of staff or players that year.

McGuire negotiated the exit agreement with Sidwell and began the public bridge-building, saying, 'His contribution to Collingwood Football Club is immeasurable. He and [wife] Nanette will always be received at Collingwood as heroes of the club. We love him.'

It was a measure of McGuire's unnatural loyalty. Others at the club wouldn't be so generous. The agreement included a commitment that Malthouse not coach anywhere else in 2012. He didn't, although he spent the year commentating for Seven and 3AW, batting away questions about his intentions with a repeated 'never say never'.

Mick Malthouse signed a three-year deal to coach Carlton in September 2012. After limp on-field performances and an abrasive relationship with an inexperienced board, Malthouse was sacked by Carlton early in 2015, two weeks after breaking Jock McHale's games record as a VFL/AFL coach. Ironically, Malthouse's fate was determined by a new Carlton board that lacked the governance and strength of Collingwood's.

Despite the ups and downs of his Collingwood presidency, Eddie McGuire's innate optimism and love of the Magpies sees his enthusiasm for the job undiminished – just like during his time at Nine, he was looking to open up new opportunities and forge ahead.

CHAPTER 17

JUMPING ON A GRENADE

Eddie McGuire became chief executive of the Nine Network in February 2006.

By every standard, it was a shock. American television executives laughed at their Australian counterparts. 'A game show host running one of your TV networks? You've got to be kidding!' A Nine executive retorted with a well-worn, 'You're the ones who elected an actor as President.'

In fact, the appointment wasn't a shock. As early as 1999, a profile of McGuire in *The Australian* speculated, 'Given his business acumen and friendship with James Packer, will he become chief executive of Nine?' It also speculated he might also 'head the Australian Football League? Or, given his political nous, and his election as the Republican movement's lead Victorian delegate to last year's Constitutional Convention, will he be prime minister?'

Football writers have since argued the Collingwood President *does* run the AFL as the most vocal president; and politics still beckons. But in 1999, *The Footy Show* host was asked whether he might end up running the Nine Network.

'That's something down the track,' he said. 'In the meantime I think I can do a lot with my company [McGuire Media].'[1] And the prime ministership? Well, he'd outlined his plans for that back at school.

The first real inkling McGuire might move into Nine management emerged in 2003, when Eddie was snapped by Sydney's paparazzi after a three-hour breakfast with Nine supremo Kerry Packer. McGuire was having breakfast with the media czar at son Jamie's Bondi Beach compound (with Carla) and denied '100 per cent' any inference he was taking a management position. Packer Snr was very keen to learn more about the man who had become his network's highest earner, and he was taking a shine to him. According to McGuire, he and Packer 'actually have a fair bit in common' and 'we're good mates'.[2]

Others weren't so sure about them having much in common. A number of his business peers believe McGuire possesses the enthusiasm and characteristics of an entrepreneur, which in themselves are valuable. Invariably, though, the traits of an entrepreneur do not mesh with the rigours of management.

Somehow, amid all the hubbub surrounding McGuire's very public football and TV lives, rumours about his Nine ascension persisted. In 2005, gossip abounded he would move to a managing director's role at GTV-9 Melbourne. Ironically, considering the scorn later heaped upon him when he actually took the management job, commentators – including Crikey founder Stephen Mayne – observed McGuire's extensive network and his close relationship with the Packers, as well as his love of the cut and thrust of the TV business, put him in a good position to do the job.[3]

Nine was a crumbling empire at the time. It remained the top-rating network but the television sector was changing, frightened rather than emboldened by the advent of the internet and the sharp exodus of advertising as marketers were dazzled by the shiny new thing. And Australian television had its own shiny new thing. The Seven Network had emerged from years of incompetence as not only a viable competitor but an aggressive adversary, charging at the market leader, Nine.

Internal management schisms at Nine during Kerry Packer's last year before his death on Boxing Day 2005 destabilised a company that son James saw, prophetically, as an asset of limited growth, as opposed to the emotional asset it had been for his father and his grandfather, Sir Frank Packer.

The mid-2000s malaise of Nine in Kerry's dying days and afterwards remains a divisive issue, with many Nine staffers still contending it was a mess of its own making rather than a consequence of a structural reshaping of the sector. Certainly a favoured son of the Packers, David Gyngell, resigned in a huff in May 2005, citing in his resignation letter 'the increasingly unhelpful and multi-layered management systems developing between Nine and PBL'.

McGuire's appointment as the next Nine Network CEO was a fait accompli. Yet he didn't apply for the job; he was quite content trying to build his own production business. He was tapped on the shoulder by James Packer, who genuinely believed McGuire's salesmanship and ability to pull together different ideas and corporate networks would be advantageous.

Packer was already thinking television was compromised and the media future in his portfolio would be focused on his digital platform, ninemsn. Television was becoming the runt of the litter, but Packer sold a plan to McGuire to rejuvenate Nine.

Nevertheless, in early 2006 recruitment agency Egon Zehnder was contracted to put forward a list of suitable candidates, a task another executive agency, Talent2, had been given the year before. In hindsight, it merely suggested transparency as Kerry had signed off on McGuire's appointment prior to his death.[4] The Packer father and son knew TV network bosses were rare and they'd seen in McGuire's dealings with advertisers and staff someone with the ability to step into the role.

The candidates duly lined up or were approached, including Austar chief John Porter, Premier Media Group's (Fox Sports) David Malone – Gyngell told James Packer Malone would be a great choice – and Foxtel chief Kim Williams, who said no to the job three years earlier, as well as some less obvious candidates including expats News Corporation's Richard Freudenstein and Tom Mockridge.

It seemed Nine was wasting everyone's time, especially when both the public broadcaster the ABC and New Zealand broadcaster TVNZ were also looking for CEOs at the time (Mark Scott would be named ABC managing director).

McGuire got his first hint during the 'selection process' that the process wasn't kosher and he was about to lead a particularly unstable media organisation. As he arrived for his 'interview' in recruitment agency Egon Zehnder's Sydney CBD office, *The Australian*'s media reporter John Lehmann was waiting for him in the foyer.

The 'recruitment' of the network's biggest star into the CEO role was playing out in the daily press. PBL's management were masters of quiet leaks to preferred business journalists, and McGuire's candidacy was leaked and gained major traction. If Packer and PBL CEO John Alexander wanted to test the financial market, the market acquiesced – at least publicly.

As one media market analyst said, 'There's deep-seated cynicism about it but no one's going to stick their head up.'[5] Another stated the company needed a 'personable chap with business acumen' like McGuire running the network because 'Alexander is a print man'.[6]

McGuire had his doubts. He sought counsel and received support from prominent Melburnians, including Fairfax chairman Ron Walker, transport magnate Lindsay Fox, AFL chief Andrew Demetriou and Victorian Premier Steve Bracks. They agreed it was the right thing for him to do at this point in his life.

Whether it was confidence or hubris, McGuire believed he could do something to right the organisation after its listing under the unstable temporary stewardship of returned CEO Sam Chisholm. Friends believed the romance of the ascension from running stats for his brother's newspaper as a teen to running Australia's dominant Australian television network entranced him.

On a personal level, McGuire also didn't shirk a challenge. He reasoned his two sons were now of a self-conscious age, and perhaps they would benefit from not having to deal with the consequences of their father being a constant presence and target on TV screens.

Weeks before the announcement, McGuire was having beers with friends and acting vague about the job when his mates proffered their opinions. A few beers bred some valour, and McGuire started opining about what he'd do to fix Nine. His friends knew, and couldn't quite believe, the rumours were true. He actually had the job to run the Nine Network, not just host some of its shows.

For McGuire, the job appeared to be a way of focusing all the skills he'd collected along the way, including his ability to make shows and stewardship of Collingwood. It would combine his knowledge of the creative side of the business with the financial aspects, bridging the murky divide between business and creative. There aren't many who have a foot in each camp. And it was the biggest gig in TV.

Within PBL, filtering down from James Packer, there was a belief Eddie McGuire's skill set and salesmanship were compelling. He was a self-made man, largely under Nine's bosom, with his own production company and fingers in many pies, including the biggest Pies in the land: Collingwood.

Internal corporate doubts were assuaged a little by the notion McGuire's friend and lawyer, Jeffrey Browne, would 'backfill' on harder-nosed business negotiations and details. Despite these perceptions of experience, McGuire and Browne didn't have the actual experience of running a network. But, as one current CEO noted, 'It's hard to find people who run television businesses.'

Despite Nine's need for stability and strength in its candidate, the job was offered on Nine's terms. The process was being stage-managed to allow Sam Chisholm to leave as 'the doyen' of Australian TV. Chisholm worked his way up to run a dominant Nine before leaving to establish pay TV in the United Kingdom for Rupert Murdoch, and returned (triumphant at first) to fix up Nine's mess.

McGuire promised to be a contrast to the despotic return reign of Chisholm – too improbable a contrast for some. A long-term Nine executive, who is still there, recalls laughing when Chisholm told them McGuire would be their next CEO. For a moment, he dismissed it as another little explosion of Chisholm madness. Then it sank in. It wasn't Chisholm's madness.

The Broadmeadows boy is a charming man who looks you in the eye as he firmly shakes your hand and asks you how your AFL team (which he remembers) is going. That might be simple Melbourne etiquette but, combined with his old-school news-breaking instincts, a new millennium ego and marketing expertise, it made him the network's biggest star. If his major failing was his omnipresence on Nine's screens; a stint in the CEO's chair could fix that.

On 9 February 2006, McGuire was confirmed as the new CEO of the Nine Network. His *Footy Show* star, Sam Newman, dropped by McGuire's Toorak mansion with two bottles of Grange Hermitage. There was good reason to celebrate: McGuire had reached the pinnacle of his profession.

Days later, McGuire sat with Newman and Marmalade in his Melbourne office and recalled being told when he became president of Collingwood that it needed to be run more like a business. He did that. He added, now he's at Nine he felt that business had to be run more like a footy club: 'a mean, lean, fighting machine that turns a profit.'

On his first day in Sydney, McGuire placed his own immediate stamp on the place. He entered Nine's Willoughby head office with a smile and shook everybody's hand as he introduced himself, beginning with the receptionists in the Nine lobby. That alone did more to pick up morale at Nine than any other recent management initiative. As did his visit to meet the *Today* show staff at 5.30 a.m. They hadn't seen an executive that early ever, but for the former breakfast radio host it was nothing. Egalitarian McGuire also decided immediately not to take temporary CEO Sam Chisholm's spacious office.

McGuire sat in Nine's Willoughby boardroom with PBL senior executives John Alexander and Chris Anderson and did what he does best: sold the story to a line of journalists queued on the telephone. Then it was off to morning tea with influential 2GB breakfast host Alan Jones.

McGuire began with enthusiasm, pointing out he had been 'hired for what I bring to the table, not what I don't bring to the table'. He wanted Nine to be the 'epicentre of young people and bright ideas', and he dismissed his weakness, noting 'it's not like I'm going to be the chief accountant here at Nine'.[7] And he knew what everyone was thinking: 'I know I've been installed as the boss of Channel Nine, not as a puppet.'[8]

The spruik of youth was a good one for Nine. The network's last big recruit, Bert Newton, was past retirement age, but within its management ranks Nine was assembling a younger team below McGuire, including Andrew Blackwell as head of entertainment, Steve Crawley as head of sport, Mark Llewellyn as director of news and current affairs, programmer Michael Healy and sales director Paul Waldren. The youth versus experience line against Seven's warhorses – former Nine managers David Leckie, Peter Meakin and John Stephens – was worth a go.

The counter-argument was McGuire's appointment took some of the magic from television. Australian TV CEOs were largely faceless – if boisterous – men until they arrived at the CEO position. Television management was all a bit Wizard of Oz-ish, which suited TV fine; the people on screen were the stars. By his own admission, McGuire rose from the factory floor, and now viewers believed anyone could run a TV station. Television wasn't so special – it looked like Nine's new reality show for a CEO.

But Nine wasn't quite so sure of itself. Media fragmentation in the advertising sector spooked the TV industry. Packer was prescient; whereas once Nine's competitors were Seven and Ten, now it was the internet and anything digital that moved. The ascendancy internet arm ninemsn had over PBL's TV and magazine arms was scaring the troops.

McGuire also appreciated that 2006 was the first time television was under pressure as the 'go-to medium'. Television was beginning to look a little dowdy next to the internet, and had changed from being a growth business to a challenged one – if not quite yet one on the slide. Unfortunately, PBL became overly excited about the possibilities of the internet, to the detriment of its core TV network.

Nine went full bore attempting to generate programming through user-generated means on ninemsn and seduce a new, cheaper generation of content providers. In this thinking, Nine went too hard too early. Even now, amidst the proliferation of user-generated media, little of it has made a legitimate cross-over to the mainstream.

And Nine's modus operandi as a broadcaster was changing. Packer remained envious of Ten's low-cost model, which was highly profitable and was chasing a distinctly younger sixteen to thirty-nine-years demographic. While Kerry had been hell-bent on being number one, no matter what the cost (and Chisholm also spent, sometimes irrationally, on his return), James was just as hell-bent on being the most profitable network, no matter what the position.

They were both right to a degree. Nine's News and Current Affairs department remained a high-cost independent state within Nine, and there were a number of outrageously expensive talent contracts not delivering results commensurate with their dollars.

Alexander and Anderson already had a further list of redundancies prepared, and the suggestion that they be implemented before McGuire was appointed was kyboshed. They believed it would send a stronger message to the market if their new boy McGuire was seen to be the sturdy, uncompromising hand at the tiller who could instigate a hard decision early.

McGuire took over as CEO during Nine's broadcast of the Melbourne Commonwealth Games, which he would have hosted. He went from being host to CEO in a day. He stepped into a reality show of someone else's making: *Survivor Willoughby*.

The appointment was greeted at Seven with mirth, relief and only a momentary touch of concern. They couldn't believe the network's key on-air star would be positioned in a manner that could only damage his profile – and audience testing ultimately showed McGuire's Q Score (a widely-used barometer of viewer likeability and awareness) fell during his tenure.

Furthermore, they were relieved Nine was again pulling focus at a time when the blowtorch should have been on Seven. It lost a 2005 ratings year it should have won, yet bludgeoned its way to secure a five percentage point ad rate increase for 2006. In the first two months of 2006, its share of advertising revenue finally drew level with Nine's at 35 per cent,[9] yet it still wasn't number one in the ratings. Seven had to deliver. If it didn't, well now the media had Eddie McGuire to kick around instead. 'Eddie McGuire was the best thing to happen to my career,' one Seven executive said laughingly.

Hindsight shows the appointment made some sense. Few realised Packer and Alexander were preparing the Nine Network for sale after private equity firms began circling Nine six months after Kerry's death.[10] The duo knew they required a likeable patsy to take the blows and sell the Nine story to staff, viewers and the market during a bruising process.

But first McGuire had to bring some stability and verve to Nine. He arrived as the official ratings year began, so he would be judged by a schedule devised by those before him. And it wasn't a great start, with the Seven Network winning prime time over summer, holding 36.8 per cent of the audience to Nine's 36.5 per cent. And then Seven launched a couple of US hits off the back of Lleyton Hewitt's march to the final of the Australian Open: *Desperate Housewives*, *Lost* and *Prison Break*. Seven couldn't have hoped for more.

During McGuire's first two weeks, it also became apparent he had a big slump in the schedule – Nine was haemorrhaging in the two-hour block from 5.30 p.m. to 7.30 p.m., with *Bert Newton's Family Feud*, *Nine News*, *A Current Affair* and *Temptation* all being beaten.

While the numbers turned the wrong way, morale at Nine lifted. Staff surmised McGuire's entrance would halt the cost-cutting that occurred under the reign of outgoing chief executive Chisholm, and McGuire was well liked internally. He had an unnatural knack for remembering names, which was especially potent in winning over studio crew.

Long-time Sydney sports presenter Ken Sutcliffe was typical of staff, later writing that, 'Eyebrows were raised at the appointment but there was hope it would be okay. Eddie was a bloke with confidence and flair, and Sam wasn't going to be here for too long.'[11]

Strong leadership was a legacy of Nine through the ages from Packer down to Chisholm and David Leckie (now at Seven). That leadership had been eroded, as had the management layer below it. Cuts meant distribution deals were being lost, vision was lacking and local content was diminishing. Heads of the Entertainment, Marketing, Communications and Drama Departments had all departed recently, and the new head of Drama, Sandra Levy, was already contemplating packing her bags. McGuire arrived at Willoughby to empty offices on a third floor usually teeming with staff. And those who were left were still shaking after the damage done. Programmer Michael Healy was a wreck after being tormented by Chisholm. McGuire thought he would need to add psychiatry to his list of management skills.

The public spin was about cost-cutting but PBL's Park Street offices were progressively filled with highly paid executives brought in to cut costs, including Ian Law, Ian Audsley, Pat O'Sullivan and Chris Anderson. Costs were squeezed at Willoughby and loaded up at Park Street. Nine was paddling madly to keep it together.

The intensity of the publicity in Sydney surprised McGuire. He was used to playing Melbourne media off against each other or taking the plaudits (*The Age* wrote that 'quite literally, Melbourne will not be the same without him'); now he had to introduce himself anew to the media, and Nine – as it always was while owned by a Packer – was a disproportionately sexy story for Sydney media. That was even more so now it was being run by an interloper from Melbourne.

In the first weekend of the new job, he was back at Collingwood watching an intra-club game, although the reality of the new job was staring him in the face. Four days later, he would miss his first Collingwood board meeting since becoming president, saying ahead of his phone hook-up:

> Don't worry, I'll be chairing it from up there. [If] I'm not contributing the way I want to, then I'll jump out straight away. When the day comes that I think somebody else is in the position to do a better job at Collingwood there will be no problem. The thing that is probably the most gratifying for me in taking up this [new] position is the thing that I've had to least worry about was Collingwood, because the place is set up and going beautifully.[12]

When McGuire moved to Sydney, he expected Nine Sydney to be the same, within reason, as Nine Melbourne. They couldn't have been farther apart. Melbourne's Bendigo Street headquarters remained largely immune to the brutalisation occurring at Willoughby. And Nine Sydney was a backwards place, having had little capital expenditure in recent years. Bendigo Street, with its eons of Nine history and shows such as *In Melbourne Tonight*, *The Don Lane Show*, *Hey! Hey! It's Saturday!* and *The Sullivans*, remained a family, of sorts. Willoughby was more like a wake. Even worse, Nine Sydney's opposite numbers at Seven were all old Nine people who wanted to destroy the place.

Nine had just lost the AFL broadcast deal – despite Kerry Packer inflating the price paid by Seven and Ten in his final bullish move before his death – and the days of yore when Nine had a big suite of executives firing on all cylinders and a gut full of grog were long gone. Nine didn't even have a sales director when McGuire started in the job. Yet McGuire thought his experience behind the camera would help him:

> The staff know I believe there are standards that have to be attained, but they'll never get into trouble for having a go under my watch. Frankly, I think it helps having been on camera. People here know I know and understand the peculiar pressures that affect people who are on air.
>
> No matter how many years you have been in the sales department, you don't understand that.
>
> To me, television today is an industry where there's a bit of gut-feel in it still. Maybe it's too rigid at times. While you don't want it to become a circus, I still think there's a time and place to go with a bit of gut.[13]

McGuire was being paid danger money, though. He had good reason to take the job. A notice to the Australian Stock Exchange subsequently revealed 500 000 new shares were allotted on 10 February at $16 each and 4 395 000 were allotted on 23

February at $16.16 with expectations they were given to McGuire, who was appointed chief executive of the network on 9 February. The share value, due to redundancies and the positive market reaction to his appointment, rose in six weeks from $8 million to almost $8.9 million.[14]

As the bank balance bulged, McGuire hoped some of the pressures of being an on-screen star would dissipate. His ego and practicalities couldn't let go straight away, though. He kept hosting *Who Wants to Be a Millionaire?* until Easter, despite a raft of auditions testing contenders as diverse as Vince Sorrenti, Mark Nicholas, Tracey Curro, Deborah Hutton, Kerri-Anne Kennerley, Richard Wilkins and Paul Vautin. 'It's really a case of us not having had time to choose a host,' he said.

'If we had decided who was going to do it, they'd be doing it tomorrow,' he told the *Herald Sun*, adding Nine should have a replacement by Easter. He could laugh at the situation, though: 'I've discovered I'm the boss's favourite personality.'[15]

He did step down as host of the Melbourne Commonwealth Games, replaced by Ken Sutcliffe. It was a bitter personal blow. The Games coverage was symptomatic of the lax network into which McGuire felt he was walking. Nine didn't convert excellent ratings for the Melbourne Commonwealth Games into commensurate revenue (the Opening Ceremony was the highest-rating show for the year with 3.56 million viewers and the Closing Ceremony came fifth with 2.73 million). Sydney-based management pilloried the Games beforehand as little more than a school sports carnival. Nine's sales department was unenthused and under-resourced to sell advertising space ahead of the subsequent strong ratings. Nine left money on the table, to McGuire's chagrin.

And money was being taken from his table. Alexander, Packer and Anderson soon told McGuire he would have to oversee more cuts to the network. McGuire was incredulous. Subsequently,

McGuire's first meeting with staff at Willoughby's canteen, Hendo's, became legend.

In what should be a Harvard Business School case study in how not to manage a business, the smiling, popular face of the network was introduced to staff as a smiling assassin.

The announcement of more redundancies was purely a corporate play to spike Nine's share price. It caught McGuire off-guard; he thought he was being brought in to reinvigorate the network, not stymie it. He argued vehemently against the cuts – saying the company slashing jobs at a moment it was trying to promise staff it was a creative organisation seeking growth was ludicrous, and the idea it should be the substance of McGuire's first major staff announcement as the new CEO was damaging.

McGuire also argued to PBL's corporate team that fronting staff – people he had known for years and who he was supposed to lead – and telling them more staff would have to go was not his style of leadership. He grew up in newsrooms and remained, at heart, a journo; this was the cruellest cut.

He was rebuked and told Nine was a public company, and that his responsibility was to shareholders, not the people with whom he worked. Then financiers were brought in to convince McGuire just how positive the consequences of a smooth sale of the network could be if Nine continued to cut costs.

Nine employees expecting a new culture after years of neglect, parsimony and meanness anticipated McGuire would, at the very least, represent a turning of the tide. Nevertheless, tensions were high as he addressed staff. McGuire announced one hundred news and current affairs staff would have to go. Worse, staff were told the cuts would make Nine's news presence 'stronger'.

That meeting at Hendo's still rankles McGuire. It represented everything he is not – 'I'm a builder, not a cutter' – and indicated to McGuire too early that this job would not be what he'd been promised. It would be one of the hardest moments of his professional life, counter-intuitive to everything he believed television should be.

The only thing in his favour was Nine employees knew this was not something McGuire would do willingly. McGuire might be their leader, but most knew from that meeting someone else was pushing the buttons and there would be more of the same cuts by a thousand anonymous executives. Morale slumped immediately, and McGuire's often-repeated catch-cries for Nine – 'Moving Forward' and 'We're All Moving Forward' – would become the subject of ridicule.

Nevertheless, some optimistic staff appreciated having McGuire's 'aura of energy and things happening' in Willoughby, as Ken Sutcliffe described it.[16] It made a change from the faceless assassins.

By March, he was making his mark off screen, appointing friends, including his manager, mentor and AFL lawyer Browne as his deputy,[17] and Nine's Melbourne-based head of sport, and former executive producer of *The Footy Show*, Cos Cardone, was also called to join him in Sydney.

But he had to say goodbye to on-air television. In March, he recorded what was meant to be his final episode of *Who Wants to Be a Millionaire?* with tears in his eyes, as Carla and his two sons, Joseph, then 5, and Alexander, then 3, watched on. McGuire wanted the kids there, at least Joseph, so they might have a memory of their dad being on television. He insisted he wouldn't return to an on-camera career:

> That's it. It's over. But this is an emotional time for me. I started in the [sport] business at thirteen, and started in television at seventeen, but this is the last official on-camera gig for me. You walk off the set and it suddenly hits you that after twenty-four years on air this is it, and it impacts on you that a significant chapter in your life has closed.[18]

Oddly enough, *Millionaire* didn't find another host. Even more oddly, McGuire was not consulted on who should replace him as *The Footy Show*'s host. Panellists Garry Lyon and James Brayshaw were separate candidates until Newman suggested a double act might work. It would send the message the new CEO of the network could not easily be replaced, while also spreading the burden of expectation on the new hosts. Brayshaw and Lyon were appointed co-hosts, although McGuire would not be entirely content with the duo. He sent them a bottle of Grange Hermitage before their first episode with the plea: 'Look after my baby.' In that first year, he couldn't help but ring a few times while the show was on air, primarily as the Nine CEO, of course. One of the conditions of his taking the Nine job was resigning his presidency of the Collingwood Football Club. McGuire asked James Packer for some time to settle things, but despite criticism internally and externally about maintaining his Collingwood duties, Packer later allowed him to retain the role. Packer appreciated it was one of the few personal bright spots in the *annus horribilis* being thrust upon McGuire.

McGuire's footy clichés grated in Sydney. He describes the TV business as like a football club, where loyalty, hype and glamour make it completely different from other businesses. And he is correct – to a degree. In other businesses, the balance sheet tells the story; in television, the words 'creativity', 'emotion' and 'loyalty' mean something tangible. But the recent death of Nine's 'coach and president' Kerry Packer had changed the dynamic at Nine. It wasn't so emotional anymore.

And it didn't take long for McGuire to realise Sydney didn't care much about Melbourne. In fact, Sydneysiders didn't think about Melbourne at all. McGuire felt like an interloper. One News Corporation journalist even told him journos at the major paper in town had been instructed to give McGuire a 'hosing'.

Another female newspaper gossip writer set the tone for McGuire's Sydney foray at his first public outing with his wife Carla in his new job, at a David Jones Winter Collection fashion show in February. The journalist approached Carla and welcomed her to Sydney, adding she hoped she'd brought the box. Carla was dumbfounded. Box? Yes, replied the journalist, the one you'll be going back down to Melbourne in.

There was no broad Sydney conspiracy to nail McGuire, although individuals had their prejudices or incredulity about a TV host from Melbourne arriving to help a Packer. McGuire also talked big about his rejuvenation of Nine, and that hurt him. The share market and advertisers saw positivity; journalists saw hubris.

Editorially, McGuire didn't get any favours from the city's two major newspapers, although it wasn't a purposeful editorial line against him – at least not from this writer's perspective, covering the media round for the *Daily Telegraph*. Indeed, the *Telegraph*'s editor, David Penberthy – an Adelaide Crows supporter leading Sydney's most popular paper – was quite looking forward to the AFL evangelist coming to town.

Rather, the editors of the two daily newspapers, the *Daily Telegraph* and the *Sydney Morning Herald*, were bemused at the appointment, and subsequently amused at the ill-discipline that led to an unprecedented gush of leaks documenting Nine's travails. Many Nine staff ended up at Seven too, so gossip was always given a push by the resurgent Seven and its effective corporate spin doctoring. Nine's internal leaking hurt McGuire, not the newspapers.

It also didn't help that McGuire was flying back to Melbourne on weekends to watch his Pies and see his ageing parents. He had to be seen to be committing to Sydney, although McGuire found Sydney's social scene unforgiving and unwelcoming. However, the most compelling pull back to Melbourne on weekends was without doubt his ailing father.

McGuire had another fight to worry about: restoring Nine. He anticipated he could build Nine back into a production powerhouse. But he had to deal with minor skirmishes first, beginning with the redundancies, which killed his plans to instil some confidence in the place while also being a messy managerial task to implement.

McGuire had some hope, though. He wanted to invest in talent. He appreciated the sector had great talent, but he felt it was let down by TV writing. He also looked at the 'Aussiewood' talent pool leaving for Hollywood and thought they should be seduced back. He assembled the country's major drama producers for a function at North Bondi Italian to say Nine was open for business.

Australian drama wasn't Nine's only fragility, although a number of shows that would rejuvenate the genre were ready to screen, including *Sea Patrol*. McGuire had a news and current affairs line-up that had been overtaken by Seven's *Sunrise* and *Today Tonight*; sport was weakened by the loss of the AFL; and the network's US production deals with the studios weren't delivering the hits Seven scored through its Disney/ABC deal, such as *Desperate Housewives*.[19]

And the sacking of so many staff had bled the business of much of its institutional memory, while those remaining were traumatised by the bullying and erratic behaviour of previous management. For instance, three news journalists in Sydney (Mike Munro, Mark Ferguson and Peter Overton) believed they had handshake agreements to follow Brian Henderson as Sydney's newsreader.

The *Sunday* program was a particular mess, a cesspit of egos and wistfulness for its 1980s heyday. Staff defied directions, and Healy and McGuire's 'radical' thought that the show might be moved to 9.30 or 10.30 on Sunday night was derided internally. *Sunday* staff were a law unto themselves, backed by a vocal chorus of ex-*Sunday* staffers sledging every change with venom to any journalist who'd listen. Host Jana Wendt didn't even speak to the man charged with running the show, former *Sydney Morning Herald* editor John Lyons. *Sunday* epitomised one of Nine's weaknesses: its highest-paid stars were working 'off peak', not in prime time.

McGuire's plan to involve Wendt more in a revamped program, selling her as its focus, lead interviewer and reporter, was met with concern she wouldn't have enough researchers or reporters for support. Wendt previously left Seven's *Witness* under the same cloud of 'role confusion'. *Sunday* had become a weeping wound: it was an expensive, high-quality program that lost its audience as Sunday became just another day of the week. McGuire asked the *Sunday* team who they thought their audience was and they replied with the standard 'high-income, older AB (demographic) audience' that drove the show in the 1980s and 1990s. McGuire countered times had changed; Sunday morning wasn't as relaxed and suitable for a magazine news program and a fifty-something viewer was no longer watching Sunday before heading off to church and coming home for a roast; they were more likely cycling down the Nepean Highway. A move to late on Sunday night would make it the last take of the weekend, preparing viewers for the week, but Wendt and then Ray Martin rebuffed the move.

Ironically, talent would prove to be an Achilles heel for McGuire. He should have understood their foibles; he had his own, and they began to show early in the piece. *Temptation* host Ed Phillips was scheduled to host a Nine function before he was yanked. The message came through from Willoughby: 'There's only room for one Ed at the launch'. (To be fair, it is not known whether the edict came directly from McGuire or was made in anticipation of his protest.)

Eddie nicknamed the foyer outside his office the 'Wailing Wall', as employees, particularly on-screen talent, lined up to dump their woes on him. Staff on the *Today* show, on and off screen, were so dysfunctional they were all called into McGuire's office for a gee-up. Production was shambolic, and Seven's *Sunrise* phenomenon was playing mental and production havoc with the team. New executive producers and directives appeared at *Today* seemingly every week.

McGuire was unhappy with the lack of protection being afforded co-host Jessica Rowe. Chisholm and Nine news boss Mark Llewellyn hired her to co-host *Today*, but her news-reading skills needed bolstering to carry three hours of live TV every morning. McGuire thought the show's producers and news chiefs – particularly Llewellyn – should be assisting Rowe more.

Throughout its history, the *Today* show has rarely hummed as a 'team' – unlike most other shows. Disparate personalities in the hosts' chairs and a carousel of producers tended to keep the show volatile. The program's woes were not healed, temporarily, until Lisa Wilkinson's appointment as co-host in 2007.

McGuire wasn't short of programming ideas across the schedule. He wanted to establish a western Sydney news bureau and hire some female Muslim reporters. That proved an idea too far from the blonde-and-blue-eyed template at Nine. The ideas could be well below his station though: he continually asked about the progress of *The Footy Show* and its weekly guests, and even suggested that Nine football callers, and mates, Dermott Brereton and Dwayne Russell get haircuts. They weren't the only ones subjected to haircuts.

McGuire and Jeff Browne were saddled with a generational change of old TV meeting new TV. And old TV was shoring up its superannuation. Browne was appointed to help McGuire on the commercial transactional side of the business. Packer and Alexander believed Browne's support would be crucial; they'd dealt with him previously in sporting rights negotiations (Browne's Melbourne-based legal practice Browne and Co. had overseen every AFL broadcasting rights deal since the mid-1980s, and represented the Australian Olympic Committee in Games deals), and knew McGuire's ideas-driven persona needed some process-driven sustenance.

A first task for Browne was reeling in salaries, which were exorbitant relative to Seven (although Nine historically had developed bigger stars). That was understandable in a culture where a 40 ratings share was expected. Nine was no longer doing 'a 40', and James Packer was more interested in the letters EBITDA (earnings before interest, tax, depreciation and amortisation) than the number 40. Implementing that very specific philosophical change at Nine from ratings-driven to balance-sheet-driven caused a lot of pain.

The next hatchet man to arrive at Nine was Ian Law from PBL's magazine arm, ACP, a manager who made his name as a cost-cutter ruling red lines through balance sheets. Management and talent salaries were targeted, as was Nine's penchant for paying too much for rights to shows and sports, often spot-buying shows in times of programming duress and above market rates. Nine also abandoned its output deal with CBS Paramount for cost reasons because it had bought ABC/Disney's news service. Nine would later live to regret losing Paramount. The addition of the studio's *NCIS* series, which was to become Ten's most successful US drama, possibly would have given Nine ratings wins in 2009 and 2010. Also under the knife was its free-spending News and Current Affairs Department.

Ratings were plummeting. In May, Nine fell to third place for the first time since people meters – the television industry's audience measurement system – were introduced in 1991, and possibly the first time for Nine in thirty years. Ten was number one with *The Biggest Loser, House, Thank God You're Here* and the start of *Big Brother 6* as Nine fell.[20]

McGuire needed to do something, and a mining tragedy in Tasmania's Beaconsfield would be the unlikely spark for McGuire's creative energy, chutzpah and conflicted roles. Sportsreader Ken Sutcliffe went into McGuire's office when it became apparent two miners, Brant Webb and Todd Russell, would be extracted from a mine collapse after being trapped underground for two weeks.

He suggested Nine go to the town and broadcast a combined NRL and AFL *Footy Show* to raise money for the family of dead miner Larry Knight. McGuire jumped at the idea. McGuire went to Beaconsfield and held sway in a town hitherto dominated by Seven's *Sunrise*, primarily because Nine's regional signal didn't carry to the town.

Beyond any charity, each network wanted to sign the miners to an exclusive interview. When McGuire saw the miners emerge and *Sunrise* host David Koch called into an ambulance to meet them, he knew Seven was in the box seat. In fact, *Sunrise* had many fans in the town, including a medical officer who was talking to the miners; he had a *Sunrise* ringtone and would leak information to the program first-hand.

McGuire branded the *Sunrise* crew 'ambulance chasers' – which, to assess the semantics of it, wasn't quite true. Todd Russell told the ambulance to stop and invited Koch inside. It didn't matter. The ratings came in and on the day of the miner's return to the surface, Seven's *Sunrise*-led coverage dominated with a peak audience of 1.02 million, with an unprecedented audience of 485 000 between 6 and 7 a.m. (to *Today*'s 332 000) and 839 000 for 7 to 9 a.m. (up on *Today*'s 529 000). Nine had been trumped and the Beaconsfield story looked like magnifying the ratings drubbing Nine received in the first three months of the year. The national secretary of the Australian Workers' Union, Bill Shorten, told *A Current Affair*'s team, 'I can't tell you how far behind Nine is in the race to get these blokes.'

McGuire knew Nine had to counter Seven's momentum, as much for the network as for his own reputation as CEO. It was important for Nine to show it could still dominate a big event. But Nine management remained so cowed by its last couple of years it could barely muster a fight. McGuire assembled his management team for a strategy meeting to determine what Nine could throw at the miners. The figure of $200 000 was suggested. McGuire blanched. That's what we get for a match-day sponsorship at Collingwood, he thought. Clearly Nine wasn't ready for a fight.

McGuire told Browne they should head down to Tasmania and make something happen despite McGuire's reticence, and advice from others that perhaps it wasn't the manner in which a CEO should act. A quick call to James Packer secured his private jet, which whisked McGuire and Browne to Tasmania. McGuire stormed into the Club Hotel and shouted the miners' local bar drinks before the night was over. He would shout the pub twice more that week.

McGuire's advice to the miners was to be wary of looking like TattsLotto winners as a colleague lay dead. He suggested a version of *The Footy Show* in Beaconsfield could raise money for the local community. Its quick production and success displayed McGuire at his best. In the process, he also became close to a local policeman who advised the family. McGuire was loving it: the thrill of the chase, the old-style journalism.

A Current Affair's Tracy Grimshaw also worked her magic, winning over the miners' wives with charm, dropping in a casserole.

The miners appointed manager Sean Anderson and the dealing began. Seven's and Nine's offers were similar in dollar terms, although Seven's was complicated when it tried to spread the financial burden across Kerry Stokes' varied companies, including a promotional deal with his Caterpillar brand of agricultural equipment.

The Nine deal involved the ACP magazine stable and internet arm ninemsn. McGuire could foresee this as a major cross-platform opportunity and a way to defray costs, just at a time when the business was exploring every opportunity to spread content across broadcast TV, magazines and the web. Calls were made to Sydney to see how far the budget would stretch.

Browne quizzed Anderson on what it would take. Anderson asked him to make an offer. Browne refused, telling Anderson he foresaw the agent only taking that offer to Seven (Anderson also represented *Sunrise*'s Koch). Seven's offer of $2.2 million wasn't far off the mark, but somehow Nine had an inkling about what Seven's offer would be. Browne raised the pressure, suggesting Anderson ask his clients what figure they would accept and then Nine would make one offer that he either accepted or rejected. If he rejected it, Nine was out.

McGuire and Browne were at the airport about to leave Tasmania when Anderson called. Browne made an offer of $2.5 million.

'You have ten seconds to answer,' Browne said and began to count down from ten. Anderson protested.

'Six ... five ... four ... three ...' Anderson agreed at three. McGuire chuckled in the background at Browne's bravado: 'Obviously we're delighted. It's a huge story, not only for Nine but for our news, ACA and magazine division,' said McGuire. 'I spent more than five hours talking to the boys, listening to their story. They confided in me and I kept their confidence.'[21]

McGuire then had to fend off the news stars desperate to do the big interview, including Ray Martin and Mike Munro, although it was obvious Grimshaw had won the right to the interview. Her program also needed the profile boost if the show was going to kick with her as host. As it happened, the two-hour interview special, *The Great Escape*, was the beginning of a buoyant run of accomplished interviews by Grimshaw and a renewed ratings run by *ACA*. The interview itself attracted an average audience of 2.79 million metropolitan viewers, making it the third most-watched TV event of the year (behind the Commonwealth Games Opening Ceremony and the AFL Grand Final). The knock-on effect for other Nine/PBL properties was just as noticeable, with *The Bulletin* selling well and website ninemsn registering a record number of hits.

The Beaconsfield experience emboldened McGuire to return to the screen sporadically, but it was a misjudgement. He jumped into the hosting chair for *The Footy Show* for a trip to Munich for soccer's World Cup. It was a disaster for the CEO, pulling less than half the expected two million viewers and costing a bundle.

'When I took the chief executive job, a lot of people said one of the downsides was that Nine was losing one of its senior on-air people,' McGuire says. 'We've taken the view now that that doesn't necessarily have to be the case and that on occasions I'll be back on air, if it makes sense.'[22]

Through the middle of 2006, incident after incident at Nine gave McGuire reason to believe being an on-air celebrity would offer respite from the pain.

In June, staff were told via email, twenty minutes after the news broke on radio, that another one hundred staff – mainly from news and current affairs – would be made redundant (the final figure was eighty redundancies and three sackings). The move of most consequence would be the appointment of *The Bulletin*'s editor-in-chief Garry Linnell as head of network news and current affairs, replacing Mark Llewellyn, who became executive producer of news and current affairs.

'The key in my mind to news is to live up to the name of the show – and that is news,' McGuire said.[23]

The reaction to the slashing of $15 million from Nine's wages bill was typical of Nine's state: hailed by media analysts who thought the changes would have been made sooner if Kerry Packer hadn't been so sentimental, and lamented by depressed staff.[24]

The cuts also further intimated that McGuire was 'a puppet of Park Street' (the Sydney CBD headquarters of Nine's parent company, James Packer's PBL).

He protested that such a thought was ridiculous. 'I had a pretty good life before this job. Why would I leave a very autonomous position to come here and be a puppet?'[25] But privately he now knew his job was not the one he'd signed up for.

The cuts meant morale was shot – not helped by a misplaced resentment among staff that everything that was good had gone to the grave with Kerry.

McGuire felt this sentiment particularly keenly among the women at Willoughby. The 'Wailing Wall' delivered a number of female employees either at their wit's end or so conditioned to a male view of television they became aggressive or combustible.

Kerri-Anne Kennerley blew up in August when erroneous reports of Seven poaching her emerged. 'I'd love to have people fighting over me, but Channel 7 have not made that telephone call to me yet,' she told the *Daily Telegraph* before expressing her disgust at the hiring of Bert Newton and the parsimony denying her business cards or Cabcharge dockets to get to work.[26]

McGuire also started a program called Women at Nine, aiming to address work–life balance issues, and he recruited former ACP magazine editor Mia Freedman as 'director of creative services' – whatever that meant.

His initiatives didn't quite work out: Freedman sparked jealousy; her talk show, *The Catch Up*, lasted four months; and McGuire's footy analogies left many women flummoxed. Drama boss Sandra Levy even asked around to see whether there was a recommended book about football or sport that might help her understand the language. She soon resigned anyway.

But if television's entrenched misogyny was going to become public, nothing could have done it better than the 'boning' incident.

The turmoil within Nine's news and current affairs department hit another crescendo after Linnell replaced Llewellyn. Linnell was a smooth operator who gave the ACP news weekly *The Bulletin* a breath of vivacity in its dying days. However, he had no TV experience. The news sent Llewellyn into a tailspin.

Llewellyn's meeting with Browne and McGuire to hear about his shifting responsibilities from news boss to 'head of news production' (sharing the major news responsibilities with Linnell) and a cut to his $750 000 salary proved calamitous for Nine.

The meeting began with discussions about the faltering performance on the *Today* show of the major talent of the day, Jessica Rowe. Some within Nine felt Rowe had been miscast as a host of three hours of live TV and was being hung out to dry with no support.

Rowe was even carrying the can for issues beyond her control, such as Nine's poor production. Pillorying Rowe became a sport, reflecting either TV's misogyny or the lingering resentment of traditional news journalists who have no respect for anyone who didn't start as a cadet or learn shorthand. Or maybe it was just easy. Whatever the case, it didn't reflect well on Nine.

A version of the conversation between Llewellyn, McGuire and Browne emerged in an affidavit filed by Llewellyn after he was summonsed to the NSW Supreme Court by Nine following his resignation and signing to the Seven Network. Llewellyn's side was concerned allegations in affidavits filed by Browne and Linnell were beyond the pale. Llewellyn's affidavit denied a number of conversations outlined in the Nine affidavits.

The explosive affidavit sent Nine's lawyers scrambling. It recounted damaging conversations including the allegation McGuire said, on 31 May 2006, of his troubled *Today* host, 'What are we going to do about Jessica? When should we bone her? I reckon it should be next week.'

Rowe was an appointee of Chisholm and Llewellyn. McGuire believed Llewellyn wasn't taking responsibility for her performance as the CEO was attending to complaints from Stefanovic, producers, directors – even an incredulous government minister, Tony Abbott, who called McGuire to ask why Rowe had been so tough with him on the show. Rowe was only trying to show her mettle. The conflict was further complicated by Llewellyn's friendship with Rowe and her husband, Peter Overton.

In his affidavit, Llewellyn explained he was worried he would be axed despite his salary cut, although he didn't make his move to Seven until he noticed his monthly salary had dropped from $24 947 per month to $16 087 per month in June 2006. It was not an edifying look among his workmates, as Llewellyn groused about his pay cut to $400 000 while more than a hundred staff under him had been sacked in the past year.

Llewellyn's team filed a statement of claim for breach of contract, with Nine claiming the $1.2 million for the remaining eighteen months left on Llewellyn's contract. The claims in Llewellyn's affidavit were promptly leaked and published. Nine's affidavits were not.

The contents of Llewellyn's affidavit remain contested yet untested by court proceedings. The parties settled. Both Llewellyn and McGuire were advised by their lawyers, against their wishes, not to pursue the matter and the settlement remains subject to a strict confidentiality agreement between the two.

Nine contested in the press a number of facts in the affidavit, but not all. McGuire's alleged 'bone' quote was one of the few statements Nine executives, including two of the three parties to the conversation, McGuire and Browne, deny to this day. No staff at Nine can recall McGuire using the term, although it was used by another senior executive.

Most at Nine maintain he did not actually use the term that would stick as a symbol of Nine's malaise and McGuire's blokey management style. Whatever the actual conversation, Llewellyn's recollection is the one on the public record.

The 'bone' term has so far proven a very lucrative colloquial verb for Llewellyn. It has also proven a particularly bitter pill for Eddie McGuire to swallow given his work to turn around sexist cultures at both Nine and Collingwood.

To be honest, the 'boned' version suited the times. It would even spark a chick-lit novel about an up and coming female TV executive, *Boned*, written by 'Anonymous'.

If only Nine had the wit to quickly move on. Nine's lawyers subsequently conceded at a board meeting the network's decision to try to quash the affidavit by issuing an injunction against other media publishing was a mistake. After all, the Llewellyn affidavit was easily transmittable (and remains online) and the injunction was for New South Wales only.

If Nine wanted to antagonise a media already kicking the network, the subsequent issuing of subpoenas to *The Australian*, the *Sydney Morning Herald* and *The Age* to surrender the document and sources was an excellent move.

The term 'bone' allowed the media to pile on the hapless McGuire. The only media support he received came from the *Herald Sun*'s Robert Fidgeon – a long-time supporter – who noted 'Llewellyn had prepared the affidavit – containing notes of what he alleges were private office conversations between him and some Nine executives – in an attempt to secure a speedy departure from Nine to Seven.' He described it as 'a giant slice of hypocrisy' by the media:

> Having led the way in criticising Rowe's performance for five months, and calling for her blood, the same media turned last week's 'Lynch Eddie' vendetta into a joint 'Save Jessica' campaign.
>
> Mark Llewellyn's affidavit was always going to be self-serving. He wanted out of Nine in a hurry. It was never going to portray Nine or its executives in a positive light.
>
> To make McGuire the scapegoat for Nine's troubles is wrong, yet that is not to say he has no case to answer.[27]

Nine subsequently dropped its legal bid to prevent Llewellyn from joining Seven after Linnell spent a week telling staff Llewellyn was contracted and going nowhere. Nine also agreed to pay the costs of both the Seven Network and Llewellyn. While curious, hindsight suggests it was wise. Subsequently, explosive affidavits became the weapon of choice for aggrieved media executives and stars, and court cases – such as James Warburton's against Seven – didn't paint either side in flattering hues.

McGuire set about shoring up the sandbags. It was now harder, with questioning staff. He had a boardroom lunch for the A-list staff of his *Sunday* program, including Wendt, that same week, assuring them *Sunday* was a goer. Wendt had already consulted her lawyers to 'review her options' after news of the redundancies and cost-cutting measures.[28]

On the Saturday of the affidavit hullabaloo, McGuire went to watch Collingwood. It was a respite from the malaise – or should have been. The Pies were thumped.[29]

McGuire subsequently cancelled a planned trip to Wimbledon with Nine advertisers and went in to bat for Rowe. 'Jessica has been the target of a malicious and unprecedented vilification campaign by our opponents in recent months,' he said. 'She has my full support.'[30] McGuire hoped to lift her credibility by allowing her to host some special reports on *A Current Affair* on issues in which she was particularly interested, but she was physically and mentally shot. By the time those on the third floor turned their attention to Rowe, the News Department had let her down.

The blows kept coming because, as the 'boning' affidavit emerged, Alexander was enjoying the corporate largesse of Nine's Wimbledon fortnight while James Packer was also in the United Kingdom playing polo at Cowdray Park in West Sussex.

The impotence of a Kerry Packer-less Nine and PBL was epitomised by the *Daily Telegraph*'s front-page headline screaming, 'He's just sacked 100 staff, his network is a mess, and he's in England for tennis and polo – HOME, JAMES'. It was Marie Antoinette writ large. The newspaper wrote:

Facing his biggest crisis since taking over his father's multi-billion-dollar empire and sacking 100 staff, James Packer has flown to Europe to enjoy playing polo, watch the Wimbledon tennis and buy a $100 million mega-yacht.

As the once-impregnable Nine Network publicly unravels, the media mogul plans to spend the next few weeks schmoozing with clients after touching down in his newly refurbished $50 million jet.

Insiders at Publishing and Broadcasting Limited, the Nine Network owner, are questioning their chairman's judgment, saying his trip and corporate spending are tasteless after embarking on brutal cost-cutting and removing 100 staff.[31]

Nine conspiracy theorists thought it was part of a concerted campaign when they realised News Corp boss Rupert Murdoch happened to be in Sydney at the same time. They put two and two together to come up with five. Certainly Nine was an easier target with Kerry gone, but the truth was the splash came from the *Daily Telegraph*'s then-editor, David Penberthy, who only happened to run it by News Corp chief John Hartigan to test whether it would cause any unnecessary corporate grief. Hartigan wasn't perturbed – indeed, he laughed – and it ran. It was highly damaging for Nine management and McGuire was the patsy left at home to defend.

McGuire was beginning to appreciate his celebrity was counter-productive because he was too easy a target, even the subject of a vendetta. But Nine just kept putting its head up to be kicked. Even in its press release announcing Linnell's appointment, Nine sought to sell its 'new vision' for news and current affairs as requiring 100 job losses. It was corporate spin deserving considerable cynicism.

The differences between Australia's two biggest cities, for the most part, are trivial. In essence, everything in Melbourne is 'world class' and everything in Sydney is 'world famous'. Melbourne lives on clubbiness – the slights, feuds and innuendoes.

It is inward-looking and takes care of its own. Sydney is egalitarian and outward-looking. If you can do the job and succeed, it doesn't matter whether you have a personality defect, criminal record or dubious history: Sydney will accept you. But it won't cop whingers. McGuire couldn't lean on his Melbourne 'club' mates as he once did to smooth paths and any protest he made sounded to Sydney like a whinge.

The boning affidavit continued a flood of leaks from, or about, Nine cascading to Sydney's four daily newspapers. Nine management was short-sighted not to realise any media organisation headed by a Packer would remain more newsworthy than one that was not – just as News Corp remained a subject of fascination because of the Murdoch family. But editors at Fairfax's *Sydney Morning Herald* can't recall any discussions 'to get Eddie' either.

In Melbourne, McGuire had the protection of the *Herald Sun* – particularly his good friend News Limited editor in chief Peter Blunden – and an open door to write any time. That paper wouldn't hurt him and a shrivelling *The Age* couldn't hurt him. Indeed, Melbourne's media respected McGuire. But in Sydney, management at the *Herald Sun* couldn't pull rank in the *Daily Telegraph*'s Holt Street headquarters and the *Sydney Morning Herald* was a more influential newspaper than its Melbourne sibling. Tellingly, McGuire often berated editors of the *Daily Telegraph*, yet didn't try it on with *Sydney Morning Herald* editors. He sometimes confused the *Sunday Telegraph* with the *Daily Telegraph*, and yelled, 'You bastards are all out to get me'. Another editor copped a spray in which McGuire pointed to seven separate negative comments about, or allusions to, him in one edition. He met another newspaper editor with the greeting at lunch, 'Are we here for a fight or a feed?'

Even editors and journalists covering the internecine battle between Seven and Nine couldn't quite get a handle on it. The two networks were brawling like Kings Cross bouncers with a level of venom never seen before.

McGuire quickly developed a siege mentality. His Melbourne modus operandi – whether as TV star or Collingwood president – was to get onto the front foot. He has a surprisingly thin skin, and would spend half an hour on the phone with anyone who dared slur him. His willingness to follow up any misdeed with a journalist didn't wash well among Sydney journos, though. Sydney doesn't work like that. You take your hits and everyone moves on.

One Sydney newspaper item in particular set him off, and had alarm bells ringing through News Corp from Melbourne. This time, McGuire was as angry as he'd ever been and it was a slight one editor concedes should not have made it to the paper.

A gossip item in the infamous Sydney Confidential pages referred to the fashion of female guests at the 2006 Brownlow Medal wearing too much fake tan. The item mentioned McGuire's wife, Carla, was among the Brownlow 'WAGs' with their 'rotisserie chicken tans'. It was a gratuitous shot, and McGuire was livid. His belief that everything – even family – seemed fair game when going after him was justified. The truth was it was just another editorial misjudgement.

Socially, McGuire lived in Darling Point and tried to inveigle his way into Eastern suburbs society, but Sydney is far more fragmented than Melbourne. The cosy Melbourne lunch clubs McGuire shares in Melbourne with AFL boss Andrew Demetriou, 3AW broadcaster Neil Mitchell, Blunden and former premier Steve Bracks had no equivalent he could see in Sydney. Nor was there anything like Village Roadshow boss Graham Burke's regular Sunday afternoon film screenings and discussion with Melbourne's movers and shakers at which McGuire often held court. He even had to call Melbourne when Carla was told there were no places available for two Melbourne boys at Sydney's Easts Auskick program. Two places freed up after Eddie called the AFL.

Back at Nine, the Rowe problem caught him in a wedge. If he axed Jessica Rowe, he was damned; if he kept her, he was damned.

Nine's media incompetence and the joy with which the tale of the underdog, Seven, was being written meant Nine couldn't find oxygen for anything positive it achieved – including a 2006 ratings win and a rising PBL share price.

Sarah Murdoch, the wife of News Corporation board member Lachlan Murdoch, was announced as an interim host of the *Today* show after Jessica Rowe departed, partly as Nine's management team knew it would stem the attacks on *Today* from the News Limited newspapers.

McGuire realised quickly he had little support at Nine. The business was in total transition, preparing for sale. Yet, among staff, the memory of a creative business run by a billionaire lingered. The internal dissent and lack of teamwork in an entrenched culture at Nine felt very much like Collingwood in 1998.

McGuire tried to shake it up. He attempted to lure Foxtel's Brian Walsh across as head of television, but negotiations foundered when McGuire couldn't clarify the new job's reporting lines, particularly with respect to Nine programming boss Michael Healy. It was apparent McGuire was CEO in name but not the boss.

He also invested in trying to create hits. The mid-year launch of *Dancing on Ice* started with a bang in the freezing, dark environs of an ice-skating rink in Sydney's Hills district. It was a handy cross-promotion of Nine talent, including Michael Slater and Karl Stefanovic (following Seven's successful strategy with *Dancing with the Stars*), and opened well with audiences of one and a half million before fading. It needed bigger numbers to justify its high cost.

Nine also banked big on its launch of its 2006–07 cricket coverage in front of 500 buyers and advertisers at the Sydney Cricket Ground (and a clumsy picture opportunity with McGuire and Rowe), and tried to sell its coming new US series, including *Kidnapped*, *Smith* and *The Nine* as well as new programs such as *The Great Weight Debate*, *What a Year*, *The Big Question*, *Overhaul*, *Rome* and *Two Twisted*. History shows none of them were stayers.

Factual specials *Turn Back Your Body Clock* and *You Are What You Eat*, and crime show *Close to Home* were all pulled after just a few weeks.[32]

Internally, some executives pilloried McGuire's appetite for one-off specials and intolerance for programs that didn't perform immediately. It was attributed to his inexperience.

The tide was turning against Eddie. By July, advertising revenue figures showed Seven was about to overtake Nine for the first time in thirty years (Seven climbed to $460 million annual revenue as Nine slid 6.1 per cent to $462 million).[33]

One of McGuire's babies would be a hit, though, and influence Australian TV drama for years. McGuire had a layman's view that Australia produced a multitude of actors, directors and crew who were winning Academy Awards and doing brilliant things on global screens but this wasn't reflected in Australian drama. And did he have a story to tell.

Previously, McGuire had arranged with *The Age* crime journalists Andrew Rule and John Silvester to pitch a TV adaptation of their bestselling series of books about the Melbourne underworld, *Leadbelly: Inside Australia's Underworld Wars* and the subsequent *Underbelly* series.

At first, the crime-writing duo thought Nine had sooled McGuire onto them just to appease its then-network star. They regarded their occasional meetings as a bore, particularly because any TV writers or producers who assessed the subject matter didn't get it. They were prisoners of their previous experience. In TV police procedurals, it is the cops, not the crims, who are always the interesting characters. Rule and Silvester knew, but no one in TV appreciated, the Melbourne gangsters of the 1990s were the interesting characters – not the faceless men of the Purana Taskforce in St Kilda Road.

McGuire got it. He was as interested in the developing crime saga as anyone else. As an ambitious young sports reporter, his nights rubbing up to footballers at King Street nightclubs were just as likely to find him in the company of a Moran or a Gangitano as a Millane or Daicos. Alphonse Gangitano (later played by Vince Colosimo) was an infamous 'star fucker' who tried to endear himself to nightclubbing footballers.

Nine's previous head of drama, Posie Graeme-Evans, knocked the crime story on the head. McGuire tried again when Sandra Levy took the drama chief's role by default. She had no power to make a decision. Silvester and Rule thought the project was dead, particularly after McGuire wheeled out the 's word': 'Sopranos'. Mere mention that this series had the potential to be a 'Melbourne Sopranos' was anathema to Nine executives. Kerry Packer might have loved *The Sopranos* but it rated poorly in Australia.

McGuire believed Nine had no faith in the idea because women would hate the dark material. Silvester and Rule knew Nine was wrong. Seventy per cent of books are bought by women, and they'd sold tens of thousands of books. Few others appreciated that women were gripped by the notion of murder and mayhem next door in humble inner-Melbourne suburbs like Carlton and leafy Moonee Ponds. The idea that gangsters who killed each other were crossing paths at parent–teacher nights was too alluring. As it happened, research later showed that young women – particularly those aged from twenty-five to thirty-five – switched on in big numbers to watch *Underbelly*.

Not that the books were unknown. The producers of *Water Rats* referred to them when looking for inspiration for their cops on the harbour drama, for instance. The problem was the *Leadbelly* series was too unwieldy to conquer within a drama series.

The third time McGuire had a crack at pitching the adaptation to Nine, he was CEO and Jo Horsburgh was head of drama. McGuire walked into Horsburgh's office and asked for the *Underbelly* file. He tells a hokey tale of retrieving the file from under a creaking pile and blowing dust off it. The fact was he gave Horsburgh a compelling pitch with vivid images and vignettes, and told her, 'We should have a look at this again but it's entirely up to you.'

Incredibly, he meant it. He displayed his passion for the project, then left Horsburgh alone. She was relieved to have such autonomy and believed McGuire, but the truth was she'd looked at the books years ago and thought there was something there too.

Horsburgh and script executive Anthony Ellis met Silvester and Rule, and raised two key issues. First, TV drama producers are brainwashed that you can't use real people. Second, the cost was prohibitive due to too many characters and locations.

Nevertheless, they approached the project with Federico Fellini in mind – the first time the words 'Fellini' and 'Channel Nine' had ever been spoken within one conversation. The Italian director's wildly baroque fantasias did not recall anything on Australian free-to-air television (maybe *Chances?*) but the *Underbelly* file was now spinning so wildly that the creative opportunities a Fellini-esque drama offered were enticing. Horsburgh asked Nine lawyers to option the books: *Leadbelly* for the content and *Underbelly* for the title.

As it happened, Screentime's telemovie of a Melbourne true-crime tale, *The Society Murders*, screened on Ten in June 2006. The tale of a son's murder of his parents behind the vaulted fences of Melbourne's moneyed Brighton won its timeslot with 1.44 million viewers – beating, as it happened, McGuire's expensive return to air in Germany during the *World Cup Footy Show Spectacular*.[34] Suddenly Nine's true crime project had reason for momentum and the power of portraying real-life characters stared Horsburgh in the face. She met writer and producer Greg Haddrick for coffee and raised the prospect of *Leadbelly*. Haddrick's face lit up; Screentime was already developing a series about the Purana taskforce.

A new Screen Australia funding program for a thirteen-part series greased the wheel for Nine, which was now wanting a series from the criminals' perspective but with a rock opera frisson:

glossy, shiny and with a sense of irreverence. The description 'tabloid' was used.

Screentime delivered a cracker. The writing on the first series was explosive and indecent. Stylistically, the show was compelling and frenetic. The casting was wonderful and the ensemble of young relative unknowns – led by Gyton Grantley, Kat Stewart and Damian Walshe-Howling – delivered more than expected of them as the young crime stars of 1990s Melbourne.

The program was made to be a 9.30 p.m. show. Screentime wanted it there, as did many within Nine. The pilot episode was certainly not for the faint-hearted. Vince Colosimo's turn as Gangitano jumped off the screen.

Horsburgh told McGuire the show would win awards, but ratings might be difficult because it was such tough material.

Before airing, *Underbelly* was generating comparisons with the seminal 1995 ABC TV mini-series about NSW police corruption, *Blue Murder*, both for their high quality and the prospect that current criminal proceedings may prevent them screening in their home state.

Justice Betty King and the Director of Public Prosecutions, Jeremy Rapke QC, asked to see the series to ensure it wasn't prejudicial, although privately they were making inferences that they did not want to ban it if it was possible to avoid doing so. Nine erred badly in its dealings with the judicial system. In an overly aggressive approach, Nine continued to tell Justice King the episodes were not finished. Yet police knew interested gangsters were already in possession of copies of the early episodes. Suggestions remain that copies were made available to Mick Gatto, a 'colourful Melbourne identity' who is judiciously portrayed as one of the few characters not involved in drug manufacture or dealing in the series. Another rumour had it that a senior Nine executive gave a copy to a rival as a favour, and it leaked from the rival network.

Nine dared Justice King to make an order to see the series. She did. Essentially, the *Underbelly* series was the Crown case for the Moran murders. King realised it was too good and too realistic to be dismissed as a dramatisation, and it was likely to affect future juries. She said she would have to ban it from screening in Victoria as it would jeopardise the upcoming trial of Evangelos Goussis, who was up for the murder of Lewis Moran. He wasn't even portrayed in the series, but was an associate of many of those dramatised, including Tony Mokbel, whose portrayal would cause subsequent legal issues.

Screentime and Nine believed they had been meticulous with the legals (many characters had been withdrawn from the show and much of the content about the crime families dropped away for legal reasons), but the show's context hurt them. Justice King banned the show in Victoria.

The original *Underbelly* could have been so much worse. Carl Williams was charged with murder as the series was in production. It was a shock to all when he pleaded guilty months before *Underbelly* aired in 2007. If he had professed his innocence, *Underbelly* might not have been seen for years.

'*Underbelly* came out and broke every rule,' said Nine programmer Michael Healy.[35] '*Underbelly* should never have worked.'

Melbourne is a parochial city when it comes to its television. When *Underbelly* premiered on Monday 13 February 2008 on Nine in all states and territories except Victoria, its audience of 1.32 million was huge across two hours. It was not unreasonable to suggest Nine could have added another 800 000 to one million viewers if it had been shown in Melbourne; it had 633 000 Sydney viewers.

Underbelly was a blockbuster that nailed the minutiae of the gangland wars in Melbourne 'based on events in Melbourne, 1995 to 2004'. Its racy nature and Victorian ban also made it a commercial success as one of the best-selling Australian DVDs of all time. And it stands alone as one of the handful of film or TV investments by Screen Australia this century to come close to returning its government investment.[36]

McGuire was no longer in the CEO chair to take the credit – although, to be fair, this success had a few parents. It was clearly his greatest success on screen in his time as CEO.

Another would come later. Again he would no longer be Nine CEO. When McGuire moved into the top job, many at Nine were still smarting that the network had lost the rights to broadcast the AFL for 2007–11. Its previous AFL free-to-air partner, Ten, dudded Nine, realising it was likely to become a junior partner in this deal after extricating such a sweet side of the Nine–Ten relationship in the AFL deal for 2002–06, giving up *Friday Night Football* in exchange for the finals series. Ten aligned with Seven on the next deal.

McGuire took stock on a whiteboard of every sporting rights deal available with his now over-stocked team of sports chiefs – including Cardone, Steve Crawley, former Seven programmer Gary Fenton and Browne. They realised the only available sports event big enough for them to launch programs off was the London Olympic Games. McGuire still rued Nine's not fully taking advantage of the Melbourne Commonwealth Games. And up to that point, Fenton had been involved in every Australian Games deal with the IOC – in fact, he was the first broadcaster in the world to go to the IOC with a multi-Games offer strategy that subsequently delivered it billions through US broadcast deals.[37] Fenton was a favoured son of the IOC and Browne was crucial because he previously negotiated rights deals with the AOC and IOC.

But if Seven learned of Nine's interest, it would increase its efforts and, as the incumbent of eighteen years, would win. McGuire appreciated Nine was leaking like the Treasurer's office before a budget, so the planning had to remain secret. He 'sacked'

Fenton and gave him the covert operation – 'Project F' – to work on his IOC contacts and investigate whether Nine was a chance. Seven was complacent, not knowing Nine was in the frame. Fenton beavered away on the project with secret trips to Geneva and the IOC headquarters in Lausanne. Meanwhile, Browne stitched up a partnership with Foxtel that he believed would be crucial to the deal.

Yet Nine foxed publicly by not committing to a bid. That was easy; no one at Nine even knew the trio's intentions. It couldn't be allowed to leak. McGuire thought Seven knowing about the bid would scupper it, but just as dire would be the opportunity for the bid to be sabotaged internally by the Finance Department or Park Street management – which was highly likely.

The Nine/Foxtel team assembled before the bid in Lausanne in October 2006. They won. McGuire received a jubilant call at home at 2 a.m. But by then – October 2007 – he was long gone from the CEO role. Nine's new CEO, David Gyngell, was in Lausanne to share the spoils.

McGuire knew he was done in the CEO job as early as mid-2006. That first meeting of staff at Willoughby, where he introduced himself and reluctantly announced redundancies, was too early to question whether the job came as advertised.

The CEO role at Nine was the first time in his life he wasn't really in control of his job. His appointments were cancelled in favour of Nine's demands. His high hopes for innovation, growth and success dissipated early. And for someone who considers himself more of a chairman than a CEO, it was debilitating. McGuire is a motivator and an ideas man, not an accountant or administrator.

James Packer came to his house to concede he had 'dropped him in the shit'. All McGuire's previous plans with Packer and Alexander were redundant: two major private equity companies, CVC Asia Pacific and KKR, were circling and Packer was inclined to sell.

When Packer told McGuire the purchase prices being discussed, McGuire agreed. Packer asked him, as a friend, if he'd be okay in the job as they pushed on. McGuire said he walked in with his eyes open, and to do the deal. As a sweetener, Packer let McGuire stay on as Collingwood president, retracting their previous agreement.

The job became about cutting, and McGuire saw himself as a 'growth man'. Despite outward appearances, most of 2006 was about preservation for McGuire: of his own future and the future of jobs, friends and programs at Nine. He became particularly keen on protecting Melbourne's GTV-9 from the ensuing cuts to make the books look more attractive. He knew how important the Nine station was to the fabric of the network's brand.

McGuire would be the public patsy for Packer, but he negotiated some danger money. In September, it became clear McGuire had added the title 'Australia's highest-paid TV executive' to his previous 'highest-paid TV star' title, earning $4.7 million according to the annual report of Nine's owner, Publishing and Broadcasting Limited.[38]

As Nine and McGuire stumbled through their dual lives trying to project strength publicly while preparing for a sale privately, McGuire found some unlikely support, including supportive calls from Seven owner Kerry Stokes. And Packer remained an enduring source of support after damaging McGuire by putting him in an unenviable role.

The unlikeliest support of all came at a Collingwood and Carlton game at the MCG. McGuire escaped Sydney to enjoy another match-up for one of the AFL's grandest rivalries. He emerged from the rooms, as he does before each game, to walk around the boundary line to his seat on the wing. He had his game face on and head down as he passed a swathe of Carlton supporters. The Sydney media could be cruel, but they had nothing on opposing AFL supporters.

The heckles came. 'Lift your head!' came one yell from a Carlton supporter. Then another. They were encouraging the Collingwood president. 'Lift your head, Eddie! Don't listen to what those bastards in Sydney are saying! Keep at it,' they yelled.

At least McGuire appreciated TV wasn't life and death anymore.

In a sign of Nine's lobbying power in Canberra, in October 2006 the Howard government relaxed cross-media laws, abolishing limits on foreign ownership. The same day, Packer's public company PBL announced a joint venture with CVC Asia Pacific that would see Nine and the ACP magazines moving into a heavily leveraged deal valuing Packer's media assets at $5.5 billion (with PBL selling half of them for $2.75 billion). Due to the huge debt obligations, Packer and his fellow shareholders took $4.6 billion from the sale.

McGuire's involvement in the negotiations for the sale was typical of his powerless period as CEO. Alexander insisted when he accepted the job that McGuire take holidays at certain times. For his mid-year break, Alexander suggested McGuire take his family to a favourite Fiji island. As they arrived at Nadi, what they presumed was a driver signalled to the couple. But he directed Eddie one way and Carla the other. McGuire was taken to Packer's plane, which was waiting on the tarmac. He had to leave the family and return to Sydney immediately for urgent meetings. He flew overnight straight into negotiations for the sale of Nine.

McGuire found the negotiations invigorating, even if he wasn't central to them. He was in an awkward predicament. He was a television person running a television company right in the middle of its biggest ever financial play. He was unlucky he won the job at the wrong time in Nine's life. Eddie was not appointed to the PBL board when James Packer sold half his company to equity firm CVC. Not that he expected to be popular with CVC when they would later realise how Packer had made them his very own Alan Bond, selling at the top of the market.[39]

McGuire turned inwards. Protecting his family became a priority. If Sydney's media had been unkind before, what sort of malarkey would they pull on hearing of the sale? Worse, he wondered whether he was even a viable on-screen commodity anymore.

Eddie's last months as CEO were spent largely preparing for life back on air. He discussed leaving in November, but was urged to stay. He wasn't happy having to deal with criticism that he was being paid to do nothing. McGuire ended the year fending off rumours he would quit and that the prodigal son, David Gyngell, would return from his role heading minor production company Granada in the United States. He told staff at the network's Melbourne Christmas party 'For the record, I'm not [resigning].'[40]

And, unlikely as it was, McGuire could celebrate another yearly ratings win for Nine. A mixture of sharp programming and milking popular series pushed Nine over the line ahead of a noisy Seven.

In an end-of-year valediction with Robert Fidgeon, McGuire claimed, 'In the race of life in television, it was a clean sweep for Nine in the toughest year we [Nine] could possibly have – and, some would argue, in the best year that our opponents could possibly have.'

On New Year's Eve, McGuire confirmed he would return to the screen to host the network's new quiz show, *1 vs 100*. The spin from Nine was that he was a reluctant host but they just couldn't find another one who would be as suitable.

As the new owners took the scythe to costs, McGuire tried to protect as much programming as he could while also figuring out the optimal moment to leave the job, personally and professionally. PBL and CVC wanted to cut Nine's costs by an estimated $55 million in 2007, which would be another cruel phase to negotiate. McGuire continued to tinker at the edges. Lisa Wilkinson was recruited from *Weekend Sunrise* to replace Jessica Rowe in early 2007.

But even at the launch of the new game show *1 vs 100* – which should have given everyone a hint he would soon step down – things went awry. In a dummy run doubling as a media launch, the technology failed, wrongly eliminating more than half the contestants, including sceptical media. Then, after the problem was rectified, media guests Tracy Bartram and Matt Tilley revived their explosive relationship as Fox FM breakfast hosts as McGuire smiled nervously.

McGuire continued to fly the flag for Nine and was mischievous as Seven and Ten took back AFL broadcasting in 2007. Despite his Pies helping Seven to early ratings victories, McGuire sold Nine as footy's 'pirate station', with Foxtel sponsoring its three AFL programs.

McGuire gave further hints of his priorities as he admitted on *The Footy Show* he would prefer to win a premiership for Collingwood than win the television ratings. 'Given the fact that Nine's dominated the ratings for 50 years, we might slip a premiership in. What do you reckon?' he smiled in answer to a question from Sam Newman.

McGuire resigned as CEO in May 2007, seventeen months after taking the job. In four years, Nine went through four CEOs (Gyngell, Alexander, Chisholm and McGuire) and five heads of news (Jim Rudder, Max Uechtritz, Garry Linnell, Mark Llewellyn and John Westacott).[41] McGuire was hardly Robinson Crusoe.

His widely anticipated departure was stage-managed to coincide with a big on-screen promotion; he would front the new game show at 7 p.m. on weeknights to replace the flagging *Temptation*.

On the morning of his departure, McGuire pulled up outside Nine's studio in Melbourne's Docklands to record fresh episodes of the show, where he resigned in public again (after saying his on-air farewells as *Who Wants to Be a Millionaire?* host a year earlier), beaming under the studio lights as he held an impromptu media conference on set.

He left with some dignity, conceding that perhaps he wasn't cut out to be the CEO – at least of a shrinking company. He also conceded mistakes had been made in a tumultuous period:

> But I'm not going to die in a ditch over a 12-month period in a job that changed so dramatically.[42]
>
> I wasn't given the flick, if that's what you're asking. They asked and wanted me to stay. No one has boned anyone here, mate.
>
> There's no animosity. There's no rancour, no one's knifed anyone, there are no Machiavellian tales to be told.[43]

He had a pleasant exit strategy and a reason to be diplomatic after locking himself in for another four years and becoming Australia's first $5 million-a-year television personality. Later that day, he elaborated in an interview with 3AW's Neil Mitchell:

> [It was] an amazing seventeen months' journey, a lot different to what I thought. When I first sort of was sounded out for the job, it was Kerry Packer who was running the show and things have dramatically changed in that seventeen months.
>
> The fact that it became far more about financial, not management, but almost mechanics in recent times, you know, isn't exactly what I wanted to do as a focus. I didn't get much of a honeymoon.
>
> I think people were always going to try to prove it was wrong.

Almost immediately, McGuire flew to the United States with his Nine team to attend the annual LA Screenings, in which Hollywood studios screen their coming programs to expectant global buyers and partners. McGuire went with a weight off his shoulders and a stomach for retribution.

Leaving the job hit him hard: McGuire hadn't failed before. It wasn't the professional baiting that was so hurtful, but the sniping that he was never home – an absent parent. And the battle was made tougher because he was watching, from afar, his beloved father age rapidly. McGuire was always going to return to Melbourne at the first opportunity. McGuire learned much about himself and about the people around him in Sydney. He would have preferred learning those lessons away from the spotlight.

While in LA, Eddie had the opportunity to vent some anger when he approached Seven's David Leckie during a night out for all the Australian TV executives. 'You wouldn't call it good-natured banter,' one observer recalled. Another executive commented, 'I thought there was going to be a stink.' McGuire had had enough of the personal nature of Seven's attacks.

'Mate, do you want me to start doing things about you and Skye?' McGuire asked, referring to Leckie's wife. 'For fuck's sake, your kids go to school with my kids! Do you want me to throw you over the balcony here? Do you want to have a fight, what do you want to do? I'll kick your head into the valley if you want.'

Obviously, Leckie was taken aback by the tirade, as was everyone else who saw it. It put Leckie on his heels for once. He returned later to apologise – some say emotionally – to McGuire before leaving early. McGuire ran out of the function full of adrenalin, catching up with PBL's Ian Law. It was a necessary cleansing. McGuire and Leckie later had dinner. No grudges on this day; it was just another evening in Australian television.

James Packer maintained the faith and friendship. In June, the McGuires joined 100 others at St-Jean-Cap-Ferrat, between Monaco and Nice, for Packer's wedding to Erica Baxter.[44] Gyngell, who was best man, would return as chief executive of Nine two months later.

It was apparent why McGuire had to leave the management job and where his interests lay when his top-floor Willoughby office was packed up. There wasn't any Nine memorabilia; rather, a boxing glove signed by Joe Frazier, a painting by Indigenous artist Ginger

Riley Munduwalawala, fourteen photos of Collingwood's fourteen premiership teams and a Collingwood life membership certificate. He was up for a fight, but he preferred fights at Collingwood than with accountants.[45] And some within Nine felt he committed more to Collingwood than Nine.

And on the same day, Gerald Stone's book *Who Killed Channel 9?* crept onto store shelves across the nation. Eddie didn't kill Nine, but Nine nearly killed him. Don't you worry about that.

CHAPTER 18

BACK TO BASICS

Eddie McGuire's 'year' in Sydney as CEO of the Nine Network flattened a man his friends knew to be irrepressible. It also knocked his family, although Carla held the strong family unit together as her husband bore the bruises.

His Melbourne friends saw him return a different person – not quite introspective but certainly operating at a gear or two below his normal enthusiasm. Some felt it was natural he would curl up and mourn, or at least brood, for some time. But that wasn't his style.

The Sydney experience was an odd one, primarily because, for the first time in his life, Eddie hadn't been his own boss. He had been an employee for many years but in effect ran his own race or was good enough to earn autonomy. In the past decade, he packaged himself as a business sold to broadcasters, so he was accountable to himself.

His Nine travails were unexpected – even shocking – speed bumps in a steady life and career progression. He expected an upward trajectory. To find himself not only battered by the experience, but then pilloried in Gerald Stone's book, *Who Killed Channel 9?*,[1] was a shattering experience. Unlikely as it sounds, it took 'Eddie Everywhere' some time to realise the only way out of his funk was to get back in front of the camera or microphone because that was his strength.

McGuire was well compensated by Nine for essentially jumping on a grenade, yet it must have stung that new Nine CEO David Gyngell was brought back in as some kind of prodigal son benefitting from the pain inflicted during McGuire's reign. Gyngell's ascension at Nine was a contentious point for some, who had worked their way up the network; they saw Gyngell – James Packer's childhood friend – as the beneficiary of Packer largesse that brought him into key roles at Nine after a career running surf shops. Nevertheless, Gyngell was very generous in acknowledging his predecessor's work, particularly as the *Underbelly* series set Australian TV screens alight. Gyngell knew he was benefitting from pains inflicted upon McGuire.

McGuire reconciled his stint as CEO as unlucky timing. Gyngell agreed, although some still left at Nine weren't so forgiving, believing McGuire didn't fully commit to the ugly grunt the job required. Even so, McGuire entered the Nine job at the wrong moment, when circumstances changed very quickly. He wasn't alone. His friend Gary Pert signed his contract at Nine the day before the sale to private equity company CVC was announced.

McGuire's broadcast career had changed from what had been two decades of regular gigs to virtually nothing. He was no longer on radio and his on-screen appearances were ad hoc, even if *Who Wants to Be a Millionaire?* had not found a suitable replacement host while he was CEO (not that anyone tried particularly hard to find one).

He realised his commercial power and the platforms he used to possess to leverage sponsors and his football club had wilted. Furthermore, his networks couldn't help him enthusiastically if he was devalued. And he'd lost his ability to control agendas. He had to get back to basics.

Yet McGuire had doubts – albeit brief – that he could return to TV undamaged by his management stint. Certainly, McGuire's Q Score rating dropped while he was CEO, although he'd dismissed such research as irrelevant.

Nine had its own doubts about how they could use its former number one star – as did others back in Melbourne who met him to talk about possible jobs. The returning McGuire was a shell of his former self, lacking self-confidence even if the Melbourne media supported their fallen star.

McGuire had two things in his favour. First, no talent had popped up or progressed quickly enough to usurp him at Nine (although Karl Stefanovic's star was rising). Second, he still had Browne in his corner as managing director at Nine and a returning Gyngell who knew his value.

He knew he had to rebuild from scratch, and he was willing to slum it. Nine didn't know what to do with him. It seemed apparent the network was embarrassed to even be dealing with him. Initially, he became a 'Mr Odd-jobs'. One of his first on-screen appearances was an on-air apology to Melbourne TV viewers before a repeat screening of *The Shawshank Redemption*, to announce that a court order precluded Victorians from watching the first episode of *Underbelly* as planned.

Gyngell's first programming move in the job was bringing back *Who Wants to Be a Millionaire?* on Monday nights with a live, $10 million version of the show. It was a big gamble and worked in generating some heat and audiences but was too expensive to sustain.

Perhaps McGuire should have disappeared for twelve months and returned fresh, but his workaholic instincts kicked in. He began pitching ideas and they were rebuffed. He became a bit player, popping up with rare and unlikely jobs, including an interview with Robert De Niro for *A Current Affair* that was seen as an audition for his own chat show.

Particularly galling was *The Footy Show*'s unwillingness to provide any option to return. He wasn't expecting to do so, but the program's inability to show any generosity to its embattled co-creator was dispiriting. Co-hosts Garry Lyon and James Brayshaw remain acquaintances, not close mates.

Such was the indifference with which McGuire was being 'greeted' in TV he began to wonder whether he was cooked. Certainly it was more difficult than he had hoped while still living in Sydney as his sons saw out the school year.

The gravity of McGuire's time in a relative wilderness was clear in 2007 when he accepted a role calling a few football matches for low-rating sports talk station SEN. He knew he needed it to get his game back up to scratch.

One of the first to nibble was Melbourne talk station 3AW, which contemplated grooming him for a role, even though the breakfast, morning and drive shifts were settled and unavailable. He told the station in no uncertain terms he would not be a fill-in presenter on weekends or for absent hosts, as it desired.

In the 2008 pre-season, McGuire's name was top of the list for AFL radio broadcasters. He signed with SEN in a surprise move. He didn't want to restrict his options for a broader radio role by signing with the higher-profile 3AW or Triple M footy teams.

Nine brought him out of hibernation in May, for a second season hosting game show *1 vs 100* against Seven's dominant Friday night schedule in Melbourne of *Better Homes and Gardens* and *Friday Night Football*. McGuire's game show was dumped after two episodes.

Then he filled in as host of *A Current Affair* and laughed off rumours that he was leaving Nine to take over from Daryl Somers as the host of *Dancing with the Stars* on rival network Seven.

The TV ideas for him that failed before fruition mounted, including a prime-time bingo program, a 5.30 p.m. news magazine show and various game show formats, including the American format, *Let's Make a Deal*.

Effectively, 2008 was a washout for Eddie McGuire, TV personality. Nine couldn't find a home for their highest paid personality and media criticism of the $4.7 million 'Eddie Nowhere' hurt him. He was trying, taking gigs he wouldn't otherwise have touched, while Nine was reticent to have him return to air in a format that would hurt him. So nothing was happening and McGuire had too much time on his hands.

Early in 2009, he continued filming pilots for Nine that didn't get to air, including the game show based on the Two-Up game, *Heads or Tails*, which was also being pitched at the US market. He recorded an interview with Greg Norman for *60 Minutes*, after meeting him at a dinner party, and he hosted the Channel Nine telethon, *Australia Unites – the Victorian Bushfire Appeal*, in February, just as a past glory niggled at him. In the same month, the second series of *Underbelly* broke a ratings record as the most successful launch of an Australian television drama series.[2]

Then McGuire and Nine went back to the well to halt a rampaging Seven at 6 p.m. The battle for viewers in the 6–7 p.m. news and current affairs hour is always the keenest for the commercial networks because the time period assembles the biggest audience of the day and establishes the evening's viewing with promotions for the following programs. News and current affairs bosses rarely acknowledge the boost they get from their 5.30 p.m. lead-in programs, or even the breakfast shows *Today* and *Sunrise*, which might be turned off at 8 a.m., with the set turned on again at 6 p.m. on the same channel. Seven's 5.30 p.m. game show *Deal or No Deal* was one of the lesser-heralded successes of Seven's ratings renaissance from 2006. It couldn't be stopped despite Nine throwing a number of alternatives against it, including *Bert's Family Feud*.

Nine knew *Who Wants to Be a Millionaire?* was a proven concept, and McGuire its accepted host. It designed a tighter format, including refined lifelines and time limits on questions, that McGuire could walk into. The reality was unspoken and unpalatable: this was possibly a last-ditch effort to bomb *Deal or No Deal*, and also risked taking its major prime-time talent into a 5.30 p.m. graveyard. Worse, recent quiz shows, including *The Rich List*, *Million Dollar Wheel of Fortune*, *Power of 10*, *National Bingo Night* and *Temptation*, had all been axed or rested by networks due to poor ratings. Conversely, the success of the Academy Award-winning movie *Slumdog Millionaire* (in which a Mumbai teenager hits the jackpot on the Indian version of the quiz show) gave Nine a little faith – although McGuire joked, 'I was a bit disappointed when the host turned out to be a prick.'[3]

It was a risk that some viewed as a step down for McGuire but he needed the on-air exposure to justify his existence on Nine's books. The risk was justified. After a slow start, *Millionaire Hot Seat*'s ratings gained ground on *Deal or No Deal* and began to beat it nationally by September.

McGuire had his mojo back, and his old networks brightened. His radio home, Southern Cross Austereo, was struggling with its Triple M network – particularly in Melbourne – and its breakfast slot was vacant after Myf Warhurst and Peter Helliar were axed in July. Triple M spoke to McGuire months earlier about options, but the station didn't have a slot available. McGuire rebuffed the one option open to him, calling Sunday afternoon AFL matches. He wanted the higher-profile Friday night or Saturday afternoon games.

With breakfast now available, McGuire and Triple M spoke again, and their views of what they could do aligned. They agreed FM breakfast was full of the same kind of light and bright duos and pop music, and believed there was space in the market for an intrinsically Melbourne-oriented talk show that focused on sport and news, with light and shade. McGuire's *The Grill Team* format did fit the bill to some degree, although it was more comedic and fluffier than Triple M needed for breakfast. He also wanted it to be a newsier format. Deep down, McGuire admired 3AW's talk titans Ross Stevenson and John Burns, and aimed to replicate their content for a younger audience. McGuire said he wanted the top-rating breakfast show in Melbourne; that was not Triple M's goal. Being number one in under-55s looked a tough enough goal as it was because Triple M was also undergoing its own format transformation from a hokey old classic rock format to sports and entertainment – and going backwards in the process.

It was perfect. Triple M needed Eddie McGuire as much as he needed Triple M.

McGuire signed in August 2009 and was on air in September, marking his territory very deliberately between the greying 3AW and 774 ABC and the pop formats at Fox, Nova and Gold:

> What we want to do is capture that ground of people who aren't quite ready for the granny flats, and at the same time, don't necessarily want to tune into the latest bubble gum song. And FM has been a bit of a stand-up comedian fest for the last five years.[4]

McGuire brought his SEN partner, former Footscray ruckman Luke Darcy, to join Tony Moclair and Mieke Buchan on *The Hot Breakfast* and pushed his networks for his first episode, which featured Julia Gillard and Premier John Brumby as guests. A week later, Triple M recorded its worst ever radio ratings share, 4.3 per cent (although McGuire's show was not part of the survey). The following ratings survey showed McGuire's *The Hot Breakfast* had a 3.6 per cent share and the critics jumped on it, with 3AW's boss Shane Healy questioning, 'Where's he going to get his audience from?' The only way was up.[5]

McGuire was trying too hard to impress with his credibility. He signed Premier Brumby for a fortnightly appearance and his daily 'Eddie-torials' on serious topics often overreached. His on-air partners certainly weren't equipped to go toe-to-toe with him on political issues, and the friction became clear as Buchan and Moclair were gradually moved aside. Buchan would leave and the remaining trio would take a full year to start sounding comfortable together considering their varied topics.

McGuire was smart, poaching Jay Mueller, the long-time producer for 3AW's 'Ross and John'. Mueller was shrewd, though, insisting on a number of 'points of agreement' before committing to work for a host infamous in the industry for his bullying of staff. Eddie worked tirelessly to bring sponsors on board. He told Triple M he would 'walk up and down St Kilda Road and empty the pockets of every advertiser in Melbourne' to help the station. And he did, with countless presentations and meetings with sponsors, although few jumped on board from the beginning.

McGuire had always been good with radio advertisers. One Triple M general manager recalled sponsors calling him to say thanks for organising McGuire to call them with personal Christmas greetings. The GM had done nothing of the sort; unbeknown to management, McGuire asked office staff to source numbers of advertisers, who he'd call from his car phone while driving home each night. It thrilled advertisers – and of course, increased McGuire's marketability.

Through Triple M, McGuire sensed his magic and the cross-promotional power of his networking was back. He boasted he would secure the only radio interview with Tiger Woods because he was hosting the golf for Channel Nine and a special dinner for the golfer. His connections were reconnecting.

McGuire was also turning the tide within Nine, as *Millionaire Hot Seat* consolidated. He travelled to Vancouver to head Nine's Winter Olympics coverage feeling confident and finally back to his pre-Sydney self. Soon enough, he was embroiled in a controversy that snowballed as he and co-host Mick Molloy scoffed at the costumes being worn by the male figure skaters. As flamboyant American figure skater Johnny Weir competed, Molloy noted, 'They don't leave anything in the locker room, those blokes', before a laughing McGuire added, 'They don't leave anything in the closet either, do they?' Molloy chided McGuire jokingly, warning him he might get into trouble. But they continued, with Molloy saying a tuxedo-style costume was something even singer Prince would not wear, while McGuire said a skater wearing a costume of overalls and a flannelette shirt was 'a bit of *Brokeback*', referring to *Brokeback Mountain*, a film about two gay cowboys.

The complaints to Nine were immediate, and social media networks hyperventilated. It was a spark that lit viewer frustration with McGuire who, as any host of an Olympic Games tends to do, had already annoyed some viewers with mispronunciations and seemingly disrespectful interviews with occasional ex-pat mogul medallist Dale Begg-Smith and former German ice-skater Katarina Witt.

McGuire defended his comments immediately with a simple 'I'm not homophobic' on his Triple M breakfast show, which was also broadcasting from Vancouver. Weir later attended McGuire's Nine program, *Vancouver Gold*, in a gracious encounter which he concluded by blowing a kiss to McGuire. Privately, Weir saw the funny side of it, wasn't perturbed and played along.

Others didn't see the funny side. Gay rights activist Gary Burns lodged a complaint with the NSW Anti-Discrimination Board, saying the comments incited hatred against homosexual males.[6] He later withdrew the complaint after he met McGuire in Sydney and said McGuire understood how his banter could impact on vulnerable gay teenagers. 'Eddie McGuire is a man of integrity,' Burns said.

McGuire had gone on a charm offensive with the LGBTQ community, appearing on the Melbourne gay and lesbian community radio station Joy FM and being interviewed for the gay men's magazine *DNA*, saying he held his 'gay-friendly' nature as 'a badge of honour' and admitting to sharing a 'wink and a nod' with gay AFL players.

The real stoush stemming from McGuire's comments was off-screen and commercial. Nine's broadcast partner for the Games, Foxtel, issued an incredible press release condemning Nine for not broadcasting the flower presentation to Australian snowboarder Torah Bright, which is held immediately after the event while the medal presentation is held later off the mountain – Nine had cut to a commercial, unaware the presentation was imminent. Foxtel was attempting to spruik its 24/7 multi-channel coverage, but the release also referred to the Weir comments, saying they were a 'calamity' for Nine, adding it was 'a disastrous 48 hours for the free-to-air network after hosts Eddie McGuire and Mick Molloy made homophobic comments about two US ice skaters'. Foxtel has a higher than industry average proportion of homosexuals in key management and programming positions, and the Weir banter grated at its North Ryde home. The press release was unbelievably inflammatory, considering Nine and Foxtel were partners in a $140 million rights deal to broadcast the 2010 Games and 2012 London Olympic Games.

Nine chief executive David Gyngell was furious when he called Foxtel chief Kim Williams. Nine issued its own release, saying Williams had apologised and had described the release as 'disgusting'.

Back in Vancouver, McGuire was beyond furious, throwing one of his grandest tantrums and threatening to get even with Foxtel. As Torah Bright entered the International Broadcast Centre to do her required interviews with both Foxtel and Nine, Jeff Browne intervened, offering her brother and manager Ben $50000 to keep her away from Foxtel. The offer caused a major kerfuffle with the Australian Olympic Committee, which couldn't allow its athlete to choose sides. It only settled when Ben Bright told Browne they didn't want the $50 000 and Torah did interviews with both Nine and Foxtel. Off screen, McGuire was in a rage, giving Foxtel's head of the Games Peter Campbell both barrels all night. If any indication of the capricious nature of television was required, it came within two years, when McGuire would be working for Foxtel.

Before that, however, Eddie consolidated his broadcast base. In 2010, Triple M's *Hot Breakfast* continued its steady ascension in the ratings, by September delivering on Triple M's expectations by jumping to a 6.8 per cent share from 5.3 per cent, and consolidating that rise with a 7.1 per cent share in the November survey – second in FM breakfast.

McGuire's stability at Nine was confirmed in November, when he was named as the host of a revamped version of *This Is Your Life*.

A measure of McGuire's returned confidence was his criticism of Chrissie Swan's Gold Logie nomination in the new year. Deep down, it must have hurt and confused McGuire that he'd not earned a Gold Logie nomination, so when the co-host of a low-rating Ten program, *The Circle*, earned a nomination, he went hard.[7]

He kept busy, launching the sports-themed game show *Between the Lines*, which was axed after a few weeks. Hindsight would tell him he was trying too hard to find a new *Footy Show* to fill a void; he attached himself to many Nine pilots and shows that were best left alone, including the game show *Million Dollar Drop*.

Nine's private equity owners were also looking to rationalise as the cuts kept coming. One of the most obvious slashes was to McGuire's $4 million-plus contract. He'd delivered the goods with *Millionaire* pulling viewers into *Nine News* – but $4 million?

Fox Sports and Nine had reconciled since the Vancouver Games, and were becoming quite entwined. McGuire was a problem, but he was also its solution. Nine could no longer afford, or justify, McGuire's salary. McGuire wasn't going to take a pay cut from Nine, particularly after the reputational damage inflicted upon him when he was CEO. And Nine wasn't in the game to win the next AFL broadcast rights deal – unlike Foxtel.

An arrangement was struck whereby McGuire would remain at Nine but also be contracted to Foxtel to become the face of its AFL coverage on the renewed Fox Footy channel. Foxtel would stump up some of McGuire's pay (up to $2 million), letting Nine off the hook for a large slab of his salary, while the Melbourne star would help Foxtel drive subscriptions in its weakest market, Melbourne. McGuire wasn't alone: NRL great Peter Sterling also stitched a deal between the two networks, alleviating Nine's costs. But he wasn't costing Nine McGuire's salary.

The deal was a bonus for McGuire because he would be able to revert to his one true love: calling football on TV. Sure enough, Foxtel subsequently picked up the rights to broadcast the AFL, on-selling the free-to-air rights to Seven. The $1.25 billion deal meant McGuire would indeed become the face of the AFL – not on Nine, but on Foxtel.

McGuire had big plans, particularly a news-breaking, agenda-setting weekly variety show on Sunday nights. *Eddie McGuire Tonight* wasn't quite the all-singing, all-dancing show the title suggested. It created some ripples, though, with strong interviews and good gets, although some reignited the perennial conflict of issue claims. His exclusive interview with troubled Aboriginal player Liam Jurrah, which he secured without going through Jurrah's club, Melbourne, a courtesy he would have expected as Collingwood president, was a case in point. McGuire defended himself as a journalist in this instance, not a club president.

'I'm not going to have another five years of this nonsense about being president of a club, which is being a glorified chook raffler these days … The only people doing it for free are the presidents,' he later said on radio.

Foxtel got its money's worth from McGuire, as it had hoped. He hit the ground running, securing an exclusive interview with the world's fastest man, Usain Bolt, ahead of the London Games. Foxtel couldn't believe its luck.

He was known to shill enthusiastically for his sponsors; even so, many were taken aback when the Nine star hosted the relaunch of the Fox Footy channel at a Melbourne function in February. 'I've seen the future of sport in this country and the future of sport is Foxtel,' McGuire smiled in front of a gathering of media and AFL stars and executives, some of whom couldn't believe what he'd said. Such was his enthusiasm, Nine seemed a distant memory.

Of course, it wasn't. McGuire's omnipresence at Nine was diminishing, though. He would be one of six co-hosts of the London Olympic Games for Nine, the very Games he, Jeff Browne and Gary Fenton had quietly schemed to win for the network. He shared the hosting duties with Leila McKinnon, Ken Sutcliffe, Karl Stefanovic, Mark Nicholas and Cameron Williams.[8] He also hosted the Games for Foxtel.

McGuire's stint with Foxtel became a professional renewal, particularly in his off-screen demeanor. Foxtel execs were mortified when he outlined his plans to juggle his Triple M radio show and Nine hosting commitments with them. He not only pulled it off but charmed Foxtel staff, acting as a cool-headed presenter and morale-builder eons away from the volatile Nine host down the hall at the Vancouver Winter Olympics.

McGuire was paired with Matt Shirvington to mentor the young host, although one of his more important, and effective, tasks was restoring the confidence of swimming commentator Susie O'Neill. The Golden Girl said what everyone was thinking in her role as a Foxtel commentator, lambasting the performance of the Australian swim team at the Games. The lack of success and later revelations justified O'Neill's comments but she was bruised by criticism and intense pressure from within the sport. McGuire and co-commentator Ray Hadley were tasked with building her back up. And they did.

The year 2012 was a triumph for McGuire on many levels. He was back in the game on television and the Foxtel relationship rejuvenated his on-screen affair with footy. *The Hot Breakfast* continued to grow with the addition of comedian Mick Molloy the previous year (McGuire had wanted him from the beginning) taking the program to another level. Teaming up with the comedy pro meant McGuire could conceivably aim for the top spot in breakfast.

In October, he celebrated his thirty years in television with a showy lunch at a favourite old haunt, St Kilda's Stokehouse. Eddie had his mitts all over the video tribute of his career, much to the consternation of harried editors and the publicity department at Nine. 'There are plenty of people here who have hated me at times, plenty of people who have hated other people here at other times, but we've all come together today to celebrate,' he told an audience that included wife Carla, James Packer, Shane Warne, Browne, Lindsay Fox, AFL CEO Andrew Demetriou, Ron Walker, Michael Gudinski, Molly Meldrum, Nathan Buckley, Molloy, Foxtel CEO Richard Freudenstein, Brigitte Duclos, Sam Newman, Tony Jones, Trevor Marmalade, Jeff Kennett, John 'Strop' Cornell and Delvene Delaney, among others.[9]

Hot Seat's dominance was confirmed the following year when Seven moved the former timeslot winner, *Deal or No Deal*, away from the 5.30 p.m. slot to be replaced by *Million Dollar Minute*. And in July, McGuire, Molloy and Darcy broke through as the kings of Melbourne's FM breakfast shift for the first time with an audience share of 9.5 per cent for *The Hot Breakfast*. The triumph was more than just numbers for a show that had been dubbed the 'low-rating *Hot Breakfast*'. It was also a triumph of format, bringing a hitherto smart talk vibe to FM breakfast and making McGuire as influential in the market as AM talk hosts Jon Faine and Neil

Mitchell, or Sydney's Alan Jones, but with a younger audience. Others have tried across Australia since with the FM talk format, yet none has approached *The Hot Breakfast*'s success.[10] The rise was even more meritorious coming before the departure of long-term rivals on Fox (Matt and Jo) and Nova (Hughesy and Kate) later that year. The subsequent flux in the market meant *The Hot Breakfast* would be unassailable for years to come. McGuire opted to join the embattled Triple M with the aim of bringing the station back to life – although, if the truth be told, he needed the broadcasting role to resuscitate himself. Four years later, both missions had been accomplished.

CHAPTER 19

A FINGER IN MANY PIES

Despite winning back his mojo on television and radio, Eddie McGuire's recovery from his period as the CEO at Nine was more protracted than he could have expected.

It might have taken him a while to get his confidence back but there was no chance he would confine his future to broadcast roles only. Eddie's historical networks were too amenable and his reach too broad to limit himself to the roles of game show host and football caller.

McGuire's entrepreneurial spirit was fuelled intermittently during his time in the CEO role, and the opportunity to show some managerial flair was one of the primary reasons he took the job at Nine. In fact, while developing and pushing programs as the head of Nine, he was enjoying the most transparent and conflict-free time of his business career. The conflict was in cutting costs and axing jobs. His business tentacles spread beyond television and radio on his return to Melbourne. They had to do so.

Some of his roles were incidental jobs. He hosted the welcoming at Telstra Dome of 40 000 Catholic pilgrims for World Youth Day in 2008. McGuire was named the official event patron of the Days in the Diocese Melbourne celebration of faith and spirituality.

Previously, the good 'Irish Mick' had hosted the Jubilee Mass in 2000 at the Telstra Dome in front of 70 000 people.

His influence in Melbourne was so pervasive he held meetings with Lord Mayor John So after others suggested McGuire could take the role of Lord Mayor of Melbourne. He contemplated the task briefly before conceding he was too busy. It showed a new maturity. A man who could never say no to a new role or job was now more discerning.

McGuire was also one of a high-profile cabal of members of the Athenaeum Club who attempted to force change at the 142-year-old club by allowing women to become members. Their attempt was stymied and the fracas saw resignations and public threats at the once-venerable institution.

McGuire pitched his tent back in Melbourne with some prominent property deals in record time, including the purchase of a reported $11 million house in central Toorak late in 2008 before securing a long-term lease on a cliff-top beach retreat at Portsea, south of Melbourne. When he took his father through his new house, his dad couldn't stop laughing at its expanse. Eddie saw it as vindication of his dad's decision to venture to Australia almost five decades before.

His appointments began stacking up. Old friend Steve Vizard eased his path onto the board of the Victorian Major Events Company, which in some way was the most suitable job of all for the boy who stood for everything Melbourne. McGuire would be a positive addition to the board, although he would also use it well.

McGuire's networking into the Collins Street financial houses resulted in his appointment to the advisory board for the broking firm Evans and Partners, alongside Foster's chairman David Crawford, former union chief Bill Kelty, corporate advisory whiz John Wylie and managing partner David Evans. Again, it would raise a minor conflict as McGuire commentated the golf for Nine, sponsored by one of Evans' competitors, J.B. Were.[1]

McGuire's enthusiasm for the city of Melbourne resulted in a few odd couplings. The AFL club president fronted a video extolling the virtues of the city to prospective recruits for the new Melbourne Rebels rugby union team.[2] And then came the cricket.

Eddie McGuire agreed to become the chairman of the fledgling Melbourne Stars Twenty20 side because he wanted strength in numbers in Melbourne sport. A solid rugby, soccer or cricket team neighbouring, or sharing facilities with, Collingwood in the Olympic Park and MCG precinct would be good for Collingwood. He also knew the impact the shortened Twenty20 game was having after Nine screened the first T20 International in 2006 to a big TV audience while he was Nine's CEO.

The new Big Bash League club needed McGuire more than he needed it, though. The Stars' management wanted to harness McGuire's profile, sponsorship prowess and networks. Just to spice it up, the Stars' cross-town rivals, the Melbourne Renegades, announced North Melbourne president and *The Footy Show* co-host James Brayshaw would be its founding chairman.[3]

Sure enough, McGuire delivered media cut-through for the team, and his mate Shane Warne joined as a 42-year-old, proving more adept and popular at the form than anyone imagined. McGuire floated the idea of the world's fastest man, Usain Bolt, joining the Stars – even as a fieldsman. He said:

> To be honest, Usain Bolt has provided as much marketing impetus to the KFC Big Bash League, probably only behind Shane Warne. If he doesn't ever come, he has done more for this game, and Cricket Australia should put on a street parade for him already. Maybe some of the people at marketing who are talking about it being a negative should come and have a chat to me and see what we're actually doing and not worry about it.[4]

It was McGuire back at his showman best.

The extracurricular connection that caused a great deal of friction within a subset of Melbourne sport was his appointment to the board of Athletics Australia, the body overseeing Athletics Victoria.

Publicly, McGuire's motive was pure. He saw a sport that was woefully under-resourced, yet every four years it became a national focus at the Olympics. It was also a poorly managed sport, which saw almost the entire board turned over after a full-scale review of the sport in 2004. After starting on the sponsorship sub-committee, he noted:

> Athletics Australia is run on a shoestring; I laugh when I look at their budget at the moment. Athletics is the biggest sport of all at the Olympic Games and it hasn't moved forward as other sports have. It seems totally factionalised.[5]

Privately, McGuire could also see the sport as a broadcast opportunity for his McGuire Media and Nine, heading towards the Olympic Games. Then there was the sport's hold over Olympic Park.

McGuire's appointment was seen by some as a stalking horse for Collingwood to gain greater control of the Olympic Park precinct. Confusing his intent was the wholesale transformation of Olympic Park from the Victorian home of athletics to Collingwood's training and administration facility and the former Olympic Pool into the Pies' indoor facility.

In February 2012, an opportunistic hack of the AFL's own website meant visitors to afl.com.au were briefly greeted with the message 'Demetriou is Eddie's bitch'. The website breach left the AFL red-faced, some amused, but Eddie had heard far worse. He shrugged it off and moved on.

CHAPTER 20

REGRETS AND RECRIMINATIONS

Eddie McGuire doesn't look back. As Nathan Buckley says, 'Eddie bites off more than he can chew and then just chews like fuck.'

He keeps moving forward. If he could take one thing back, though, it is his on-air brain fade that Sydney Swans footballer Adam Goodes might be used to promote the *King Kong* musical. He knows it is the one stain in his life that is indelible. It is devastating to him, and it can't be undone.

Before this radio faux pas, McGuire had done much for Indigenous Australians. He wrenched Collingwood's label as a racist club from it, and even the night before he put his foot in his mouth, Eddie spoke at a dinner raising funds for Indigenous school kids.

The Collingwood Football Club wasn't alone in not recruiting Indigenous players during the VFL era, and it would be a slight to the club to suggest it did so with intent. But when Wally Lovett debuted for Collingwood in 1982, it was the last of the Melbourne-based clubs to select an Indigenous player. And some before him at other clubs, including Syd Jackson, Graham 'Polly' Farmer and Barry Cable, had ignited the game.

The environment at Victoria Park back then reflected an Anglo-Celtic disregard for Indigenous players. The venue was a cauldron of invective for any opposition players, not the least being Indigenous players. Magpie David Cloke acknowledged as much in a game during the 1980s when he tapped North's Jimmy Krakouer on the head before the first bounce and said he couldn't control the supporters but if any player resorted to racial abuse, to tell him and he'd sort it out.

That was something because years earlier Carlton's Indigenous brilliant forward flanker Syd Jackson defended his report for striking Collingwood flanker Lee Adamson by saying he had taunted him with racial abuse. He won a reprimand.

It is no coincidence that arguably the most striking image in Indigenous sport – of St Kilda star Nicky Winmar raising his guernsey to point to his dark skin – was snapped at Victoria Park. It was his damning response to racial abuse from Collingwood supporters, who had begun their abuse even as St Kilda players walked the ground before the game. Winmar made a pact with an Indigenous teammate, Gilbert McAdam, to show them and they did, splitting the three and two Brownlow votes between them in a famous victory.

Then Collingwood president Allan McAlister exacerbated the controversy by noting that, 'As long as they conduct themselves like white people, well, off the field, everyone will admire them and respect them.'

McAlister's words as much as Nicky Winmar's actions sparked the AFL's move to address racism on and off the field, which accelerated two years later when Essendon's Michael Long reported racial abuse from Collingwood's Damian Monkhorst and the AFL code of conduct on racism was established.

That was the kind of club McGuire stepped into as president in 1998/99. McGuire led the way in turning the racism around. His sense of social justice is undeniable, and it comes from parents who were themselves shunned in their own ways in the religious troubles of Ireland and Scotland.

It was not a token role when, in 2008, McGuire was appointed to one of Prime Minister Kevin Rudd's thought bubbles, the Social Inclusion Board, and its first meeting was in Broadmeadows.

His charity work remains prolific and, for the most part private. In 2005, it was notable that McGuire's citation for becoming a Member of the Order of Australia cited his 'service to the community, particularly through support for health care and welfare organisations, and to broadcasting'.

Much of his community work at Collingwood was not only turning the culture of the football club around, but ensuring the club's strength was directed to help the community's weakest members.

'We should not be just a football club. We should be a talisman for community standards, good or bad, so when the bad things happen we can get in and make an impact,' he said.[1]

McGuire helped to establish the Collingwood Football Club Foundation, which aims to be 'the biggest philanthropic sporting organisation in Australia, with an emphasis on youth and inspiring young people to do their best'. One of its initiatives, AFL SportsReady, is a program designed to increase Indigenous participation in employment and education, with a strong community football and local government involvement. McGuire launched the program in 2012. The Barrawarn program (Barrawarn denotes 'magpie' in Woi wurrung, the language of the Wurundjeri people) provided fifteen Indigenous kids with the chance to kick-start their careers with traineeships.

Within Collingwood, McGuire always ensured the personal well-being of his Indigenous players, taking a particular shine to Leon Davis, who became a two-time All-Australian in a 225-game career. At a pre-game function before Davis's two-hundredth game in 2010, McGuire conceded the club stood for 'anyone who's disassociated', but it couldn't deny regrettable parts of its history that did not reflect that. He said at a pre-game function:

> We did go the wrong way. We were racial vilifiers, not standing up for the people who we should be looking after, which are the people being vilified.
>
> We've turned that around, and Leon Davis is the personification of that in our team – a young man from Western Australia who's played exciting, great football.
>
> And now at 29 years of age, he plays his 200th game and becomes the first Indigenous player to wear the black and white stripes in 200 games.
>
> It's a wonderful landmark day for our club. Do not underestimate what it means to all of us close to Collingwood. We love Leon Davis, we love what he stands for and we know that he has made our club such a better club for his patronage of our football club.[2]

Early in McGuire's presidency, he also led the campaign, through the annual Anzac Day AFL match with Essendon, to have Indigenous servicemen recognised.

Beyond Collingwood, McGuire became patron of the Michael Long Foundation, which focuses on Indigenous causes, and he took up many individual causes, including some quiet patronage of former North Melbourne star Jimmy Krakouer after he was released from prison.

Which is not to mitigate his one dreadful misstep – merely to note it didn't come from an impure place.

McGuire was so sensitive to Collingwood's dark past on racial issues that he jumped on a St Kilda supporter who chastised the Magpies' new Aboriginal recruit, Andrew Krakouer, at an MCG match in 2011. McGuire angrily rebuked the supporter, although it later became clear the supporter was not racially abusing the player but rather dredging up Krakouer's sixteen-month jail stint for serious assault.

'It was a very demeaning way to speak of any person, whether they're black, white or brindle,' McGuire said of the 'borderline racial abuse'.[3] Andrew Krakouer remained on the club's books in 2013 in its 'philanthropic arm' as an Aboriginal liaison officer after he suffered injury, as well as personal and financial problems.

Two months after the supposed abuse of Krakouer at the MCG, Collingwood began running advertisements on scoreboards at games warning fans not to be abusive to the opposition, in response to abusive chants directed at St Kilda player Stephen Milne. Coach Mick Malthouse was a conscientious objector to the scheme.

Despite the club's best efforts, two events in 2013 would scrawl a 'black' mark across McGuire and Collingwood and haunt Sydney Swans star Adam Goodes, who the following year was named Australian of the Year.

As the fizz left the final quarter of a Swans win against Collingwood at the MCG on a cool May Friday night in 2013, Goodes ran across the boundary line chasing a ball. He pulled up sharply after hearing someone call him an 'ape', turned around and pointed to the Collingwood supporter sitting behind the fence, calling security staff to eject her from the ground. Goodes reacted instantly and wasn't to know the offender was only thirteen years old. McGuire didn't know either until later that night. The fact wasn't even apparent to TV viewers or the Seven Network, which continued to screen vision of the incident throughout the telecast. The fan was escorted from the ground by police and Goodes, distressed, left the field immediately after the final siren.

It wasn't the first time a player had asked for a fan to be ejected. Two years earlier, Magpie Dale Thomas pointed out a Collingwood fan in the crowd who had racially vilified Gold Coast player Joel Wilkinson. That wasn't in prime time or during the

AFL Indigenous Round, though – or in a game in which Goodes dominated with thirty disposals and three goals, including his four-hundredth. Television footage later showed the teen was not the only Collingwood supporter to racially abuse Goodes and teammate Lewis Jetta that night.

McGuire rushed to the Sydney rooms after the game to apologise to Goodes and reiterate Collingwood had 'zero tolerance' for racial abuse. They shook hands, although Goodes was bamboozled by the age of the child and the abuse coming in that week, of all weeks. That same week, Goodes was also one of the leaders of a campaign launched to recognise Aboriginal people in the Constitution.

The thirteen-year-old called Goodes on Saturday to apologise, telling him she did not realise the word 'ape' was racist. McGuire also spoke to the girl, who was young and naïve, not even realising it was the Indigenous Round, let alone that the term used was offensive. Goodes was worried she would become a scapegoat; cruelly, history would show that her age would be used against him by racists condemning him as a bully.

Later that week, McGuire was speaking at a function raising funds for Indigenous school scholarships, while on crutches and painkillers for a leg injury. In front of an audience of businesspeople and philanthropists, he spoke of the danger of transplanting Indigenous kids in southern schools away from their home communities. He had been heartbroken previously when interviewing Cyril Rioli, as the Hawthorn star recounted crying himself to sleep every night while he was on scholarship at Melbourne's Scotch College. A subsequent initiative with Michael Long aimed to build footballing facilities in Darwin for kids from remote communities to gradually get used to being away from home before contemplating moving south to play.

The following morning, McGuire was on air as usual on Triple M's *The Hot Breakfast*, talking to Luke Darcy in that pre-7 a.m. fog known to most breakfast radio announcers.

Darcy mused how the gorilla hand perched on the top of the Eureka Tower had been an effective promotion for the stage production of *King Kong*.

'Get Adam Goodes down for it, do you reckon?' McGuire retorted.

'No, I wouldn't have thought so,' Darcy replied. 'Absolutely not.'

'You can see them doing that, can't you?'

'Who?' Darcy asked, fearing the worst already.

McGuire: 'Goodsey.'

'What's that?' said Darcy, still not experienced enough to shut McGuire down but looking at him alarmed.

'You know, with the ape thing, the whole thing,' McGuire continued. 'I'm just saying the pumping him up and mucking around and all that sort of stuff.'

The conversation moved on and McGuire was none the wiser to the implications of what he had just said.

Those outside the studio were, though. Co-host Mick Molloy was preparing to come on air (his breakfast radio contract stipulated a 7 a.m. start) and was incredulous. He rushed in to producer Jay Mueller and asked, 'Did he just say what I think he said?'

Mueller and Molloy suggested to McGuire this one 'wasn't going to go through to the keeper', and he might want to get on the front foot and apologise in order to muzzle it immediately. Those in the studio felt McGuire wasn't quite there when he said it.

McGuire wasn't so convinced, primarily because in his own mind he hadn't meant anything by it. Initially, he didn't see the offence because he hadn't meant to offend. To him, it was a bit of light banter that touched on the old Broadway ways of using anything topical to promote a musical while he thought he was also contrasting how far we had progressed.

Radio veterans could see the various thoughts swirling around in search of a gag but the synapses not connecting. Timing is everything in comedy and radio and McGuire couldn't have mistimed a 'gag' so badly, both in the moment and in that week.

Producers cut to a song and the control room was a panic station. McGuire checked what he'd said and returned to the studio to retract the statement and apologise. He said, 'I wasn't racially vilifying anyone' – which wasn't the point. It didn't matter how *he* felt. Prior to breakfast radio's prime time of 7.30–8.30 a.m., McGuire felt the moment might pass without note. His workmates knew otherwise.

McGuire continued the shift and met a friend for a pre-arranged catch-up at South Melbourne's St Ali café afterwards. He was melancholy and over-tired, having worked himself to the bone. He asked his friend for some advice that had nothing to do with that morning's broadcast but his overcommitments: 'If I had to dump something, what would you suggest?'

McGuire's phone started ringing. He ignored it. Then the messages became more frequent. McGuire told his friend, off-hand, that it might have something to do with something he'd said on air that morning – 'a passing comment'. He suggested that it would blow over. It didn't.

As anticipated by others at Triple M, 3AW's Neil Mitchell replayed the offending excerpt. The story wasn't going away. The incident was propelled into the national consciousness by a simple tweet from Goodes – 'Morning Australia, this is what I have woken up to' – linking to an article about the gaffe and McGuire's on-air apology.

McGuire was realising the gravity of the situation. Swans chairman Richard Colless texted him: 'I think we need to talk urgently. You know what I'm talking about. This is a very serious matter.'

McGuire responded by telling Colless he thought the transcript took the comments out of context. Colless didn't agree, and told McGuire he had nowhere to go on this one. It was indefensible.

McGuire spoke to a Southern Cross Austereo lawyer, who advised him that he should buckle in for a rough week. McGuire brushed him off, saying the controversy would pass in a day. They spoke a week later and McGuire conceded the lawyer had been right.

McGuire made the call to Goodes to apologise and try to explain. Goodes was distraught – way more so than in the previous week when insulted by the thirteen-year-old Collingwood supporter. He was particularly let down considering the work on racial tolerance the duo had done together, telling McGuire he couldn't believe he could say such a thing 'after all that we've been through'.

Later in the day, McGuire called a press conference, hoping to clear the air. It was bold but his obfuscation and lack of clarity only worsened his plight. In the twenty-four-minute press conference, he used the phrase 'slip of the tongue' sixteen times. He said in a statement he had contacted the Sydney Swans and Goodes, and 'Adam was gracious enough to take my call and expressed his disappointment. Adam accepted my apology and acknowledged my strong commitment and record in tackling racial vilification, not just on the football field but in the wider community.'

That was the most positive reading of Goodes' reaction. He was saddened and furious, and the Swans didn't take kindly to McGuire using their conversation so boldly.

Karma would deeply hurt McGuire. The Sydney Swans was the wrong club for McGuire to offend. The club despised him before that moment, and was disgusted with McGuire's comment. They would not allow him any wriggle room from this one, as the Swans' management could see how his comments had devastated their player.

Eddie McGuire's feuds with other clubs and the AFL were part of his presidential modus operandi. Many were manufactured for cynical or show business means, hyped up to make his Collingwood members and sponsors feel good. Other feuds stemmed from his serious beliefs about the future of the game and the protection of players and his club. And others were just personal.

Brisbane had years of enmity after its Grand Final victories over Collingwood, accusing McGuire of poaching players and then asking for him to be banned from calling Brisbane matches after he fought successfully against the salary cap concessions given to Brisbane and Sydney. In 2003, McGuire's taunting message ('The AFL Lions With salaries to spare/Fix'em up Pies/Make 'em look like Bears') on a Magpie banner was banned by the AFL before a match against Brisbane.

All clubs lambasted McGuire for Collingwood's recalcitrance about wearing an alternate guernsey – most particularly Port Adelaide, which blued with McGuire for years about rights to the black-and-white striped jumper.

Essendon fought with him after renaming the 'Coventry' end of the Docklands stadium the Lloyd end, and McGuire accused the club of cheating the salary cap under coach Kevin Sheedy.

Richmond said McGuire didn't respect its club[4] and later criticised him for muck-raking in suggesting coach Terry Wallace would be replaced by Kevin Sheedy.[5] North Melbourne had jumper issues with Collingwood too, as well as personal issues concerning president James Brayshaw and CEO Eugene Arocca, not to mention McGuire's occasional dismissiveness of the club.

McGuire didn't warm to the new clubs, criticising draft concessions to the Gold Coast Suns and Greater Western Sydney (GWS), and later criticising GWS as trying to make a go of it in 'the land of the falafel'. Coach Kevin Sheedy responded, recalling McGuire's troubled stint as Nine CEO: 'Just because you couldn't handle Sydney doesn't mean the whole of Australia can't.'[6] McGuire later accused the GWS of cheating when it announced its first signing, Adelaide's Phil Davis.

Melbourne earned McGuire's ire by asking for extra draft picks for Tom Scully and then poaching one of Collingwood's uncontracted recruiters. Geelong had its spats with McGuire, particularly after he accused president Frank Costa of barracking for the Brisbane Lions instead of Collingwood during a Grand Final, as discussed previously.

Carlton was a long-time nemesis, and he baited its history of salary-cap cheating and questionable third-party deals between sponsor Visy and Chris Judd. Smaller clubs, including North Melbourne and the Western Bulldogs, despised McGuire's seeming control of the AFL equalisation fund, which he said drained money from wealthy clubs to prop up struggling clubs.

But McGuire's feud with the Sydney Swans topped them all, and has soured relations between the two clubs, or at least key figures at the two clubs, to a point beyond reconciliation. McGuire needled Sydney throughout his presidency.

Initially, they were mere mischiefs. In 1999, he warned of a fiasco, and a possible forfeiture of the four points, if crowds disrupted the Magpie game at the SCG in which Tony Lockett would kick his record-breaking 1300th goal.[7]

A year later, Sydney sought legal advice after McGuire said Collingwood was now treating Sydney 'like our worst enemies' after it put forward a deal to play a game in Sydney but 'tried to stitch us up'. 'As long as they try to stitch up Melbourne clubs and try and pull one over us, of course they are going to be looked on with distrust,' McGuire retorted. Sydney chairman Richard Colless claimed McGuire was incorrect and offensive:

> Mr McGuire preaches leadership and cohesion. It would be constructive for him to actually apply those principles ... The club, as a result of this, has no desire to have any association whatsoever with the Collingwood Football Club in relation to a Collingwood home game in Sydney. The club believes Mr McGuire sadly misunderstands his club's status in the Sydney market.[8]

Collingwood, at its lowest ebb, subsequently presented a proposal to the AFL Commission to play three games in Sydney (two against the Swans and one against the financially weak North Melbourne).

McGuire later said the proposal would only go ahead if the Magpies were guaranteed eighteen games in Melbourne. The president thought the proposal would help the broader game by boosting Sydney attendances. Sydney thought it was condescending. Subsequently, McGuire began a campaign against Sydney and Brisbane that would ferment ill-will for years and prompt Colless, in 2002, to send a one-finger cheerio to McGuire, direct to a TV camera.

McGuire said the salary-cap advantages enjoyed by Brisbane and Sydney resulted in a 'grossly unfair playing field' (the AFL granted the Lions and Swans extra room in their salary caps to allow them to recruit and retain players in 'non-football' states). 'Don't worry about where the AFL will be turning to get the money (to help Sydney and Brisbane),' he said. 'They'll be turning straight to Collingwood and straight to Essendon.'[9]

McGuire united the Melbourne clubs in their opposition to new draft concessions for Sydney and Brisbane, giving them priority access to local players. He had a head of steam, accusing the AFL of attempting to shoehorn both teams to success.

The draft concessions were dropped and Sydney went ballistic in an open letter to the AFL from Richard Colless and chief executive Kelvin Templeton describing McGuire's comment, in which he labelled the AFL Commission as cheats, as 'a low point in the history of our game'.[10]

The vitriol continued in what at times appeared to be a Punch and Judy show starring McGuire and Colless. In 2003, McGuire described Sydney as Australia's 'bullshit capital' when its higher cost of living was used to justify Sydney's higher salary cap.[11] Months later, Colless tried to plant a kiss on McGuire's cheek ahead of a financially lucrative match.[12]

The fracas continued as the AFL's 'equalisation' plans developed and McGuire saw the Swans still receiving concessions. 'As George Orwell said, "All animals are equal, but some animals are more equal than others",' he said.

McGuire's long campaign against the northern clubs eventually resulted in the cost of living allowance for the Swans being phased out by the end of 2016, to be replaced by a rental subsidy scheme, and, worse, being banned from the trade and free agency periods at the end of 2014 and 2015 after the club recruited Lance Franklin and Kurt Tippett.

The Sydney Swans had financial reason to despise McGuire's efforts, although his constant criticism the club was an AFL 'favoured state' also hurt and diminished the club's toil and savvy planning. So when McGuire attacked one of their own players, there were, as it used to be said, 'no beg pardons'. The Swans quietly kicked as he was down.

The day of the Goodes gaffe did not pan out as McGuire had anticipated. His waffly press conference – in which he would normally quell criticism with a mixture of transparency and defiance – did not play well. He looked in bad shape and clearly still did not understand the gravity of his offence. He refused to acknowledge he had racially vilified Goodes – a position he changed later that night on Fox Footy's *AFL360*. He added he would not resign as Collingwood president after an unreserved apology: 'It has cut me to the core. I put my foot in it. I'm happy to cop any criticism. I could not be more sorry. I did the wrong thing – not intentionally – but nevertheless it caused hurt.'

He called AFL chief Andrew Demetriou and federal Sports Minister Senator Kate Lundy on that Wednesday to offer his *mea culpa*. He also called Michael Long to offer to resign as chairman of the Michael Long Foundation, an offer Long rejected.

Demetriou said the AFL would not censure McGuire, yet later that day the AFL confirmed it would launch an AFL racial vilification investigation after criticism mounted, including from Collingwood player Harry O'Brien.

'I think Eddie's going to live with this for a long time,' Colless said, and that fact was beginning to dawn on McGuire.

McGuire used the *Herald Sun* the next morning to explain himself:

> Last night I looked my sons in the eye and told them two things. The first was that they know what their dad stands for.
>
> The next was that I had made a massive mistake, and I deserved the fall-out ... I find myself in the exact opposite position to every belief I have, and it cuts me to the core.
>
> Last Friday, I stood for what I believed in, and yesterday I made a simple, if devastating, mistake.
>
> To everyone who believes in me and what I stand for, I apologise, and I will continue to fight for equality for all.[13]

He also emailed Collingwood's 75 490 members, saying, 'I would like to offer my sincerest apologies to the entire Collingwood family ... I am sad that my words have cast a shadow on this great club.'

The vitriol came from all corners. Even the thirteen-year-old girl who ignited the controversy branded McGuire a hypocrite. 'Why would he say it again after all the trouble I got into? And he said something like that should never be repeated again, and then he goes and says it,' she said. 'I don't understand why.'[14]

The story kept rolling, and McGuire kept fuelling it with his running commentary. He wanted to show remorse and openness, but hindsight says he should have disappeared for a week or two after his initial apology.

The AFL ordered him to mediation with Goodes and to take tolerance classes, and McGuire said he would stand down from any of his roles if asked: 'I'd cop that blemish on my impeccable record.'

A tearful McGuire apologised again on Thursday during his Triple M breakfast show, even if it didn't sound wholly convincing:

> I think I've just about ticked every element of [the AFL's racial and religious vilification mediation process]. That is, shown remorse, squared up with Adam Goodes, which is the key point, and apologised. But I will go through it and do it ... even to be seen to be doing it.
>
> It's hard to be portrayed as the opposite of what you are,' he added. 'If I'm feeling it this morning, I can only imagine what Adam Goodes has felt all his life, and Harry O'Brien. I've copped it and, you know what, maybe I'm getting a feel for what they cop every day of their lives.

Comparing his plight to that of Indigenous Australians did not help. No one stood beside McGuire and only a few backed him. The Collingwood board unanimously supported his retention of the presidency and coach Nathan Buckley expressed his support, saying:

> It's a respect issue. Does Eddie respect Indigenous people? Absolutely. He's done so much good work and he's done so much positively to impact on the opportunities of Indigenous people as he has for discriminated people in all walks of life. That's part of what he's stood for in his time and I think his record should stand for itself in that regard.[15]

Buckley also gave his players Andrew Krakouer and Harry O'Brien the option of sitting out that week's game.

Away from the club, the *Sydney Morning Herald*'s Peter FitzSimons mused:

> The best [excuse] I can get to is the one he offered, that in a fog of exhaustion where everything upside down is also back to

front, he totally misjudged things. What he thought might be a light laugh was actually a powder keg of poison, and he will wonder forever how he could have got them mixed up.

And *Herald Sun* journalist Andrew Rule noted, 'There but for the grace of God goes everyone in talk radio' in giving a fair rendering of McGuire's gaffe as 'a clumsy association of ideas: "King Kong" links with "ape" links with the Adam Goodes footy fan drama already on his mind … Before his brain filtered and deloused a loose train of thought, the machine-gun tongue kicked in.'[16]

McGuire was as rattled as friends had ever seen him. They tried to encourage him, telling him he'd weathered public storms before and it would pass. 'No,' he replied. 'This one goes on my permanent record.' Goodes told McGuire he would take it to his grave and now he knew that to be true. After thirty-five years in the business, in which his broadcast ubiquity was relatively gaffe-free, it all came down to a few seconds of pre-dawn radio banter.

He was mortified anyone could believe he was capable of such thoughts. Nevertheless, McGuire is of a generation growing up in the 1970s that would not have encountered a black person, particularly in Broadmeadows. School friends recall McGuire defending the vilified, even in the schoolyard, but the very white Australia of the 1970s and 1980s was still clumsy, offensive and coming to terms with racial sensitivities. And the vilified were Greek and Italians; Aboriginals weren't part of a Melbourne schoolboy's world.

It has been a slow transformation. Broadly, baby boomers have entrenched attitudes to race and religion while Gen Y and Millennials have grown up with tolerance and respect. McGuire's Generation X is the generation that, in some regards, had to be taught and adapt.

Throughout it all, Goodes was silent. However, McGuire couldn't be. In August, Goodes told Seven he had forgiven McGuire but they had yet to talk it out.

'No one can explain why he said the things that he said. But people make mistakes. I have done that before and I know that he will hopefully learn from it as well,' Goodes said.[17]

On the same day, at a pre-match function at Sydney's ANZ Stadium, McGuire put his foot in it again, blaming the media for the 'absolute injustice' of his treatment after his King Kong gaffe.

Furthermore, when quizzed by Colless – who noted that McGuire did 'not have a racist bone in his body' – he said he felt he'd now walked a mile in the shoes of Indigenous Australians. Again, the comparison was misjudged:

> The absolute injustice I felt the moment of being done over by the media was an insight into the life of Adam Goodes and Aboriginals in Australia on a daily basis. That's what they get: people making rash judgments like that on a daily basis. For the rest of my life I'll have people thinking, 'There's that bogan, idiot, imbecile president of Collingwood.'
>
> Okay, I'll cop that. Because what happened, happened. As unintentional as it was … again, I apologise.[18]

Without doubt, the media's 'hazing' of McGuire was a heavy, perhaps arguably over the top, torrent of doubt, schadenfreude and vitriol, but that was not for McGuire to say or judge.

It allowed anyone who despised McGuire to kick him – and they queued up. Other unsubstantiated examples of drunken bigotry from yonder swirled. Even Carlton coach Mick Malthouse said he was 'totally shocked' by the comments, and that his former president should not be portrayed as a victim. When asked whether he thought McGuire was a racist though, Malthouse responded coolly, 'I would say, "No", but by his own admission he said it was a racist comment.'[19]

McGuire couldn't ask for sympathy. He was not the victim.

The incident coloured future relations between McGuire and the Sydney club. And subsequent circumstances meant the gaffe could not be forgotten.

In 2015, Hawthorn supporters openly booed Goodes in a distasteful expression of ignorance and emotion that gained momentum in the following weeks. Some fans justified their action by saying they didn't like the way the dual Brownlow medallist played (raising the justification that he slid into or tripped opponents) and that he was an umpire's pet. Many other players could be labelled thus, but they are not booed. Others booed Goodes because they despised a strong, Indigenous man who was named Australian of the Year in 2014. They justified their bigotry by saying Goodes picked on a thirteen-year-old girl, despite Goodes subsequently saying that was the element of the event that most haunted him. He tried to ensure she was not ridiculed (he tweeted after talking to her and accepting her apology, 'Let's support her please'). 'When something is said to you like that, it cuts you to your core and cuts you to your core more when it's a young girl,' he said.[20]

Behind the boos in 2015 was latent racism. And anyone who joined in the booing, for whatever reason, was complicit.

It also meant that when Goodes performed an innocuous war dance after scoring a goal at the SCG during an Indigenous Round match against Carlton in 2015, the context was more volatile than it otherwise might have been.

McGuire, hosting Fox Footy's coverage of the match, said at half-time, 'We've never seen that [celebration] before and I don't think we ever want to see it again to be perfectly honest, regardless of what it is.'

It is hard not to believe the comment was fuelled by two years of regret and a bucket full of bitterness about his treatment by the Swans – and a little ignorance. No one appreciated what Goodes was doing until he spoke afterwards. The Swan merely danced towards a bay of 'opponents', Carlton fans, as war dances do.

The following morning, McGuire tried to explain himself, saying he was on Goodes' side:

> Had we known before the game that Adam or the Indigenous players were planning to do some sort of war cry, we could have been able to educate and understand the situation. It's almost like what the government has to do as far as the equal rights marriage situation is concerned. There are people out there who are frightened, people don't understand, you have to put it into context and take people along for the ride.[21]

Again, the damage had been done before McGuire could apologise, and again, anyone had a lash. The NSW Parliament's Legislative Council passed a motion, put forward by Greens MP Jeremy Buckingham, declaring support for Goodes and condemning McGuire.

'As a lifelong Collingwood supporter, I'm embarrassed by Eddie McGuire's blunders and racial gaffes, so I'm glad the NSW Upper House has officially condemned Mr McGuire for being a "continual boofhead",' Buckingham said.

The misspelt motion, after recognizing Goodes' achievements and the role of war dances, finally said: 'That this House condemns Mr Eddie Macguire [sic], the President of the Collingwood Football Club, for his comment that "This is a made-up dance, this is not something that has been going on for years", and being a continual boofhead.'

If McGuire had any doubt about whether the King Kong gaffe would remain on his permanent record, there it would be, forevermore in the political *Hansard* of the NSW State Parliament.

Whether these latest criticisms and his desire to prove people wrong will be the impetus to take steps towards the political ambitions Eddie harboured as a child or are enough to discourage him from them, forever, only Eddie knows.

CHAPTER 21

BUILDING ON SUCCESS

Eddie McGuire foxes when asked about any political ambitions, noting he wouldn't know which party to choose.

In 1999, he admitted, 'I'd struggle to fit into either party. I'd like to see a government that ran the economy like the Liberals but with a Labor Party conscience.'[1]

Colleagues know he's being disingenuous. His upbringing and instincts point towards the ALP. As do occasional comments, such as one to a friend at the 2000 Brownlow Medal, as the Victorian election result hung in the balance, that a Labor victory could prove a problem because 'we haven't got all the good people ready yet' to form government. 'It wasn't meant to happen so soon,' he explained.[2]

His Melbourne lunch clubs have tended to feature Labor politicians before Liberals. His regular monthly lunch in the front room of Chinatown's Bamboo House with a group of prominent Melburnians including 3AW's Neil Mitchell, the *Herald Sun*'s Peter Blunden, Qantas's Ken Ryan and AFL's Andrew Demetriou featured Liberal warhorse Peter Costello and ALP premier Steve Bracks. Union boss and Labor aspirant Bill Shorten also featured for some time.

McGuire is a progressive in action and politics, though. He wanted to move on from that old Melbourne gathering and establish another lunch club with a younger batch of tyros, including the AFL's Gillon McLachlan and current Labor premier Daniel Andrews.

McGuire was open about his ambition to be prime minister as a youngster, pleasing Sister Therese with his call for increased pay for teachers. Even as a young journalist at Ten he spoke of his major political ambitions, although he wasn't alone in aiming that high as a young man. He is different in being able to do so now without a lifetime's slog getting to pre-selection, although he has watched warily as celebrity candidates Peter Garrett and Malcolm Turnbull have not met their own expectations.

Colleagues aren't unified on whether McGuire will, or should, enter politics. He is far more effective outside the political realm and they feel such an outcome-driven person would not cope with the elaborate machinations of the political process.

Certainly, both parties would take McGuire and his personal appeal 'on the hustings'. His popularity and cut-through was clearly displayed while campaigning for the republic where he was compared to Bob Hawke. If the Republican push had been successful with a directly elected president model, some friends suggest he could have, and would have, had a crack.

He told *The Age* in 2002, 'Politics is not something I harbour at the moment. But you never say never.'[3] And in the week before the 2003 Grand Final, he admitted he could see himself in federal politics, although 'probably the answer at the moment is no'.

He conceded he was unsure 'that I'm prepared to put in danger the well-being of my family for politics', and at Collingwood 'we can actually make an impact in society and we're able to do that without going through all the party politics and the nonsense. I don't know whether I'd have the patience or the temperament for all the back-room lobbying and the time spent on the back bench to make an impact.'[4]

McGuire has told staff and advisers that his personal and financial affairs should be scrupulous enough to withstand the scrutiny of a prime minister, although it is unsure whether that is a consequence of piety, his already public profile or future ambition. Undoubtedly, examples of previous Kevin Rudd-like tantrums and abuse of staff will emerge were he to run for political office, although nothing too debilitating.

The chance to make an impact was there for the taking in 2005 when the ALP leadership, under Kim Beazley, publicly dangled the safe northern Melbourne federal seat of Scullin in front of McGuire. He said politics interested him 'but it's just not something that's on my radar at the moment.'[5] It wasn't the first or last approach by either side, merely the most public.

Instead, his brother Frank was parachuted into the safe state seat of Broadmeadows in an unprecedented deal. Frank McGuire was given the seat, despite not even being an ALP member, at the behest of the ALP national executive, led by union chief Bill Shorten and Senator Stephen Conroy. Four unions, led by Health Services Union boss Kathy Jackson, contested the decision in the Supreme Court, and lost. Jackson said ALP executives Shorten and Communications Minister Stephen Conroy (funnily enough both Collingwood supporters) were 'faceless and shameful men'.[6]

In the same year, McGuire was 'absolutely flabbergasted' by being named a member (AM) in the general division of the Order of Australia in the year's Queen's Birthday honours list. 'The irony wasn't lost, I can tell you, absolutely,' the republican said and laughed. 'Somebody up there's got a sense of humour in the Governor-General's office.' He didn't consider declining it.[7]

He seems – at least at this moment – sanguine about a political future. He disingenuously believes he is too old and repeated in 2013, 'I don't think the political life is for me. It puts too much pressure on families.'[8]

McGuire's entrepreneurial spirit would be deadened by politics. His company McGuire Media had played around in the shallow end of the TV pool for years, picking up special offshoots from Nine and keeping brother Frank busy after he had a tough run.

After McGuire concluded his stint as Nine CEO and Frank left to become a politician, the company began to step up a few gears and is now at a juncture where McGuire can begin to plan for another career as a media mogul. The business took baby steps after Eddie returned from Sydney, producing minor TV shows under its TV arm, Jam TV, such as a caravan travel show hosted by Nicky Buckley and Murray Bingham for Ten, *Making Tracks*.

The company was a beachhead for McGuire's broadcast ambitions as much as anything. When the AFL broadcast rights beyond 2002 were being negotiated, he believed his company could be the one production house packaging footy for the networks. It would take more than a decade for McGuire Media to show it was capable of broadcasting abridged league seasons.

The elevation of the company would come in the form of a reality football show and the return of McGuire's old producer on *The Footy Show*, Cos Cardone.

Gradually, the company broadened its reach in areas with which it was familiar. It began broadcasting the World Tennis Classic from Adelaide in 2008, the Essendon Football Club program *The Hangar* and Collingwood's *The Club*, the Stawell Gift and then Athletics Australia meetings and, from 2013, the Australian Premier League Bowls. Small beer but it was stacking up.

The reality show *The Recruit* was a similar format to *Football Superstar*, which was created by North One Television and previously aired on Foxtel. Its source remains a contentious issue. *Football Superstar* sifted a group of young soccer players to find one capable of winning a professional contract with an A-League club.

Similar concepts had been pitched to the AFL previously and withered in development. McGuire thought the concept could work and he was one of the few who could open doors throughout TV and the AFL to make it happen. It took his dogged negotiation skills through 2012 and '13 until, the AFL and clubs eventually acquiesced to a proposal where winning players would be eligible for a special rookie draft.

McGuire was mooted as host, although that created issues, until former player turned radio host Ryan 'Fitzy' Fitzgerald took the gig, aided by coaching mentor Michael Voss. McGuire Media's delivered episodes were a little too rough for Foxtel and another company, The Media Tribe, was brought in to spruce it up. It worked and the show became a major ratings hit for Foxtel in 2013 and elevated McGuire's company as a production force. It should have returned the following year but didn't as Voss moved to an AFL coaching role.

Simultaneously, Cardone worked on a package to broadcast the dormant South Australian football league, the SANFL. McGuire Media presented to the SANFL a deal in which it would have its production costs underwritten by broadcast sponsors (in this instance the Motor Accident Commission, Bank SA, IGA and RAA) and the broadcasts would be on-sold to Seven or Nine. Seven picked up the package that reinvigorated live coverage of, and interest in, Adelaide's local league, including record TV audiences for SANFL matches, doubling previous ABC audiences.

Parochialism worked and McGuire Media was ready to pounce upon the rights to the Western Australian Football League and Victorian Football League as the cash-strapped ABC looked to off-load them after federal government budget cuts in 2014. Again, McGuire did the deal with Seven which could promote the local leagues off its AFL coverage.

McGuire was expanding his horizons for the company and did, contentiously, into cycling. Like many smaller Australian sports, cycling broadcasts had been the domain of a steady few, most particularly Beyond International's sports arm, Beyond Action, which broadcast the annual Tour Down Under. Beyond was readying to broadcast the special Cadel Evans Great Ocean Road Race in 2014 until McGuire Media snaffled the rights late in the piece. The event was staged by the Victorian Major Events Company, of which McGuire is a board member.

McGuire Media and Jam TV's tentacles began to stretch into all sports in 2013–15, including the opening ceremonies of the ICC Cricket World Cup in 2015. But McGuire Media's step up to partner with Gearhouse Broadcast and HBS to form a syndicate, ACBS (Asian Cup Broadcast Services), to become the host broadcaster of the AFC Asia Cup was wholly unexpected and appeared, initially, perhaps beyond McGuire's reach.

HBS provided the technical facilities and crew and McGuire Media produced the broadcasts, including camera plans, graphics, opening/closing sequences and production management. It covered 32 matches across five Australian cities without a hitch for a successful tournament that delivered windfall ratings to Fox Sports and the ABC as the Socceroos won their first major trophy. The tournament was McGuire Media's coming of age and McGuire's decade-old plan to take over broadcasting of an AFL season suddenly didn't look so ridiculous. McGuire Media and Seven combined well to boost VFL and WAFL coverage in 2015 and McGuire's company was chosen to be host broadcaster of the 2015 Netball World Cup.

The year couldn't have been better for the business but, off screen, the business was causing immense tension with Eddie's broadcast partners. His conflicts of interest had a material bearing on competitive and complementary commercial interests. McGuire's various roles as broadcaster, host and political player intertwined clumsily.

Essentially, Foxtel, and to a lesser extent Nine, asked themselves how McGuire could take their coin as a TV host while also taking production jobs away from them as broadcasters competing for events and broadcast rights. The time was coming for McGuire to decide, again, whether he wanted to be a TV host or a broadcast executive. He also had to choose with whom McGuire Media was competing.

The Foxtel relationship was complicated by personality clashes at Fox Footy, with a headstrong bunch of former players bitching about who worked, or wouldn't, with McGuire on *Friday Night Footy*. Mysteriously, his Sunday night Fox Footy program *Eddie and Derm's Big Week in Footy* didn't return in 2015 as these tensions simmered.

In 2015, his business was humming, his Triple M *Hot Breakfast* was the top FM breakfast show in Melbourne and Nine's *Hot Seat* continued to spoil Seven and deliver audiences to National Nine News.

McGuire's value to free-to-air television hadn't diminished, though. Nor had his desire to call AFL. Seven, in the form of chairman Kerry Stokes and CEO Tim Worner, made another major play for McGuire in mid-2015. Seven was anticipated to renew its AFL broadcast deal later that year but the network had problems elsewhere. *Seven News* was being smashed by *Nine News* in the eastern markets and Nine's *Hot Seat* at 5.30 p.m. was a contributing factor.

Seven made a multi-million-dollar offer to recruit McGuire, allowing him to host the AFL (Seven's caller Dennis Cometti was retiring), move into a game show format at 5.30 p.m. on Seven and, tellingly, become the face of Seven in Melbourne, a city in which it was languishing.

Seven was worried how McGuire would explain his presence on the network after years of belittling it while at Nine. But McGuire had no qualms, invoking footy talk again when discussing how he would 'smash' Nine.

He might have trash-talked behind closed doors – and been too expensive for Seven – but, in another instance of McGuire's loyalty perhaps outweighing his good sense, he re-signed with Nine, on a slightly reduced fee. McGuire had enjoyed a period of bounteous contracts at Nine but times were tight. He remained the best-paid TV and radio star in the country though, with, give or take, $1 million from Nine, $2 million from Foxtel and $3 million to package the *Hot Breakfast* for Triple M (of which half would go to his team and production).

The Australian broadcast sector still valued Eddie McGuire more highly than any other personality and Eddie knew when opportunity comes along you have to grab it while you can.

EPILOGUE

THE SON KEEPS RISING

Eddie McGuire has learned to appreciate life a little more since his Sydney adventure.

In 2012, at the celebration of his 30th anniversary in television at St Kilda's Stokehouse restaurant, he noted, with some comfort, 'The people of Melbourne and the culture of Melbourne have inspired me over the past 30 years.'[1]

Typically, he spoke off the cuff and mentioned by name pretty much everyone in the room while making them feel as though they were one of only a few in the room. He was back in his domain. And his father's death in December 2011 would have shown, yet again, how important family is.

He's a club man and Melbourne hosted his clubs, whether it be his wine group with best mate Rob Sitch, or an increasingly outrageous lunch club comprising former CUB exec Peter Scanlan, restaurateur Frank Van Haandel, and Just Jeans founder Craig Kimberley.

McGuire is enjoying the spoils of his toil and he is a different person in such settings, great company and not always 'on'. Close friends see an Eddie McGuire who is loyal to the point of absurdity and thoughtful in unexpected ways. They muse he doesn't ask for or expect anything in return. Eddie's reward is activity, progress and success. Just like his father, he lauds 'goers'.

Eddie McGuire turned 50 in 2014 and Carla and friends spent months compiling a book of inspirational messages for him. The book contained greetings, words and signatures from friends, acquaintances and legends, and was the product of someone with an unfeasibly rare and broad global network.

After his birthday party, Eddie went home, relatively early, and sat down and thumbed through the messages from President Obama, Shane Warne, Muhammad Ali and many more. He quietly reflected, swimming in their inspiration.

A key to Eddie McGuire's life demonstrated by that book is he understands success: what it requires in sacrifice, stamina and patience. He reaches for it, knows its rhythms and not only seeks it but seeks successful people. But the real key to Eddie McGuire is the foundations of his character that were laid by his parents. Before Edward Senior died in December 2011 his family gathered around his bedside and spent the day with him as he was given the last rites of the Catholic Church. When that was done, Eddie's father told his son to go to work and 'get on with it'.

That's what Eddie McGuire is doing – getting on with it.

ACKNOWLEDGEMENTS

Eddie McGuire's life has been a relentless forward movement and I trust I've gone some way to reflect that in this book, in style as much as content. It careers along, just as he has.

Also, this book didn't set out to offer a mélange of opinions about the man, merely piece together the key events in his life, as best can be done.

Many background interviews were undertaken to fill the story, validate the public record – which at the time often suits the participants rather than the truth – and corroborate facts. For most, talking about Eddie was a joy; for a few it was too much. Eddie's influence and power, particularly in Melbourne, was obvious enough in some reactions.

All efforts have been made to corroborate interviews and properly source material.

This is not an authorised biography although I owe Eddie a thank you for not standing in its way. He was gracious, eventually, without giving his imprimatur or oversight.

I understand his reticence but, to be honest, it is ridiculous that his life, which spans so many areas of public life, hasn't been chronicled before now. I trust I've done it justice.

To the many who spoke to me, I owe great thanks. Many, particularly in the AFL milieu, had little reason to trust me yet they were generous and illuminating.

To Mick Warner who pushed me to write the book, a mighty thanks. Mick should have co-written the book but life and a monumental year of events in the AFL intervened. It would have been much better with him, although he's kicking enough of his own goals in print.

And to Peter FitzSimons who was generous with his insight and crucial in motivating me to get off my arse and begin.

A big thanks to a few people who greased wheels and made things happen when they might not have, particularly Sarah Allen, Steve Price and Mick Molloy.

To those who provided shelter and occasional food at various times during the writing process – Jamie Gorton and Nicole Nabout, Olivia McCarron, Tony and Di Boland, and Sebastian and Charlotte King – a hearty thanks.

A few of my highly respected colleagues – Peter Lalor, Kate Legge, Jim Middleton, and Nick Leys – offered wise counsel, assistance, and were occasionally unwitting psychologists for me.

My publisher Vanessa Radnidge is a dream editor, backing me to get the job done and cajoling when it wasn't. Her relentless positivity and wisdom is a blessing any writer would cherish.

And thanks also to Kate Stevens and the production team at Hachette who dealt with my abrupt manner, crunched deadlines and edited the copy with a light touch.

And finally, to the people who pay the price when a book is written: my family. To Finnegan and Maisie, for their good humour and empathy as Dad turned into a monster for six months. And thanks, Finny, for picking up that embarrassing mistake.

To Michaela, who makes everything happen, all the time. And tolerates me – not just when a book is made. I'd still be writing nonsense while hunched in a deck chair in Melbourne were it not for you. I love you.

ENDNOTES

Author's Note
1. 'The world according to Eddie', Konrad Marshall, *The Age*, 27 August 2010, p. 44.
2. 'Eddie Talks', Chris Beck, *The Age*, 9 June 2005, p. 3.
3. Ross MacDowell, *Inside Story: 20 Famous Australians tell their story*, Hobson Dell, Melbourne, 2001.

Chapter 1 – A Broady Boy
1. 'How Eddie achieved his goals', Doug Aiton, *The Age*, 11 September 1994, p. 4.
2. 'Back in Broady, another Eddie is all smiles', Rachel Kleinman, *The Age*, 10 February 2006, p. 2.
3. 'The night all my dreams came true', Aaron Langmaid, *Sunday Herald Sun*, 21 June 2015, p. 11.
4. Kate Legge, *The Australian Magazine*, 13 May 2006, p. 1+.
5. 'There is no grey in Eddie's view, he sees it all in black and white', Frank McGuire, *Herald Sun*, 24 September 2010, p. 42.
6. 'Man for all seasons', Gay Alcorn, *The Age*, 3 January 1998, p. 1.
7. 'Mr Multimedia', Richard Yallop, *The Australian*, 23 September 1999, p. M01.
8. *Herald Sun*, 24 September 2010, p. 42.

Chapter 2 – Eddie McGuire, Boy Reporter
1. Ross MacDowell, *Inside Story: 20 Famous Australians tell their story*, Hobson Dell, Melbourne, 2001.
2. Good Weekend Magazine, *The Age*, 23 September 2001.

Chapter 3 – Counting on Ten
1. 'InterView', *The Age*, 31 July 1994, p. 17.
2. 'Mr Multimedia', Richard Yallop, *The Australian*, 23 September 1999, p. M01.
3. Ross MacDowell, *Inside Story: 20 Famous Australians tell their story*, Hobson Dell, Melbourne, 2001.
4. 'Tough bike classic speeds into the space age', B Hitchings, *Sun News-Pictorial*, 13 October 1988, p. 51.
5. *Herald Sun*, 24 September 2010, p. 42.
6. McGuire and Steve Pritchard would also write, produce, host and edit the video *The Road to Victory*, the review of Collingwood's 1990 Grand Final year.
7. 'McGuire gears up for pranks', K Collier, *Herald Sun*, 2 April 1992, p. 75.
8. *Herald Sun*, 28 July 1993.
9. 'Zero out of ten', Jon Anderson, *Herald Sun*, 8 September 1993, p. 89.

Chapter 4 – Eddie Everywhere
1. 'Man for all seasons', Gay Alcorn, *The Age*, 3 January 1998, p. 1.
2. *The Australian Magazine*, 10 September 2005, p. 14.
3. 'Andrew tops the most wanted list', *Herald Sun*, 6 February 1991, p. 15.
4. Kate Legge, *The Australian Magazine*, 13 May 2006, p. 1.
5. 'Eddie still kicking goals', L Hetherington, *Herald Sun*, 13 March 1991, p. 47.
6. 'Crux club chaps real good sports', J Romney, *Herald Sun*, 30 April 1991, p. 31.
7. 'Footy big shots on the ball', Ross Brundrett, *Herald Sun*, 24 June 1994, p. 16.
8. 'Eddie's rings of confidence', L Hetherington, *Herald Sun*, 19 January 1995, p. 15.
9. 'Man for all seasons', Gay Alcorn, *The Age*, 3 January 1998, p. 1.

Chapter 5 – More than a Nice Haircut and a Good Smile
1. 'Hot Eddie', Jon Anderson, *Herald Sun*, 27 May 1994, p. 91.
2. 'FM station joins footy big league', Paul Dowsley, *Herald Sun*, 28 August 1996, p. 14.
3. 'Price puts boots in but Eddie set to kick goals', Mike Sheahan, *Herald Sun*, 12 December 1996, p. 107.
4. 'Nasty feud on air', L Hetherington, *Herald Sun*, 13 July 1995, p. 15.
5. 'Man for all seasons', Gay Alcorn, *The Age*, 3 January 1998, p. 1.
6. 'Man for all seasons', Gay Alcorn, *The Age*, 3 January 1998, p. 1.
7. 'Grill Team feels the heat', Paul Dowsley, *Herald Sun*, 27 May 1998, p. 8.
8. 'McGuire switches off radio gig', Genevieve Lally, *Herald Sun*, 14 November, 1998, p. 3.

Chapter 6 – Nine Comes After Ten
1. J Miller, *The Herald*, 4 September 1989.
2. 'McGuire swap', Brian Meldrum, *Herald Sun*, 30 December 1993, p. 63.
3. 'Man for all seasons', Gay Alcorn, *The Age*, 3 January 1998, p. 1.
4. 'Luck of the Irish holds out', *Herald Sun*, 15 July 1994, p. 18.
5. 'Footy for the masses', Garry Mansfield, *Herald Sun*, 19 May 1994, p. 79.

Chapter 7 – *The Footy Show*
1. 'Man for all seasons', Gay Alcorn, *The Age*, 3 January 1998, p. 1.
2. 'How Eddie achieved his goals', Doug Aiton, *The Age*, 11 September 1994, p. 4.
3. 'Nine's player of the year', Robert Fidgeon, *Herald Sun*, 25 September 1996, p. 3.
4. 'Footy team makes its midweek mark', Debi Enker, *The Age*, 1 May 1994, p. 10.
5. 'Flying high', Dugald Jellie, *The Age*, 12 May 1994, p. 1.
6. 'Mr Multimedia', Richard Yallop, *The Australian*, 23 September 1999, p. M01.
7. The Sunday sports programs were allowed AFL vision in a swap with Seven for its NRL footage.
8. 'Luck of the Irish holds out', *Herald Sun*, 15 July 1994, p. 18.
9. 'Grand final climax for Seven's heaven', Dugald Jellie, *The Age*, 3 October 1994, p. 5.
10. 'The winner, and not a footy clip in sight', Philip Johnson, *The Age*, 29 June 1995, p. 14.
11. 'Cracker of a finale', Jon Anderson, *Herald Sun*, 30 September 1996, p. 91.
12. 'The night all my dreams came true', Aaron Langmaid, *Sunday Herald Sun*, 21 June 2015, p. 11.
13. 'A footy tale of two cities' sports codes', *Herald Sun*, 21 August 1996, p. 8.
14. 'There's a draft warming up the commentary box', Peter Wilmoth, *Sunday Age*, 8 September 1996, p. 3.
15. 'Sporting Life', Geoff McClure, *The Age*, 9 March 2004, p. 13.
16. Leigh Matthews, *Accept The Challenge: The Autobiography*, Random House, Sydney, 2013, p. 321.
17. 'How Seven stole The Footy Show . . . and went for gold', *The Age*, 31 January 1998, p. 1.
18. 'Chief goes in TV footy war', Robert Fidgeon, *Herald Sun*, 31 January 1998, p. 9.
19. Robert Fidgeon, *Herald Sun*, 4 February 1998, p. 7.
20. 'Footy's state of play', Eddie McGuire, *Herald Sun*, 31 January 1998, p. 25.
21. 'The show goes on but . . . fans are turning off', Mark Robinson, *Herald Sun*, 25 April 1998, p. 38.
22. 'Dermie rides in to challenge Sam and Eddie', Caroline Wilson, *The Age*, 13 November 1999, p. 1.

Chapter 8 – Outrageous Fortunes
1. 'Footy Show ad anger', D Jarvis, *Herald Sun*, 27 September 1994, p. 3.
2. 'Newsman a sport', Eddie McGuire, *Herald Sun*, 27 September 1997, p. 22.
3. 'Newsman a sport', Eddie McGuire, *Herald Sun*, 27 September 1997, p. 22.
4. 'Club director slams TV pair for ridiculing woman', Jason Dowling with Phillip Hudson, *Sunday Age*, 9 May 2004, p. 3.
5. 'Saints call for Footy Show boycott over Newman', Michael Gleeson and Lyall Johnson, *The Age*, 11 July 2005, p. 2.
6. 'Mr Multimedia', Richard Yallop, *The Australian*, 23 September 1999, p. M01.
7. 'Newman dumped as Winmar declares war', Daryl Timms, Michelle Coffey, Sasha Baskett, *Herald Sun*, 30 March 1999, p. 3.
8. 'Footy Show in new face-off', Benjamin Haslem, *The Australian*, 4 June 1999, p. 5.
9. Chip Le Grand, *Weekend Australian*, 16 June 2001, p. 48.

Chapter 9 – Man on the Rise

1. 11 a.m. on Sundays, Nine Network, 1995.
2. 'Good sports in new positions', Robert Fidgeon, *Herald Sun*, 12 April 1995, p. 5.
3. 'And on and on and on', Robert Fidgeon, *Herald Sun*, 17 May 1995, p. 2.
4. 'Double act for Midday', *Herald Sun*, 29 May 1995, p. 7.
5. 'Life after Brian', Gary Tippet, *Sunday Age*, 19 October 1997, p. 1.
6. 'Legends show is all go', Scot Palmer, *Sunday Herald Sun*, 19 May 1996, p. 74.
7. 'Nine's player of the year', Robert Fidgeon, *Herald Sun*, 25 September 1996, p. 3.
8. 'Rating high in ego-land', Kay O'Sullivan, *Herald Sun*, 21 September 1996, p. 15.
9. Ken Sutcliffe with Ian Deads, *The Wide World of Ken Sutcliffe*, Allen & Unwin, Sydney, 2009.
10. 'Telly's cast of millions', Robert Fidgeon, *Herald Sun*, 11 March 1998, p. 4.
11. 'Sporting Life', Geoff McClure, *The Age*, 10 April 1998, p. 8.
12. 'Slap for award bashers', Eddie McGuire, *Herald Sun*, 25 April 1998, p. 20.
13. 'Nine quizzes Seven tactics', *Sunday Herald Sun*, 11 April 1999, p. 31.
14. 'When money talks', *The Age*, 29 April 1999, p. 6.
15. 'Big night a ripper', Eddie McGuire, *Herald Sun*, 17 April 1999, p. 124.
16. 'So, who wants to be a millionaire …?', Robert Fidgeon, *Herald Sun*, 22 June 1999, p. 1.
17. 'The sharp and the glamourous are summoned for a grand union', Melissa Fyfe, *The Age*, 20 October 1999, p. 10.
18. 'Nine rockets ABC in new year war', Amanda Meade, *The Australian*, 6 January 2000, p. 3.
19. 'McGuire kicks goals for Nine', *The Age*, 20 July 2000, p. 6.
20. 'Mr Multimedia', Richard Yallop, *The Australian*, 23 September 1999, p. M01.
21. 'Who wants to be Eddie McGuire?', Garry Linnell, Good Weekend Magazine, *The Age*, 22 September 2001, p. 14.
22. 'Ed on the block', Robert Fidgeon, *Herald Sun*, 7 May 2003, p. 6.
23. Author interview, 2015.
24. 'Steady, Eddie, who wants to be such an unfunny Logies host', Amanda Meade, *The Australian*, 12 May 2003, p. 7.
25. 'Eddie's humility (really) saves the day; The Logies', Jonathan Green, *The Age*, 12 May 2003, p. 3.
26. A national audience of 2 802 000 – 320 000 more viewers than in 2003.
27. Adam Boland, *Brekky Central: Behind the smiles of Australian breakfast television*, Melbourne University Press, Melbourne, 2014.

Chapter 10 – 'Austraya'

1. 'The Broady boys got to the barricades', James Button, *The Age*, 11 October 1997, p. 1.
2. Malcolm Turnbull, *Fighting for the Republic: The Ultimate Insider's Account*, Hardie Grant, Melbourne, 1999, p. 29.
3. 'Man for all seasons', Gay Alcorn, *The Age*, 3 January 1998, p. 1.
4. 'Republicans believe diversity is their ticket to ride Constitutional Convention', Tony Stephens, *Sydney Morning Herald*, 10 October 1997, p. 9.
5. 'Man for all seasons', Gay Alcorn, *The Age*, 3 January 1998, p. 1.
6. 'Colourful cast tackle the great national drama', Michelle Grattan, *Australian Financial Review*, 11 November 1997, p. 1.
7. 'Populist pitch just the ticket for ARM', Stuart Rintoul and Stuart Honeysett, *The Australian*, 30 October 1997, p. 4.
8. Eighteen of the top twenty federal electorates with the highest percentage returns were in Victoria.
9. 'McGuire team claims win', Claire Heaney, *Herald Sun*, 12 December 1997, p. 12.
10. 'Republicans win lion's share of votes', AAP, *Australian Financial Review*, 23 December 1997, p. 6.
11. 'Delegates start the fighting early', Adrian Rollins, *The Age*, 24 December 1992, p. 2.
12. 'The great divide', Virginia Trioli, *The Age*, 13 December 1997, p. 8.
13. 'Idealism put aside as realism becomes buzzword for delegates', Stuart Rintoul and Roy Eccelston, *The Australian*, 9 February 1998, p. 5.
14. Malcolm Turnbull, *Fighting for the Republic: The Ultimate Insider's Account*, Hardie Grant, Melbourne, 1999, p. 1.
15. 'Pulling back for the good of the cause', Gervase Green, *The Age*, 7 February 1998, p. 7.
16. *Sunday Herald Sun*, 7 November 1999, p. 5.
17. Malcolm Turnbull, *Fighting for the Republic: The Ultimate Insider's Account*, Hardie Grant, Melbourne, 1999.

Chapter 11 – Collingwood Forever
1. Wren, a prominent architect, fixed a deal between the football and cricket club over rights to Victoria Park and wangled a state government subsidy to pay for new clubrooms in the late 1930s as well as get a Tivoli Club licence moved to Collingwood in 1939.
2. Garrie Hutchinson and John Ross, *The Clubs: The Complete History of Every Club in the VFL and AFL*, Viking, Melbourne, 1998, p. 84.
3. Allan Oakley, *The Phoenix Rises*, Slattery Media Group, Melbourne, 2014, p. 229.
4. 'Dreaming in black and white', Scot Palmer, *Sunday Herald Sun*, 7 July 1996, p. 74.
5. 'Feathers fly in Magpie boardroom', Eddie McGuire, *Herald Sun*, 13 December 1997, p. 24.
6. Bob and Kevin were both former champions, with Kevin then president.
7. 'TV footy war erupts', Chloe Saltau and Greg Denham, *The Age*, 27 June 1998, p. 18.
8. 'Now the boot's on the other foot', Eddie McGuire, *Herald Sun*, 27 June 1998, p. 26.
9. 'Hungry eyes on Pies', Michael Horan and Tony De Bolfo, *Herald Sun*, 25 June 1998, p. 94.
10. 'Magpies in turmoil', Stephen Linnell, *The Age*, 26 June 1998, p. 1.
11. 'AFL wary of McGuire', Daryl Timms, *Herald Sun*, 10 September 1998, p. 94.
12. 'McGuire team to pounce on Pies', Daryl Timms and Mike Sheahan, *Herald Sun*, 8 September 1998, p. 3.
13. 'My plan to fix the Pies', Eddie McGuire, *Herald Sun*, 10 September 1998, p. 4.
14. 'All or nothing says Eddie', Mike Sheahan, *Herald Sun*, 7 October 1998, p. 78.
15. 'Black and white and seen all over', Doug Aiton, *Sunday Age*, 13 September 1998, p. 17.
16. 'Broady boy on a hiding to nothing', Mike Sheahan, *Herald Sun*, 10 September 1998, p. 94.
17. 'McGuire passion seduces Collingwood faithful', Jamie Walker, *The Australian*, 23 October 1998, p. 9.
18. 'Masses unite for change', Daryl Timms, *Herald Sun*, 30 October 1998, p. 113.

Chapter 12 – Rumblings
1. 'Magpie McGuire has a finger in every "Pie"', Tim Pegler, *The Australian*, 10 September 1998, p. 18.
2. Eddie McGuire, *Herald Sun*, 10 September 1998, p. 94.
3. 'Fast Eddie slows down a little', Caroline Wilson, *The Age*, 19 November 1998, p. 8.
4. Ashley Browne, *The Age*, 22 July 1999, p. 14.
5. 'Who wants to be a president?', *The Age*, 24 April 1999, p. 2.
6. 'Who wants to be a president?', *The Age*, 24 April 1999, p. 2.
7. 'Conflict of interest for Eddie McGuire: fans', Rohan Connolly, *The Age*, 27 March 2001, p. 1.
8. 'The Eddie Empire – So who wants to be a multi-millionaire?', Caroline Wilson, *Sunday Age*, 24 December 2000, p. 1.
9. 'No call yet on McGuire role', Andrew Dodd, *The Australian*, 4 October 2001, p. 3.
10. 'Footy split unsettled', *Herald Sun*, 29 May 2002, p. 15.
11. 'McGuire slams Demon "wimps"', *Sunday Age*, 29 April 2001, p. 3.
12. 'McGuire's firm wins right to run government footy-tipping', *The Age*, 20 December 2000, p. 3.
13. 'MultiEmedia grabs sport stake', *The Age*, 15 February 2000, p. 3.
14. 'McGuire looks to Net profits', AAP, *The Age*, 25 February 2000, p. 1.
15. 'Dotcom keeps buying to staunch bleeding', Jane Schulze, *The Australian*, 8 May 2001, p. 19.
16. 'Magpies warn of war over TV rights', *The Age*, 20 March 2000, p. 3.
17. 'League blasts Magpies over stadium', *The Age*, 30 March 2000, p. 3.
18. 'Jackson belts "Bib and Bub"', Andrew Ramsey, *The Australian*, 6 July 2000, p. 18.
19. 'Eddie, Mick face fines', Mike Sheahan, *Herald Sun*, 26 April 2002, p. 108.
20. 'Magpies take frustrations to the top', Emma Quayle, *The Age*, 24 July 2004, p. 3.
21. '"Biased" Eddie bagged for call', Jon Anderson, *Herald Sun*, 28 May 2002, p. 70.
22. 'Eddie's not centimetre perfect', Liz Gooch, *The Age*, 29 May 2002, p. 1.
23. 'Eddie bites back', Jon Anderson, *Herald Sun*, 30 May 2002, p. 58.
24. 'Being Eddie McGuire, written, directed and starring Eddie McGuire', Sally Jackson, *The Australian*, 27 June, 2002 p. M01.
25. 'McGuire may face action over comment', Peter Ker and Daniel Ziffer, *The Age*, 10 April 2004, p.3.
26. 'Collins a lame duck president without dome to call home', Patrick Smith, *Weekend Australian*, 15 May 2004, p. 53.
27. 'Journalists' chief blasts McGuire', Steve Butler with Alan Shiel, *The Age*, 16 July 2004, p. 12.

28 'With an eye on the box, Magpie chief urges night grand final', Caroline Wilson, *The Age*, 18 February 2005, p. 1.
29 'With an eye on the box, Magpie chief urges night grand final', Caroline Wilson, *The Age*, 18 February 2005, p. 1
30 'Nine threatens to walk away from AFL', Neil Shoebridge, *Australian Financial Review*, 23 March 2005, p. 1.
31 'Eddie's attack pathetic: Ten boss', Annie Lawson, *Sunday Age*, 3 April 2005, p. 9.
32 'HIH money went to Magpies', Malcolm Maiden and Jake Niall, *The Age*, 17 July 2002, p. 1.
33 'Brad Copper paid for Magpies deal', Kylie Walker, *The Age*, 25 July 2002, p. 4.
34 'It's all there in black and white: Eddie', Nick Papps, *Herald Sun*, 18 July 2002, p. 3.
35 'McGuire sticks to oval ball', Michael Lynch, *The Age*, 14 February 2004, p. 5.
36 'It's there in black and white, McGuire has hijacked the AFL', Patrick Smith, *The Australian*, 10 June 2005, p. 27.
37 'Malcolm Turnbull's biggest mistake was joining the wrong party', *Herald Sun*, 29 November 2009, online.
38 'Malcolm Turnbull's biggest mistake was joining the wrong party', *Herald Sun*, 29 November 2009, online.
39 Mark Dunn, *Herald Sun*, 11 November 2010, p. 23.
40 'Fight to make Pies pay', Mark Dunn, *Herald Sun*, 11 November 2010, p. 23.
41 'Time for Collingwood to move on from Eddie McGuire', Stephen Mayne, *Crikey*, 17 December 2008.
42 'Bad week gets worse for Pies', John Ferguson, *Herald Sun*, 8 August 2008, p. 7.

Chapter 13 – Eyes on the Prize
1 'Worst Woods I've seen', Scot Palmer, *Sunday Herald Sun*, 18 April 1999, p. 1.
2 'McGuire: Pies not looking flash', *The Age*, 6 April 1999, p. 5.
3 'High profile president under pressure; Steady Eddie facing battle', Michael Davis, *The Australian*, 19 April 1999, p. 25.
4 'Who wants to be a president?', *The Age*, 24 April 1999, p. 2.
5 Scott Burns and Mal Michael joined Buckley.
6 'McGuire asks Pie fans to stay loyal', Karen Lyon, *The Age*, 3 May 1999, p. 1.
7 'Worst Woods I've seen', Scot Palmer, *Sunday Herald Sun*, 18 April 1999, p. 1.
8 'No shows not the die hards', Eddie McGuire, *Herald Sun*, 19 June 1999, p. 116.
9 'Footy coup', Michelle Coffey, *Herald Sun*, 14 June 1999, p. 1.
10 'Coach falls on his sword', Terry Brown, *Herald Sun*, 25 June 1999, p. 8.
11 'A Magpie first and foremost', Eddie McGuire, *Herald Sun*, 26 June 1999, p. 124.
12 *Sunday Herald Sun*, 29 August 1999, p. 9.
13 'Pies put $1.5m up for top jobs', Rod Nicholson, *Sunday Herald Sun*, 27 June 1999, p. 3.
14 Christi Malthouse, *Malthouse: A Football Life*, Allen & Unwin, Sydney, 2012, p. 157.
15 'How Eddie got his man', Mark Stevens, *Herald Sun*, 23 September 1999, p. 109.
16 Mick Malthouse and David Buttifant, *The Ox is Slow but the Earth is Patient*, Allen & Unwin, Sydney, 2011, p. 7.
17 Mick Malthouse and David Buttifant, *The Ox is Slow but the Earth is Patient*, Allen & Unwin, Sydney, 2011, p. 7.
18 'Mick: Eddie goes, I go', Trevor Grant, *Herald Sun*, 11 July 2002, p. 90.
19 'Mick: Eddie goes, I go', Trevor Grant, *Herald Sun*, 11 July 2002, p. 90.
20 'Malthouse and McGuire play it low key', Stephen Reilly, *The Age*, 14 March 2000, p. 4.
21 'The club that won't lie down', *Sunday Age*, 2 July 2000, p. 16.
22 'Magpie legionnaires' infection fears grow', *The Age*, 1 July 2000, p. 1.
23 'Magpies to test Sydney market', Chip Le Grand, *The Australian*, 12 May 2000, p. 20.
24 'Pies take the right tack on Buckley', Caroline Wilson, *Sunday Age*, 19 November 2000, p. 1.
25 'Collingwood profits from losing season', Stephen Reilly and Jake Niall, *The Age*, 16 November 2000, p. 3.
26 'McGuire pleads for Pies stability', Jake Niall, *The Age*, 6 December 2000, p. 2.
27 'Sporting Life', Geoff McClure, *The Age*, 1 November 2000, p. 6.
28 'McGuire endorsed by Pies and rivals', *The Age*, 18 December 2001, p. 3.
29 Chip Le Grand, Michael Davis, Scott Coghlan, *The Australian*, 17 April 2002, p. 18.
30 'Magpie Davis may leave manager, claims McGuire', Melissa Ryan, *The Age*, 19 April 2002, p. 3.
31 'Humble Pies; The inside story of the most important three years in Collingwood's proud history', Trevor Grant, *Herald Sun*, 11 July 2002, p. 90.

32 'As long as they conduct themselves like white people, well, off the field, everyone will admire and respect . . . As long as they conduct themselves like human beings, they will be all right. That's the key,' McAlister said on Nine's *Sports Sunday* TV program, 25 April 1993.
33 'Pies' good-luck charm', Michael Horan, *Herald Sun*, 18 June 2002, p. 76.
34 'Magpies lobby for Vic Park', Fay Burstin, *Herald Sun*, 19 July 2002, p. 17.
35 'Humble Pies', Trevor Grant, *Herald Sun*, 11 July 2002, p. 96.
36 'Knocking on heaven's door', Michael Davis, *Weekend Australian*, 21 September 2002, p. 43.
37 'How finals feats started at dinner; Eddie's recipe a meal, a laugh', Michael Stevens, *Herald Sun*, 23 September 2002, p. 49.
38 'I didn't feel as if I had lost the biggest thing in my life', Mark Robinson, *Herald Sun*, 30 September 2002, p. 42.

Chapter 14 – Bullets, Booze and Lies
1 'Losers drown their sorrows; Magpie duo in pub wobbly', Michael Warner and Cameron Smith, *Herald Sun*, 30 September 2003, p. 3.
2 'Sporting Life', Geoff McClure, *The Age*, 28 March 2003, p. 8.
3 'The rookie who cost Collingwood $500,000', Karen Lyon, *The Age*, 10 January 2008, p. 1.
4 'Saints call for Footy Show boycott over Newman', Michael Gleeson and Lyall Johnson, *The Age*, 11 July 2005, p. 2.
5 'Rookie's drink drive charge costs Pies. Magpies wipe off $500,000', Michael Warner and Karen Collier, *Herald Sun*, 10 January 2008, p. 1.
6 'The rookie who cost Collingwood $500,000', Karen Lyon, *The Age*, 10 January 2008, p. 1.
7 'A minority trash the Magpie brand', Trevor Grant, *Herald Sun*, 3 August 2006, p. 92.
8 'Pie-eyed night leaves Eddie with a mess to clean up', Chip Le Grand, *Weekend Australian*, 10 July 2004, p. 47.
9 3AW, 2 August 2006.
10 'No end to McGuire–Shaw spat', Caroline Wilson, *Sunday Age*, 6 August 2006, p. 3.
11 'Magpies "rat" rift worsens', *Herald Sun*, 7 August 2006, p. 1.
12 'Tarrant escapades put him on brink', Caroline Wilson, *The Age*, 4 August 2006, p. 2.
13 'Eddie's wild footy show', Sam Edmund, *Herald Sun*, 12 September 2006, p. 2.
14 'Pies go from cell to spoils', Chloe Saltau and Len Johnson, *The Age*, 7 October 2006, p. 3.
15 'Bikies, guns and strippers: Magpie star regrets big night out with accused killer Hudson', John Silvester and Dan Silkstone, *The Age*, 29 June 2007, p. 1.
16 'No more chances for Didak', Michael Horan, *Herald Sun*, 30 June 2007, p. 34.
17 'Jeers bring no cheer to Didak', Samantha Lane, *The Age*, 2 July 2007, p. 2.
18 '"Stupid" Magpie admits to being reckless', Greg Denham, *The Australian*, 4 July 2007, p. 20.
19 'Didak's night of booze, bullets', John Silvester, *The Age*, 4 July 2007, p. 1.
20 'Didak's deal lifts Magpie curfew', Sam Edmund, *Herald Sun*, 18 July 2008, p. 114.
21 'Magpie lies humiliate McGuire', Lyall Johnson and Andrea Petrie, *The Age*, 5 August 2008, p. 1.
22 'THEY LIED! Didak was with Shaw in crash car', Mark Robinson, Sam Edmund and Carly Crawford, *Herald Sun*, 5 August 2008, p. 1.
23 'McGuire humiliated over Didak, Shaw lies', Mark Robinson, Jon Ralph and Sam Edmund, *Herald Sun*, 6 August 2008, p. 1.
24 'Footy stars easy prey Magpies' fears after young gun "king-hit"', Michael Warner and Kelly Ryan, *Herald Sun*, 14 December 2009, p. 1.
25 'Pies stick by fallen stars', Emma Quayle, *Sunday Age*, 10 August 2008, p. 2.
26 'Didak regrets crash, lying', David Hastle, *Herald Sun*, 19 September 2008, p. 110.
27 Ben Cousins with Malcolm Knox, *My Life Story*, Pan Macmillan Australia, Sydney, 2010.
28 Ricky Nixon and James Weston, *It's a Jungle Out There*, Pan Macmillan Australia, Sydney, 2010.
29 'How a party night turned sour; Magpies 16 hours of flag celebrations', Nick Leys, *Herald Sun*, 5 October 2010, p. 5.
30 *Mornings with Neil Mitchell*, 3AW, 7 October 2010.
31 'Pies dump night owl Dane for 2 weeks', Glenn McFarlane, *Herald Sun*, 8 August 2012, p. 7.

Chapter 15 – The Handover
1 Wayne Carey, *The Truth Hurts*, Macmillan, Sydney, 2009.
2 'Lowe brothers on a Pies high', Darryl Timms, *Herald Sun*, 26 May 2003, p. 42.
3 'A hi from Lowe surprises', Fiona Byrne, Alice Coster, Nicola Webber, *Herald Sun*, 17 July 2010, p. 108.

Endnotes

4 'McGuire has stars Pie-eyed', Fiona Byrne, Alice Coster, Nicola Webber, *Herald Sun*, 25 September 2010, p. 108.
5 'Pies may share nest', Shaun Phillips, *Herald Sun*, 29 May 2003, p. 69.
6 'Magpies spread their wings into travel market with the power of Eddie', Stephen Dabkowski, *The Age*, 5 April 2003, p. 4.
7 'Magpie mania nears record', Mark Stevens, *Herald Sun*, 10 April 2003, p. 68.
8 'Eddie: Holland set up', Mark Stevens, *Herald Sun*, 27 August 2003, p. 84.
9 'Cat lets his pro-Lion feelings out of the bag', Len Johnson, *The Age*, 18 November 2003, p. 10.
10 'Mick stays a Pie', Shannon McRae, *Herald Sun*, 17 December 2003, p. 118.
11 'Magpies pave way for massive deal', Stephen Reilly, *The Age*, 16 March 2004, p. 12.
12 'Magpie Sally breaks down the barriers', Caroline Wilson, *The Age*, 9 March 2004, p. 1.
13 'Molly hands it to Eddie', Mike Edmonds, Peta Hellard, Luke Dennehy, *Herald Sun*, 5 December 2002, p. 22.
14 'Magpies step into the future', Linda Pearce, *The Age*, 8 April 2004, p. 12.
15 'McGuire concedes defeat on oval name', Martin Boulton, *The Age*, 28 July 2004, p. 1.
16 'McGuire blames squatters', Martin Boulton, *The Age*, 7 April 2005, p. 8.
17 'Magpies' season hangs on the line', Peter Lalor, *The Australian*, 22 June 2004, p. 16.
18 'Eade, Wallace to decide soon', Stephen Reilly, Caroline Wilson, *The Age*, 30 July 2004, p. 14.
19 'Record Pie profit', AAP, *The Age*, 17 November 2004, p. 23.
20 'Magpies on the hunt for players who can make a difference – McGuire', Emma Quayle, *The Age*, 16 May 2005, p. 9.
21 'Low-flung Pies are still high flyers', Chip Le Grand, *The Australian*, 19 May 2005, p. 35.
22 'Tarrant mauled, says McGuire', Dan Oakes, *Sunday Age*, 22 May 2005, p. 5.
23 'McGuire lays down the law to his coaches', Jake Niall, *The Age*, 22 July 2005, p. 3.
24 'Magpies call on outside help', Michael Gleeson, *The Age*, 23 July 2005, p. 3.
25 'Magpies football review could cost jobs: McGuire', Dewi Cooke, *Sunday Age*, 24 July 2005, p. 4.
26 'Eddie everywhere really is, just ask Mick', Michael Gleeson, *The Age*, 8 August 2005, p. 2.
27 'Dome coaching box substandard, says McGuire', Emma Quayle, *The Age*, 9 August 2005, p. 5.
28 '"Useless" picks in past: Pies', Dan Oakes, Jake Niall and Stephen Reilly, *The Age*, 14 December 2005, p. 2.
29 'Collingwood review sees heads roll in', Chip Le Grand, *The Australian*, 29 September 2005, p. 37.
30 'Pies $2m profit', Mike Sheahan with Mark Robinson, *Herald Sun*, 21 November 2006, p. 73.
31 'Pie chief poached in Pratt coup', Michael Gleeson, *The Age*, 24 March 2007, p. 3.
32 'McGuire rejects criticism after Pert gets job', Martin Boulton, *The Age*, 11 May 2007, p. 2.
33 'McGuire shaken but hardly stirred', Caroline Wilson, *Sunday Age*, 13 May 2007, p. 6.
34 'Magpies forgot Shaw', Daryl Timms, *Herald Sun*, 8 September 2007, p. 34.
35 'Judd right in the mix for Magpies', Mark Robinson, *Herald Sun*, 25 September 2007, p. 86.
36 'Get Juddy', Jake Niall, *The Age*, 26 April 2008, p. 1.
37 'Magpies go to water in desert', Caroline Wilson, *Sunday Age*, 10 February 2008, p. 3.
38 'Olympian slams Eddie; Clarke's plea to save historic track', Michael Warner, *Herald Sun*, 6 March 2008, p. 19.
39 'Welcome to Maggieland', Michael Gleeson, *The Age*, 30 April 2008, p. 2.
40 'Black-and-white deal more a murky shade of grey', *The Age*, 13 August 2009, p. 14.
41 'Sponsorship deal to keep Magpie juggernaut rolling', Andrea Petrie, *The Age*, 25 March 2009, p. 5.
42 'Pies get park back', Terry Brown, *Herald Sun*, 23 July 2009, p. 10.
43 'Alisa jumps at chance to join Pies' board', Georgie Pilcher, *Herald Sun*, 9 December 2009, p. 7.
44 'Collingwood to part with major naming sponsor', Caroline Wilson, *The Age*, 17 November 2009, p. S03.

Chapter 16 – Changes Brewing
1 'Pies the club for coach Bucks', Jon Pierik, *Herald Sun*, 18 April 2006, p. 75.
2 'Eddie looking unsteady as leader of the Pies', Caroline Wilson, *The Age*, 6 March 2009, p. S03.
3 'McGuire retaliates by denying Age access', *Sunday Age*, 8 March 2009, p. S03.
4 'Buckley may learn on the job', Samantha Lane, *The Age*, 16 March 2009, p. S02.

5   'Buckley coy about McGuire's coaching revelation', Samantha Lane, *The Age*, 17 March 2009, p. S02.
6   'Bucks no sure thing for Pies', Jon Ralph, *Herald Sun*, 21 March 2009, p. 28.
7   'Choco in Pie mix', Mike Sheahan, *Herald Sun*, 25 April 2009, p. 31.
8   'Amicably into the unknown', Mike Sheahan, *Herald Sun*, 29 July 2009, p. 69.
9   'Malthouse will stay or be sued: McGuire', Jon Pierik, *Sunday Age*, 4 April 2010, p. S03.
10 'Malthouse Theatre – Collingwood', Caroline Wilson, *The Age*, 28 August 2010, p. C08.
11 'Ed in full cry', Mark Robinson, *Herald Sun*, 4 October 2010, p. 91.
12 'Mick to go Sheahan says: Malthouse won't be a Magpie next year', Mike Sheahan, *Herald Sun*, 26 August 2011, p. 1.
13 'Malthouse rebuilt the Pies: McGuire', Jon Pierik, *Sydney Morning Herald*, 29 September 2011, p. 17.

Chapter 17 – Jumping on a Grenade

Much of Eddie McGuire's time at Channel Nine was revealed in the author's book, *Broadcast Wars* (Hachette Australia, Sydney, 2011). Information in this chapter has been drawn from pp. 98-127, 128, 138-146, 206-212 of *Broadcast Wars* as well as from the sources below.

1   'Mr Multimedia', Richard Yallop, *The Australian*, 23 September 1999, p. M01.
2   'Sporting Life', Geoff McClure, *The Age*, 3 September 2003, p. 23.
3   'Who wants to be Eddie?', Wendy Tuohy, *The Age*, 14 May 2005, p. 3.
4   Paul Barry, *Who Wants to Be a Billionaire? The James Packer Story*, Allen & Unwin, Sydney, 2009, p. 289.
5   Interviews with author, February 2006.
6   Interviews with author, February 2006.
7   Interview with author, February 2006.
8   Interview with author, February 2006.
9   'The Diary', Amanda Meade, *The Australian*, 23 March 2006, p. 42.
10 Interview with author, February 2006.
11 Ken Sutcliffe with Ian Deads, *The Wide World of Ken Sutcliffe*, Allen & Unwin, Sydney, 2009.
12 'Right time, right place: McGuire ready to kick network goals', Samantha Lane with Daniel Ziffer, *Sunday Age*, 19 February 2006, p. 4.
13 'Eddie's agenda', Robert Fidgeon, *Herald Sun*, 1 March 2006, p. 3.
14 'Executives at PBL ahead on new shares', Lisa Murray, *The Age*, 22 March 2006, p. 3.
15 Robert Fidgeon, *Herald Sun*, 21 February 2006, p. 9.
16 Ken Sutcliffe with Ian Deads, *The Wide World of Ken Sutcliffe*, Allen & Unwin, Sydney, 2009.
17 'McGuire lures lawyer to Nine', Caroline Wilson, *The Age*, 24 March 2006, p. 3.
18 'Teary Eddie's final farewell', Robert Fidgeon, *Herald Sun*, 2 March 2006, p. 15.
19 Its Warner Brothers deal gave Nine the forgettable US series *The Evidence, Closer to Home* and *Invasion* in 2006.
20 'McGuire keeps head down as Nine slides', Neil Shoebridge, *Australian Financial Review*, 2 May 2006, p. 14.
21 'Deal done: Eddie gets his men', Robert Fidgeon, *Herald Sun*, 17 May 2006, p. 5.
22 'I'm no one's puppet, says Nine chief', Neil Shoebridge, *Australian Financial Review*, 19 June 2006, p. 1.
23 'Nine to cut 100; High-profile shows get breaking news', Robert Fidgeon, *Herald Sun*, 7 June 2006, p. 6.
24 'Nine boss gets tough on costs', Nabila Ahmed, *The Age*, 10 June 2006, p. 7.
25 'I'm no one's puppet, says Nine chief', Neil Shoebridge, *Australian Financial Review*, 19 June 2006, p. 1.
26 'Kerri-Anne's anger at Nine's regime', Marcus Casey, *Daily Telegraph*, 5 August 2006, p. 1.
27 'Ed on the block; Who wants to be a TV boss', Robert Fidgeon, *Herald Sun*, 5 July 2006, p. H03.
28 'Eddie lays on Sunday roast', Janet Fife-Yeomans and Marcus Casey, *Herald Sun*, 4 July 2006, p. 2.
29 'Struggling Nine braces for new chiefs', Angela Kamper, *Herald Sun*, 3 July 2006, p. 5.
30 'Eddie's Wimbledon KO', Robert Fidgeon, *Herald Sun*, 29 June 2006, p. 7.
31 'He's just sacked 100 staff, his network is a mess, and he's in England for tennis and polo - HOME, JAMES', Janet Fife-Yeomans, *Daily Telegraph*, 30 June 2006, p. 1.
32 'Nine still looking for the big one', Annie Lawson, *The Age*, 10 August 2006, p. 3.
33 'Jessica and Eddie present united front in TV war', Ben Cubby and Paul McIntyre, *The Age*, 26 July 2006, p. 3.

34 'Nine fails to score with biff', *Daily Telegraph*, 20 June 2006, p. 5.
35 Michael Bodey, *Broadcast Wars: The Money, the Ego, the Power Behind Your Remote Control*, Hachette Australia, Sydney, 2011.
36 Screen Australia invested $2.938 million in *Underbelly* and recouped $2.59 million by April 2011.
37 In the mid-1990s, Fenton pitched for Seven to the IOC what he thought might be an inadequate offer to broadcast the 1996 Atlanta Olympic Games. Atlanta was expendable but Fenton feared that if Seven didn't win the US Games, its prospects would diminish when later bidding for the holy grail, the 2000 Sydney Olympic Games. He suggested to the IOC that Seven should present a double Games bid. Seven's offer of US$75 million locked up the rights to Atlanta and Sydney and sparked a frenzy among US broadcasters sensing multi-Games pitches were logical. It quickly led to NBC stumping up US$1.2 billion for Atlanta and Sydney, and before the year was out paying a further US$2.3 billion for the next three Games.
38 'Who wants to be a very well-paid TV executive?', Helen Westerman, *The Age*, 27 September 2006, p. 1.
39 Kerry Packer once noted 'You only get one Alan Bond in your lifetime, and I've had mine' after the WA entrepreneur paid him $800 million and $250 million of subordinated debt in Bond's company for his Nine stations in 1987, only to have Packer get back the stations for a substantially smaller 'price' after Bond went under.
40 'Quit rumour denied; I'm still the one – Eddie', Robert Fidgeon, *Herald Sun*, 9 December 2006, p. 2.
41 Paul Barry, *Who Wants to Be a Billionaire? The James Packer Story*, Allen & Unwin, Sydney, 2009, p. 301.
42 Michael Bodey, *Broadcast Wars: The Money, the Ego, the Power Behind Your Remote Control*, Hachette Australia, Sydney, 2011.
43 'I wasn't given the flick; Eddie's $10 million exit', Darren Devlyn, *Herald Sun*, 19 May 2007, p. 1.
44 'Packer walks into wedded life a second time around', Sophie Tedmanson, *The Australian*, 21 June 2007, p. 3.
45 'Eddie's wall of fame', Steve Perkin, *Herald Sun*, 28 May 2007, p. 44.

Chapter 18 – Back to Basics
1 Gerald Stone, *Who Killed Channel 9?: The Death of Kerry Packer's Mighty TV Dream Machine*, Pan Macmillan Australia, Sydney, 2007.
2 The first episode of *Underbelly: A Tale of Two Cities* notched a national audience of 2.58 million.
3 'Eddie has a Hot date', Darren Devlyn, *Herald Sun*, 15 April 2009, p. 5.
4 'Eddie in the hot seat; War of words erupts over new radio gig', Ashley Gardiner, *Herald Sun*, 1 September 2009, p. 11.
5 'McGuire shrugs off low radio ratings', Michael Lallo, *The Age*, 3 November 2009, p. 5.
6 'Eddie's gay joke probe', Geraldine Mitchell, *Herald Sun*, 27 February 2010, p. 19.
7 'TV mag pours scorn on Eddie's Swan dive', Alice Coster, Nicola Webber and Kate McMahon, *Herald Sun*, 5 April 2011, p. 23.
8 'Eddie's world stage', Alice Coster, Kate McMahon, Jackie Epstein, *Herald Sun*, 8 March 2012, p. 27.
9 'Eddie's friends channel praise', *Herald Sun*, 12 October 2012, p. 27.
10 'Eddie now radio king', Luke Dennehy, Jackie Epstein, Nui Te Koha, *Herald Sun*, 3 July 2013, p.22.

Chapter 19 – A Finger in Many Pies
1 'McGuire masters broker clash', John Beveridge, *Herald Sun*, 17 November 2009, p. 49.
2 'McGuire to help promote Rebels', Russell Gould, *Herald Sun*, 19 March 2010, p. 105.
3 'McGuire may try a new ball game', Chloe Saltau, *The Age*, 9 July, 2011 p. S03.
4 'Bolt backed as guest Star', Martin Blake, *The Age*, 22 August 2012, p. 21.
5 'Eddie on board in hunt for millions', Jenny McAsey, *The Australian*, 11 March 2005, p. 32.

Chapter 20 – Regrets and Recriminations
1 'Eddie McGuire', John Stensholt, *Australian Financial Review*, 23 September 2011, p. 65.
2 *ABC News*, 1 August 2010.
3 3AW, 6 June 2011.
4 'Eddie hits out at Tigers', *Herald Sun*, 28 March 2003, p. 124.

5   'Eddie clears air on Kevin', Mark Stevens, *Herald Sun*, 28 March 2009, p. 40.
6   'Sheeds, Ed get personal', Chris de Kretser and Daryl Timms, *Herald Sun*, 11 February 2011, p. 87.
7   'Pies voice safety fears', Mark Robinson, *Herald Sun*, 5 June 1999, p. 35.
8   'Angry Colless blasts Collingwood chief', AAP, *The Australian*, 16 May 2000, p. 17.
9   'Even salary cap: McGuire', AAP, *Sunday Age*, 1 September 2002, p. 4.
10 'Swan fury over draft backdown', Alan Kennedy, *The Age*, 3 October 2001, p. 2.
11 'Pies, Dons renew their cap attacks', Lyall Johnson, *The Age*, 28 June 2003, p. 3.
12 'Colless, McGuire birds of feather', Peter Lalor, *The Australian*, 20 August 2003, p. 18.
13 'Boot in mouth but I'm no racist', Eddie McGuire, *Herald Sun*, 30 May 2013, p. 5.
14 'I may step aside', Rebekah Cavanagh, Christopher Gillett and Angus Thompson, *Herald Sun*, 30 May 2013, p. 1.
15 'Collingwood stands by "magnificent" McGuire', Emma Quayle, Stathi Paxinos, *Sydney Morning Herald*, 31 May 2013, p. 4.
16 'Eddie a victim of morning sickness', Andrew Rule, *Herald Sun*, 31 May 2013, p. 27.
17 'The Diary', Leesha McKenny, *Sydney Morning Herald*, 12 August 2013, p. 15.
18 'McGuire's "injustice"; King Kong saga still grates Pies honcho', Glenn McFarlane, *Herald Sun*, 12 August 2013, p. 4.
19 'Mick: Eddie not a victim', Sam Edmund, *Herald Sun*, 1 June 2013, p. 85.
20 *Living Black*, NITV, 29 October 2013.
21 'Swans chairman tells Eddie McGuire to butt out of latest Adam Goodes debate', Andrew Wu, *The Age*, 1 June 2015, online.

Chapter 21 – Building on Success
1   'Mr Multimedia', Richard Yallop, *The Australian*, 23 September 1999, p M01.
2   'The Eddie Empire – So who wants to be a multi-millionaire?', *Sunday Age*, 24 December 2000, p. 1.
3   'In top form', *The Age*, 25 September 2002, p. 6.
4   'Father Ed', Tim Lane, *The Age*, 20 September 2003, p. 1.
5   'Beazley quiet on McGuire seat talk', Gosia Kaszubska, *The Australian*, 11 April 2005, p. 5.
6   'Union fury at Conroy, Shorten', Pia Akerman, *Weekend Australian*, 29 January 2011, p. 2.
7   'There's a new order in Mount Eliza', Larry Schwartz, *The Age*, 13 June 2005, p. 1.
8   *Open Mike*, Fox Footy, 13 March 2013.

Epilogue – The Son Keeps Rising
1   'Eddie's friends channel praise', Jackie Epstein, *Herald Sun*, 12 October 2012, p. 27.

BIBLIOGRAPHY

Bodey, Michael, *Broadcast Wars: The Money, the Ego, the Power Behind Your Remote Control*, Hachette Australia, Sydney, 2011.

Boland, Adam, *Brekky Central: behind the smiles of Australian breakfast television*, Melbourne University Press, Melbourne, 2014.

Buckley, Nathan, *All I Can Be*, Penguin, Melbourne, 2008.

Carey, Wayne with Happell, Charles, *The Truth Hurts*, Pan Macmillan Australia, Sydney, 2013.

Cousins, Ben with Knox, Malcolm, *My Life Story*, Pan Macmillan Australia, Sydney 2010.

Griffin, James, *John Wren: A Life Reconsidered*, Scribe, Melbourne, 2004.

Hardy, Frank, *Power Without Glory*, Random House Australia, Sydney, 2000.

MacDowell, Ross, *Inside Story: 20 Famous Australians tell their story*, Hobson Dell, Melbourne, 2001.

Malthouse, Christi, *Malthouse: A Football Life*, Allen & Unwin, Sydney, 2012.

Malthouse, Mick and Bullifant, David, *The Ox Is Slow but the Earth is Patient*, Allen & Unwin, Sydney, 2011.

Martin, Ray, *Ray: Stories of my life*, William Heinemann, Sydney, 2010.

Maxwell, Nick with Gleeson, Michael, *One Grand Week: A captain's tale of the 2010 triumph*, Weston Media and Communications, Melbourne, 2010.

Matthews, Leigh, *Accept the Challenge: The Autobiography*, Random House Australia, Sydney, 2013.

McFarlane, Glenn and Roberts, Michael, *Collingwood at Victoria Park*, Lothian, Melbourne, 1999.

McFarlane, Glenn and Roberts, Michael, *The Machine*, Slattery Media Group, Melbourne, 2004.

McGuire, Eddie with Main, Jim, *Pants: The Darren Millane Story*, Celebrity Publishing, Melbourne, 1994.

Niall, Brenda, *Mannix*, Text Publishing, Melbourne, 2015.

Nixon, Ricky and Weston, James, *It's a Jungle Out There*, Pan Macmillan Australia, Sydney, 2010.

Oakley, Ross, with Green, Jonathan, and Slattery, Geoff, *The Phoenix Rises*, Slattery Media Group, Melbourne, 2014.

Richards, Lou with Phillips, Stephen, *Lou: My Wonderful Life*, Slattery Media Group, Melbourne, 2012.

Ryan, Peter, *Side by Side: a season with Collingwood*, Slattery Media Group, Melbourne, 2009.

Silver, Harvey, *Behind The Footy Show*, Five Mile Press, Melbourne, 1997.

Stone, Gerald, *Who Killed Channel 9?: The Death of Kerry Packer's Mighty TV Dream Machine*, Pan Macmillan Australia, Sydney, 2007.

Sutcliffe, Ken with Heads, Ian, *The Wide World of Ken Sutcliffe*, Allen & Unwin, Sydney, 2009.

Turnbull, Malcolm, *Fighting for the Republic: The Ultimate Insider's Account*, Hardie Grant, Melbourne, 1999.

Vizard, Steve, *Two Weeks in Lilliput: Bear Baiting and Backbiting At the Constitutional Convention*, Penguin, Melbourne, 1998.

Weston, James, *Cakewalk: The inside story of Collingwood's 1990 Premiership*, Weston Media and Communications, Melbourne, 2010.

INDEX

1 vs 100, 279–80, 287
2GB, 242
3AK, 40
3AW, 57, 59–60, 63, 84, 146, 192, 195, 268, 281, 287, 290–1, 310
3GL, 59
3LO, 60
3UZ, 109
3XY, 152
5AA, 177
60 Minutes, 288
774 ABC, 290

A Current Affair, 99, 245, 257–9, 265, 286–7
Abbott, Tony, 119, 262
ABC, 31, 45, 60–1, 105, 115, 239, 273, 290
Ablett, Gary Snr, 75
Aboriginal Australians *see* Indigenous Australians
ACP magazines, 256, 258, 261, 278
Adamson, Lee, 304
Adidas, 49
AFC Asia Cup, 327
AFL SportsReady program, 305
AFL/VFL, 7, 15, 30–4, 38, 141–4, 169–70, 236
   All-Australian squad, 212–13
   broadcasting rights, 36, 66–7, 70, 77, 86, 99, 105, 129, 137–45, 149, 247, 255, 275, 280
   Collingwood *see* Collingwood Football Club
   Fosters International Cup Qualifying Final, 36
   interstate clubs, 123
   Media Association, 139
   Media Awards, 37
   Middle Eastern debut 2008, 214
   newspaper reporting, 19–24
   North Melbourne Kangaroo Under-19s, 24
   Players' Association, 165
   Tribunal, 148

The Age, 24, 26, 44, 70, 103, 108, 117, 127, 140, 174, 210, 217, 222, 246, 264, 270, 323
Ahmat, Robbie, 178
Aitken, Ian, 36
Alberti, Susan, 92
Alexander, John, 239, 242, 244, 248, 255, 265, 276, 278, 280
Ali, Muhammad, 6, 7, 331
Allan, Graeme, 132, 158
Allen, Paul, 144
Allis, Janine, 92
Allis, Jeff, 61–2, 100
Allison, Annette, 25
Anderson, Adrian, 146
Anderson, Chris, 242, 244, 246, 248
Anderson, John, 142
Anderson, Jon, 43, 79
Anderson, Sean, 258–9
Andrew, Bruce, 45
Andrews, Daniel, 323
Anti-Discrimination Commissioner, 92
Anzac Day AFL match, 177, 210, 223, 306
Arocca, Eugene, 156, 189, 210–12, 214, 218, 312
Asian Cup Broadcast Service (ACBS), 327
Asper, Izzy, 38
Astbury, Rob, 31, 33
Athenaeum Club, 300
Athletics Australia, 153, 215, 302, 325
Athletics Victoria, 215–17, 302
Audsley, Ian, 246
Aussie Home Loans, 219
Australia Unites: Reach Out to Asia, 109
Australia Unites – the Victorian Bushfire Appeal, 288
The Australian, 108, 147, 208, 224, 236, 239, 264
Australian Associated Press (AAP), 21
Australian Grand Prix, 102, 152
   celebrity race, 51

Australian Journalists Association, 148
Australian Premier League Bowls, 325
Australian Republican Movement, 112–19
Australian Shareholders Association, 211–12
Australian Soccer Association, 152
Australian Sports Medicine Association, 60
Australian Survivor, 108
Awake the Sleeping Giant, 171
awards, 37
Azzaro, Luciano, 161

Baillieu, Ted, 143
Ball, Luke, 21, 227
Ball, Ray, 21
Balme, Neil, 165, 168, 173–4, 178, 206
Bana, Eric, 59
Banks, Dean, 57, 60
Banks, Dennis, 41, 52–3
Banks, Tony, 26
Barassi, Ron, 114
Barham, David, 207
Barker, Trevor, 50
Barnes, Jimmy, 151
Barrawarn program, 305
Bartram, Tracy, 280
Baxter, Erica, 282
The Beach Hotel, 154–5
Beaconsfield mining tragedy, 256–9
Beale, Edward, 50
Beams, Dayne, 194
Beasley, Simon, 52
Beazley, Kim, 324
Become the AFL's Most Hated/Respected Team, 171
Begg-Smith, Dale, 292
Beitzel, Harry, 37, 45, 90
Bertrand, John, 208
Better Homes and Gardens, 287
Between the Lines, 294
Big Bash League, 301
Big Brother, 108, 256

347

The Big Question, 269
The Biggest Loser, 256
Bingham, Murray, 325
Bishop, Julie, 120
Blackwell, Andrew, 242
Blethyn, Geoff, 7
Blight, Malcolm, 165, 231
Blofeld, Henry 'Blowers', 22
Blue Heelers, 85
Blue Murder, 273
Blunden, Peter, 267–8, 322
Board, Peter, 155
Boland, Adam, 109
Bolt, Usain, 296, 301
Bond, Alan, 278
Bracks, Steve, 239, 268, 322
Brad 'The Young Idiot', 57
Brayshaw, James, 92, 251, 287, 301, 312
Brennan, Bridget *see* McGuire, Bridget 'Bridie'
Brereton, Dermott, 50, 60, 62, 69–70, 76, 82–3, 86, 127, 165, 197, 255
Bright, Ben, 294
Bright, Torah, 293–4
Broadmeadows, 1, 3–7, 11, 13–14, 16–18, 22, 24, 111
  Swimming Centre, 7
Brokeback Mountain, 292
broken nose, 48
Brother McCarthy, 15
Brown, Alf, 20, 23
Brown, Bryan, 114
Brown, Gavin, 75, 133–4, 158, 173, 205, 208
Brown, Jonathan, 204
Brown, Mal, 70
Browne, Jeff, 107, 130, 140, 181, 240, 250, 255–6, 258–9, 262–3, 275–6, 286, 293–4, 296, 297
Brownlow Medal, 78, 95, 179, 200, 304, 322
Brumby, John, 192, 215, 216, 290–1
Buchan, Mieke, 290–1
Buckingham, Jeremy, 321
Buckley, Nathan, 43, 85, 134, 158–9, 163–5, 167–8, 173–8, 192, 198, 200, 213, 214, 220–35, 297, 303, 317
Buckley, Nicky, 59, 325
Burke, Graham, 268
The Bulletin, 119, 259–61
Burns, Creighton, 24
Burns, Gary (gay rights activist), 292
Burns, Gary (Nine director of sport), 81
Burns, John, 290
Burns, Scott, 174, 175, 190
Burrows, Mark, 32
bus 'hijack', 53

Business Review Weekly Top 50 Australian Show Business Earners, 101
Butterss, Rod, 92–3
Buttifant, David, 208, 223, 229

Cable, Barry, 303
Cain, John, 113, 152
Campbell, Peter, 294
Campbell, Wayne, 85
Campese, David, 42
Camplin, Alisa, 155, 219
Capp, Sally, 156, 201, 219
Cardone, Cos, 88, 95, 250, 275, 325, 326
Carey, Wayne, 75, 138, 197–8, 207
Carlyon, Les, 30
Carman, Phil 'Fabulous', 12
Carroll, Ernie, 87
Cartoon Corner, 13
Casey, Clinton, 141
Casey, Darren, 59
The Catch Up, 261
Ceberano, Kate, 114
Centenary of Federation, 112
Champion, Greg, 50
Chances, 272
Channel Nine, 26, 61, 63–110, 114, 127, 129, 132–4, 137–8, 140–1, 147–9, 151, 156, 171, 238, 246–7, 256, 263, 267, 269–76, 280, 288, 291–6, 325
  'boning' affidavit, 262–5, 267
  CEO, 156, 210–12, 236–86, 299, 325
  commentator on, 175, 176, 291–3, 296, 329
  cricket, 301
  deal with Foxtel, 294–5
  News, 97–8, 245, 294
  ninemsn, 238, 243, 258
  ratings, 237, 244, 248, 256–7, 259, 269, 274, 279, 288
  sale, 210, 212, 244, 249, 269, 276–9, 285
  telathon, 288
Channel Seven, 25–6, 36, 40, 42–3, 58, 65, 67, 69–70, 72, 77–8, 83–6, 98–9, 103–5, 109, 129, 137–8, 140, 144, 149, 237, 243–5, 247, 252–4, 256, 258–9, 261–5, 267, 270, 275–7, 280, 282, 287–8, 328
Channel Ten, 6, 25–44, 47–8, 64–7, 77, 81, 83, 86, 99, 105–6, 108–9, 121, 140, 147, 149, 199, 206, 243, 247, 256, 272, 275, 280

cadetship, 27–36
news reading, 37
charity work, 40, 52, 78, 86, 97, 109–10, 257, 305
Cheers, 79
Chevron Club, 52
childhood, 5–18
Chisholm, Sam, 240–3, 245–6, 255, 262, 280
Christian Brothers College, St Kilda, 14–18, 22–3
Christian, Michael, 41, 130
Clark, Ed, 142–3
Clarke, Ern, 123
Clarke, Ron, 153, 216
Clarkson, Alastair, 36
Cleary, Phil, 117–18
Clement, James, 175, 213, 221
Cleo Bachelor of the Year competition, 51, 54
Clifton, Jeff, 126
Cloke, Cameron, 183, 187
Cloke, David, 127, 162, 304
Cloke, Jason, 175, 179
Cloke, Travis, 193, 196, 205, 210, 213
Close to Home, 270
The Club, 156
The Club, 325
Club 10, 75
Coach and Horses, 156
Colless, Richard, 310, 313, 314, 316, 319
Collier family, 122, 157
Collier, Harry, 122
Collingwood Football Club, 7–12, 16, 23, 31, 33–5, 40–1, 75, 80–1, 91, 100, 104, 106, 121–235
  altitude training, 208–9
  annual meetings, 209
  assaults on players, 193
  betting by players, 195–6
  coaches, 41, 52, 122–3, 126–8, 139, 141, 146, 158–69, 206–7, 220–35
  community work, 305
  culture, 182–96, 304
  drafting new players, 174–5, 213
  EGM, 135
  enmity with other clubs, 311–13
  feud with Sydney Swans, 311–14
  finances, 174, 175, 178, 200, 204, 210, 218–19
  Foundation, 305
  Grand Final 2002, 179–82
  Grand Final 2003, 182, 184, 200
  Grand Final 2009, 219
  Grand Final 2010, 194, 229–31
  Grand Final 2011, 233–4

INDEX

Hollywood stars visiting, 198–9
home ground, 9–11, 41, 121–5, 128, 151, 164–9, 171
Indigenous players, 178, 303, 305–6
liquor licence, 154–5
losing streak, 159–2
Maggieland, 125, 218
New Magpies, 31, 121, 123
Olympic Park, 152–3, 165–6, 199, 201, 202–3, 214–15
player drunkenness and misconduct, 182–96
premierships, 40–1, 51, 68, 106, 121–5, 157–8, 194–5, 231, 283
presidency, 45, 47, 63, 94, 100, 107, 124–50, 158–236, 240–1, 246, 251, 268, 277, 304
pubs, 154–6, 218
social club, 121, 134, 162
sponsorship, 81, 91, 126, 128–9, 148–50, 161, 167, 170–2, 174, 183–4, 201, 205, 219, 227, 285
Sydney, 173
theme song, 135, 165
Transport Accident Commission sponsorship, 183–4
wooden spoon, 12, 122, 165, 168, 206
Collingwood Football Club Foundation, 305
Collins, Ian, 36, 169
Colosimo, Vince, 271, 273
Cometti, Dennis, 147, 328
commentating, 36–7, 39–40, 59–60, 63, 85, 99–100, 107, 140–2, 147–8, 287, 289
Commonwealth Games
 Malaysia, 63, 100–1, 132
 Melbourne, 152, 244, 248, 259, 275
conflicts of interest, 134, 136–56, 211–12, 300
Conroy, Stephen, 324
Constitutional Convention, 63, 84, 100, 112, 114–20, 125, 236
The Coodabeen Champions, 50, 59
Cooper, Brad, 130–1, 150, 174
Copeland Trophy, 181, 188
Corfe, Jeff 'Joffa', 187
Cornell, John 'Strop', 297
Cosser, Steve, 38
Costa, Frank, 140, 200, 313
Costello, Peter, 99, 322
Costello, Rev. Tim, 115–16
Cousins, Ben, 194
Coventry family, 122, 154, 157

Cover, Ian, 50
Cox Plate, 54
Crawford, David, 300
Crawford, Shane, 95
Crawley, Steve, 242, 275
cricket, 4, 16, 21–2, 37, 46, 50, 77, 109, 269
 Big Bash League, 301
 ICC Cricket World Cup, 327
 Melbourne Stars Twenty20 side, 301
Crosisca, Gavin, 173
Crowe, Russell, 209
Crown Casino, 60, 81–2, 181, 194, 230
Cruise, Tom, 198
The Crux Club, 52
Cudmore, Vicar-General Monsignor Gerald, 89–90
Curro, Tracey, 248
Curry, John, 212
CVC Asia Pacific, 276, 278–9, 285
cycling broadcasts, 326–7

Daffy, Nick, 141
Daicos, Peter, 41, 165, 207, 271
Daily Telegraph, 252, 261, 265–7
Dal Santo, Nick, 204
Dancing on Ice, 269
Dancing with the Stars, 269, 287
D'Aquino, Nuno, 201
Darcy, Luke, 290, 297, 308–9
Davidson, Tom, 185
Davies, Ben, 205
Davis, Bobby, 69, 74
Davis, Leon, 175, 229, 305–6
Davis, Nick, 175, 176
Davis, Phil, 312
Dawes, Chris, 231
Days in the Diocese Melbourne, 299
De Niro, Robert, 286
Deal or No Deal, 288–9, 297
Delahunty, Mary, 115–16, 118, 120
Delaney, Delvene, 297
DeLutis, Colin, 50–1, 181
Demetriou, Andrew, 149, 165, 214, 239, 268, 297, 302, 315, 322
Denton, Andrew, 103, 108
DePledge, Amanda, 43
Desperate and Dateless Ball, 51
Desperate Housewives, 245, 253
D-Generation, 57, 59, 61
Diamond Creek Tavern, 154–6
Dibbs, Mary-Anne, 43
Didak, Alan, 175, 187–94, 210, 232
Dimsey, Clem, 31
DiPierdomenico, Robert, 51
Docklands Stadium, 134, 137, 145

Doing the Rounds, 34, 38, 64
The Don Lane Show, 69, 109, 247
Donegan, Peter, 31, 43
Doran, Jenny, 113, 116
Drum, Damian, 127, 162
Duclos, Brigitte, 57, 62, 78, 297
Dugina, Mike, 208
Dunne, Jack, 21
Dunstall, Jason, 72, 76, 83, 85, 95
Dutton, Kevin, 126
Dyer, Jack 'Captain Blood', 45, 69, 74

Eade, Rodney, 203, 234
Eddie Everywhere, 49, 56, 109, 285
Eddie McGuire Tonight, 295
Eddie-torials, 291
Edwin Flack Oval, 153
Egan, Chris, 205
Egon Zehnder, 238–9
Elliott, John, 94, 145–6
Ellis, Anthony, 272
Emdur, Larry, 98
Emerson, David, 170–1
Emirates Airlines, 199, 205, 213, 214, 227
Evans and Partners, 300
Evans, David, 300
Evans, Ron, 130–1, 137
Ewe, Jiin-Wen, 92
Eyewitness News, 30, 32, 38, 40, 48, 64

Faine, Jon, 297
Fairfax, Russell, 43
Family Feud, 245, 288
Farmer, Graham 'Polly', 303
Farr-Jones, Nick, 42
Fawlty Towers, 77
federal election night coverage, 99
Fellini, Federico, 272
Fenton, Gary, 275–6, 296
Ferguson, Mark, 253
Fevola, Brendon, 204
Fidgeon, Robert, 264
Fitzgerald, Ryan 'Fitzy', 326
FitzSimons, Peter, 317
Fletcher, Adrian, 206, 208
The Flying Doctors, 50
Football Superstar, 325
Football Writers' Association Awards, 45–6
Footy Classified, 92
Footy Millions, 139, 143
The Footy Show, 44, 47, 52, 58, 60, 68–100, 103–6, 113–14, 131, 139, 141–2, 146, 148, 151, 154, 166, 171, 176, 184, 198, 204, 228, 232, 236, 241, 250–1, 255, 257, 280, 287, 294

Awards, 90
Beaconsfield mining tragedy fundraiser, 256–8
Didak's apology on, 193
Flinders Park stadium broadcast, 79
London edition, 87–8
NRL, 78–80, 257
radio segments, 91
ratings, 79, 85–7, 90, 105, 260
sponsors, 72, 80–2, 90–1
World Cup edition, 260, 272
Footytips website, 144
Ford Superquiz, 109
Fordham, David, 42
Four Quarters, 58, 78
Fox FM, 59, 61–2, 280, 290, 298
Fox, Lindsay, 115–16, 239, 297
Foxtel, 105–6, 140, 149, 239, 269, 276, 280, 293–6, 326–9
  commentating for, 295–6
  Fox Footy, 295, 296, 315, 320, 328
Franklin, Lance 'Buddy', 184, 315
Fraser, Josh, 175, 229
Frasier, 79
Frazier, Joe, 282
Freeborn, Glenn, 161
Freedman, Mia, 261
Freudenstein, Richard, 239, 297
Friday Night Football, 275, 287
Friends, 79, 103

Galbally, David, 125
Galbally family, 122
Galbally, Frank, 122
Galloway, Carla *see* McGuire, Carla
The Game, 86, 105
Gangitano, Alphonse, 271, 273
Gangitano family, 271
Gardner, Paul, 17
Garrett, Peter, 323
Gatto, Mick, 273
Gell, Rob, 32
George, Jennie, 113
Get Smart, 59
Gibbs, Phil, 39
Gibson, Mike, 42
Gillard, Julia, 290
Gillies, Max, 114
Glasgow Celtic Football Club, 2, 9, 124
Gold, 290
golf, 50, 291
Goodes, Adam, 200, 303, 307–11, 315–21
Gordon, Peter, 38, 123
Gotch, Brad, 206, 208

Goussis, Evangelos, 274
Graeme-Evans, Posie, 271
Grant, Trevor, 20
Grantley, Gyton, 273
Grattan, Michelle, 24
The Great Escape, 259
The Great Weight Debate, 269
The Grill Team, 59, 61–3, 85, 97, 100, 106, 290
Grimshaw, Tracy, 98, 258–9
Gudinski, Michael, 297
Gutnick, Joseph, 142
Gyngell, David, 149, 238–9, 276, 279–80, 282, 285–6, 293

Haddrick, Greg, 272
Hadley, Ray, 297
Hafey, Tom, 123
Hall, Tony, 78
Hamer, Rupert, 115
Hamilton, Fiona, 47
Hamilton, Jack, 45, 47
Hamish and Andy, 58
Hammond, Peter, 131–2, 135
Handy, Chris, 52
The Hangar, 325
Hanson, Pauline, 90
Harmer, Wendy, 108
Hartigan, John, 266
Haupt, Robert, 24
Hawke, Bob, 323
Hawke, Hazel, 113
Hawkins, Doug, 60, 72, 75–6, 83–6
Hayes, Lenny, 229
HBS, 327
Heads or Tails, 288
Healy, Michael, 242, 246, 253, 269, 274
Healy, Shane, 290
Heartland, 77
Helliar, Peter, 289
Henderson, Brian, 253
Hendo's, 249
Hensley, Lisa, 59
Herald, 19–24, 26, 50, 111, 156
Herald Sun, 43, 47, 62–3, 71, 79, 85, 87, 101, 132, 134, 153, 159, 187, 232, 248, 264, 267, 316, 318
Hewitt, Lleyton, 245
Hey! Hey! It's Saturday, 8, 70, 77, 87, 247
Higher School Certificate, 26
HIH Royal Commission, 149–50
Hird, James, 78, 83, 85, 138
Hitchener, Peter, 98
Hogg, Bob, 114
Holland, Brodie, 175, 185, 199, 221
Holmes, Katie, 198
Holmes à Court, Peter, 209
Holt, Harold, 6
homosexuals, 201–2, 292–3

Honey, Nick, 215
honeymoon, 54
Horowitz, Ralph 'Racetrack Ralphy', 59, 86
Horsburgh, Jo, 271–3
Hot Breakfast, 290, 297–8, 308, 328, 329
Hot Seat, 289, 291, 297, 328
House, 256
Housing Commission home, 3, 5, 11
Howard government, 278
Howard, John, 104, 119
Hudson, Anthony, 43
Hudson, Christopher Wayne, 188–9
Hughes, Dave, 109
Hughes, Graeme, 32
Hughes, Robert, 112
Humphreys, Bill, 18
Hunt, Rex, 60, 63, 147
Hutton, Deborah, 248
Hyde, Don, 40

In Melbourne Tonight, 43, 69, 247
Indigenous Australians
  AFL Indigenous Round, 308, 320
  AFL players, 178, 295, 303–11
  AFL SportsReady program, 305
  Barrawarn program, 305
  Michael Long Foundation, 306, 315
  racism, 303–11, 315–21
internet ventures, 139, 143–5
Irwin, Steve, 109

Jackson, Kathy, 324
Jackson, Mark, 70
Jackson, Syd, 303, 304
Jackson, Wayne, 129, 136–7, 143, 145–6, 169–70
Jacotine, Craig, 161
Jakovich, Allen, 77
Jakovich, Glen, 75
James, Glenn, 94
JamTV, 325, 327
Jess, Peter, 93–4
Jetta, Lewis, 308
Joffa, 80
Johnson, Ben, 175, 182–5, 187, 191
Johnson, Ian, 65–7, 69–70, 72, 81, 83–5, 87–8, 99, 102, 104, 114, 129, 137, 140, 142, 181
Johnson, Mark, 185
Johnston, David, 25, 27, 31–2
Jolly, Darren, 227
Jones, Alan, 242, 298
Jones, Clem, 118
Jones, Tony, 66, 68, 179, 191, 297

INDEX

Joy FM, 293
Jubilee Mass, 300
Judd, Chris, 213, 313
Judkins, Noel, 174, 206
Jurrah, Liam, 295

K-Rock, 59
Kath and Kim, 109
Kearney, Neil, 32
Kekovich, Sam, 70
Kelly Country, John, 178
Kelly, Craig 'Ned', 37, 41, 60, 75, 130, 210
Kelly, Ros, 217
Kelty, Bill, 113, 300
Keneally, Tom, 113
Kennedy, Alan, 148
Kennedy, Graham, 43, 69, 73–4, 102, 110
Kennedy, Jack, 126, 131–2, 135, 156, 174
Kennedy, Jane, 59, 114, 181
Kennerley, Kerri-Anne, 248, 261
Kennett, Jeff, 90, 113, 297
Kernahan, Stephen, 36
Kerr, Dr Robert, 95
Keyte, Jennifer, 32
Kidnapped, 269
Killigrew, Alan, 13
Kimberley, Craig, 330
King, Justice Betty, 273–4
King Kong incident, 303, 309–20
King, Poppy, 115–17
KKR, 276
Kleiman, Mark, 206
Knight, Beverly, 91
Knight, Larry, 257
Koch, David, 257, 259
Korda, Mark, 155
Kozaris, Chris, 133
Krakouer, Andrew, 306–7, 317
Krakouer, Jimmy, 304, 306

LA Screenings, 281–2
Landy, John, 216
Landy, Peter, 65
Lane, Cassie, 187
Lane, Don, 73, 110
Lane, Tim, 141–2
Lane, Tyson, 161
Larkins, Peter, 60
The Last Supper, 89
The Late Show, 61
Law, Ian, 246, 256, 282
Leadbelly: Inside Australia's Underworld Wars, 270–2
League Teams, 69, 74
Leaping Larry L, 57
Leckie, David, 81, 109, 140, 242, 245, 282
Leckie, Skye, 282
Leeds, Paul, 155
Let's Make a Deal, 288

Levy, Sandra, 245, 261, 271
Lexus Centre, 201, 215, 216, 217, 225
Licuria, Paul, 163, 175, 213, 221
Lim, Eddie, 151
Linnell, Garry, 260–2, 264, 266, 280
Live and Kicking, 85–6
Llewellyn, Mark, 242, 255, 260–5, 280
Lloyd, Matthew, 85
Lockett, Tony 'Plugger', 35–6, 313
Lockyer, Tarkyn, 163, 213, 229
Logie Awards, 68, 80, 99–101, 103, 108–10, 191, 294
Long, Michael, 304, 308, 315
Longmire, John, 231
Lonie, Ryan, 175, 221
Lord Mayor of Melbourne, 300
Lost, 245
Loveless, Tim, 126
Lovett, Wally, 303
Lowe, Chad, 199
Lowe, Rob, 198–9
Lowy, Frank, 38, 152
loyalty, 35, 54, 65, 104, 228, 235, 251, 329, 330
Lundy, Kate, 217, 315
Lyneham, Paul, 98–9
Lyon, Garry, 92, 165, 251, 287

McAdam, Gilbert, 304
McAlister, Allan, 41, 123, 125–6, 164–5, 178, 214, 218, 304
McAlpine, John, 149
McAvaney, Bruce, 31, 33, 36–7, 64–5, 98, 147
McCann, Stephen, 36
McCarthy, Brother, 15
McCarthy, John, 194
Macdonald, Ranald, 31
Macedon Ranges Telegraph, 27
McFarlane, Peter, 22, 44
McGuane, Mick, 40, 165
McGuinness, Tony, 123
McGuire, Alexander, 107, 250, 287
McGuire, Bridget 'Bridie', 1–6, 9–11, 14–15, 17, 19, 252
McGuire, Brigitte, 5
McGuire, Carla, 53–5, 60, 107, 114, 160, 180, 231, 237, 250, 252, 268, 278, 284, 297, 331
McGuire, Edward (Snr), 1–6, 8–11, 13–14, 19, 25–6, 40, 180, 252, 282, 300, 330, 331
McGuire, Evelyn, 3, 5, 8, 14, 19, 27
McGuire, Frank, 2–3, 5–9, 14, 16, 18–23, 25, 59, 90, 111–14, 149, 324, 325

McGuire, Joseph, 107, 180, 250, 287
McGuire Media, 87–8, 90, 100, 106, 127, 137–8, 149, 236, 325–7
McHale family, 122
McHale, Jock, 122, 157, 227, 231, 233–5
McHale Stadium, 165
Machin, Wendy, 113
McKenna, Guy, 78, 205, 208, 221, 228
McKenna, Peter 7–9, 12, 231
McKinnon, Leila, 296
McLachlan, Gillon, 323
McManus, Rove, 109–10
McMullin, Ian, 131, 134–5, 155–6
Macpherson, Elle, 51
Madden, Justin, 178
Madden, Simon, 41
Magic, 60
The Magpie Monochromes, 51
Main, Jim, 40, 68
Major, Ian, 45
Making Tracks, 325
Malone, David, 239
Malthouse, Christi, 166, 206
Malthouse, Mick, 141, 146–7, 166–9, 173–9, 185, 189, 192–4, 197–8, 200, 202–13, 220–35, 307, 319
Malthouse, Nanette, 235
Mann, Neil, 158
Mannix, Dr Daniel, 122
Marmalade, Trevor, 51, 58–9, 62, 70, 73–4, 76, 86, 171, 241, 297
marriage, 54, 60
Marshall, Steve, 58–9
Martin, Ray, 99–101, 104, 254, 259
Martin, Tony, 61–2
Martin/Molloy program, 61–2
Massey, John, 128
Matthews, Leigh, 41, 52, 82, 123, 148, 158–9, 224, 231
Maurice, Ian, 97
Maxwell, Nick, 195, 210, 225, 229–31
May, John, 165, 168
Mayne, Stephen, 237
MCG, 9–12, 20–2, 40, 137, 164–5, 171
Meade, Amanda, 108
Meakin, Peter, 242
Meares, Jodhi, 104
Medhurst, Paul, 229
Melbourne Cup, 37
Melbourne, enthusiasm for, 301
Melbourne Football Club, 73
Melbourne lunch clubs, 322
Melbourne Rebels rugby team, 301

Melbourne Stars Twenty20 side, 301
Meldrum, Molly, 201–2, 297
Member of the Order of Australia (AM), 305, 324
Merlino, James, 217
Merrett family, 122
Micallef, Shaun, 108–9
Michael Long Foundation, 306, 315
Michael, Mal, 163, 174, 186
Midday, 98
Millane, Darren 'Pants', 41, 52–3, 68, 271
Millennium Live, 105, 143
Miller, Neil, 34
Millichamp, Stephen, 53
Million Dollar Chance of a Lifetime, 103
Million Dollar Drop, 294
Million Dollar Minute, 297
Million Dollar Wheel of Fortune, 289
Millionaire Hot Seat, 289, 291, 297, 328
Milne, Stephen, 228, 229, 307
Minogue, Kylie, 85–6
Mitchell, Neil, 195, 268, 281, 297, 310, 322
Mockridge, Tom, 239
Moclair, Tony, 290–1
Mokbel, Tony, 274
Molloy, Jarrod, 175
Molloy, Mick, 61–2, 292–3, 297, 309
Monkhurst, Damian, 304
Montague, Greg, 130
Moran family, 271, 274
Moran, Lewis, 274
More Than a Game, 106, 127
Morgan, Anthony, 59
Morphett, Drew, 45–6
Morrison, Chad, 183
Motley, Geof, 168
Mouse Pack, 50
Mueller, Jay, 291, 309
MultiEmedia, 145
Munduwalawala, Ginger Riley, 282–3
Munro, Mike, 253, 259
Murdoch, Lachlan, 269
Murdoch, Rupert, 29, 32, 38, 241, 266–7
Murdoch, Sarah, 269
Murphy, Paul, 174

National Bingo Night, 289
National IQ Test, 108
Natrass, Sue, 92
Naylor, Brian, 68, 98
NCIS series, 256
Neos Kosmos, 152
Netball World Cup, 327
Nettlefold, Michael, 52
New Faces, 109
Newcombe, John, 32

Newman, Sam, 46–8, 52, 60, 63, 68–76, 79, 81–7, 90–6, 102, 105, 166, 171, 198, 241, 251, 280, 297
News Corporation, 17, 239, 251, 266–9
News Limited, 129, 267, 269
  Super League, 129
newspaper journalism, 19–27, 33, 45–6
Newton, Bert, 69, 73, 102, 109–10, 242, 261
  Family Feud, 245, 288
Nicholas, Mark, 248, 296
nickname, 49
nightclubs, 46–52
Nightline, 98
The Nine, 269
Nine Network *see* Channel Nine
Nine News, 97, 98, 245, 294
ninemsn, 238, 243, 258
Nixon, Ricky, 60, 75, 83, 176, 194
Norm Smith Medal, 200, 229
Norman, Greg, 288
Nova, 58, 290, 298
NRL, 69, 77, 129
  Footy Show, 78–80, 257
NSW Anti-Discrimination Board, 292
NSW State Government motion, 321
NYPD Blues, 77

Oakes, Laurie, 99
Oakley, Allan, 164
Oakley, Ross, 38, 123
Obama, Barack, 331
Oborne, Brad, 161
O'Bree, Shane, 175, 229
O'Brien, Harry, 210, 223, 316, 317
O'Brien, Paddy, 118
O'Donnell, Simon, 69, 83
O'Keefe, Andrew, 110
O'Lone, John, 25, 27
Olsen, Jimmy, 19
Olympic Games, 65, 255, 275–6, 292, 302
  London 2012, 275–6, 293, 296–7
  Melbourne 1956, 216
  Seoul 1988, 37, 42
  Sydney 2000, 99–100, 104–5
  Vancouver Winter Olympics, 291–3, 296
Olympic Park, 152–3, 201–3, 214–18, 302
  AFL taking over, 214–17
  Athletics Victoria ousted from, 215–17
  Collingwood training ground, 152, 165–6, 199, 201–3, 214

  redevelopment, 152, 178, 199, 214–18, 302
  Trust, 137, 153, 202, 217
  VIS ousted from, 214–17
O'Neill, Susie, 296
Orchard, Mark, 161
O'Sullivan, Pat, 246
Overhaul, 269
Overton, Peter, 253, 263

Packer, Sir Frank, 238
Packer, James, 81, 100, 102–5, 114, 129, 133, 198, 199, 210, 236–40, 243–4, 248, 252, 255–6, 258, 260, 265, 276–8, 282, 285, 297
Packer, Kerry, 90, 92, 102, 104–5, 107, 130, 137, 149, 237–8, 243, 244 246–7, 251, 260–1, 266, 271, 281
Pagan, Denis, 24, 165–6
Palmer, Scot, 159
Pandazopoulos, John, 143
Pannam family, 157
Pants: The Darren Millane Story, 53, 68
Parer, Damien, 17
Parkin, David, 70
Patterson, Mark, 152
Pearce, Wayne, 42
Pearson, Jo, 31
Penberthy, David, 252, 266
Pendlebury, Scott, 193, 207, 210
Perfect Match, 32
Peris, Nova, 120
Perkin, Steve, 87–8, 94
Perkins, Kieren, 42
Pert, Gary, 155, 190, 192, 210–14, 226, 229, 230, 232, 285
Philbin, Regis, 105
Phillips, Ed, 254
Pie in the Sky Travel, 199
Player, Gary, 71
politics, 63, 84, 100, 112–20, 291, 322–5
Porter, John, 239
Power of 10, 289
Power Without Glory, 13, 92, 111
Pratt, Richard, 130, 213
Premier League, 152
Prestigiacomo, Simon, 163
Price, Barry, 126, 132
Price, Steve, 60
prime minister ambition, 14, 29, 111, 236–7
Prison Break, 245
Pritchard, Darrin, 35
Pritchard, Steve, 43, 58
Pro Squad, 75
property deals, 300

352

INDEX

Publishing and Broadcasting Limited (PBL), 114, 129, 133, 238–40, 242–3, 246, 249, 256, 259–60, 265, 269, 277–9, 282
Purana taskforce, 270, 272

Q Score, 244, 286
Quartermain, Stephen, 31, 37, 42–3, 47–8, 50, 53, 60
Quartermaine, Matt, 59

racism, 303–11, 315–21
  Goodes incident, 303, 307–11, 315–21
radio, 40, 49, 56–63, 91, 97–8, 139, 285, 289–90
Radio City Australia Pty Ltd, 139
Ralph, Lynn, 92
Rapke, QC Jeremy, 273
Ratten, Brett, 199
Real Republican Party, 115–16
The Recruit, 325
Red Eagle Hotel, 58
republican, 84, 112–20, 236, 323, 324
Reyne, David, 98
Rhys-Jones, David, 60
Ricciuto, Mark, 200
The Rich List, 289
The Richard Stubbs Breakfast Show, 49, 57, 62, 98
Richards, Lou, 41, 45–6, 68–70, 74, 122
Richards, Ron, 122
Richardson, Alan, 207, 221
Richardson, Graham, 99
Richardson, Wayne, 40
Right the Sinking Ship, 171
Rioli, Cyril, 308
RMIT Journalism course, 26–7, 30
RMIT University honorary doctorate, 30
Roach, Michael, 40
Robbins, Glenn, 59
Robbins, Tim, 198
Roberts, Michael, 52
Roberts, Neil, 45
Roberts, Sandy, 65, 78
Rocca, Anthony, 163, 175, 198
Rocca, Saverio, 174
Rocchiccioli, Roland, 59
Rome, 269
Roos, Paul, 78, 231
Roosevelt, Theodore, 193
Rose, Bob, 123, 130–2, 153, 158
Rose family, 31, 126–7, 157, 162
Rose, Kevin, 124, 126–8, 130–1, 135–6, 175
Rose, Lionel, 7
Rowe, Jessica, 255, 262–5, 268–9, 279

Rowe, Stephen, 177
Rowntree, Catriona, 108
The Roy Hampson Show, 25
Rudd, Kevin, 305, 324
Rudder, Jim, 280
Rui, 201
Rule, Andrew, 270–2, 318
Rumour File, 60
Rusling, Sean, 205
Russell, Dwayne, 255
Russell, Todd, 256–7
Ryan, Ken, 322
Ryan, Marise, 120

St Dominic's Catholic school, 5–6, 14
St Kilda's Stokehouse, 297, 330
Sale of the Century, 102
Salmon, Paul, 85
Samuel, Graeme, 137, 140, 153
Samuel, Grant, 137
Sarandon, Susan, 198
Scanlan, Peter, 330
school, 6, 11, 13–18, 21–3, 26
Screema!, 106
Schwarz, David, 95
Sciessere, Rick, 174
Scotland, Heath, 163, 175
Scott, Brad, 221
Scott, Chris, 234
Scott, Mark, 239
Screen Australia, 272, 275
Screentime, 272–4
Scully, Tom, 312
Sea Patrol, 253
SEN, 287, 290
Shaw family, 154
Shaw, Heath, 190–2, 195, 210
Shaw, Ray, 12
Shaw, Rhyce, 175, 184, 190, 192, 210
Shaw, Tony, 35, 126–7, 133–4, 139, 158–63, 185–6, 192
The Shawshank Redemption, 286
Sheahan, Mike, 50, 134, 136, 232
Sheedy, Kevin, 70, 165, 312
Shepherd, Tony, 17
Sherrin family, 122, 157
Shirvington, Matt, 296
Shorten, Bill, 217, 257, 322, 324
Sidwell, Peter, 223, 227, 228, 232, 235
Silvagni, Stephen, 76, 85, 207
Silver, Harvey, 70, 75, 83–4, 87
Silvers discotheque, 46
Silvester, John, 270–2
Simon, Lee, 57
The Simpsons, 79
Sister Matthews, 15
Sister Therese, 14, 323

Sitch, Rob, 57, 181, 330
Slater, Michael, 269
Slumdog Millionaire, 289
Smith, 269
Smith, Patrick, 153
Smith, Tim, 57
Smorgon, David, 94
So, John, 300
soccer, 152
  AFC Asia Cup, 327
Social Inclusion Board, 305
The Society Murders, 272
Somers, Daryl, 8, 13, 17, 87, 101–2, 110, 287
The Sopranos, 271
Sorrell, John, 65
Sorrenti, Vince, 248
South Australian Football League (SANFL), 326
Southern Cross Austereo, 59, 61, 100, 289
Sowada, Karin, 113
The Sports Show, 42
Sports Tonight, 42–3, 64
Sportscenter, 42
Sportsview.com.au, 139, 144–5
Sportsweek, 42
Starcevich, Craig, 35
Startin, Andrew, 84
Stefanovic, Karl, 262, 269, 286, 296
Steinfort, Carl, 175
Stephens, John, 242
Sterling, Peter, 295
Stevens, Anthony, 197
Stevenson, Nicole, 59
Stevenson, Ross, 57, 290
Stewart, Craig, 130
Stewart, Kat, 273
Stokes, Kerry, 129, 258, 277, 328
stolen 1970 Premiership Cup, 67–8
Stone, Gerald, 283–4
Strachan, Graeme 'Shirley', 50
Streisand, Barbra, 85
Stremski, Richard, 132
Stubbs, Richard, 57–8, 62, 78, 98
The Sullivans, 247
Sunday, 253–4, 265
Sunday Footy Show, 70–1
Sunday Observer, 21, 33, 57
Sunday Press, 21, 33
Sunday Scoreboard, 97
Sunday Telegraph, 267
Sunrise, 109, 253–4, 257, 259, 288
Superbowl, 99
Sutcliffe, Ken, 98, 100, 102, 245, 248, 250, 256, 296
Swan, Chrissie, 294
Swan, Dane, 175, 185, 193, 196, 210
Swan Premium Sun Tour bike race, 36

353

Swann, Greg, 167–71, 173, 175–9, 204, 206, 211, 213, 214
Sydney, 151, 156, 241, 246, 251–2, 266–8, 277–9, 282, 284, 287
Sydney Morning Herald, 252, 254, 264, 267, 317
Sydney Swans, 303, 311–14
Symond, John, 219

Talent2, 238
Talking Footy, 138
Tancred, Mike, 31, 33, 47, 54, 71, 121
Tape, Jamie, 161
Tarrant, Chris, 146, 163, 182–7, 205
Tattersalls, 143, 155
Taylor, Brian, 59–60, 99, 130
Taylor, Simon, 184
Ted Whitten Legends game, 99
Templeton, Kelvin, 314
Temptation, 245, 254, 280, 289
Thank God You're Here, 256
Theodossi, Nick, 174
This Is Your Life, 7, 294
Thomas, Dale, 207, 210, 211, 231, 307
Thompson, Mark, 234
Thompson, Robert, 17
Tilley, Matt, 280
Tippett, Kurt, 315
TipStar, 142–3
Today, 242, 254–5, 257, 262, 269, 288
Today FM, 58
Today Tonight, 253
Tonight Live with Steve Vizard, 40
Topo Gigio, 46
Transport Accident Commission, 183–4
Trioli, Virginia, 117
Triple M, 49, 51, 57–63, 97, 100, 106, 114, 138–9, 141, 195, 235, 287, 289–94, 296, 298, 308–10, 317, 329
   Hot Breakfast, 290, 297–8, 308, 328, 329
Triple M Breakfast Team, 97
Triple R, 57
Trippett, Graham, 181
Turn Back Your Body Clock, 270
Turnbull, Malcolm, 112–13, 115, 118–20, 323
TV Week Logie Awards *see* Logie Awards

Two Twisted, 269
Twomey family, 157

Uechtritz, Max, 280
Uncle Toby's Iron Man Super Series, 42
Underbelly, 270–4, 285–6, 288

Van Haandel, Frank, 330
Vancouver Gold, 292
Vancouver Winter Olympics, 291–3, 296
Vautin, Paul 'Fatty', 79, 248
VFA, 39–40, 118
VFL *see* AFL/VFL
Viatel, 128
Victoria Park, 9–11, 41, 121–2, 124–5, 128, 164–9
   Collingwood leaving, 178, 202, 219
   dispute with Yarra Council over, 203, 219
Victorian Institute of Sport, 178, 202, 214–17
Victorian Major Events Company, 152, 300, 327
Video Entertainment Group, 106
Vizard, Steve, 113, 115–19, 144–5, 152, 300
Voss, Michael, 224, 326

Waislitz, Alex, 130–1, 134–5, 155–6, 174, 228
Wakelin, Shane, 221
Waldren, Paul, 242
Waley, Jim, 98
Walker, Max, 68, 70
Walker, Ron, 142, 239, 297
Wallace, Terry, 312
Walls, Robert, 88
Walsh, Brian, 269
Walsh, Geoff, 190, 192, 194, 224, 226, 229
Walshe-Howling, Damian, 273
Warburton, James, 265
Warhurst, Myf, 289
Warne, Shane, 297, 301, 331
Warren, Ray, 32
Warrick, Frank, 103
Warry, Glen, 204
Wasley, James, 161
Water Rats, 271
Watson, Tim, 72, 75–6, 78, 147
Webb, Brant, 256
Webster, Tim, 32, 43, 64, 109
Weekend Sunrise, 279
Weideman family, 157
Weideman, Murray, 123, 158
Weir, Johnny, 292

Wellingham, Sharrod, 183–4
Wendt, Jana, 253–4, 265
Were, J.B., 300
West, Morris, 17
Westacott, John, 280
Westaway, Greg, 17
Western Australian Football League (WAFL), 326, 327
What a Year, 269
White, Peter, 130, 132
Whitten, Ted, 41, 45, 49, 68, 70, 98–9
Who Killed Channel 9?, 283–4
Who Wants to Be a Millionaire?, 102–3, 105, 108, 141, 151, 179, 181, 248, 250–1, 280, 285–6, 289, 294
Wide World of Sport, 69
Wilkins, Richard, 98, 248
Wilkinson, Joel, 307
Wilkinson, Lisa, 255, 279
Williams, Cameron, 296
Williams, Carl, 274
Williams, Kim, 239, 293
Williams, Mark, 225
Williams, Paul, 174
Wilson, Caroline, 92, 222
Wilson, Jim, 138
Wilson, Rebecca, 138
Wimbledon, 265
Windy Hill, 7, 9, 10, 13, 22
Winmar, Nicky, 91, 93–4, 304
The Winners, 45
Winter Olympics, Vancouver, 291–3, 296
Witness, 254
Witt, Katarina, 292
Wizard Home Loans, 205
Women at Nine, 261
Woods, Tiger, 291
World of Sport, 45, 58, 70–1
World Tennis Classic, 325
World Youth Day, 299
Worner, Tim, 103, 328
Wran, Neville, 113
Wren family, 122
Wren, John, 92, 122, 219
Wren, John Jnr, 122
Wylie, John, 300

The X-Files, 73, 77

Yarwood, Graeme, 87
You Are What You Eat, 270